Focus: Music in Contemporary Japan

Focus: Music in Contemporary Japan explores a diversity of musics performed in Japan today, ranging from folk song to classical music, the songs of *geisha* to the screaming of underground rock, with a specific look at the increasingly popular world of *taiko* (ensemble drumming). Discussion of contemporary musical practice is situated within broader frames of musical and sociopolitical history, processes of globalization and cosmopolitanism, and the continued search for Japanese identity through artistic expression. It explores how the Japanese have long negotiated cultural identity through musical practice in three parts:

- Part I, "Japanese Music and Culture," provides an overview of the key characteristics of Japanese culture that inform musical performance, such as the attitude towards the natural environment, changes in ruling powers, dominant religious forms, and historical processes of cultural exchange.
- Part II, "Sounding Japan," describes the elements that distinguish traditional Japanese music and then explores how music has changed in the modern era under the influence of Western music and ideology.
- Part III, "Focusing In: Identity, Meaning and Japanese Drumming in Kyoto," is based on fieldwork with musicians and explores the position of Japanese drumming within Kyoto. It focuses on four case studies that paint a vivid picture of each respective site, the music that is practiced, and the pedagogy and creative processes of each group.

The accompanying CD includes examples of Japanese music that illustrate specific elements and key genres introduced in the text. A companion website includes additional audio-visual sources discussed in detail in the text.

Jennifer Milioto Matsue is an ethnomusicologist at Union College specializing in modern Japanese music and culture. She has conducted research on numerous music cultures in contemporary Japan and is author of the monograph *Making Music in Japan's Underground: The Tokyo Hardcore Scene* (Routledge 2008), as well as several articles on related topics.

> The **Focus on World Music** Series is designed specifically for area courses in world music and ethnomusicology. Written by the top ethnomusicologists in their field, the Focus books balance sound pedagogy with exemplary scholarship. Each book provides a telescopic view of the musics and cultures addressed, giving the reader a general introduction on the music and culture of the area and then zooming in on different musical styles with in-depth case studies.

Visit the companion website for this edition:

www.routledge.com/textbooks/focusonworldmusic

This website includes further resources for both instructors and students.

FOCUS ON WORLD MUSIC

Series Editor: Michael B. Bakan

Focus: Music, Nationalism, and the Making of the New Europe
Second Edition
Philip V. Bohlman

Focus: Music of Northeast Brazil
Second Edition
Larry Crook

Focus: Afro-Caribbean Music
Katherine J. Hagedorn

Focus: Music of South Africa
Second Edition
Carol A. Muller

Focus: Gamelan Music of Indonesia
Second Edition
Henry Spiller

Focus: Irish Traditional Music
Sean Williams

Focus: Music in Contemporary Japan

Jennifer Milioto Matsue

Union College, USA

NEW YORK AND LONDON

First published 2016
by Routledge
711 Third Avenue, New York, NY 10017

and by Routledge
2 Park Square, Milton Park, Abingdon, Oxon, OX14 4RN

Routledge is an imprint of the Taylor & Francis Group, an informa business

© 2016 Jennifer Milioto Matsue

The right of Jennifer Milioto Matsue to be identified as author of this work has been asserted by her in accordance with sections 77 and 78 of the Copyright, Designs and Patents Act 1988.

All rights reserved. No part of this book may be reprinted or reproduced or utilized in any form or by any electronic, mechanical, or other means, now known or hereafter invented, including photocopying and recording, or in any information storage or retrieval system, without permission in writing from the publishers.

Trademark notice: Product or corporate names may be trademarks or registered trademarks, and are used only for identification and explanation without intent to infringe.

Library of Congress Cataloging in Publication Data
A catalog record for this book has been requested

ISBN: 978-1-138-79138-1 (hbk)
ISBN: 978-1-138-79140-4 (pbk)
ISBN: 978-1-315-76285-2 (ebk)

Typeset in Minion Pro
by Swales & Willis Ltd, Exeter, Devon, UK

Dedication

To my husband Ryota, who is the air in my lungs, and my son Hikaru, who is the spring in my step. Thank you for your perseverance and patience. Our year in Kyoto changed all our lives and brought me closer to you than you can ever possibly know. None of what follows would have been possible without the two of you.

Contents

List of Figures	ix
List of Musical Examples on Compact Disc	xi
List of Musical Examples on Companion Website	xiii
About the Author	xv
Series Foreword by Michael B. Bakan	xvi
Preface	xviii
Acknowledgments	xxii
A Word About Translations and Languages	xxiii
Maps	xxiv
East Asian Historical Periods	xxviii

Part I   Japanese Music and Culture — 1

1 Japanese Music in Geographical, Historical and Cultural Context — 3
2 Japanese Cultural Identity and Musical Modernity — 36

Part II   Sounding Japan — 65

3 Performing Music of Pre-modern Japan — 67
4 Making Music in the Modern Era — 108

PART III   Focusing In: Identity, Meaning and Japanese Drumming in Kyoto — 147

5 *Taiko* and the Marketing of Tradition in Kyoto — 149
6 Four Case Studies and Some Conclusions — 175

Tosha Rōetsu and the Pontochō *Okeiko* (Lesson) 176
Basara and the One-room Schoolhouse 190
Matsuri-shū and the Kyoto Taiko Center 198
Murasaki Daiko and the Proper *Dōjō* (Studio) 206

Conclusion: The Future of Japanese Music 220
Appendices 224

   A "Echigojishi" (*Yoshizumi Kojūrō-fu* for *shamisen*) 225
   B "Echigojishi" (*Kineya bunkafu* for *shamisen*) 226
   C "Echigojishi" (Japanese score for *ko-tsuzumi* and *ō-tsuzumi*, by Tosha Rōetsu) 227
   D "Echigojishi" (Western score for *ko-tsuzumi* and *ō-tsuzumi*, by Yamauchi Reach) 228

Glossary 233
Additional Resources 245
Index 267

Figures

Map 1	Asia	xxiv
Map 2	Japan (prefectures)	xxv
Map 3	Japan (topographical) (Courtesy of the University of Texas Libraries, The University of Texas at Austin)	xxvi
0.a	East Asian Historical Periods	xxviii
1.1	Commemorative light display in Kobe	8
1.2	Kennin-ji garden in Kyoto	9
1.3	Miyajima *torii*	17
1.4	Basara performing "*Shishi-mai*"	18
1.5	Kongōbu-ji garden at Kōya-san	19
1.6	Gravestones at Kōya-san	21
1.7	"Rishukyō"	22
1.8	*Ryūkyū* scale	31
2.1	East Asian zithers	39
2.2	Tokyo Tower and Zōjō-ji	42
2.3	Tokyo urban landscape	45
2.4	Hardcore girl on guitar	50
2.5	Urban cherry blossoms	54
3.1	James Nyoraku Schlefer at Columbia University (photo by Lenny Pridatko)	74
3.2	"Choshi" (Japanese score)	75
3.3	"Choshi" (Western score) (provided by James Nyoraku Schlefer)	76
3.4	Stanley Jiang (Union College '16) and the author on *nagauta shamisen*	78
3.5	Yamauchi Reach on *tsugaru-jamisen*	79
3.6	*Ryo* and *ritsu* scales	85
3.7	*In* and *yō* scales	86

ix

x • List of Figures

3.8	Koizumi's tetrachords	86
3.9	Koizumi's scales	87
3.10	*Yabusame* (archery on horseback) at Shimogamo-jinja in Kyoto	91
3.11	"Chū no Mai" (transcription)	96
3.12	*Bugaku* performance at Shiramine-jingū in Kyoto	102
4.1	*Yonanuki* pentatonic scales	112
4.2	"Akatonbo" (vocal melody) (JASRAC 出 1414514-401)	113
4.3	Hardcore band Jug	123
4.4	Hatsune Miku (Illustration by KEI (C) Crypton Future Media, INC. www.piapro.net)	129
4.5	NAMCO "*Taiko no Tatsujin*" (©BANDAI NAMCO Games Inc.)	136
4.6	Asano Kaoly, leader of Gocoo with additional members (photo by Mark Dozadzillo)	140
4.7	Kenny Endo on *ō-daiko* (photo by Raymond Yuen)	142
5.1	*Mikoshi* from Yasaka-jinja on display	150
5.2	Crowds at *Gion Matsuri*	151
5.3	*Gion Matsuri yamaboko*	152
5.4	*Matsuri* at Ichihime-jinja in Kyoto	153
5.5	*Matsuri* at Genbu-jinja in Kyoto	154
5.6	Kiyomizu-dera in Kyoto	156
5.7	Kamo-gawa	156
5.8	Kyoto Tower	160
6.1	Tosha Rōetsu	176
6.2	*Geiko* Gionkōbu Mamechizu on *ko-tsuzumi* at *okeiko*	182
6.3	Tosha Rōetsu (with Imafuji Misuzu), instructing *geiko* Miyagawa Yachiho on *ō-tsuzumi*	183
6.4	"Echigojishi" (Japanese score by Tosha Rōetsu)	188
6.5	Notation key (by Tosha Rōetsu)	188
6.6	"Echigojishi" (Western score by Yamauchi Reach)	189
6.7	Basara rehearsing	191
6.8	Ōtsuka Takeshi of Basara on *shinobue*	194
6.9	Basara performing "Narushima"	196
6.10	Matsuri-shū performing "Konjichō"	199
6.11	Yamauchi Reach on *shime-daiko*	199
6.12	Kawarazaki Yoshihiro on *katsugi-oke-daiko*	201
6.13	Osoda Miho of Murasaki Daiko performing at Heian-jingū	207
6.14	Murasaki Daiko *dōjō*	209
6.15	Akane Fujino	211
6.16	Murasaki Daiko dancing	213
6.17	Murasaki Daiko drumming	214
7.1	Vendors at a *matsuri*	220

Musical Examples on Compact Disc

1. "Rishukyō" by Kōya-san shōmyō no kai from *Kōya-san no shōmyō / daimandaraku*, VZCG-249, 2002. Licensed by Victor Entertainment.
2. "The hack-driver's song of Hakone" by a Hakone man from the recording entitled *Traditional Folk Songs of Japan*, FW04534, courtesy of Smithsonian Folkways Recordings. ℗ © 1961. Used by permission.
3. "Kagoshima Ohara bushi" by a group from Kagoshima Prefecture from the recording entitled *Traditional Folk Songs of Japan*, FW04534, courtesy of Smithsonian Folkways Recordings. ℗ © 1961. Used by permission.
4. "Kasuga Sanbasō" by Vocals: Kasuga Toyoeishiba, *shamisen*: Kasuga Toyokisen and Kasuga Toyoshibashu from *Kasuga Sanbasō*, VZCG-763, © 2012. Licensed by Japan Traditional Cultures Foundation.
5. "Japan: Traditional Vocal & Instrumental Pieces: Ōgi no Mato (voice *biwa*)"; performed by Handa Ayako / Explorer Series: East Asia ℗ 1976. Produced under license from Nonesuch Records Inc.
6. "(Futaiken) Tsuru no Sugomori" by James Nyoraku Schlefer from *Flare Up*, NRCD-102g, © 2003 James Nyoraku Schlefer.
7. "Yaraiya" by Yamauchi Reach, performed by Wakana, © 2011 Yamauchi Reach.
8. "Rokudan" by *sangen*: Gunji Etsuko, *koto*: Iseki Kazuhiro and Nishi Yoko from *Japon Splendeur du Koto*, Playasound PS 65131, © 1993 Kyoto Records.
9. "Etenraku" by The Music Department of the Imperial Household Agency from *The Sounds of Japan*, Victor Entertainment VICG-60067, 1997. Licensed by Victor Entertainment.
10. "Kagura" from *Japanese Noh Music* performed by The Kyoto Nohgaku Kai, LYRCD-7137 © 1994, Lyrichord Discs Inc. Used with permission.

11 "Yobikake" ("The Calling") by Kenny Endo from *Hibiki*, Bindu BIN-9801/2, © 1998 Kenny Endo.
12 "Akatonbo" by vocals: Tsuji Teruko from *Yamada Kosaku no Isan 6*, Nippon Columbia COCA-13176, © 1996 Licensed by Nippon Columbia Co., Ltd.
13 "Lied" by Hosokawa Toshio, performed by flute: Kolbeinn Bjarnason, piano: Members of Caput Ensemble from *Toshio Hosokawa Flute Music*, Naxos 8.572479, © 2010. Courtesy of Naxos of America.
14 "Love Maniac" by Demi Semi Quaver (vocal, accordion: Eleonola Emi; bass: Yokoyama Hidenori; guitar: Terashi Toru; drums: Naka Koichiro; percussion, metals: Eto Steve; keyboards: Kuwajima Genya; produced by Kamiyama Hoppy) from *Demi Semi Quaver*, God Mountain Records GMCD-008, © 1994. Released under license from God Mountain Records, Tokyo.
15 "Woodpecker No. 1" by Merzbow from *Pulse Demon*, Relapse Records RR-6937, © 1996. Courtesy of Relapse Records.
16 "Japan: Kabuki & Other Traditional Music: Echigojishi (The Echigo Lion)" performed by Ensemble Nipponia / Explorer Series: East Asia ℗ 1987. Produced Under License From Nonesuch Records Inc.

Musical Examples on Companion Website

1. "Megitsune" performed by Babymetal © 2013. https://www.youtube.com/watch?v=cK3NMZAUKGw.
2. "Kohama-bushi" by vocals and *sanshin*: Takamine Mitsu, *koto*: Ishigaki Kyoko, *fue*: Haino Kiyoshi. https://www.youtube.com/watch?v=nieFRFi4-ZQ.
3. "Koten-chōshi" by Kaoru Watanabe; recorded in New York City by the author, May 5, 2014.
4. "Utamono" by Kaoru Watanabe; recorded in New York City by the author, May 5, 2014.
5. "Duet" by drums: Kenny Endo, *fue*: Kaoru Watanabe; recorded at red Elephant in Honolulu, HI, February 9, 2007. https://www.youtube.com/watch?v=FOSVrgom51s.
6. "Choshi" performed by James Nyoraku Schlefer; recorded in New York City by the author, May 4, 2014.
7. "Musume Shirasagi" by lyricist: Takeshiba Kanisuke, composer: Kiyomoto Umekichi IV, choreographer: Fujima Syuusen, dancer: Hanayagi Michikaoru, *jōruri*: Kiyomoto Umejyudayuu, *shamisen*: Kiyomoto Shiyou, *narimono*: Mochizuki Kimi, with other performers; recorded by Ezawaat Sendai Denryoku Hall in Sendai, November, 7, 2004.
8. "In Scale" performed by James Nyoraku Schlefer; recorded in New York City by the author, May 4, 2014.
9. "Chū no Mai" (unifying rhythmic exercise) with Tosho Rōetsu and the author; recorded in Kyoto by the author, June, 2010.
10. "Chū no Mai" (excerpt of the piece) with Tosho Rōetsu and the author; recorded in Kyoto by the author, June 2010.
11. "Lady Gaga Telephone cover TEAM KOZAN" by Team Kozan; directed by Yuasa Hiroaki. https://www.youtube.com/watch?v=ZZ06aVZpGYA.
12. "Sai-bo" by Kirihito, P-Vine, Inc. https://www.youtube.com/watch?v=dWhxz-yXLIM.

13 "Kiyari and Miyake" by Kodō; excerpt from DVD *Kodō HONOKA*, OD-007, © 2012 Otodaiku Co., Ltd.
14 "DKN" by DaiKeN and J. Suzuki; performed by Gocoo, recorded during Gocoo's European tour in 2012 by Tarow M. and Masaki H.
15 "Kaoru Watanabe Taiko Ensemble featuring Kenny Endo in NY" by Kenny Endo and Kaoru Watanabe; filmed and edited by Lia Chang, at the Metropolitan Museum of Art, May 16, 2009. https://www.youtube.com/watch?v=Nn9aHziCZ70; video courtesy of www.liachangphotography.com.
16 "Echigojishi" by *ō-tsuzumi*: Tosha Rōetsu, *shamisen*: Imafuji Misuzu, *ko-tsuzumi*: Yamauchi Reach; recorded by the author at Tosha's studio in Kyoto, 2010 during a lesson.
17 "Semi Shigure" by Banba Tomoko; performed by Basara, recorded by the author at Basara's rehearsal space in Kyoto, 2010.
18 "Konjichō" by Yura Hidenori; performed by Matsuri-shū, excerpt from DVD *Matsuri-shū End of the Year Performance 2007* © 2008 Kyoto Music Center, Inc. http://www.wawawa.ne.jp.
19 "Hannya" by Akane Fujino; performed by Murasaki Daiko, recorded by Akane Fujino.

About the Author

Jennifer Milioto Matsue (B.A. Wellesley College and M.A. and Ph.D. University of Chicago) is an ethnomusicologist specializing in modern Japanese music and culture. She has conducted research on a variety of music cultures in contemporary Japan including the Tokyo hardcore rock scene, *nagauta* (a type of traditional chamber music featuring the three-string lute *shamisen*), raves, the increasingly popular world of *taiko* (Japanese ensemble drumming), and most recently, Vocaloid Hatsune Miku. She is interested in how performers find meaning through participating in such worlds, with a particular focus on women's roles in music making. She is the author of the monograph *Making Music in Japan's Underground: The Tokyo Hardcore Scene* (Routledge 2008), as well as several articles on related topics. She is Director of the World Musics and Cultures Program, and serves as Associate Professor in Music, Asian Studies and Anthropology at Union College in Schenectady, New York.

Series Foreword

The past decade has witnessed extraordinary growth in the areas of ethnomusicology and world music publishing. With the publication of both the ten-volume *Garland Encyclopedia of World Music* and the second edition of the *New Grove Dictionary of Music and Musicians* (2001), we now have access to general reference resources that ethnomusicologists and world music enthusiasts of even just a few years ago could only have dreamed of. University and other academic presses—Chicago, Oxford, Cambridge, Illinois, Temple, Wesleyan, Indiana, California, Routledge—have produced excellent ethnomusicological monographs, edited volumes, and smaller-scale reference works in ever-increasing numbers, many accompanied by CDs, DVDs, and other media that bring the musics described vividly to life. A host of new introductory-level textbooks for freshman/sophomore-level world music survey courses have come out too, along with new editions of long-established textbooks catering to that market. New instructional resources for teaching these same kinds of introductory survey courses have been created in addition, the Oxford Global Music Series perhaps most notable among them. And the Internet has of course revolutionized everything, with thousands upon thousands of Web-based resources—from superb scholarly and educational resources such as Smithsonian Global Sound (www.smithsonianglobalsound.org) and *Grove Music Online* to the wild frontiers of YouTube and myriad commercial online music providers—all now available from your desktop at the click of a mouse.

Yet for all of this profuse and diverse publishing activity, there remains a conspicuous gap in the literature. We still lack a solid corpus of high-quality textbooks designed specifically for area courses in world music, ethnomusicology, and interdisciplinary programs with a strong music component. The need for such texts is greatest where courses for upper-division undergraduate and entry-level graduate students are taught, but it extends to courses at the freshman and sophomore levels as well, especially those enrolling music majors and other students who are serious and motivated.

What has been needed for such courses are books that balance sound pedagogy with exemplary scholarship, and that are substantive in content yet readily accessible to specialist and non-specialist readers alike. These books would be written in a lively and engaging style by leading ethnomusicologists and educators, bringing wide interdisciplinary scope and relevance to the contemporary concerns of their readership. They would, moreover, provide a telescopic view of the musics and cultures they addressed, zooming in from broad-based surveys of expansive music-culture areas and topics toward compelling, in-depth case studies of specific musicultural traditions and their myriad transformations in the modern world.

This is precisely what Routledge's *Focus on World Music* series delivers, with books that are authoritative, accessible, pedagogically strong, richly illustrated, and accompanied by a compelling compact disk of musical examples linked integrally to the text. I am delighted to be part of the team that has brought this exciting and important series to fruition. I hope you enjoy reading these books as much as I have!

Michael B. Bakan
The Florida State University

Preface

My journey through Japanese music began in high school when I took a course on world literature. Intrigued by the philosophical underpinnings of Asian poetry, my first semester in college I studied Asian religion and took Japanese language. By the end of the term, I declared Japanese Studies as my major, while also continuing my study of Western music on the cello and in courses. I found a way to bring both these interests together through ethnomusicology, and embarked on graduate study focused on contemporary music in Japan. I put down the cello and picked up a *shamisen* (a three-stringed Japanese lute) and never turned back. While a graduate student, I first learned of *taiko* (Japanese ensemble drumming also known as *wadaiko*) when I completed a project on a local Buddhist group, and shortly thereafter I first saw the famous Japanese professional group Kodō perform live. I found myself in Japan in the mid-1990s, studying the unexpectedly similar worlds of underground rock for my dissertation and *nagauta* (a chamber music featuring the *shamisen*) to expand my understanding of art musics in general. I never suspected that I would someday find myself actually directing a college Japanese drumming ensemble (Union College's Zakuro-Daiko) and focusing my research energies on understanding the origins and movements of this performance style within the broader context of Japanese performing arts and contemporary culture.

The Goals of Music in Contemporary Japan

Music in Contemporary Japan explores a diversity of musics being performed today reaching far beyond *taiko*, ranging from court genres to the underground rock that first brought me to Japan. Discussion of contemporary musical practice is situated within broader frames of musical and sociopolitical history, processes of globalization and cosmopolitanism, and the continued search for Japanese identity through artistic expression.

Though there are many fine studies of Japanese music, this book in part is a result of my own frustration at finding suitable texts for teaching bright and eager undergraduate students that raise theoretically complex ideas, but do not alienate the students through excessive jargon and complicated terminology. This is particularly complicated in the case of Japanese music, as the Japanese themselves have a penchant for labeling every minute detail, and there has been a similar focus within much scholarship on cataloging numerous genres, or couching analysis in a theoretical language that is too complicated for anyone but the specialist to dissect. This book therefore intends to introduce the amazing intricacies of Japanese music and theoretical joy of ethnomusicology in a way that undergraduates, graduate students and specialists alike can engage with in a critical and thoughtful manner. Thus rather than offer an introduction to Japan and Japanese music that outlines major musical elements and genres or an ethnography that only the specialist can appreciate, this work combines both approaches, by first reviewing music in Japan in general today, and then focusing in on fieldwork with drummers in Kyoto. This approach is unified in the desire to better understand how Japanese identity is expressed through and shaped by music.

Music in Contemporary Japan is further inspired by my own course in Japanese ensemble drumming. Therefore this is a book that can be used for either teaching elements of Japanese music in general, a seminar on Music and Culture or East Asian Music Cultures, for which there are limited ethnographies that the upper-level undergraduate can digest in a limited amount of time, or a more specific course on Japanese ensemble drumming.

Thus *Music in Contemporary Japan* is about a great variety of musics and related social practices that are currently performed in Japan. "Performance" here refers to a breadth of social activities—both on stage and off, in line with Small's seminal work *Musicking* (1998) and the broader field of Performance Studies—required for the production of musical sound. All the musics introduced in the following discussion are actively *performed* in contemporary Japan, even if they first developed centuries ago. Therefore, rather than title the work as "Japanese music," "Music in Japan," or "Modern and/or Contemporary Music in Japan," I consciously choose to word the title as "Music in Contemporary Japan," as this phrasing best reflects my interest in a diversity of musics currently being performed, ranging from court music with origins dating back to the sixth and seventh centuries to avant-garde underground music making in vibrant urban centers.

How This Book is Organized

Music in Contemporary Japan explores how Japanese have long negotiated cultural identity through musical practice in three parts. Part I "Japanese Music and Culture" first overviews key characteristics of Japanese culture that inform the performance of many musics, addressing how geography and the attitude towards the natural environment, changes in ruling powers, dominant religious forms, and historical processes of cultural exchange have shaped the quality of Japanese artistic expression. This opening further breaks down the myth of a homogeneous Japan, instead highlighting a diversity of cultural practices that are reflected in music making. Part I also asks just what is "Japanese" about Japanese music, a particularly complicated question given that Japan has long adapted foreign cultural forms, transforming them to serve local Japanese tastes and needs. Japanese cultural identity became increasingly complicated to isolate in the modern era. This approach to understanding Japanese culture contextualizes the ensuing introduction to the key aesthetic principles and major genres of Japanese music.

In Part II, "Sounding Japan," the elements that distinguish Japanese music—that make Japanese music actually "sound" Japanese—such as broad concepts of what actually is conceived as "musical," the use of *ma* (an intriguing understanding of "emptiness"), concepts of pitch and melody, vocal qualities, free rhythm, and specific forms (for example, *jo-ha-kyū*), are explored in some detail. The actual voicing of these principles is analyzed in a range of significant traditional genres with origins in the pre-modern era, including court music, theatrical forms, instrumental genres, and narrative and poetic vocal styles. Part II also explores how, since the late nineteenth century, the Japanese learned to make new music in the modern era, through the rapid and extensive transformation of culture in general, as Japan embraced Westernization. Part II ends with a look at the development of increasingly popular Japanese ensemble drumming (*taiko* or *wadaiko*), which reflects modernizing processes that the nation as a whole has undergone in the twentieth century. Originating Japanese groups, including Ondekoza, Kodō, O-Suwa Daiko and Sukeroku Daiko, for example, were initially motivated by a nationalist agenda that continues to resonate in contemporary performance, but which is complicated as the genre developed and continues to transform through transnational flows. This discussion of *taiko*'s particularly rich engagement with the search for Japanese cultural identity sets the stage for the following section.

Part III, "Focusing In: Identity, Meaning and Japanese Drumming in Kyoto," based on fieldwork with musicians primarily from 2009–10, explores the position of Japanese drumming within Kyoto, a city steeped in tradition. Part III focuses on four case studies that paint a vivid picture of each respective site, the music that is practiced, the pedagogy and creative processes of each group, and the motivations of the people involved, while also connecting with larger issues at play in the performance of music in contemporary Japan. The first case study looks at the formal lesson environment of traditional Japanese drumming and the master performer and formidable teacher Tosha Rōetsu. The second, in contrast, explores a semi-professional *taiko* group, Basara, and what motivates their practice in a one-room schoolhouse on the outskirts of Kyoto. The next looks at the professional group Matsuri-shū, and the connection of two of its members, Yamauchi Reach and Kawarazaki Yoshihiro, with the hugely popular Kyoto Taiko Center and its strategies to spread Japanese ensemble drumming to the masses. The final study introduces an entirely different interpretation of the genre through the all-female professional group Murasaki Daiko directed by Akane Fujino, whose work is heavily influenced by commercial interests. Each case study tells a compelling story that collectively reveal the diversity of Japanese drumming while intersecting with larger theoretical issues important to the field of ethnomusicology.

Supporting Materials

Sources cited within the text are included in an alphabetical reference list at the end of each chapter. To facilitate further research, most of these citations, plus additional sources, are organized by topic under "Additional Resources" at the end of the volume.

The accompanying CD includes representative examples of Japanese music that illustrate specific elements and key genres introduced in the text. The professionally recorded tracks have been included with permission from the artists themselves and/or with licensing through the appropriate institutions. Details on these recordings are provided in the opening list of "Musical Examples on Compact Disc," and within the chapters. A companion website features additional audio-visual sources discussed in detail in the text, including fieldwork recordings, and both professional and informal video examples. These items as well are included with permission from the various artists and institutions involved in their production. The book's companion website can be found at http://www.routledge.com/textbooks/focusonworldmusic. Details on these audio-visual materials are provided in the opening list of "Musical Examples on Companion Website," and within the chapters. Whenever possible, complete recordings have been included to provide a sense of how this music is heard in real life contexts—to make the listening experience as visceral as possible. All the examples discussed in detail when appropriate will have corresponding times in either the CD tracks or website examples marked in parentheses throughout the remainder of the text. Additional songs mentioned in the text should be available through a quick search on the Internet. Similarly, images of instruments and ensembles not included here are also readily available through the Internet.

Photographs

All photographs, unless otherwise noted, are by Ryota Matsue.

References

Small, Christopher. 1998. *Musicking: The Meanings of Performing and Listening.* Middletown, CT: Wesleyan University Press.

Acknowledgments

This book would not have been possible without the American Council of Learned Societies (ACLS), which granted me a fellowship to support a year of research in Kyoto. As always, I must first and foremost acknowledge the kind generosity of all the performers who shared their knowledge, music and patience with me throughout the process of researching while on that fellowship and the writing of this book. North American performers Kenny Endo, James Nyoraku Schlefer and Kaoru Watanabe, in particular, continue to challenge me intellectually and inspire me musically. Tosha Rōetsu, the members of Basara, Kawarazaki Yoshihiro and Yamauchi Reach of Matsuri-shū, and Akane Fujino of Murasaki Daiko were exceptionally patient with me as I first navigated Japanese music and drumming in Kyoto. I would also like to thank the many scholars and enthusiasts of Japanese music who took the time to discuss parts of the text, debate philosophical concepts over e-mail, and support my work, especially Bruce Deschênes, Yuko Eguchi, Richard Emmert, David Hughes, Justin Hunter, Jay Keister, David Locke, Anne Prescott, Cathleen Read, Bonnie Wade and Lawrence Witzleben. I am simply a vehicle bringing these voices together in hopefully a new and helpful manner. My editors Michael Bakan and Constance Ditzel, who first recruited me to write this text, and convinced me that I had something more to say about Japanese music, must also be thanked, and the external reviewers who provided such thoughtful commentary. My two research assistants, Amanda Laven and Stanley Jiang, were immensely helpful pulling everything together. And last but not least, to all my students, who motivate my research and writing about Japan. I prepared the final manuscript while teaching "Popular Music in Modern Japan" as a Visitor at Kansai Gaikokugo Daigaku in Osaka, Japan in fall 2014. The students in this class in particular offered wonderful feedback on all the examples and discussion that follows.

A Word About Translations and Languages

The author completed all the translations, with assistance from Ryota Matsue. Translations were made with an emphasis on general intent in order to maintain the original tone. *Kanji* (Chinese characters), *hiragana* and *katakana* (the two Japanese alphabets) have been romanized in the modified Hepburn system, with long vowels indicated with a macron (for example, oo or ou = ō), except in the case of words now commonly found in English in an alternate spelling (for example, nō = noh), and with people's names, when the individual prefers that his or her name be romanized in a certain way. The use of hyphens in compound nouns is rather subjective in romanized Japanese, though the general trend in publishing is to include them sparingly (Society of Writers, Editors and Translators, Tokyo 1998). I choose to insert hyphens in order to highlight roots (for example, *noh-hayashi*, where "*hayashi*" is a general term for an ensemble), while other compounds are rendered as one word. Japanese names appear in customary fashion with the surname first, followed by the given name, unless otherwise indicated. Professional names are also included as typically rendered in Japan. Other names, including those of U.S.-born Japanese performers, appear with given name first. Foreign terms appear in italics throughout the text, except for song titles, personal, ensemble and place names. There is a glossary containing key terms and Japanese vocabulary at the end of the text.

References

Society of Writers, Editors and Translators, Tokyo. 1998. *Japan Style Sheet: The SWET Guide for Writers, Editors and Translators*. Berkeley, CA: Stone Bridge Press.

Maps

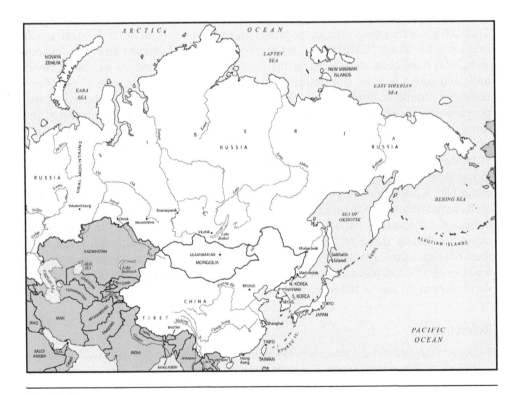

Map 1 Asia

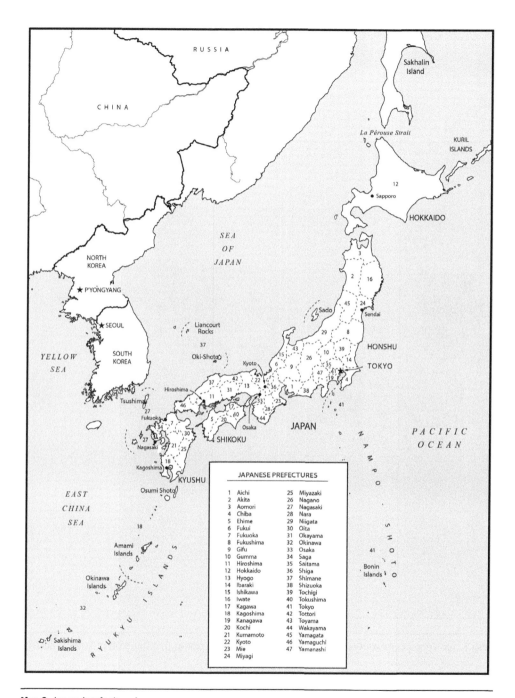

Map 2 Japan (prefectures)

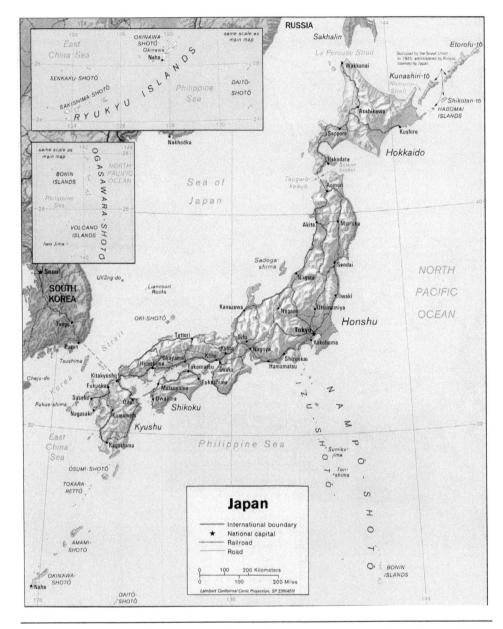
Map 3 Japan (topographical) (Courtesy of the University of Texas Libraries, The University of Texas at Austin)

East Asian Historical Periods

Year	CHINA	KOREA
B.C.E 200	Han Dynasty..................202 B.C.E–220 C.E.	Three Kingdoms
100		–Koguryo..............
C.E. 100		–Paekche..............
200	Three Kingdoms........................220–280	–Silla..................
	Jin...265–420	
300		
400	Northern and Southern	
500	Dynasty..................................420–589	
	Sui..581–618	
600	Tang..618–907	Unified Silla Dynasty..
700		
800		
900	Five Dynasties..........................907–960	
	Northern Song......................960–1127	Koryo Dynasty.......
1000		
1100	Southern Song......................1127–1279	
	Yuan Dynasty.......................1279–1368	
1200	Ming Dynasty......................1368–1644	
1300		
1400		Choson Dynasty......
1500		
1600	Ching Dynasty.....................1644–1911	
1700		
1800		
	Republic of China.................1912–1916	
	Warlord Era..........................1916–1927	
	Nanjing decade....................1927–1937	Modern Korea
	Anti-Japanese War / World War II	–Japanese Colonial
	1937–1947	–Republic of South
1900	Civil War.............................1947–1949	–Democratic People's
	The People's Republic of China 1949–	–(North)..............
2000		

Figure 0.a East Asian Historical Periods

	JAPAN
	Jōmon period.*ca.*10,000 B.C.E.–300 B.C.E.
	Yayoi period……………………*ca.* 300 B.C.E.–300 C.E.
……………………?–668	
……………………?–660	
……………………?–668	
	Kofun period………………………*ca.* 300–552
	Asuka period……………………………552–710
……………………669–935	
	Nara period………………………………710–784
	Heian period……………………………794–1185
……………………918–1392	
	Kamakura period……………………1185–1333
	Kemmu Restoration……………………333–1336
……………………1392–1910	Muromachi (Ashikaga) period……………1336–1573
	Azuchi-Momoyama period………………1573–1600
	Edo (Tokugawa) period…………………1600–1868
Period……………1910–1945	Meiji period……………………………1868–1912
Korea……………1948–	Taishō period…………………………1912–1926
Republic of Korea	Shōwa period…………………………1926–1989
……………………1948–	Heisei period……………………………1989–

PART I
Japanese Music and Culture

Part I, "Japanese Music and Culture," launches this exploration of Japanese music and cultural identity first by introducing geographical, historical and cultural characteristics of Japan that contextualize musical expression, and then focusing in on religious and folk musics. The search for Japanese cultural identity in music becomes increasingly complicated in the modern era, as Japan rapidly Westernized, but here I suggest ways that we may still locate some essence of "Japaneseness."

Part I

Drama & Music and Culture

CHAPTER 1

Japanese Music in Geographical, Historical and Cultural Context

Black-and-white images of a drum set on an empty wooden stage flash across the screen, followed by a close-up of the drummer, face obscured by long black hair and a white mask. The music thumps along in classic rock fashion, but these drums clearly are not Western. Images of several women in black, each holding the same mask to her face, are interspersed with those of the drummer, as one by one they gradually approach the viewer down a narrow hallway. A similarly garbed man is seen with a string instrument, which he is playing like a guitar, but even at a quick glance there is something unexpected here again. Suddenly several young girls appear, the same mysterious ladies, but now brightly displayed in color as two of them literally "unwrap," the third from a large sash around her waist to reveal black and red costumes. She will soon assume her role as the lead-singer of this trio. Both she and her companions are backed by the drummer and four men, faces yet unseen, jamming on the same string instrument introduced above, thrashing and flipping their hip-grazing long hair as if each one were the lead guitarist for the latest speed metal band. But surely none of them are actually playing? Throughout the video the red and white image of the mask—clearly meant to depict a specific animal—is seen again and again, either floating on its own or on the faces of various performers. The music moves through various sounds, some in-line with mainstream Japanese popular music, and others not, begging us to ask—just what is going on here?

"Megitsune" (Website Example 1) is a confusing amalgamation of iconic references to Japanese traditionalism melded with modern popular music idioms. The video juxtaposes traditional Japanese settings, instruments, and costumes with the sounds of electric guitars, synthesizers, and a pounding dance rhythm to create a new style that is capturing the global imagination. Babymetal, the three Japanese young women featured here, indeed perform a highly "poppified" version of metal that is gaining steam. And whether consciously or not, Babymetal's performance of "Megitsune" both celebrates and exacerbates stereotypes of Japan, down to the strangeness of it all. The oddness of this mix actually may account for its immense global popularity, with close to 10 million hits on YouTube as of October 2014. This video has gone viral, representing an important image of Japanese music making that has spread abroad. The following journey hopes to introduce ways to make sense of the sounds and images of "Megitsune" within the context of music making in Japan more broadly, and we will head back to Babymetal at the end of this volume.

Music and Japanese Identity

There is no doubt that music and dance are fully integrated into the daily lives of Japanese. As children, Japanese are exposed to music on television in educational programming, *anime*, and commercials. They learn to sing Western-style songs at school, some dating back to the late nineteenth century, and they play piano and violin from a young age. Whole families gather to watch contests with regional folk music competing against mainstream popular songs, or variety shows featuring top talents and favorite new hits on television every week. If everyone cannot come together on an average Sunday due to busy schedules, then certainly on New Year's Eve when millions, rather than welcoming the new year with a glass of champagne and a kiss, gather around to watch "The Red and White Song Contest" (*Kōhaku Uta Gassen*) on public television (NHK). Both children and adults may find themselves in the neighborhood Japanese drumming group (*taiko*), and performing at the annual fall festivals (*matsuri*) for the local shrine.

The mother whose children have grown may enjoy taking a lesson on the Japanese three-string lute (*shamisen*) in a small studio, learning traditional Japanese dance (*nihon buyō*), guitar, or even South American panpipes. Young adults may find themselves spending hour after hour rehearsing with a rock band, dancing all night at the hot new club, sharing a *karaoke* box with friends, or even drinking at a pub amongst a sea of Western faces while an Irish band jams. The retired gentleman may pick up the Western flute, or sing along to his favorite Japanese popular song, as he imagines a rural, pristine homeland that no longer exists, if it ever really did (*enka*). There is an endless list of ways for Japanese to engage with the diversity of music and dance that inhabits contemporary Japan. And in so doing, individual, communal, and national identities are produced.

Music assumes such an important role in many cultures precisely because it is a powerful and immediate way to negotiate our own individual identities and come to a better understanding of how others view themselves. Ideas of identity should not be seen as fixed, however, but rather are in constant flux, transforming over time, and as we move between social contexts. Identity itself is a performance, not absolute, but rather something individuals, communities, and nations enact through various behaviors, including creating and consuming music. With its complex history of intercultural exchange, flexibility, and hybridity, music is a particularly rich and complicated practice through which to explore Japanese cultural identity (Naka 2002; Rawski 2002). And recognizing just how this "Japaneseness" is expressed, through sounds and actions that are somehow understood as uniquely Japanese, becomes ever more complicated in the contemporary moment, as globalization, and especially the Internet, shrink the distance amongst peoples and obfuscate the boundaries between nations.

Nonetheless, music remains a particularly compelling marker of identity because of its connection with the body, a relationship that has not changed despite technological innovation. Whether pounding away on percussion on stage, dancing in the audience, or tapping a toe to a beat in one's headphones—music remains visceral—something we individually experience in our bodies. But through this immediate experience, national identity may be asserted. Surak (2013), in her study of Japanese tea ceremony (sadō), argues that after completing school, in Japan embodied practices are one of the most potent means of affirming ideals of national identity, whether one practices the art in question personally or not; an awareness of the meaning of necessary movements and the common values they express is enough to transmit knowledge and create shared identity. Music involves a similar engagement with the body, and therefore is a powerful means of creating identity.

This is true whether one is primarily a "listener" or a "musician," roles that we may shift between, even finding ourselves at times simultaneously hearing and making music. De Kloet, in his study of bootleg recordings in China, argues identity work is possible through listening to recordings, as doing so

> . . . is a reflexive and performative act. Sounds are integrated into lives and used as technologies of the self. The audience is engaged in a constant dialogue with musicians, and music is used as an important topic of conversation among friends, as a way to enact one's identity.
> (de Kloet 2010: 163)

We often introduce ourselves to others through the music we enjoy listening to, as a way to quickly say "this is who I am."

Musicians may take even more active roles in creating Japanese cultural identity. Mathews explains Japanese musicians "whether playing the *koto* [a Japanese zither] or chanting hip-hop odes . . . are, at least indirectly, depicting, describing, or defining Japaneseness" and in turn revealing the transformation of this category throughout time (2004: 336). Given its ephemeral nature—its ability to reflect changing tastes, intersections of different peoples throughout time, and advances in technology and modes of production—music exposes the history of a people and the ways in which their collective identity similarly transforms. Music nevertheless remains capable of eliciting strong emotional responses and inspiring fierce debates about its artistic qualities. Thus music connects with both the deeply personal and the broadly national. The following pages attempt to explore how music has been used both to shape and express who the Japanese are as individuals and a nation. This identity work is possible precisely because music of course does not exist in a vacuum (an expression my own students are probably weary of hearing) but rather is informed by the unique geographical, historical, and cultural context in which it is produced.

The Natural Environment of Japan

Japan is an archipelago of some 6,852 total islands within East Asia, located between the Sea of Japan on the west and Pacific Ocean on the east (see Map 1).

Japan has four major islands—Hokkaidō, Honshū, Shikoku, and Kyūshū—and a fifth group collectively referred to as either the Ryūkyū, the name of the ruling family of this area prior to colonization, or the Okinawan islands (see Map 2, which also indicates the prefectures, equivalent to states in the United States). Japan's weather is temperate in general, with varied temperature and weather patterns, which are most noticeable in winter when the climate ranges from extreme cold in northern Hokkaidō, with some of the heaviest snowfalls in the world recorded on the coast of the Sea of Japan, to tropical warmth in the southern Ryūkyū islands.

Japan's total area of approximately 146,000 square miles, which is smaller than California, is home to an estimated 126.66 million people as of 2013 (a number that is actually decreasing) (World Population Statistics 2013). Japan, however, is 80 percent mountainous and only 16 percent of its lowland coastal areas are inhabitable, which results in immense numbers of people crammed into relatively small spaces on the coastal margins (see Map 0.3). To put this into perspective, the population of the United States in 2013 was approximately 317.29 million (World Population Statistics 2014), but spread across nearly 25 times the land area. The Japanese therefore are tightly hemmed in by mountains to one side and oceans on the other, with both, not surprisingly, taking on great symbolic importance in their daily lives. The popularity of images of Japan's most iconic mountain—the snow-covered Fuji-san (where "san" means "mountain").

The natural environment of Japan, which is quite varied from region to region, exerts tremendous influence on Japanese sensibilities (Karan 2005: 9). In general, however, Japanese suffer from limited natural resources. Karan notes:

> Japan's natural resources are meager, and important materials such as oil and metals are scarce. Areas of good arable land are also severely limited. The main renewable resources are plants, forests, and fish. These are declining, however, primarily because of human activities such as overexploitation, shrinking acreage due to rapid urbanization, often-short-sighted land development policies, and largely unconcerned public.
>
> (ibid.: 26)

Although forests cover approximately 67 percent of Japan, given the overall small landmass, actually this is not very much, and they have been heavily exploited throughout Japan's history as a result of the popular consumption of and appreciation for wood and paper products (ibid.). Massive amounts of trees, for example, were used in the construction of Kyoto centuries ago. Reforestation efforts were made in the Edo period, but rapid deforestation increased once again during the Meiji through to the post-World War II period. And even when reforestation projects have been pursued, commercially profitable trees are planted, rather than those most appropriate to the location: "In this gloomy picture, nature serves commerce" (ibid.).

Nature is also made to serve culture. A mainstay of the Japanese diet is of course fish, but the nation must import from elsewhere, as local fishing grounds can no longer supply the demand, exacerbated by the concerns over contaminated water off the coast of Fukushima (see further discussion below). Japan is often critiqued for still being one of the few countries that practice whaling, as well as the now-infamous mass "dolphin kill" that occurs annually off the coast of Wakayama, as depicted in the documentary

The Cove (2009). But the demand for eel is also causing a lesser-known crisis, as the eel population decreases to the point of extinction, yet Japanese are encouraged to continue consuming this diminishing resource as this is considered part of their "culture."

Other mineral resources are similarly scarce, causing especially great concern as the nation debates how best to meet its citizens' energy needs. Despite Japan's continued reliance on coal as a fuel, for example, there is a minimal domestic mining industry, which met only 0.6 percent of the need in 2010, resulting in the importation of the remaining 99 percent from Australia (62.3 percent), Indonesia (19 percent), Russia (6.1 percent), and Canada (5.6 percent) (Japan Coal Energy Center n.d.). Japan imported 97.1 percent of its required natural gas in 2012 (Tokyo Gas. n.d.), and only produced 0.4 percent of its oil needs, importing the rest from abroad, with the majority coming from the Middle East (83.4 percent) (Fuha 2013). This lack of natural resources of course fuels, no pun intended, the current controversy over nuclear power.

On Friday, March 11, 2011 an earthquake with magnitude 9.0 hit some 70 kilometers (43 miles) off the coast of Tōhoku. Now commonly referred to as the "Great East Japan Earthquake," or simply "3/11," it remains the most powerful earthquake ever recorded in Japan. Even more devastating, the earthquake was followed by a *tsunami* with waves reaching 40.5 meters (133 feet) high, traveling up to 10 km (six miles) inland. To date, nearly 16,000 casualties have been recorded, with over 6,000 injured and still close to 3,000 people still missing. Countless buildings, roadways, and other structures were damaged, none more catastrophically than the Fukushima Daiichi Nuclear Power Plant, which suffered Level 7 meltdowns. The treatment of the nuclear crisis at the time and Japan's reliance on nuclear power continue to be debated (*Nova: Japan's Killer Quake* 2011; Kingston 2013).

Nuclear power has long been controversial in many parts of the world, but such concerns are made all the more provocative when we remember that Japan is the only nation to suffer the devastation of nuclear weaponry; therefore, as a people, Japanese are especially sensitive and aware of the destructive power of nuclear technologies (even if "the bomb" and energy-producing plants rely on remarkably different means of harnessing nuclear power). Following the disaster in Fukushima, all of the approximately fifty nuclear power plants in Japan were gradually shut down for "maintenance" and safety evaluation, and have remained off-line since. However, with such limited natural resources, Japan may have little choice but to continue upgrading its nuclear power facilities and bringing them back on-line. Manabe notes that not all Japanese are meeting this prospect with positive attitudes and that music

> ... has been an integral part of antinuclear demonstrations: here, music functions not only as an expression to be heard, but also—and perhaps more importantly—as a mechanism for encouraging participation and building solidarity among antinuclear citizens.
>
> (2013:1)

The controversy surrounding nuclear power was becoming increasingly heated as Japan prepared to bring several nuclear power plants back on-line in 2015.

Although this nuclear crisis results from advanced technology, it was of course an earthquake and the subsequent *tsunami* that were the impetus, and the Japanese have long faced similar natural disasters that have shaped cultural identity. The islands are part of the "Pacific Ring of Fire," a horseshoe-shaped area in the basin of the Pacific

Ocean prone to large earthquakes and volcanic eruptions, which can happen at anytime anywhere—indeed, Japan is constantly quaking and shaking. Historically, however, Japan has suffered from three immense earthquakes. Massive fires that destroyed the city and marked one of the most important historical moments in Japan's early modern history followed the first, the "Great Kantō Earthquake" in Tokyo in 1923. The "Hanshin Earthquake" in Kobe in 1995 shocked the world, and generated much critique of Japan's surprisingly slow acceptance of foreign assistance. Even today, Kobe commemorates this earthquake with an elaborate display of lights, attracting hundreds of thousands to the city every winter season (see Figure 1.1).

At the time of writing, the "Great East Japan Earthquake," followed by the massive *tsunami* in Tōhoku in 2011, remains the fifth largest quake in the world in recorded history, and hopefully for a long time into the future. Masuda suggests that the world may have a lot to learn from the Japanese in the aftermath of "3/11," as people "waited patiently for food, water, and medical attention" (2011: 62). Story after story emerged of selfless acts of support for strangers, behavior he attributes to the admirable Japanese traits of *ganbaru* (to persevere with patience and determination) and *gaman suru* (to suffer through hardship patiently); traits that the Japanese may have developed as a result of both human-made and natural disasters.

Japan's 124 volcanoes, many of which are dormant, including the iconic Fuji-san, are a constant reminder of not only the immense power of nature but also the concomitant insignificance of human life in its path. In Fall 2014, Ontake-san in Nagano suddenly erupted on September 27, killing 57 people who were ascending the mountain at the time. Japan's extensive mountain ranges also make travel difficult, while

Figure 1.1 Commemorative light display in Kobe

in contrast, navigable waterways are abundant in Japan, including rivers, lakes, and of course seas, which have collectively facilitated the movement of people throughout history. The abundant rivers, however, also often overflow as they drain from mountains, and heavy rains from monsoons in early summer and typhoons in the late summer and early fall regularly bring flooding and mudslides. In August 2014, 74 people, including schoolchildren, perished in sudden mudslides in Hiroshima, following a major typhoon.

The inadequate natural resources and destructive potential of much of Japan's environment, however, actually generates a great deal of respect for nature amongst the Japanese. Karan once again reminds us that

> The Japanese attitude toward these hazards illuminates an interesting fact in the life of the country. In other industrial countries, nature seems to exist only as a half-forgotten backdrop to life. In Japan, a personal relationship is recognized between humans and nature. Nature is a reality, not an abstraction. It brings beauty and calamity to everyday life . . . The Japanese seem to be eager to cooperate with nature and help to nourish and embellish its various forms, because they respect them and consider them so important.
>
> (2005: 33).

Natural disasters are so common that historically Japanese believed new eras were marked by such catastrophes (ibid.: 36). Thus nature becomes a "beloved enemy," greatly admired precisely because of its constant presence and destructive potential (ibid.: 33).

Figure 1.2 Kennin-ji garden in Kyoto

Suikinkutsu, Shishi-odoshi, *and the Sounds of Japanese Gardens*

Japanese gardens range from the potted plant outside the front door of a 30th-floor high-rise apartment in Tokyo, to the grandest Zen-inspired designs of thousand-year-old temples (see Figure 1.2). Nature is invited into the lives of Japanese not only through the visual appearance of such foliage, but also the sounds that inhabit these natural spaces. Many gardens contain ornaments designed to bring the listener into a greater state of awareness of what is around them and the importance of nature in our everyday lives. Created in the Edo period, the *suikinkutsu* (water pot), for example, is an upside-down jar buried underground. As water slowly drips through a hole and lands in the water pooled below, a soft pinging sound echoes, creating a most serene and appealing effect. The *suikinkutsu* is even used in concert by artist Tamura Hikaru, who appreciates the unique quality of each droplet (http://www.youtube.com/watch?v=enfTsvBCJfA). Also involving water, the *shishi-odoshi* (deer-scarer) brings a different timbral quality into the garden as water softly trickles into a bamboo stalk, which, once filled, gently tips forward to release its contents, snapping back to make a clacking sound as the end of the bamboo tube strikes a precisely positioned rock (http://www.youtube.com/watch?v=cvwHph4bFN0). Whether this actually scares away any deer is not the point; rather the differing quality of sounds combined is quite pleasing, inviting the listener into the natural environment of the garden through sound (Blasdel 2005:43).

Zen master and *shakuhachi* player Watazumido explains:

> Music cannot be limited to one form. It is all around you if you listen carefully. The sounds of water are music, or the wind in the trees, or children in the fields, or birds singing and crying. That is all music. Even the sound of boiling water can be music. The sound of *sukiyaki* cooking makes vibrations in the air and that is music. All these are just parts of one sound.
> (Sukiyaki and Chips 1984)

The Japanese, constantly faced with nature's immense power, as well as the presence of potential nuclear devastation, have come to appreciate the ephemeral nature of life—a way of thinking deeply informed by the dominant religious beliefs of Shintō and Buddhism (see further discussion below), as well as the cycle of the seasons. Although many cultures celebrate four seasons, the Japanese strongly differentiate between them, which they mark by celebratory and ritual events, songs and dances, varying patterns and colors on clothing, different foods, and subtle-to-overt themes in artwork. From the brightly colored fall foliage of maple leaves to the cherry blossoms in the spring, both of which attract hordes of viewers who gather in parks to drink and make merry, the Japanese remember the transitory nature of life, which in turn fosters a great appreciation for every moment of every day.

The effects of the natural environment on Japanese identity cannot be denied, but who the Japanese are today is of course also informed by whom they once were. The following discussion therefore summarizes key developments in the cultural history of Japan, introducing major musical genres along the way.

The Cultural History of Japan

There is little early written history of Japan, with the exception of the *Kojiki* and the *Nihon Shoki* (or *Nihongi*), the two oldest chronicles, both believed to be completed in the eighth century. Within these works, Japan is depicted as originating with a pair of deities—husband Izanagi and wife Izanami—who descend to earth along a rainbow serving as a bridge, and give birth to numerous additional gods, as well as the Japanese islands and other elements of nature. Music and dance inhabit even these earliest of mythological stories of Japan, most famously in the tale of Amaterasu. Daughter of Izanagi and Izanami, the sun goddess Amaterasu, who shared her light and warmth with the world, quarreled with her brother Susano-o, the storm god, blocking herself in a cave and casting the world into darkness. Other gods tried to entice her to appear, but it was not until her sister Ama no Uzume danced before the cave, drumming her feet loudly on the ground, that Amaterasu glimpsed outside, caught her own radiant reflection in a mirror and returned to the world. Music and dance enticed the gods then, just as it continues to be performed for the gods today (see further discussion below). Amaterasu is an ancestor of Emperor Jimmu, who is believed to be the first emperor of Japan, to whom the royal family continues to trace an unbroken lineage. Thus the royal family was positioned as descendants of the gods, a belief that would persist until the end of World War II, and amongst some Japanese even today.

Historical periods in Japan dating farther back than the eighth century, however, have been identified through archeological research, and in several ancient Chinese writings. These sources establish the origins of the Japanese people actually on mainland Asia, and a portrait of Japan's changing identity, often based on exchanges with foreign neighbors, begins to emerge (see Map 1 Figure 0.a; East Asian Historical Periods of East Asia). Japanese history is typically thought to begin with the Jōmon period (*ca.* 10,000 B.C.E.–300 B.C.E.). A specific type of clay figurine (*dogū*) recovered from ruins of this period suggests Japan's early identity was deeply connected with shamanistic beliefs and nature, which may have later developed into Shintoism, the dominant indigenous religion. Other archeological evidence indicates that Jōmon culture revolved around hunting and gathering, including the emergence of fishing techniques and thus launching Japan's long passion for marine products and seafood. The Japanese language also presumably began to develop in this period. Japanese culture, however, is generally believed to truly arrive with the development of wet rice cultivation in the Yayoi period (*ca.* 300 B.C.E.–C.E. 300). In the following years, new technologies, social systems, and economies continued to emerge.

Archeological evidence of great tombs (*kofun*) indicates various regional leaders began to merge under powerful rulers, the supposed descendents of Amaterasu, in the Yamato region who had the wealth and power to construct such monuments. These tombs were peppered with terracotta sculptures (*haniwa*) of objects found in daily life, such as houses and animals. The Kofun period (300–552) and subsequent Asuka period (552–710) are thus marked by the establishment of a centralized governing system controlled by an imperial line of divine origin. This resulted in the formalization of a stratified society, and a capital through which to manage the new unified land and its people, who, modeled after the Tang Dynasty, were now seen as property of the state. Exchanges with China and Korea became increasingly pronounced, with Buddhism finding its way into Japan around the mid-sixth century. And with Buddhism came the highly musical chanting of sutras (*shōmyō*) and related ideas of music theory that would inform Japanese music making for years to come (see further discussion below).

At this point, until the advent of the modern era, historical periods were named after the seat of government, emphasizing the importance of centralized governance and emerging urbanization. And of course these locations changed with each major natural disaster. Nara was established as Japan's capital by the beginning of the eighth century, launching the Nara period (710–84), a time when a vast array of artistic practices were imported from China and Korea, including architecture, visual arts, calligraphy, lacquering, and silk-making. Buddhism continued to flourish, resulting in the creation of some of the greatest Buddhist temples and sculpture in Japan's history (Karan 2005: 53). Musical instruments and genres of course were also imported, including court music (*gagaku*), and new ideas of music theory, which also would be highly influential in the future (see Chapter 3).

During the Heian period (794–1185), the capital was established in Heiankyo (now Kyoto), which remained the home of the imperial family until the court moved to Edo (now Tokyo) in 1868. During this period, Japan's geographical base expanded through all of Honshū, while outlying areas were seen as ancillary, establishing an understanding of center and periphery that continues to permeate Japanese identity. Modeled once again on urban design in China, Kyoto was laid out in a grid pattern, with the palace to the north, aristocrats housed nearby, and lesser folk in the social hierarchy, such as merchants, farther away. "The establishment of Kyoto marks the opening of the Heian age (794–1185), a period of remarkable artistic sophistication of the court and metropolitan aristocracy" (ibid.) illustrated with the fine poetry of early collections such as the *Man'yōshū* and *Kokin Wakashū*, and beautifully captured within the world's first great novel *Genji Monogatari (The Tale of Genji)* written by a lady of the royal court, Murasaki Shikibu (late tenth-century to early eleventh-century). *Genji Monogatari* in particular is replete with musical episodes, as the Lothario Prince Genji repeatedly falls head-over-heels in love with different women, one infatuation based solely on the sound of the lucky lady's performance on the Japanese zither (*koto*).

In subsequent years, the warrior class in Japan would gain increasing power over the court, first as the Fujiwara family married into the imperial line, resulting in positions of political power they would maintain for 200 years (Hendry 2003:13), and later as the relationship between the centralized state and local agriculture was replaced by the reliance of regional farmers on local governing families instead (ibid.: 13):

> In stark contrast to the artistic occupations of court life, these provincial rulers were concerned with the acquisition of military skills, and they developed a code of ethics that has become another major source of Japanese pride and identity. The *samurai* warriors, as they became to be known, valued deprivation and rigorous discipline in the interest of building an impenetrable inner strength of spirit. They trained themselves to conquer fear and be ready to die at a moment's notice.
>
> (Ibid.:14)

Though "[t]he principles of *bushidō* (or the way of the *samurai* warrior) were not specifically articulated until much later . . . the military leaders who developed this set of values gradually came also to wield greater political power throughout Japan" (ibid.), perhaps accounting for the nation's strong militaristic identity that would continue through the middle of the twentieth-century and has recently been resurfacing (see further discussion below).

In 1185, the great warrior clan Minamoto defeated other families who were then vying for power; they established the governing system known as the "*bakufu* (meaning 'curtain government' or 'ruling from behind the scenes'), at Kamakura, far from the imperial capital of Kyoto" (Karan 2005: 54) and thus initiated the Kamakura period (1185–1333). The emperor granted the head of the Minamoto family, Minamoto no Yoritomo (1147–99), the title of *shōgun*. He became commander of the military forces, essentially assuming rule over the country, while the emperor was rendered more of a figurehead. Later, Emperor Go-Daigo attempted to return the nation to a civilian-run as opposed to military government during the Kemmu Restoration (1333–36); however, rule was quickly assumed by another military family in the Muromachi period (1336–1573). Civil war ensued for the next 250 years, but "the period was also marked by economic growth and artistic achievements ... painting, classical drama, architecture, landscape gardening, ceramics, the tea ceremony, and flower arrangement—a great deal of what is recognized today as Japan's magnificent cultural heritage—blossomed in these stormy years" (ibid.: 55).

Noh, the oldest and arguably most elegant of the three great theatrical arts of Japan (the other two being *bunraku* and *kabuki*) represents a highly refined synthesis of literature, theater, dance and music (Kishibe 1984: 48). The art form was founded in the fourteenth century by two playwrights—Kan'ami Kiyotsugu (1333–84) and his even more famous son Zeami Motokiyo (1363–1443)—under the sponsorship of *shōgun* Ashikaga Yoshimitsu; it reflects Zen Buddhist philosophy and complex aesthetic ideas that have influenced not just music, but numerous artistic practices.

The years of fighting continued nonetheless until Oda Nobunaga (1534–82) and his loyal servant and successor Toyotomi Hideyoshi (1537–98) began to impose order in the Azuchi-Momoyama period (1573–1600), setting the stage for the unification of the country under the Tokugawa family. A new *bakufu* was established in Edo (now Tokyo) that would last until the mid-nineteenth century. The Edo (Tokugawa) period (1600–1868) is often depicted as a time of relative peace, as the *shōgun* of the Tokugawa clan, Ieyasu, solidified his rule and strategically placed family members in significant ruling positions throughout Japan. Essentially in the same fashion as European feudalism, regional leaders (*daimyō*), who answered to the *shōgun* and governed over other *samurai*, controlled Japanese culture (Hendry 2003: 14; Karan 2005: 56).

The Tokugawa family thus established a firm social hierarchy with class distinctions between *samurai* (the highest rank and the only people allowed to carry swords), farmers, artisans, merchants, and outcasts: "... there were also itinerant entertainers and others who remained outside the system at a lower level" (Hendry 2003: 15). Each class within this social order "had distinct rules by which to live, and all activities, from cultivation to trade, were registered and controlled" (ibid.: 16). The way of the *samurai* became increasingly esoteric, and although the merchant class was positioned low in the social hierarchy, they expanded their activities and increased in wealth and power, with commerce and agriculture both flourishing. Rice farmers produced a certain yield for their regional leader in exchange for protection. Rice (measured in *koku*; 1 *koku* = about 180.39 liters) became the primary currency, with one's power determined by the number of *koku* in one's coffers. These systems were far from perfect, especially as merchants amassed greater wealth in the face of the *samurai*'s progressively impotent position in society, and began to break down by the middle of the nineteenth century.

As part of exerting control over the nation and maintaining this relative peace (at least on the surface) Japan closed its doors to European traders and Christian missionaries. This isolation was motivated in large part by the cultural domination the government witnessed in other areas of Asia, "which was seen as a threat to the new social order" (Hendry 2003:15). With the exception of the Dutch, "who were allowed to occupy one island off the coast of Kyūshū, and provided a continuing trickle of knowledge from Europe" (Hendry 2003:5), the Japanese did not import new foreign goods or ideas. The Japanese were also banned from traveling abroad, thus launching the much-discussed period of Japan's isolation, which would last 250 years.

This condition, which similarly restricted the importation of musical ideas, actually allowed Japanese arts to flourish, taking on especially unique Japanese sensibilities. The *samurai* class continued to cultivate high arts such as *noh* as a Zen Buddhist practice, and solo instruments including the bamboo flute (*shakuhachi*), Japanese zither (*koto*) and the three-string lute (*shamisen*) developed expansive repertoires. Systems, resembling the hierarchical organization that characterized the society as a whole, for the transmission of these new performance techniques and types of music soon emerged (see further discussion in Chapter 3). Two more major theatrical genres, *bunraku* and *kabuki*, appeared in the seventeenth century. Unlike *noh*, which developed as a reified court style, common people generated these new theatrical forms as popular entertainment. *Bunraku* is distinguished by the use of puppets (*ningyō*), which are incredibly emotive and not seen as children's entertainment in any way (there are numerous puppetry traditions throughout Asia which are similarly perceived as high art). The music features the *shamisen* and a narrator (*gidayū*), who relates topics of interest for the masses—including current events, tales of class conflict in the Edo period involving *samurai* and *geisha*, and dramatic accounts of ritual suicide. The works of famous playwright Chikamatsu Monzaemon (1653–1725) are now read as classical literature. *Kabuki*, which also set numerous Chikamatsu plays, was also formalized in the seventeenth century, drawing on the instrumental music of *noh* and the narrative singing and *shamisen* of *bunraku*, but with human actors, stylized dancing, elaborate costumes and dramatic staging. Though both theatrical forms, strictly speaking, were deemed inappropriate for the *samurai* class, many would disguise themselves as merchants in order to attend these immensely popular performances, hinting at the failure of governmental policies to maintain the desired strict divisions of society and the changes to come in the modern era.

Japan's relative isolation came to an abrupt close when the doors were opened by Commodore Perry's arrival in 1853 with a directive from U.S. President Millard Fillmore to engage in trade. In 1854, Perry returned with the now-iconic nine "black ships" (large gunboats), essentially forcing Japan into international trade first with the United States and then the United Kingdom, Russia and France. Japanese identity would subsequently undergo major transformation as the people grappled with new technologies and ideologies of the West, launching the Meiji reformation of 1868 (see further discussion in Chapter 2). At the time, the Meiji emperor was "figuratively" restored to power, ending the rule of the Tokugawa *shōgun*. The name of historical periods since has changed with each new emperor.

Japan's complicated negotiation of modernism will be further discussed both as an ideology and in regards to musical modernity in Chapter 2. Nonetheless, it is important to note here, in this account of Japan's cultural history, that the Japanese began reshaping education, business, legal and military practices in line with new Western ideas from Europe and the United States. The old ruling system and social order of the Edo period was abolished, replaced in 1889 by a constitution establishing a parliamentary government with an aristocratic House of Peers and an elected House of Representatives. A railway system was installed, a postal service established and schools constructed throughout Japan. Western cultural products, from food to fashion, were readily consumed.

"In an incredibly short time, Japan became a modern, industrialized, military power" (Karan 2005:63), attacking China in 1894 and taking control of Korea and Formosa (now Taiwan). With the defeat of Russia in the Russo-Japanese War in 1904, Japan became the dominant imperial force in East Asia, growing increasingly militaristic during the Taishō period (1912–26), though not without some debate, as the nation joined the Allies in World War I, and crushed uprisings in Korea.

According to Karan, three different groups vied for leadership of Japan in the 1920s (2005:64). The *zaibatsu*, great industrial conglomerates, advocated for "peaceful economic penetration of Asia." Liberals, comprising primarily university professors and students, worked to broaden suffrage, encourage unionization, and decrease military power, "[b]ut the long tradition of passive submission to authority on the part of the masses made liberal reforms difficult" (ibid.). The third group, the military, were bent on increasing their own power and destroying "all democratic processes of government and civil rights" (ibid.: 65), and eventually they corrupted the *zaibatsu* with lucrative military contracts.

Riding the wave of the military's power, Emperor Hirohito ushered in the Shōwa period (1926–89), leading Japan through increasing imperialism. All "people were encouraged to think of themselves as ultimately related through their ancestors to the imperial family" and by extension the Shintō gods (Hendry 2003:18). *Samurai* ideals "were held up as personal qualities to emulate in the pursuit of the Confucian principles of loyalty and filial piety" and extended to the nation (ibid.:18). Japan's military machine peaked in World War II, but would not last. After the destruction of Hiroshima and Nagasaki by nuclear weaponry, and the complete desolation of Tokyo by fire bombing, Japan surrendered on August 15, 1945. Hirohito was allowed to remain emperor, although he had to publicly present himself as human and no longer a god.

Since World War II, Japanese have largely re-imagined themselves "victims" rather than "aggressors." Numerous wartime actions are downplayed or completely denied, including the "Nanjing massacre," during which hundreds of thousands of Chinese were executed in Nanjing, "biological experiments on prisoners of war" or forced labor of prisoners, and the controversial "comfort women" "in which [as many as 200,000] Asian and European women were forced to provide sex to Japanese soldiers" (Karan 2005:67). Many of these atrocities are only cursorily considered in Japanese school textbooks, if at all, causing continued outcry from both the individual and national victims.

Following the war, Japan once again experienced a massive influx of foreign influence from the United States. From 1945 to 1952, U.S. forces occupied Japan, creating a democratic constitution, demilitarizing the nation, restoring civil liberties and working to expand the economy. And indeed Japan's economic recovery in this time period is nothing short of astounding, as the Japanese labored long hours to rebuild the nation out of the ashes of World War II. Already by the 1960s, Japan had risen to become the third greatest industrial nation, with one of the most impressive train systems in the world, thriving massive urban centers, and emerging leaders in technological and automotive industries. By the 1980s, Japan was the second largest economy in the world. Emperor Hirohito would witness this remarkable rebirth prior to his death in 1989, which marked the beginning of the Heisei period. Japan's booming "bubble" economy of the 1980s collapsed in the early 1990s, and the country has since struggled to recover. In 2009, China surpassed Japan to become the second largest economy in the world; nonetheless, Japan is still holding on as the third.

This economic stagnation is in large part due to the nature of legislative power that has been in place in Japan since Occupation, comprising a Diet with elected officials in both the House of Representatives and the House of Councilors, the latter replacing the earlier House of Peers. "Administrative power falls to the Cabinet, a body of ministers, headed by the Prime Minister, responsible to the Diet, but supported by a very strong bureaucracy of civil servants" (Hendry 2003:213). The prime minister is chosen from members of the Diet. There are different parties constantly vying for majority power—just as with Republican and Democratic parties in the United States. However, with the exception of a few years in 1993 and 2007, the largest conservative party—ironically named the Liberal Democratic Party (LDP), as opposed to the Social Democratic Party (SDP)—has held the majority since its inception in the 1950s.

Political change moves roughly at the speed of glaciers in Japan, as decisions are often reached by consensus in the Cabinet (Hendry 2003:214), and the general populace remains quite apathetic towards the government's inability to recharge the sluggish economy. In 2014, Prime Minister Abe Shinzō had been making waves with what some saw as a return to imperialist policies, with the reinstatement of Japan's ability to have an active military (that is, one beyond self-defense), and of course plans to bring nuclear power plants back on-line as well in 2015. Japan's cultural history thus continues to inform contemporary identity.

Religious Practices in Japan

Throughout the above account, brief mention has been made of specific religious beliefs, in particular Shintō and Buddhism, the latter of which was imported from abroad, bringing with it musical and broader philosophical ideas that continue to resonate. It actually can be difficult to differentiate between religion and philosophy in Asia in general, and especially in Japan, where so many people do not consider themselves active adherents of any particular practice. Most Japanese in fact would probably tell you that they are not "religious" and do not "believe"; however, when asked if they visit a Shintō shrine on New Year's Day, or invite the local priest to bless a groundbreaking ceremony for a new home, or whether they expect to have a Buddhist cremation, they likely would respond "yes," seemingly adhering to the tenets of one system in the morning and another at night. This is reflective of the typical relationship that Japanese have with religious beliefs—they are pervasive in everyday life, but not necessarily something that someone *actively practices* as it were. Nonetheless, as we have already seen, these specific religious traditions exert tremendous influence on Japanese cultural identity.

Shintō and kagura

Shintō, which translates as "the way of the gods," is an indigenous, animistic religion that is flexible enough to allow for local beliefs with loose practice to flourish, as well as serving the needs of the imperial court, which again claims lineage to the gods, and requires numerous prescribed rituals. Japanese national identity is linked to Shintō, with "state Shintoism" reaching its peak in conjunction with the nationalistic fervor leading up to

Figure 1.3 Miyajima *torii*

World War II. There are many Shintō shrines (*jinja*) in which different deities reside that people visit for guidance and assistance, ranging from the smallest shelf in the corner of one's house (*kami-dana*) to the grandest of globally recognized living national treasures (see Figure 1.3). These shrines are entered through the iconic gate (*torii*), typically constructed of wood painted bright red, or recently of more practical concrete, which delineates the sacred space beyond. Both a healthy connection with nature and emphasis on purity are particularly important in Shintō aesthetics. In general, Shintō can be understood as marking major moments in life, such as the birth of a child, coming of age, marriage, building a home, etc., which are celebrated in numerous rituals and festivals (*matsuri*). Shintō in general is less involved with the afterlife, an area of concern that falls under Buddhism's care, thus feeding the ability for these two religions to happily coexist (Reischauer and Jansen 1995:203–215; Hendry 2003:126–143; Karan 2005:70–76).

As noted, the gods of Japan have long enjoyed music, which remain central to religious practices today. Shintō music, in general known as *kagura*, accompanies rituals in courtly, refined contexts (*mikagura*), large national shrine events (*okagura*) and community-oriented local folk festivals (*satokagura*) (Malm 2000:48–49). All these performance styles trace their origins to the dance of Ama no Uzume to attract the sun goddess Amaterasu from her self-imposed hiding in a cave and thus dancing is also a common component of Shintō rituals. Larger shrines, for example, may have female attendants (*miko*) who perform dances for the gods (*miko-mai*). This ritualized *kagura* is performed to the accompaniment of wooden clappers (*shakubyōshi*), a six-string zither (*wagon*), a type of transverse bamboo flute (*fue*) and an oboe-like double reed instrument (*hichiriki*). This type of esoteric performance is less common in the everyday life of contemporary Japanese, many of whom will never experience the courtly music and dance first-hand (ibid.:47–65).

Festivals, generally known as *matsuri*, on the other hand, remain a significant part of life in both rural and urban areas of Japan. *Matsuri* are often associated with particular times of the year, with many in the autumn as the harvest season comes to a close, and of course New Year's Day, which is celebrated quite differently than the North American penchant for "drinking until the ball drops" in Times Square. Although these *matsuri* vary tremendously throughout Japan, the music is generally known as *matsuri-bayashi* and typically consists of a small ensemble (*hayashi*) comprising a bamboo transverse flute (*shinobue*), two small double-headed drums with skins affixed by ropes, somewhat resembling a snare (*taiko*), a larger double-headed barrel drum (*ō-daiko*) and a small gong (*atarigane*) or cymbals (*chappa*). The *matsuri-bayashi* accompanies numerous dances, including the lion dance (*shishi-mai*). In *shishi-mai*:

> Like the dragon costumes in festivals in China and elsewhere in East Asia, the lion costume covers one or several people inside the lion's body and has a carved wooden head with jaws that clack together ferociously. Bringing good luck to the inhabitants and to the dancers themselves, the lion dances through the village and visits stores and homes.
>
> (Alves 2013:311)

In Winter 2010, the Kyoto-based *taiko* group (here referring to *taiko* as the modern ensemble style that relies on Japanese drums) Basara (see further discussion in Part III), donned

Figure 1.4 Basara performing "*Shishi-mai*"

the *shishi* costume and performed the *shishi-mai* in a small town just to the north of Kyoto (see Figure 1.4). The group visited several shops including a bakery, electronics store, hair salon, restaurant and even a private residence, each time performing in a neighboring small parking area or street, attracting stares from those passing by on foot or in cars. Some of these performances were pre-arranged, while some establishments agreed on the spot after a member of Basara offered their services, performing *shishi-mai* and receiving donations in small envelopes upon completion. The *shinobue* set the atmosphere and announced the arrival of the star of the show, the *shishi*, before performing a high-pitched repetitive melody, with wooden clappers (easier to carry about the town than a drum) to supply the accompanying, often syncopated rhythms, as well as hand-held bells (*suzu*), all of which would improvise as the *shishi*'s dancing became increasingly energetic. The *shishi* leaped and bounded, clapping and chomping its large wooden mouth near the bent heads of spectators who approached, appreciating the novelty of the event, as they exclaimed "*mezurashii*" (how rare!), and bringing good luck and fortune to all. Certainly this is not something one sees every day in this sleepy suburban town! Presumably the stores that agreed to the performances outside their doors felt they would benefit by receiving good luck from the gods in the form of customers coming to watch the performance and staying to purchase something after. One manager, who was extremely happy to see the group, in the end exclaimed "Wonderful, now I will have good fortune!" and handed over an envelope, which one of the staff stuffed into the *shishi's* mouth, the ritual way of showing one's appreciation. Thus the tradition continues in modern life.

Buddhism and shōmyō

Buddhism also exerts a strong presence both in the cultural history of Japan, evidenced by the number of Buddhist-inspired artworks and sculptures, as well as in contemporary

Figure 1.5 Kongōbu-ji garden at Kōya-san

society. First introduced during the Nara period, Buddhism was promoted as the state religion and today there are now 220,000 Buddhist monks (*sō*) and 84,000 temples (*tera* or *jiin*) (Relnet Corporation n.d.), though it can be difficult to separate Shintō shrines from Buddhist temples, as they often inhabit the same grounds (Reischauer and Jansen 1995:203–215; Hendry 2003:126–143; Karan 2005:70–76). There are many sects of Buddhism, but they share a general understanding that there is one Buddha who found enlightenment and was released from the cycle of suffering (Steinnilber-Oberlin 2011). According to Reischaeur and Jansen, Buddhism is similar to Christianity with its concern about the afterlife (1995:203–215). In the simplest terms, Buddhists believe in a never-ending cycle of suffering lives (*samsāra* in Sanskrit, or *rinne* in Japanese). This suffering derives from worldly attachment and desires. But one can be freed from suffering through Buddha's teachings, be released from *samsāra* and reach *nirvana* (*nehan* in Japanese).

The many sects of Buddhism share the key practice of chanting sutras (*shōmyō*), imported from China and Korea in the early Nara period. Early components of Japanese music theory, including scale types *ryo* and *ritsu* (see further discussion in Chapter 3), came from China to Japan through *shōmyō*, which is both meditative and incredibly musical. *Shōmyō* was formalized in the Heian period "when two Japanese priests, Saichō and Kūkai brought Chinese chants from the mainland and established the Tendai sect and the Shingon sect respectively. These two sects have been responsible for the major kinds of *shōmyō* we know today" (Kishibe 1984:45). Later sects, including Zen Buddhism, developed their own modes of chanting based on these two earlier styles. The following discussion explores more closely the practice of *shōmyō* at Mt. Kōya (referentially referred to as "Kōya-san" in Japanese), where the headquarters of the Shingon sect of Buddhism are now located (see Figure 1.5).

Kūkai (also known as Kōbō-Daishi) established Shingon Buddhism on the sacred mountain Kōya-san in the early ninth century. It is believed that he traveled to China, where he received the Shingon doctrine and then threw a "Buddhist implement" (a metallic object used in Buddhist rituals) across the sea, where it landed on Kōya-san, indicating where he should go and build his temple. Upon returning to Japan, he eventually established Shingon Buddhism and founded the Kōya-san monastery. He is generally celebrated as a great saint and is believed not to be dead, but rather resting silently in "eternal meditation" at Kōya-san, waiting for the next Buddha to return (Steinilber-Oberlin 2011:93–125). Attendants still bring meals twice a day and a change of clothes once a year to the temple where he rests, approached by walking through the largest graveyard in all of Japan (see Figure 1.6).

To reach Kōya-san by train, one travels south from Osaka and then takes a cable car, which ascends the mountain side at an alarming angle, passing through trees to the misty mountaintop, transporting the passenger from the reality below to the religiosity of Kōya-san above; a romantic depiction, yes, but also an actuality. Today, there are four thousand permanent residents in Kōya-san, a thousand of whom are monks. There are 117 temples at the top of the mountain, with 52 offering accommodations for devoted pilgrims, as well as the curious tourist, to stay and experience the life of the monk. Rengejo-in, for example, a sprawling temple on the outskirts of the tiny town, offers such accommodations and features the vegetarian cuisine that developed amongst the monks (*shōjin-ryōri*). Within this Buddhist temple, there is a large altar with offerings for the

Figure 1.6 Gravestones at Kōya-san

Shintō gods (*kami-dana*), once again revealing the blurred lines between these two religions—and their ability to coexist in harmony. All are invited to join private meditation at 5:30 in the evening, and morning chanting of the sutra at 6 a.m., an experience not to be missed despite the early hour, for some. In fact, it is hard to avoid, as a large bell struck with a hammer (*ō-gane*) rings at 5:55 a.m., calling all to prayer. The sound of other *ō-gane* can be heard echoing in the distance as neighboring temples similarly call their residents and guests to morning service. The main hall is ornate and highly decorated with flowers, lanterns, and colorful tapestries and scrolls. The monks sit in an inner chamber, while the practitioners face them from a separate seating area. The main priest begins the service, facing the altar with his back to the practitioners throughout the chanting, until at its conclusion he turns and delivers what is essentially a sermon—this particular day's being about the connection between the present world and the afterlife.

It is impossible to capture the smell of the incense and collective energy of the sleepy participants at the morning ritual, nevertheless an entire 17-minute recitation of the "Rishukyō" sutra, explaining the way to reach full enlightenment, is included in Track 1 with the intention of pulling the listener into the movement from opening incantation to increasing inward reflection of all in attendance (note this is not the sutra that was recited at the ritual described above, hence the following sermon covered a different topic). This recitation within Shingon Buddhism reflects many of the common characteristics of *shōmyō*, such as responsorial performance: a lead singer chants a statement, followed by choral response, both in slow tempo with a predominantly free rhythmic feel. Even when there are moments when a pulse seems discernible, there is no sense of

序

歸命毘盧遮那佛　無染無着眞理趣
生生値遇無相教　世世持誦不忘念
弘法大師增法樂
大樂金剛不空眞實三摩耶經
般若波羅蜜多理趣品
　　　　大興善寺三藏沙門大廣智不空奉　詔譯
如是我聞一時薄伽梵成就殊勝一切
如來金剛加持三摩耶智已得一切如來
灌頂寶冠爲三界主已證一切如來
一切智智瑜伽自在能作一切如來
切印平等種種事業於無盡無餘一切
衆生界一切意願作業皆悉圓滿常恆

Figure 1.7 "Rishukyō"

meter, but rather a spilling-forth of the sutra through what Malm describes as a "liquid, sliding movement between pitches" (Malm 2000:70). The recitation is supported at times with bells (*suzu*), and a thumping sound here, or by strikes on a small hanging gong (*kei*), resonating bowls (*kin*), or even the clashing of cymbals (*nyōhachi*), which mark the passage through different parts of the sutra. The priest at the recitation in the Rengejo-in introduced above, for example, strikes a bell or gong to signal the change to the next section, which he presents and to which the monks respond, each on their own pitch, thus creating a thick collection of tones.

The text is read from top to bottom and right to left (see Figure 1.7; the complete sutra can be found at http://www.nbn.ne.jp/~club88/risyukyou.pdf). Since the sutras originate in India and traveled through China to Japan, they can be sung in an Indian dialect, or Chinese or Japanese. And "[b]ecause the Japanese adopted Chinese ideographs for their written language, giving them Japanese pronunciations, it is possible for them to sing Chinese songs with their own pronunciation" (Malm 2000:67). Here the sutra is rendered in Chinese with the pronunciation written in Japanese to the right of each character in *furigana* (the "sound" of the characters in one of the Japanese alphabets, here *katakana*). The Shingon sect reads the sutra in *kan'on* reading, the way the monks learned in China in the seventh to eighth centuries. The monks only chant the Chinese characters (*kanji*) with the *furigana* running alongside.

The first section (lines 1–5) serves as an introduction to the sutra in which devotees pledge to keep searching for the truth and to increase the amount of joy one gains in the world by believing in Buddha's teaching. Sometimes the text repeats itself, such as when the chorus of monks responds, sometimes not. The head priest intones the name of "Kōbō Daishi" from 3:37–4:05 in the recording and the third line of the text, though the vowels are elongated like slow-pouring molasses in a melismatic fashion, and the monks respond in turn. There is an indented line of slightly smaller text, crediting the temple and monk who translated this sutra, and separating the introduction and recitation, but which is not read. Rather the introduction moves directly into the main recitation, which starts on the first line of the second block, at 4:48 with no break. To open the narrative, the head priest chants "*jo shi ga bun,*" roughly translated as "So I heard the story this way. . . ." The tempo increases and the rhythm becomes more pulsative, when the chorus of monks enters at 5:01 on "*isshi fuwakya fuwansei shu shu shō issei,*" the first line of text in the second section, thus beginning the tale of how Buddha found enlightenment.

Even if not actively participating in community festivals or chanting sutra, Shintō and Buddhism inhabit the daily lives of Japanese. Other religions and philosophical practices have entered Japan as well, exerting differing degrees of influence on Japanese cultural identity as a whole. Confucianism, for example, although not strictly speaking a religion, continues to influence Japanese society and moral codes, for example, emphasizing loyalty to the family, which extends to one's place of employment, and fulfilling one's expected roles in society. Christianity, on the other hand, was first introduced in the mid-sixteenth century, but was then expelled by the Tokugawa *shōgun* during Japan's period of isolation. Today, only between 1 and 2 percent of the population claims Christianity as their religion, likely due to the inability of the restrictive requirements of monotheistic belief to blend well with existing religions and the need for flexibility by the Japanese. Even those who embrace Christianity often participate in Buddhist and Shintō practices. In contrast, 43 percent of the Korean populace practices Christianity. The message within the gospel of Matthew "Blessed are the meek: for they shall inherit the earth" (Matthew 5:5) may have been particularly attractive to Koreans, given their history of colonial domination. Christianity's limited influence through conversion, however, belies its impact via the many schools and universities of Christian origin established there (Reischauer and Jansen 1995:203–215).

While there are only a few dominant religions with numerous sects in Japan, many more folk practices are relied upon in selecting auspicious names, suitable marriage partners, dates for major events, etc. (Hendry 2003:126–143), in turn highlighting the actual multiplicity of Japanese people.

Folk Song (*Min'yō*) and Regional Diversity

Japan may be understood as being relatively homogenous when compared to the supposed "melting pot" of the United States. Minorities in Japan comprise less than 3 percent of the total population. These include the Ainu, an indigenous people numbering anywhere from the official estimate of 25,000 to an unofficial tally of over 200,000 (Science Council of Japan 2011), who live primarily in Hokkaidō, 1.4 million Okinawans residing throughout the southern Ryūkyū islands, 2.1 million registered foreigners (Ministry of Internal Affairs and Communications 2014b) and an estimated 2–3 million *burakumin*, a low-caste people similar to the "untouchables" in

Hinduism (the Ainu are not typically included in minority statistics of Japan, because their status is not based on distinct ethnic boundaries). This relatively low number of minorities in part feeds the myth of a homogeneous and unique Japanese cultural identity, that developed as part of nation-building processes in the modern era (see further discussion in Chapter 2).

Diversity in Japan, however, is created by other means than ethnicity and class distinctions. Reigning social policies that restricted movement of peoples during the Edo period also fostered much regional variance, enhanced by the sheer number of islands and Japan's geographical terrain, with its immense mountain ranges; the result was numerous areas with distinct identities expressed through dialects, localized cultural practices and of course regional folk performing arts (*minzoku geinō*).

Labeling Genres of Japanese Music

Generic labels reveal much about the ways Japanese musics are organized, based on at times complicated perceptions of cultural origins and artistic hierarchies. For example, whether a music is considered Japanese (*hōgaku*) or Western (*yōgaku*) can be confusing, a result of "the failure of the modern ontological separation of Japanese culture into native and foreign categories" that does not consider the modernist incorporation of Western styles into indigenous practice nor continuous circulating flows of influence globally (Novak 2013:130). Kitagawa explains that in general these terms distinguish music (*gaku*) as Japanese (*hō*) or Western (*yō*), based on musical style rather than origin. Simple enough on the surface, as for example "[t]he *koto* music (termed *sōkyoku*) composed by Yatsuhashi Kengyō (1614–85), is *hōgaku*," while "the orchestral works written by Japanese composers trained in Western music, such as Takemitsu Tōru (1930–96), are seen as 'Japanese *yōgaku*'" (Kitagawa 2009:261). Different criteria, however, are used in determining whether a popular music is *hōgaku* or *yōgaku*: "Works written by a Western composer and performed by Western musicians fall into the *yōgaku* category, but if Japanese lyrics are attached to the same tunes and sung by Japanese singers, they are regarded as *hōgaku*" (ibid.:262). Thus a song produced in North America and sung in English is *yōgaku*, while its cover by a Japanese artist is considered *hōgaku*—the language and ethnicity of the performers here determine Japaneseness. "Moreover, *yōgaku* within the category of popular music also includes songs sung, for example, by artists from Turkey or Singapore . . . and *yō* means 'apart from Japan,'" rather than necessarily Western (ibid.).

Nihon ongaku may literally translate as "Japanese music," but is actually quite complicated. It most often "refers to *hōgaku* within the art music domain, as well as Japanese folk music, but does not extend to popular music" (ibid.), such that even recently composed *koto* music would be labeled Japanese, while a music deemed popular, even if written a century ago, would not. Therefore "time" is not really a criteria here, but rather there are other markers of Japanese cultural identity.

The development of popular music in Japan is seen as heavily influenced by Western styles. This is not to say that there were no broadly consumed musics for the purpose of entertainment before the Meiji period. After all, *kabuki* theater featured star performers and bawdy audiences long before Commodore Perry's "blackships" appeared on the horizon. But "popular" in this context refers to musics that are perceived as "modern"—"born out of urbanization, industrialization, and rationalization of people's lifestyles and values since the nineteenth-century in Europe and elsewhere" (Yano and Hosokawa 2008:345)—out of the same processes that define modernization (see further discussion in Chapter 2).

Popular music has been referred to by a number of terms throughout the modern era. Fujie translates *minshū ongaku* and *taishū ongaku* as "popular music" or "music of the masses" (1989:198), though these are not used in common parlance today. The term *kayōkyoku* was and still remains a term to refer to popular song in general, though is probably used most often to refer to Japanized Western popular song of an older style. The term *popyurā myūjikku*, which renders the English "popular" and "music" into Japanese phonetically, is likely the most common term.

As noted above, *minzoku geinō* refers to folk performing arts with immediate, regional ties, while *koten* refers to classical genres including court music, dance and the theatre as well as other styles that are considered to have high artistic merit (see further discussion below). Though both *min'yō* and *koten* are easily understood as Japanese musical categories, the classical arts are in general seen as more privileged (Arisawa 2012:181).

The difficulty, even futility, of isolating genres into East vs. West or indigenous vs. foreign dichotomies, or into distinctions between categories like art, classical, traditional, folk and popular only increases as musics blend and blur all such boundaries. Nonetheless, it is difficult to avoid such labels when considering music in contemporary Japan.

Min'yō on mainland Japan

Folk performing arts certainly are rich and plentiful in Japan. Folk songs specifically, most commonly referred to as *min'yō* (Hughes 2008:9), were sung in pre-modern Japan while people

> ... planted the rice in spring, threw their fishnets into the sea, wove cloth, and pounded grain. Folk songs accompanied many daily activities, serving to relieve boredom, to provide a steady beat for some activity, to encourage a group working at some task, to provide individual expression, and so forth.
> (Fujie 2002:356)

Min'yō thus can be further divided into nearly unlimited categories including work songs, dance songs, bawdy songs and children's songs.

Min'yō have changed over time and differ greatly by region and function; nevertheless, Hughes identifies certain general characteristic elements that survive and serve to unify the broad genre today (2008:26–39). Several of these musical qualities, such as pitch and scale, will be discussed in the context of other genres of Japanese music in Chapter 3. But there are points best raised here in order to understand the musical identity of Japanese folk song. For example, *min'yō* can be performed in free or fixed rhythm, although sometimes the boundaries can be difficult to discern. When metrical, *min'yō* are usually duple in simple (2/4) or compound (6/8) meter, sometimes with a swinging quality akin to jazz (ibid.:26); whereas in comparison, Korean folk song is predominantly in triple time, creating a decidedly different feeling.

Historically, *min'yō* were often unaccompanied, but instrumentation is now standardized, particularly for party songs and festival dancing, which includes simple hand-clapping, drums struck with sticks (*taiko*), different hand gongs (*kane*), or a variety of transverse bamboo flutes (*fue*) and the three-string lute (*shamisen*), or more rarely, the end-blown bamboo flute (*shakuhachi*) (ibid.:29–30). When present, the *shamisen* accompaniment usually keeps a regular rhythm while vocal lines arrive ahead or behind the instrumental phrasing (a voicing that will be further discussed in Chapter 3). Phrase lengths are not standard and can differ between the dance and music within the same piece (ibid.:28).

Min'yō are sung solo, or by a group in unison or in responsorial style, with a leader and chorus. In the latter case, the choral response (*hayashi-kotoba* or *uta-bayashi*) delivers "words of encouragement," and in some cases the chorus interjects vocal calls (*kakegoe*) (ibid.:30). No doubt one of the most distinguishing, and entrancing, qualities of *min'yō* are the incredibly ornamented vocals (*kobushi*). Hughes describes vocal melody as ornamented "horizontally":

> In place of elaboration in the vertical dimension, as it were, through Western style polyphony, instead the folk singer elaborates horizontally, ornamenting the vocal melody line to a far greater extent than in Western classical music. Polyphony and ornamentation often stand in an inverse relationship cross-culturally: too much of one tends to inhibit the other. Further, by using a relatively "straight" tone as their point of departure—rather than a constant *bel canto* vibrato—Japanese singers can bring their melodic twists and turns into greater prominence.
>
> (Ibid.:31)

The quality of *kobushi* depends on the individual singer. Hughes explains: "As Japanese singers are very proud of this element of their art, the topic arises frequently in conversation with foreigners, who are told that Western folk song has no *kobushi* and thus is rather insipid" (ibid.:32). Hughes further argues against the common assessment of *min'yō* vocal timbre as "nasal," yet a "tense throat" is common. However, it is the ornamentation that is key in assessing the quality of a folk song. He concludes: "In aesthetic evaluation of *min'yō* performance, the term used overwhelmingly is *aji*, 'flavour': this person's voice has *aji*, that way of ornamenting that song has no *aji*, etc." (ibid.:32). Not only are *min'yō* diverse by region, but they also vary even by individual performer and their particular ornamental style, that is, their *aji*.

Most *min'yō* not surprisingly are sung in regional dialects. Texts, however, are typically in strophic form, with a common syllable per line arrangement of 7-7-7-5 for a total of 26 syllables per verse (ibid.:33). Variables do exist and this pattern can be obscured in the ornamentation of performance (ibid.:33). Though ballads, often tragic tales, are sung, the "'folk-lyric,' a song of indeterminate length lacking a coherent, developed narrative" is common (Wilgus 1959:432, quoted in Hughes 2008:33). The "folk-lyric" is generally a shorter song, comprising independent verses that can be interchanged and expanded, theoretically indefinitely. And given the common organization of lines of text with 7-7-7-5 syllables, it is possible to set any text to any melody as long as the number of syllables roughly aligns. This system allows great variance, depending on the individual performer's tastes and ability (ibid.:34). Nevertheless, even though verses may be interchanged with other songs, many well-known *min'yō* are titled with the name of the community in which they originated, reinforcing strong regional associations.

Both the common qualities and diversity of *min'yō* are evident through comparison of two songs from different areas of Japan. "Hakone Mago Uta" (Track 2) is from the Hakone region on the island of Honshū, which is considered "eastern" Japan, while "Kagoshima Ohara-bushi" (Track 3) is from Kagoshima prefecture on the island of Kyūshū, which is considered "western" Japan. Both *min'yō* are from the collection of Ryūtaro Hattori, who compiled some 36 songs he felt represented a comprehensive sampling of the range of Japanese folk song, split into eastern and western Japan, and released by Folkways in 1966. The lyrics are included below first in Japanese and then romanized, both organized to highlight the 7–7–7–5 syllable pattern (please note "n" and extended vowels count as syllables in Japanese), and lastly translated to English with explanatory notes. However, the use of local dialects of course complicates the ability to accurately represent the original intent of the song (unless otherwise indicated, all lyrics will be presented in a similar fashion throughout the remainder of the text).

"Hakone mago uta" illustrates well the extensive *kobushi* that characterizes *min'yō*. The melody stretches each of the syllables in the standard 7–7–7–5 pattern, accompanied by simple *fue*, and some sort of *suzu* jangling, as if on the harness of a horse plodding along, hooves clacking on the cobblestones. Intermittent *kakegoe* punctuate the phrases of the main vocal line:

箱根　馬子唄
"Hakone mago uta"
("The hack-driver's song of Hakone")

(:20)
箱根八里は　馬でも越すが　こすにこされぬ　大井川
Hakone hachiri wa   uma de mo kosu ga   kosu ni kosarenu   Ōigawa
You can walk Hakone's 20 miles with a horse, but even if you want, you cannot cross Ōi river.

(1:40)
咲いて見事な　小田原つつじ　もとは箱根の　山つつじ
saite migoto na   Odawara tsutsuji   moto wa Hakone no   yama tsutsuji
Odawara's azaleas are flowering beautifully, but they used to be Hakone's mountain azaleas.

"*Hakone hachiri*" in the first line of the song refers to the distance from a specific inn in Odawara to Mishima, one of the stretches on the Tōkaidō—the famous thoroughfare between Edo (now Tokyo) and Kyoto in the Edo period. Thus "Hakone mago uta" is a simple song harkening back to an important moment in Japan's history.

"Kagoshima Ohara-bushi" offers a different style of *min'yō*, with less *kobushi*, but a lively *shamisen* accompaniment and *taiko*. The lines containing "*oharahā*" are the main song. "Hara" is a contraction of "Harara," a village in Kagoshima; the "o" means "little." Here the singer provides her own *uta-bayashi*, with the lines that begin "ē," though more typically another singer or chorus often provides these interjections. She also supplies her own *kakegoe* "ha yoi yoi yoiyasa," which again is usually sung by someone else. Every line contains some humor or play on words. For example, in the first line of text, the flowers are beautiful, the tobacco is tasty, and then the volcano erupts—juxtaposing delightful thoughts with disaster—not so surprising perhaps in the context of Japan's volatile natural environment. Fujie adds that "a certain outlandish sense of humor" is greatly appreciated by Japanese (2002:381) and is certainly well-illustrated in this example:

鹿児島おはら節
"Kagoshima Ohara-bushi"
("Kagoshima Ohara Song")

(:04)
（ハ　ヨイヨイ　ヨイヤサ）
花は霧島　煙草は国分　燃えて上がるは　オハラハー　桜島
（ハ　ヨイヨイ　ヨイヤサ）
(ha yoi yoi yoiyasa)
hana wa Kiri-shima tabako wa Kokubu moe te agaru wa oharahā Sakura-jima
(ha yoi yoi yoiyasa)
Beautiful flowers from Kiri-shima, tasty tobacco from Kokubu, and the volcano on Sakura-jima is erupting.

(:30)
雨の降らんのに　草牟田川濁る　伊敷原良の　オハラハー　化粧の水
ame no furan no ni Somuta-gawa nigoru Ishiki Harara no oharahā keshō no mizu
Even though it is not raining, the Somuta River's water is cloudy (rain makes the river cloudy with mud). Probably from the women of Ishiki Harara washing their makeup into the river.

(:49)
エー道端大根　引かずばどすかい　好いたすさまの　袖引かずばどすかい
（ハ　ヨイヨイ　ヨイヤサ）
ē michibata daikon hikazu ba dosukai suita susama no sode hikazu ba dosukai
(ha yoi yoi yoiyasa)
If you find a radish (*daikon*) on the side of a road, you pull it out. If you like someone, you pull his or her arm.

(1:07)
伊敷原良の　巻揚（まきゃげ）の髪を　髪を結うたなら　オハラハー　なおよかろ
（ハ　ヨイヨイ　ヨイヤサ）
Ishiki Harara no makyage no kami o kami o yuta nara oharahā nao yokarō
(ha yoi yoi yoiyasa)
The curly hair of the women of Ishiki Harara is pretty but even prettier when tied.

(1:31)
見えた見えたよ　松原越しに　丸に十の字の　オハラハー　帆が見えた
mieta mieta yo Matsubara goshi ni maru ni ju no ji no oharahā ho ga mieta
Beyond Matsubara I can see the cross crest of the house of Shimazu on a ship's mast. Welcome home lord.

(1:50)
エーヤッサヤッサ 大根(でこん)のヤッサ 切らすの高さ おかべたかどん 金もうけ
じゃんさお こげなこっつぁ めってなござらん めってござれば
からだもたまらんさ
(ハ ヨイヨイ ヨイヤサ)
*ē yassa yassa dekon no yassa kirasu no takasa okabe takadon kane mōke jansao
kogena kottsua mette na gozaran mette gozareba karada mo tamaransa
(ha yoi yoi yoiyasa)*
As for the radishes, if you don't have them you have to pay a lot at Okabe [this term is difficult to translate, but possibly a shop name here, or it could even refer to tofu in Kagoshima dialect] which are overpriced. This better not happen a lot, because if it does, I will fall apart.

(2:20)
桜島には 霞がかかる 私や貴方(おはん)に オハラハー 気がかかる
Sakura-jima ni wa kasumi ga kakaru wataya ohan ni oharahā ki ga kakaru
It is foggy over Sakura Island. I am foggy [have feelings] for you.

Min'yō such as "Hakone mago uta" or "Kagoshima Ohara-bushi" continue to be performed today, providing an important bridge with the past, while connecting Japanese people to their community and creating a sense of shared identity. Hughes introduces the common phrase "*Min'yō wa kokoro no furusato*" (Folk song is the heart's hometown) (ibid.:1), locating the important connection between Japanese identity and *min'yō* in the all-important *furusato*—an often imagined rural hometown that all Japanese long to return to and which therefore symbolizes community and belonging. Folk songs remain popular because of their ability to capture the Japanese desire to connect both with pastoral life in the countryside and a simpler past (Fujie 2002: 356). Fujie explains:

> Despite increasing geographic mobility and cultural homogenization, the Japanese identification of people and songs with their original home area is still very strong ... *Furusato*, or the concept of a home community, maintains a strong emotional grip on today's urban dwellers—even those who left home several decades earlier. The folk song, with its associations and allusions to a particular region, expresses their nostalgia for a faraway place. Thus, nostalgia not only for a different time but also for a different place underlies their popularity.
>
> (Ibid.:357)

Min'yō thus bring together communities in both rural and urban contexts within Japan, often expressing the idea of a bucolic home even for those born in the heart of one of the country's numerous cities.

As a result, Hughes argues *min'yō*

> ... is seen as quintessentially Japanese, even by those who consider it to represent a provincial or backward aspect of Japanese culture unsuitable for international exposure. The Japanese perceive a close link between 'Japaneseness' and *min'yō*.
> (2008:300)

Min'yō in fact may survive in contemporary Japan because of its role in the formation and maintenance of identity in a rapidly changing society:

Elderly rural residents find that joint participation in preservation societies [*hozonkai*] reaffirms their life experiences and thus raises their self-esteem. New urban migrants turn to songs from their home regions to recapture their identities amidst the sea of superior strangers. Newly formed neighborhoods often feel the need for a 'new folk song' to create a sense of community. Urban residents of longer standing may join a *min'yō* class in order to find a group to belong to outside the family—an important need in a society which puts so much stress on belonging, and one which *min'yō* with its communal orientation is particularly well qualified to fill. Increasingly, participation in *min'yō* contributes to one's sense of identity as Japanese: it is a uniquely Japanese form of music, often considered uniquely difficult for foreigners and thus a symbol of the superiority of Japanese culture. (Ibid.:303)

Hughes suggests, however, that the same difficulty that leads to great pride may also be preventing some young people today from performing *min'yō* because they are intimidated by the regional lyrics and required vocal skills (ibid.:28). In contrast, the genres *tsugaru-jamisen* (a narrative style from the Tsugaru region that features a flashy *shamisen* part) and *taiko* (here referring to the modern ensemble drumming style) enjoy popularity in large part by being instrumental genres—and

> ... the fact that the young are not required to make potentially embarrassing attempts at singing seemingly old-fashioned lyrics in a difficult traditional style. Japan's guitar-playing youth are ready to tackle "*[t]sugaru-jamisen* in a way that singers of pop music and *fōku songu* [post-World War II popular music influenced by the North American folk boom] are definitely not prepared for with *min'yō*.
> (Ibid.:281)

Similarly *taiko* "provides a sense of contact with tradition that does not, however, require any embarrassing attempts at 'traditional'-style singing" (ibid.:282).

Nonetheless, *min'yō*, at least for now, is secure in its ability to capture certain characteristics important to Japanese national identity, including the assortment of regional practices. And interest in *min'yō* may even be enjoying a slight revival given the popularity of Okinawan folk music in recent decades.

Okinawan min'yō *and musical identity*

People who claim Okinawan heritage are actually one of the largest populations of Japanese minorities. The Okinawan people, however, were actually part of the independent kingdom of Ryūkyū from 1429 until incorporation into Japan in 1879. Okinawa was officially occupied by Allied forces from 1945 until 1972, and the U.S. military continues to exert a controversial presence in Okinawa, with over half the 47,000 U.S. troops in Japan stationed on the islands in over thirty bases. Concerns about environmental damage, crimes committed by servicemen and accidents rage on (Okinawa Prefectural Government 2011; McCurry 2014). Okinawans thus have long struggled to assert a distinct identity in the face of colonizing forces; however, in the end, this situation may in fact help preserve their uniqueness.

Historically cultural markers of Okinawan identity once were criticized, but as the desire to assimilate the southern islands into mainland Japan (including Honshū,

Hokkaidō, Shikoku and Kyūshū) increased in the early twentieth century, connections between the two cultural areas were highlighted. In more recent years, regional Okinawan identity came to be celebrated and even has been used to construct a national Japanese cultural identity (Gillan 2012a:47–48). National recognition of Okinawan performing arts as so-called "Intangible Cultural Properties" (a designation for arts deemed of great cultural significance), for example, not only establishes their legitimacy as art forms (Gillan 2012b:227), but also affirms Okinawa's recognition as part of mainland Japan. As Okinawan popular musics that drew on elements of folk music began to enjoy success in world music markets, first with Kina Shōkichi in the 1970s and a later boom in the 1990s and 2000s, Okinawan minority musical practices came to represent Japanese culture as a whole. So the minority comes to represent the majority musically, both within Japan and in global contexts.

In the process of constructing local and national identity through Okinawan music the image of "Okinawa as [an] historical root of Japan" became common (Gillan 2012a:151). Gillan explains:

> Okinawa has often been portrayed in the [twentieth] century as a link to ancient Japanese "roots," and this cultural image has been frequently referenced in the context of the Okinawa music boom. Much of the cultural representation of Okinawan in the Japanese media has presented the islands as an antithesis to the harsh realities of modern Japanese city life—as a region rich in spirituality where gods and ancestors are still revered.
>
> (Ibid.: 151)

An impression of Okinawa as pristine, ancient and tropical was created and widely marketed through song, both inside Japan and internationally.

While mainland *min'yō* may seem "old-fashioned" to many young people, Okinawan folk song (called *min'yō*, or *koten min'yō*, or *shimauta*) is thus at once both familiar and exotic. As Hughes explains, "For mainlanders, Okinawa is the most accessible and comfortable 'foreign' culture. Okinawan language, music, dance, clothing—all are related to those of the mainland, yet sharply different" (2008:282–283). Okinawan music, able to express a common Japanese cultural identity for many people, is nevertheless still fresh and interesting.

As an island chain extending south of the Japanese mainland to Taiwan, Okinawan music shares characteristics with both Chinese and Japanese music. The unique identity of Okinawan music is created in large part by the use of a distinctive pentatonic scale type that dominates music of the Ryūkyū islands (see Figure 1.8). This scale type sounds similar to those found in South East Asia and hence distinguishes this music in general from that produced in mainland Japan, which is largely based on different scale types primarily imported from China (see further discussion in Chapter 3).

Ryūkyū Scale

Figure 1.8 *Ryūkyū* scale

Okinawan musical identity is located not only in the quality of the "*Ryūkyū* scale," but also in the three-string, snakeskin-covered *sanshin*, which itself has become an important "symbol of Okinawan cultural identity" (Gillan 2012a:31). Related to the Chinese *sanxian*, the *sanshin* is believed to have entered Okinawa in the late fourteenth century, although clear references are not found of the instrument until the sixteenth century. The *sanshin* would later develop into the *shamisen* in mainland Japan and thus serve as an important bridge connecting Okinawan and mainland musical identity. But the instrument was modified to create a different timbre, has a larger body, and is covered with cat or dog skin, likely as there were not the same large snakes as found on Okinawa (ibid.:32–33). In Okinawa, the *sanshin* held a strong association with the Ryūkyū court and the elite well until the mid-twentieth century, so much so that in the past, the instrument and its practice were looked down upon by farmers, as mastering the techniques and learning repertoire requires a great deal of time—time that could be better spent in the fields (ibid.:34):

> The instrument currently enjoys a position of cultural distinction throughout the prefecture as a symbol of Okinawan cultural identity. A well-known saying makes the point that, while the literary Chinese commonly display a poetry scroll in the main room of their houses, and the *samurai*-influenced Japanese display a sword, music-loving Okinawans still commonly display a *sanshin* as the focal point of their living rooms. While it would be an exaggeration to say that all Okinawans have direct experience of, or even interest in, the *sanshin*, it is nevertheless a "popular" instrument in a way that is rarely seen for traditional instruments in other parts of Japan.
>
> (Gillan 2012a: 32)

Many of these issues and musical elements are illustrated in "Kohama-bushi" (Website Example 2), an example of *koten min'yō*, or "classical folk song," from Yaeyama in Okinawa (also known as *fushiuta* (melodic song) or simply as *min'yō*), with Takamine Mitsu on vocals and *sanshin*, Ishigaki Kyoko on the 13-string zither (*koto*) (which is much less discernible than the distinctive plucking of the *sanshin* in this recording) and transverse bamboo flute (*fue*) by Haino Kiyoshi.

The piece is in a *Ryūkyū* scale similar in sound to scales within South East Asian music, especially the Balinese *pelog*, and actually this performance feels remarkably like those one may hear in the many temples of Bali. As an offering song, the text is poetic, thanking nature and the gods for the rice harvest. The lyrics in the original Yaeyaman are included below. The romanization of Okinawan is difficult, however, as there are many dialects even on a single island. Yaeyaman also contains a vowel sound between "i" and "u," which is romanized with "ï," while consonants "f/h" and "w" differ by village and island. Long vowels are romanized with the modified Hepburn macron (Gillan 2012a:xv). Given the complicated process translating this text, please find the original in Yaeyaman dialect, followed by romanization, translation into mainland Japanese and finally English:

小浜節
"Kohama-bushi"
("Kohama Song")

(:20)
小浜てる島や果報の島やりば大岳ばくさで白浜前なし（ヨオンナ　以下略す）
くもまてぃるしぃまや　かふぬしぃまやりば　うふだぎばくさでぃ　しるぱまいなし
kumoma tïru shïma ya kafu nu shïma yariba ufudagi ba kusadï shirupama mainashi
小浜という島は果報の島であるから大岳を背にして白浜を前にしている
The island called Komoma has the good fortune to have tall mountains in the back and white beaches in the front.

(1:48)
大岳に登てうし下し見りば稲粟のなうり弥勒世果報
うふだぎにぬぶてぃ　うしくだしみりば　いにあわぬなうり　みるくゆがふ
ufudagi ni nubuti ushikudashi miriba iniawa nu nauri mirukuyugafu
大岳に登って下を見ると稲粟がよく実り豊年満作である
When you climb up the mountain and look down, you can see the fields of millet ready to be harvested.

(3:21)
稲粟の色や二十頃美童粒美らさあてど御初上げる
いにあわぬいるや　はたちぐるみやらび　ちぃぶぢゅらさあてぃどぅ　うはつぃあぎる
iniawa nu iru ya hatachi guru miyarabi tsïbu jurasa atïdu uhatsï agiru
稲粟の色は二十頃の娘のように色艶が良く粒ぞろいで初穂は神仏に捧げる。
The color of the millet resembles the skin of young women and the grains are all shiny and the same size. The first harvest is a gift to the gods.

Not surprisingly, there are many versions of this song available on the Internet, including an interpretation by well-known Yaeyaman popular musician Ara Yukito, who added guitar, thus creating a style that helped propel these local musics to the global stage. The recording on the website here is not made by professionals, however, and I make no attempt to evaluate the quality of this performance—indeed, this is not the point. Rather, I include this version because of the honesty of the vocal; a reminder that these musics exist in the everyday lives of the people who sing them.

Okinawan music today, just as with the *min'yō* discussed above, varies greatly with each island possessing its own identity and even on the same island, further distinctions by village. And just as images of the islands came to represent Japanese culture as a whole in the past, Gillan argues Okinawan music is now being used to represent a multiplicity of minority identities:

> To give one example, the Charanke *matsuri*, an annual festival held in Tokyo's Nakano district since 1994, was established to promote cultural links between Okinawan and Ainu groups in the Japanese capital, and features performances of traditional music and dancing, food and crafts from both regions.
> (2012a:180)

Okinawan music has been linked through concerts with other minority groups in Japan, including Koreans, collectively "presenting images of Japan's cultural minority groups" (ibid.).

Although beyond the scope of detailed consideration here, each of the minority groups introduced at the beginning of this section similarly have unique and varied musical practices with a compelling story to tell about Japanese cultural identity (UNESCO 2009; Bender 2012; Pilzer 2012; de Ferranti 2013). As interest in minorities in general increases in Japan, no doubt more studies of the role of music making amongst these communities will also develop, and in so doing will thoroughly and finally debunk the mythology of homogenous Japan—a myth that resulted as part of the search for Japaneseness in the modern era, the topic of the following chapter.

References

Alves, William. 2013. "Japan." In *Music of the Peoples of the World*, 3rd Edn., pp. 309–333. Stamford, CT: Cengage Learning.

Arisawa, Shino. 2012. "Dichotomies between 'Classical' (*koten*) and 'Folk' (*min'yo*) in the Intangible Cultural Properties of Japan" In K. Howard, ed., *Music as Intangible Cultural Heritage: Policy, Ideology, and Practice in the Preservation of East Asian Traditions*, pp. 181–196. Farnham: Ashgate.

Bender, Shawn. 2012. *Taiko Boom: Japanese Drumming in Place and Motion*. Berkeley: University of California Press.

Blasdel, Christopher Y. 2005. *The Single Tone: A Personal Journey into Shakuhachi Music*. Tokyo: Printed Matter Press.

The Cove. 2009. 92 minutes. Louie Psihoyos, dir.

de Ferranti, Hugh. 2013. "Music-Making among Koreans in Colonial-Era Osaka." In H. de Ferranti and A. Tokita, eds., *Music, Modernity and Locality in Prewar Japan: Osaka and Beyond*, pp. 229–254. Farnham: Ashgate.

de Kloet, Jeroen. 2010. *China with a Cut: Globalization, Urban Youth, and Popular Music*. Amsterdam: University of Amsterdam Press.

Fuha, Raizō. 2013. "Which countries Japan is importing oil from?" *Yahoo Japan News* (August 30, 2013): http://bylines.news.yahoo.co.jp/fuwaraizo/20130830-00027687 (accessed November 10, 2014).

Fujie, Linda. 1989. "Popular Music." In R. Powers and H. Kato, eds., *Handbook of Japanese Popular Culture*, pp. 197–220. New York: Greenwood Press.

———. 2002. "East Asia - Japan" In J. Titon, ed., *Worlds of Music: An Introduction to the Music of the World's Peoples 4th Edn.*, pp. 331–384. Belmont, CA: Schirmer/Thomson Learning.

Gillan, Matthew. 2012a. *Songs From the Edge of Japan: Music-Making in Yaeyama and Okinawa*. Farnham: Ashgate.

———. 2012b. "Whose Heritage? Cultural Properties Legislation and Regional Identity in Okinawa." In Howard, Keith, ed., *Music as Intangible Cultural Heritage: Policy, Ideology, and Practice in the Preservation of East Asian Traditions*, pp. 213–228. Farnham: Ashgate.

Hendry, Joy. 2003. *Understanding Japanese Society*, 3rd Edn. New York/London: Routledge.

Hughes, David. 2008. *Traditional Folk Song in Modern Japan: Sources, Sentiment and Society*. Folkestone: Global Oriental.

Japan Coal Energy Center. n.d. "Japan's Coal Usage." *Japan Coal Energy Center* (n.d.): http://www.jcoal.or.jp/coaldb/country/06/post_9.html (accessed November 10, 2014).

Karan, Pradyumna P. 2005. *Japan in the 21st Century: Environment, Economy, and Society*. Lexington: University of Kentucky Press.

Kingston, Jeff. 2013. *Contemporary Japan: History, Politics, and Social Change Since the 1980s*, 2nd Edn. Malden: John Wiley & Sons Ltd.

Kishibe, Shigeo. 1984. *The Traditional Music of Japan*. Tokyo: The Japan Foundation.

Kitagawa, Junko. 2009. "Music Culture." In Y. Sugimoto, ed., *The Cambridge Companion to Modern Japanese Culture*, pp. 261–280. Cambridge: Cambridge University Press.

Malm, William P. 2000. *Traditional Japanese Music and Musical Instruments*. Tokyo: Kodansha.

Manabe, Noriko. 2013. "Music in Japanese Antinuclear Demonstrations: The Evolution of a Contentious Performance Model." *The Asia-Pacific Journal* 11(3).

Masuda, Norman, T. 2011. "Why Japan Matters." *Education About Asia* 16(2):61–62.

Mathews, Gordon. 2004. "Fence, Flavor, and Phantasm: Japanese Musicians and the Meanings of 'Japaneseness'." *Japanese Studies* 24(3):335–350.

McCurry, Justin. 2014. "US promises to reduce burden of military presence in Okinawa." *The Guardian*. (February 12, 2014): http://www.theguardian.com/world/2014/feb/12/us-promises-reduce-military-okinawa-airbase-futenma (accessed August 12, 2014).

Ministry of Internal Affairs and Communications. 2014b. "Statistic of Foreign Residents in Japan." *Ministry of Internal Affairs and Communications* (June 1, 2014): http://www.e-stat.go.jp/SG1/estat/List.do?lid=000001127507 (accessed November 20, 2014).

Naka, Mamiko. 2002. "Cultural Exchange." In R. Provine, Y. Tokumaru and J. Witzleben, eds., *East Asia: China, Japan and Korea. The Garland Encyclopedia of World Music Vol. 7*, pp. 49–52. New York/London: Routledge.

Nova: Japan's Killer Quake. 2011. 60 minutes. PBS. NOVA6224

Novak, David. 2013. *Japanoise: Music at the Edge of Circulation*. Durham, NC: Duke University Press.

Okinawa Prefectural Government. 2011. "US Military Base Issue in Okinawa." *Okinawa Prefectural Government* (September 2011): http://www.pref.okinawa.jp/site/chijiko/kichitai/documents/us%20military%20base%20issues%20in%20okinawa.pdf (accessed August 12, 2014).

Pilzer, Joshua D. 2012. *Hearts of Pine: Songs in the Lives of Three Korean Survivors of the Japanese "Comfort Women."* Oxford: Oxford University Press.

Rawski, Evelyn S. 2002. "Cultural Interactions in East and Inner Asia." In R. Provine, Y. Tokumaru and J. Witzleben, eds., *East Asia: China, Japan and Korea. The Garland Encyclopedia of World Music Vol. 7*, pp. 9–38. New York/London: Routledge.

Reischauer, Edwin O. and Marius B. Jansen. 1995. *The Japanese Today – Change and Continuity, Enlarged Edn*. Cambridge, MA: Harvard University Press.

Relnet Corporation. n.d. "Religion in Japan." *Relnet Corporation* (n.d.): http://www.relnet.co.jp/relnet/brief/r10.htm (accessed November 20, 2014).

Science Council of Japan. 2011. "Ainu Political Moves and People's Acknowledgement." *Science Council of Japan* (September 15, 2011): http://www.scj.go.jp/ja/info/kohyo/pdf/kohyo-21-h133-1.pdf (accessed November 20, 2014).

Steinilber-Oberlin, E. 2011/1938. *The Buddhist Sects of Japan: Their History, Philosophical Doctrines and Sanctuaries*. New York/London: Routledge.

Sukiyaki and Chips. 1984. 60 minutes. Shanachie 1213.

Surak, Kristin. 2013. *Making Tea, Making Japan: Cultural Nationalism in Practice*. Stanford: Stanford University Press.

Tokyo Gas. n.d. "Secret about Natural Gas." *Tokyo Gas* (n.d.): http://www.tokyo-gas.co.jp/kids/genzai/g1_2.html (accessed November 10, 2014).

UNESCO. 2009. "Traditional Ainu Dance." *UNESCO*. (2009): http://www.unesco.org/culture/ich/RL/00278 (accessed May 14, 2014).

Wilgus, D.K. 1959. *Anglo-American Folksong Scholarship Since 1898*. Rutgers University Press.

World Population Statistics. 2013. "Japan Population 2013." *World Population Statistics* (September 27, 2013): http://www.worldpopulationstatistics.com/japan-population-2013/ (accessed November 10, 2014).

——. 2014. "Population of the United States 2014." *World Population Statistics* (May 19, 2014): http://www.worldpopulationstatistics.com/population-of-the-united-states-2014/ (accessed November 10, 2014).

Yano, Christine R. and Shūhei Hosokawa. 2008. "Popular music in modern Japan" In A. McQueen Tokita and D. Hughes, eds., *The Ashgate Research Companion to Japanese Music*, pp. 345–362. Farnham: Ashgate.

CHAPTER 2

Japanese Cultural Identity and Musical Modernity

The audience is brought to attention by a resounding wooden clapper, first playing a sparse rhythm, but gradually increasing in frequency, reaching a peak, before diminishing back to silence. This opening rhythmic contour is mimicked on a medium-sized barrel-shaped drum, struck with long, narrow sticks on the skin head and wooden body, before a rhythm played with both sticks begins, energetic, bouncing and brief, but poignant—known as "yose-daiko," this drummer's call opens the sumō match in the morning, just as it opens the exploration of Japanese cultural identity and musical modernity here.

Sumō, a wrestling match in a small, sand ring, between two, typically quite large, men in minimal attire, is widely considered a national sport of Japan; it is steeped in tradition and therefore expresses a unique Japanese cultural identity. But the elements that mark this traditionalism are actually modern conventions, assigned as a result of extensive intercultural exchange and the influence of the West (Tierney 2007). Prior to the advent of the Meiji period (1868–1912), when Japan suddenly ended a long era of isolation and threw open its doors to Western trade, and concomitantly imported ideologies of nationhood, wrestling took place as popular entertainment throughout the country and was not seen as traditional nor representing a unified national identity in any way. Tierney argues that it was in fact Westerners, invited to *sumō* matches in the mid-1900s, who began to frame the sport as representing the nation (2007:71). However "foreign observers regularly wrote about *sumō* wrestling as indicative of Japan's backwards and uncivilized position in the evolution of cultures," which was embodied in the violent acts and naked bodies of wrestlers (ibid.:71). *Sumō*, at that time perceived from outside Japan as a national sport, was thus fashioned as a barbaric practice, as a way of degrading the country as a whole, and the wrestlers' bodies came to be viewed by critics as representing a negative, pre-modern past (ibid.:74).

In the late 1900s, *sumō* therefore was refashioned to represent a more respectable, healthy body and in turn a progressive, modernized nation, ironically by embracing tradition. Tierney explains, "What was once a popular display to be watched now became a moral ideology and the 'way' to both bodily and spiritual improvement and purity" (ibid.:76). During the Meiji period:

> The wrestlers who had once been an embarrassment of Japan were now role models for their fellow citizens—the embodiment of a primordial Japanese spirit. These developments were part of a turn to 'tradition.' While these imbricated categories of 'sport' and 'tradition' have often been contrasted, it should be noted that the Japanese word for tradition, *dentō*, was resuscitated at this time and mobilized for nationalist projects.
>
> (Ibid.:76)

Thus the nation of Japan, and hence Japanese cultural identity, was equated with ideas of "traditionalism" in the face of what was perceived as Western "modernism." In the twentieth century, this modernist desire to construct an appropriate national sport resulted in many markers of tradition being assigned to *sumō*. The costume of the referee, for example, was designed to look like clothing from the fourteenth century, and he was allowed to carry a short sword, a practice that had been banned decades earlier: "With these new outfits and the re-addition of the short sword, the referees were transformed from contemporary Japanese to historical figures" (ibid.:79). Even though today *sumō* takes place indoors, there is a roof in place designed to appear like that found in a famous seventh-century temple in Nara, "furthering the link between *sumō* and a primordial Japan" (ibid.:79). *Sumō* came to express a national Japanese identity in which modernity is consciously wrapped in traditional garb.

Essentially, modernization froze *sumō* in time (ibid.:83), so much so that, "by the 1930s, *sumō* had fully transformed into a reified tradition. What had been a marginal popular performance at the center of popular culture was turned into a central symbol of the Japanese nation" (ibid.:83). What happened with *sumō* encapsulates broader modernizing processes in the late nineteenth and twentieth centuries, through which Japanese identity *vis-à-vis* the West came to be equated with tradition—at times derided as old-fashioned and even barbaric, and at others celebrated as representing an essential, prized Japaneseness. The idea that in order for something to be perceived as representing an ideal Japanese cultural identity, it must be grounded in long-standing local practices, however, ignores the historical impact of outside influences (ibid.:84), and the fact that Japanese culture has of course long been shaped by intercultural interaction and hybridity.

The Japanese are amazingly adept at importing and adapting foreign musical ideas and instruments—from the *shōmyō* of Buddhism to the *sanshin* of Okinawa in the proceeding chapter—to meet local aesthetic and social needs, and in the end creating something uniquely Japanese. This process was complicated with the rapid exposure to Western musical forms and ideology that arrived with the Meiji period. Like *sumō*, as Japanese engaged with modernity, ideas of just what music should represent the nation drastically changed. Traditional musics, here meaning those that originated prior to the Meiji period, whose "traditional garb" is always apparent, were similarly at times dismissed as representing an outdated Japan and others celebrated. The markers of tradition contained in these musics would occasionally mix with new Western styles, in an attempt to assert a Japanese identity much like the short sword or the seventh-century temple roof in *sumō*. But unlike *sumō*, whose constructed traditionalism allows it to survive today, Western-style musics in fully modern clothes are more prevalent. Throughout much of the modern era, the Japanese in fact have struggled to find a way to make these new musics speak in a uniquely Japanese voice.

This modern history complicates our ability to define Japanese music in the contemporary moment. Though perhaps possible with musics that originate prior to the Meiji period, it is difficult to locate Japaneseness in the *sound* of music alone, as so much music created since the late nineteenth century, on the surface at least, immediately appears Western. Nor can we easily argue that Japaneseness requires a musical form and its related practices to have originated in Japan. Both approaches are particularly problematic given Japan's history of interculturality, and when we recognize that even what has been conceived as "Japanese music" once emerged from diverse musical elements and myriad national origins, a process that has characterized Japanese culture for centuries.

Hybridity as Japanese Culture

While musics may develop through hybridization throughout the world, this process has particular meaning within the context of Japan. From early court orchestra (*gagaku*) to modern popular song (*enka*), Japanese have adopted and adapted sounds, instruments and bodily practices from abroad, which initially complicates the ability to identify uniquely Japanese qualities. Scholars of Japanese music, however, have come to question the framing of a false dichotomy of foreign (and especially Western) vs. Japan in musical practice, instead arguing that Japanese music has in fact been defined by fusions of diverse musical sources and adaptations of foreign forms long before globalization became the "hip" term that it is today (de Ferranti 2002; Mathews 2004; Peluse 2005; Wade 2005; Tokita and Hughes 2008; McClimon 2011; Cook 2014). Respected Japanese musicologist Koizumi Fumio explains that Japanese music

> ... is a kind of patchwork, something new that emerges from the joining of elements brought together from all over the place. That is something which can be seen not only in popular song, but as one of the patterns of Japan's traditional culture: We don't make something entirely new by *combining* things that are new with things we already had; rather, we take familiar and borrowed things just as they are, then make something by patching and darning them together— this is one characteristic of the way Japanese culture is constructed.
> (Quoted in de Ferranti 2002:205)

If we accept that Japanese culture as a whole is hybrid in nature, through combinations of both internal and external forms (Wade 2005), then Japanese music is easily understood as necessarily hybrid as well. Indeed, this hybridization may voice the essence of Japanese music (Mathews 2004) and the combining of styles may prove to be one of the most Japanese of characteristics.

The circulation and cross-fertilization of such varied items as language, arts, religion, and even systems of governance between China, Korea and Japan can be traced to centuries past (see East Asian Historical Periods). This exchange of culture within East Asia is readily apparent through a comparison of how similar instruments are acculturated in each area. There are, for example, three zither types of East Asia: the *guzheng* from China, the *gayageum* from Korea, and the *koto* from Japan (Track 8).

All three instruments share similar zither construction, featuring a long, wooden sounding box with strings laid across the top of diagonally placed bridges and thus resembling the back of a dragon. Each, however, is quite different from its compatriots (see Figure 2.1 with the guzheng, gayageum and koto arranged from top to bottom). The most obvious variance is the instruments' length, with the *koto* at around 72 inches while the *guzheng* is slightly shorter at an average 62 inches, and the *gayageum* varies from 55 to 62 inches. The number of strings also notably differs, with 21 on the *guzheng*, 12 on the *gayageum*, and 13 on the *koto* (the number of strings can vary within the same country depending on the type of zither and music being performed, especially as instruments have adapted to modern works in Western scales). Not surprisingly, the tuning of each instrument fits with the dominant modes in each respective cultural area and therefore sounds unique. The *guzheng* is most commonly tuned in a pentatonic scale [D E F# A B], the *gayageum* is turned to a different pentatonic scale [E♭ F A♭ B♭ C], while the *koto* uses a distinct pentatonic scale with its inclusion of semitones [D E♭ G A B♭].

With all three instruments, the strings are plucked with the right hand to the right side of the bridges, while the left hand presses down to bend pitch and create numerous other effects. But which fingers on the right hand are used to do so actually changes, as do the types of gestures possible on each instrument. This is due in part to the varying quality of materials to create the bridges and strings with steel or steel core and nylon for the *guzheng*, silk for the *gayageum*, and historically silk and now nylon for the *koto*. The position of the *guzheng* on a stand, with the player seated on a chair, is also distinct from the *gayageum*, where the end of the instrument is placed in the lap of the player seated on the floor. With the *koto*, the player traditionally also sits on the floor, but with the instrument positioned in front. In modern performance venues, particularly when

Figure 2.1 East Asian zithers

the *koto* is inserted into larger ensemble settings, the player may sit on a chair with the instrument on a stand much like the *guzheng*.

All three of these instruments have long, varied and interesting histories within their respective cultural homes; thus the story that each tells is unique, relaying immediate social and political influences. Within Japan, the ways in which instruments were adapted—what elements of design were kept and what was modified—is a reflection of aesthetic preferences that connect with our understanding of Japanese identity more broadly. Minoru (2008), for example, argues the importance of maintaining a connection with the natural environment informed instrument design and performance technique:

> In the ninth century, as instruments imported from abroad were modified to Japanese tastes, two distinguishing characteristics emerged. First, all low-pitched instruments disappeared, as their easily produced harmonics destroy subtle pitch inflections, which may have been seen as an undesirable trait or deemed unnatural. Second, the sustained sound of bowed instruments was disliked. Perhaps this was due to the poor acoustics of indoor spaces in Japan, where the instruments did not resonate well. It may also have been a resistance to the sound of a bow scraping over a string, or that this was also perceived as being somehow unnatural.
>
> (2008:4)

Through the avoidance of the "unnatural," the Japanese developed ways to maintain harmony with nature suited to the country's particular setting:

> In the East, especially in Japan, the union of human culture and nature has been held as an ideal since ancient times. In buildings made from stone, where the outside is completely separated from the inside, sounds echo for extended periods of time and rich harmonics are born. In buildings open to the outside, however, such as those found in traditional Japan, or even present-day spaces, which use materials such as *tatami* (straw-mat flooring) and *fusuma* (sliding doors) that absorb the sound, one cannot hear high harmonics. In traditional Japanese music, bright sounds rich in harmonics were considered undesirable. As a result, sounds containing percussive elements become important. These aesthetic preferences are considered evidence demonstrating that in Japan, there is no conception of creating an artificial sound world in confrontation to nature.
>
> (Ibid.:4)

The technique used with Japanese instruments and conceptions of ideal sound thus are deeply informed by Japan's natural environment, and in turn we begin to see the ways in which music, even when imported from abroad, may be made to actually sound uniquely Japanese.

Of course today, Japan continues to negotiate its musical practices within flows unique to East Asia (Craig and King 2002; Iwabuchi 2002; Chun, Rossiter and Shoesmith 2004). As noted above, however, since the Meiji period Japanese have predominantly defined cultural identity *vis-à-vis* the West—a complicated process in which Japan is often positioned as traditional and the West as modern. The following discussion therefore further problematizes Japanese modernity before turning to consider Japanese music in a less theoretical context.

Japanese Cultural Identity in the Modern Era

> It is such juxtapositions of symbolic images of the past with the present that help exemplify a culture that so often displays contiguous identity as part of East Asia on the one hand and the West on the other. Observers may experience a dissonance, or disruption, about the performance of culture and identity, and visitors to Japan can hardly fail to notice the seeming violence with which the modern and the traditional co-exist and permeate each other in sometimes perplexing and contradictory ways.
>
> (Jaffe and Johnson 2008:1–2)

Goto-Jones productively approaches modernity as an *ideology* rather than an *era*. Modernity therefore refers to "a more-or-less specific constellation of intellectual, social, political, and scientific norms and practices," in contrast to a specific time period (2009:7). These practices may have been happening simultaneously in different locations, but ideas of just what defines modernity were formalized in the nineteenth century, spreading throughout the world primarily through Western imperialism. Modernity does not exclusively refer to Westernization: instead, any society

> ... might be considered modern, for instance, if it exhibits signs of industrialization and urbanization. An economic system might be modern if it boasts a market economy organized according to capitalist principles. A modern political system should be organized around a central nation-state, supported by popular nationalism, and a representative system of government (perhaps a democracy) that gives voice to the will of the people ... It supposes a level of literacy and access to information ... that enables people to make rational choices about their best interests.
>
> (Ibid.:8)

Modernity also implies access to science and technology, adequate health care, mechanization and technological power (ibid).

Goto-Jones argues that many of the trappings of modernity were in place in Japan by the end of the Edo period, such as a centralized government "with a nation-wide state apparatus under the secular control of the *bakufu* in Edo ... [and] a sophisticated market economy" (ibid.:36). The country, however, was suffering from conflict, as its isolationist and domestic social stratification policies crumbled. Modernity is therefore typically viewed as beginning with the arrival of Commodore Perry and his notorious blackships, ushering an abrupt and total transformation that continues to intrigue us today:

> Indeed, the history of modern Japan, since the end of its apparent international isolation in the mid-[nineteenth] century to the present day, is the document of a nation grappling with the effects of its encounter with Western powers and its simultaneous exposure to the ideas and technologies of modernity. Negotiation, both in the political and intellectual senses, has been a key feature of this period ... [And t]he experience of Japan provides us with a fascinating lens on the myriad ways in which nations respond to the complex problems of cultural, intellectual, social, political, and scientific change, especially as occasioned by the sudden (and uninvited) arrival of American gunboats.
>
> (Ibid.:5)

Figure 2.2 Tokyo Tower and Zōjō-ji

Japan, as the first non-Western nation to modernize, and in such a dramatic and compelling way, thus serves as a model for exploring how this process happened elsewhere.

As the opening discussion of *sumō* illustrates, for example, the need to establish tradition only emerged as Japan modernized. Waswo argues the equating of tradition with Japan and modernization with Westernization was easily established in the Meiji period, as Japanese institutions actively suppressed the "old" traditions and replaced them with "new" Western practices (2007:46). And even though questioned later in the twentieth century, as the "revival of interest in indigenous tradition and the search for ways of synthesizing and blending tradition and modernity" occurred (ibid.:46), these assumptions still influence how Japanese cultural identity is conceived.

Transforming Traditions

The positioning of tradition as something old and fixed in the history of Japanese music is troubling on numerous levels. And several ethnomusicologists offer a more flexible, value- and process-focused approach that may expand our understanding of tradition in more positive directions. Bakan defines tradition as a

> . . . *process of creative transformation whose most remarkable feature is the continuity it nurtures and sustains*. This definition emphasizes the fact that traditions, wherever they are found—which is in fact everywhere that human communities exist—are dynamic rather than static, flexible rather than fixed, resilient yet adaptable to change. (2012:xx, original emphasis)

This continually foregrounds the idea that tradition is an "active process" (ibid.:xxxi). Spiller similarly dismisses the idea that traditions must originate in a primordial past, arguing that what marks "music as traditional is not how old it is, but rather how well it teaches, reinforces, and creates the social values of its producers and consumers" (2008:4). Traditional music therefore grows and changes in line with the culture that is producing it:

> Truly traditional music, then, exploits new resources, acknowledges new requirements, and responds to new situations. It provides a place for people to try out new approaches to their existing values, to experiment with new ideas, and to synthesize the new with the old. It is rooted in enduring musical processes—the general ideas about how people organize their musical activities—but is not limited to particular musical instruments, sounds, or repertoires. (Ibid.:4)

Both Bakan and Spiller thus offer an extremely flexible approach to reading tradition that concentrates more on cultural values and social functions and less on sonic codifications and limitations. These principles may connect with the past, but don't preclude the modern.

In the 1920s and 1930s, some Japanese intellectuals recognized that "Japan needed to break away not from modernity but from modernity as defined and exemplified by the West" and purported the need for a "new cultural order at home and in East Asia" (Waswo 207:51). Following Japan's defeat at the end of World War II, however, "Modernization was once again equated with Westernization, modernity once again viewed as the opposite of tradition" (ibid.:53). As Japan recovered from the war and began its ascent to becoming a leading world power, the Japanese would of course again "search for what was both modern *and* Japanese," with two important themes emerging (ibid.). The West came to be questioned as a valid model for Japan to follow, while "the direct bearing of Japanese cultural traditions on Japan's contemporary achievements" was reified (ibid.). Thus what was once dismissed as inferior was now lauded as a crowning achievement of Japanese culture.

In the 1970s and 1980s, the Japanese search for self intensified once again, encapsulated in the discourse of *nihonjinron* (theories of Japaneseness), a body of scholarly and public literature devoted to the study of Japanese cultural identity (Befu 2001; Sakai 2002; Sugimoto 2010). Despite the fact that, historically, Japan was characterized by diversity, following World War II and the end of Occupation, a new "monoethnic nationalism" emerged (Bigenho 2012:140). In an attempt to distinguish Japanese culture from all others, writings within *nihonjinron* presented the Japanese as possessing a unique cultural identity common amongst an essentially homogenous population. Certain traits are stressed as exclusive to Japanese, for example, an emphasis on group dependency and connection with the natural environment, and everyone is purported to share a single cultural history and language. Japan is thus conceived as an "island country" (*shimaguni*), "isolated, unique, and homogenous, a land and culture unto itself" (Yano 2002:21). Within the discourse of *nihonjinron*, "Japanese culture is predominantly identified in comparison or in configuration ... with the putative traits of the West" (Sakai 2002:357), resulting generally in positive stereotypes of Japan's superiority celebrated by Japanese authors, and critiqued by Western ones: "Yet, the basic operation is always the same in that the West and Japan are figured in reference to one another" (ibid.:357).

Often dismissed as absurdly stereotypical, uncritical, and skewed, the discourse of *nihonjinron*, nevertheless, may actually be a sincere attempt "on the part of the Japanese to recapture a sense of their own history and formulate their own cultural identity" (Waswo 2007:52), following the end of Occupation. Waswo ultimately argues that these changing perceptions of who the Japanese are as a people in the modern era were all attempts to "reconcile foreign borrowing" with Japanese cultural identity (ibid.:55). Modernity required the Japanese to engage with foreign influences at unprecedented speed—adopting, adapting, or even rejecting them, as Japan asserted a modern sense of self suitable for the new world order (see Figure 2.2). Japanese people have long been obsessed with the search for self, precisely because Japanese culture is rooted in foreign input, constantly looking to the outside to understand the inside. And of course, these ideological debates of the modern era are both reflected in, and expressed by, music as well.

Musical Modernity

Japanese musical history accordingly can be divided into the pre-modern era, comprising the development of traditional musics of Japan that originate prior to 1868, and the modern era marked by the advent of the Meiji period and subsequent rapid transformation of musical styles and related performance practices. Just what "Japanese music" would become in the modern era was heavily directed by and enforced through

> ...educators, policy-makers and intellectuals who recognized the interrelationship between Western music and the ideology and policy of modernization-Westernization. Many elites debated the question of which music Japan should choose: Western, Japanese or some kind of blended synthesis. The universal (represented by Western music) and the particular (Japanese "traditional," vernacular music) could be theoretically fused in a blended synthesis that was supposed to inherit the advantages of both cultures.
> (Yano and Hosokawa 2008:346)

All three modes of music making ultimately came to coexist in Japan in the twentieth and twenty-first centuries.

The Japanese continued to acculturate foreign musical ideas into traditional practices, for example, modifying Japanese instruments to facilitate performing new Western music elements. Flautist Kaoru Watanabe explains that there are now two types of *shinobue* (a traditional transverse bamboo flute): the *koten-chōshi*, the "classical" flute where the holes are basically all the same size intended to play Japanese scales (Website Example 3) and the *utamono*, where the size and placement of the holes was modified to ease playing of Western scales (Website Example 4). The latter is obviously a modern development, while any regional, indigenous festival likely uses the *koten-chōshi* flute, and thus sonically maintains ties with Japan's pre-modern past (interview May 5, 2014).

Numerous scholars, however, have standardized the story of Japan's musical modernization as beginning with the introduction of instruments and musical styles of Western brass bands and related military songs (*gunka*). The hymnody of missionary choral groups also entered Japan, bringing with it ideas of harmony and choral singing (Malm 2000; Fujie 2002; Wade 2005; Hebert 2012). And when the education system as a whole was refashioned after North American models, both these forms and Western music more broadly became an important part of the new curriculum, with songs assuming a particularly significant role. The newly formed Ministry of Education, Science and Culture (*Monbushō*) promulgated the Education System Order (*gakusei*) in 1872 and established *Monbushōshōka* (school songs), with the goals of modernism in mind and songs created that combined the Western diatonic scale and tunes with Japanese lyrics (Kitagawa 2009:263–264). Indeed,

> The government invested heavily in education, including music education, regarding it as a cornerstone of producing modern citizens. Singing school songs became a way to teach the lessons of the nation, intellectually through the content of the lyrics, aurally through the sounds of the music, as well as bodily through the very act of unison singing.
>
> (Yano and Hosokawa 2008:346)

Although the importance of music in shaping Japan's new modern identity was clearly recognized, essentially Japanese music that originated prior to the Meiji period was not seen as relevant to schoolchildren's education—as central to shaping new modern citizens—thus feeding the read of modern as Western, with Japanese music positioned as something antiquated and inferior. Other types of children's songs developed in the early twentieth century that blended elements of Japanese and Western music in increasingly musical ways, which in turn would challenge this presupposition (see further discussion in Chapter 4). Nonetheless, Western music, including the quality of scales, rhythm and form, quickly established a strong presence in the minds of modern Japanese, who eagerly consumed numerous imported styles of both art and popular music in the late nineteenth and early twentieth centuries. This early engagement with Western music set the stage for all the musical moments that shape the daily lives of the Japanese today (see Figure 2.3).

Figure 2.3 Tokyo urban landscape

Multiple Modernities

De Ferranti and Tokita caution against distinguishing between traditional and modern musics, arguing instead that modernization affected both. For example, traditional Japanese musics became commoditized products through the introduction of new technologies including recording capabilities and the expansion of radio. Both Japanese and Western musics thus were "transformed as music journalism, music publishing, public concert performances and music marketing permeated daily life" (2013:13), feeding the read of tradition as something alive and changing, not fixed and static.

Japanese people of all classes in many major urban locations in the early twentieth century had access to a broad range of styles:

> Interest and active engagement with any or several of these musics as amateur practitioners, audiences and consumers was simply part of modern life, and, unlike in the early postwar decades, no justification was needed for involvement in both musical worlds.
>
> (Ibid.:4)

The standard story of Japanese musical modernity does not adequately consider such coexistence of Western and non-Western musics in Japan prior to the war.

De Ferranti and Tokita also explore the "distinctive regional modernities" constructed through musical performance in Osaka and the surrounding Hanshin region, a counter to the Tokyo-centric view of modern Japanese music history (ibid.:3). Prior to the establishment of Tokyo as the center of media around 1930,

> ... the profound changes in Japanese people's experience of music—changes in forms of exposure to and media for enjoying music, as well as the shaping of musical sensibility through education—during the prewar decades were characterized by a significant degree of regional variation.
>
> (Ibid.:4)

Thus musical modernity in Japan is not one monolithic experience, but rather differed by region, shaped

> ... largely by local forces, as a product of history, geography and socio-economic contingencies. Such forces include the prominence of regional music traditions or local manifestations of nationwide performance traditions [that is, musics seen as traditional Japanese] ... the attitudes of local elites toward Western expressive culture as well as the input of various foreigners.
>
> (Ibid.:4–5)

De Ferranti and Tokita call for new localized approaches to looking at musical modernity, expanding our understanding of this process in Japan beyond the typical concentration on activities in or disseminated from Tokyo only. The focus on *taiko* within Kyoto in Part III hopefully adds to this discussion.

Popular Music in Modern Japan

Japan's complicated negotiation of musical identity *vis-à-vis* Western influence is readily apparent in the development of popular musics, which reflect both modernizing processes and major political and ideological shifts in Japan's history (IASPM-Japan 1990; Hosokawa 1994; Stevens 2008; Yano and Hosokawa 2008). Atkins argues, for example, that the "*sōshibushi* of the 1870s and 1880s, sung on street corners and in political plays, expressed the satirical, anti-government ideologies of the 'Freedom and People's Rights' activists" at the time (Atkins 2001:49). These politically charged yet humorous songs became "the precursor of mass-manufactured and mediated popular songs after the late 1920s" thus paving the way for the mass dissemination of popular culture to come (Yano and Hosokawa 2008:347). Also called *enka*, following World War II, this early popular song transformed into the genre as we know it today, synthesizing elements of Western and Japanese music (see further discussion in Chapter 4). At the same time, already established Japanese musical styles intended for entertainment, including the *shamisen*-based narrative genre known generally as *rōkyoku* or *naniwa-bushi*, persisted well into in the early twentieth century, although with new stories suitable for the times.

During the Taishō period (1912–26), direct importation of foreign popular musics increased. The 1923 Kanto earthquake marked a period of rapid change in popular culture leading up to the Manchurian war, as Japan rose as a political and economic power. It is during this period that an assembly-line approach to producing Japanese popular music is established that would continue until the 1970s. A dance craze took over the nation and American recordings were readily imported. "Jazz," a category capturing the "exotic" nature of these new styles, came to designate a breadth of foreign musics. And by the end of the Taishō period, Western popular music was firmly woven into Japan's sonic tapestry.

During the period leading up to and through World War II (1931–45), sanctions were placed against music of "the enemy," and the rapid importation of much foreign music temporarily subsided. Japanese composers in these styles had to either find other methods of making a living, leave Japan, or create patriotic music; censorship expanded and song lyrics became increasingly nationalistic. Abruptly, in 1945, the war era came to an end, and American military forces occupied Japan.

Stevens describes the Allied Occupation as the most significant event in modern Japanese history (2008:38). The Occupation controlled the mass media and the dissemination of songs on the radio and recordings. American GIs in Japan wanted to hear live music from home, and thus many Japanese musicians found themselves learning the latest music rages on the military bases, and bringing these styles to the local youth. Western popular music forms once again bombarded the Japanese. As a result, Japanese popular music would be defined in relation to Western popular music well into the 1990s (Stevens 2008; Bourdaghs 2012).

Similar to the United States, the period following the war was marked by continued urban migration, growth in youth culture that had unprecedented access to leisure time and income, and increased ease of exchange and access to recorded materials (initially quite expensive and exclusive, but quickly falling in price). Styles such as boogie-woogie and, soon thereafter, rockabilly, enjoyed great popularity, and paved the way for later forms of rock and roll. While North American-style country music was consumed by the educated and elite, who had the leisure income and time to pursue purchasing records and instruments. Jazz, which had enjoyed popularity prior to the war, once again boomed during the Occupation, now aligning more closely with North American styles, and it remains immensely popular, with regular live performances.

The 1950s also saw the emergence of a star-based system of production in which power and creative control was centralized with specific companies (Stevens 2008:41) This system would influence the development of "idol" (*aidoru*) management companies that continue to dominate Japanese popular music (see further discussion in Chapter 4). And diverse media, especially television, came to play a more significant role in the creation of hit songs.

As Japan attempted to find a new identity following the end of Occupation, the 1960s welcomed a music called *wasei* pop or "made in Japan pop," that "integrated American style with Japanese sensibility" by introducing pentatonic scales and Japanese tunes (ibid.:41). Stars of this era began appearing on a variety of television shows that featured music, dance and comedy, and which were becoming increasingly popular with urban white-collar workers and their families as the booming economy took flight (ibid.:42). Later in the 1960s, there would be an even greater diversification of Japanese produced popular music. Groups like the Ventures (and their emphasis on the guitar) and the Beatles inspired the "electric boom" (*ereki būmu*), through which electric guitars became standard instrumentation in Japan. With the addition of vocals, the short-lived but important genre known as "group sounds" (*gurūpu saunzu*) emerged. In the beginning, these performers were mainly imitators, but then began to introduce unique contributions, moving from copying the Beatles to creating more psychedelic styles. Inspired by the folk-music boom of the United States, Japanese singers developed similar styles of acoustic guitar-based popular and protest "folk song" (*fōku songu*), not to be confused with traditional Japanese *min'yō*. The sentimental song style known as *enka* arose in response to the sound and image of these Anglo-American inspired popular musics that dominated Japan by the 1960s (see further discussion in Chapter 4).

Western-style singer-songwriters, nevertheless, now under the broad umbrella category of "new music" (*nyū myūjikku*), would continue to flourish with introspective and personal lyrics in the 1970s, self-producing music and challenging the top-down systems of control long in place in the industry. In the late 1970s, Japan would lay claim to the great pioneers of electronic music, the Yellow Magic Orchestra (YMO), whose early explorations in the new technology of the synthesizer would tremendously influence techno throughout its history on a global scale. By the beginning of the 1980s, a tradition of Japanese-produced popular music had been firmly established.

Idols (*aidoru*) boomed in the 1980s, riding the optimistic wave of economic prosperity, and saturating diverse forms of media (see further discussion in Chapter 4), with catchy pop-tunes easy to sing at the local *karaoke* box. A rebellious rock developed in response to the insipidness of the idols—with a number of groups whose "songs appealed to the audience's sense of social reality with lyrics about disappointment and struggles in superficially successful and materialistic 'bubble' Japan" gaining steam (Stevens 2008:51). Underground (*angura*) and other independent musics continue to comment on pressing issues of the day and challenge the sounds of mainstream Japanese popular music (see further discussion in Chapter 4). When the bubble burst in the early 1990s, the *aidoru* temporarily lost their glow, though they quickly climbed back to the top of the J-pop pile where they remain today. "J-pop" in fact became a standardized and now globally recognized term to designate Japanese-produced popular musics, with "J-Rap," "J-Rock" and other specific styles similarly indicated with a "J-" soon to follow.

Japanese popular music thus has reached a point where it no longer needs to define itself in terms of its Western counterpart. And while older Japanese artists may identify with Western-produced popular musics, younger Japanese now may locate themselves only within a trajectory of Japanese-produced popular musics (ibid.:65). Certainly, many musicians continue to negotiate musical identity within both systems, but the proceeding discussion highlights both how Japanese engaged with Western styles throughout the twentieth century, revealing a gradual process of increasing acculturation, and the ultimate acceptance of previously imported styles as now thoroughly Japanese.

Hōgaku and *Yōgaku* today

Over a century ago, Japanese traditional (*hōgaku*) music was "old" and "familiar," while Western musics (*yōgaku*) were "new" and "exotic." Throughout the twentieth century, however, with the prime position of Western music in school education, the rise of choruses and brass bands, and later orchestras, operas and all forms of European art music, and the regular consumption of popular musics from around the world—the tables have turned and *hōgaku* is now the "new" and "exotic" in Japan (Kitagawa 2009:278). Western music is in fact so ubiquitous today that it sounds more "traditional" than traditional Japanese music, which many Japanese have never seen live, nor have any interest in doing so. Some Japanese may in fact continue to view traditional Japanese music as inferior to Western art music, perpetuating the modernist strategies of well over a century ago (Blasdel 2005:88):

> Many educated and highly cultured Japanese lack awareness or respect for Japanese traditional music. And herein lies a deep paradox in the musical perceptions of the Japanese. Western classical music represents the apex of all that is refined and cultured, while Japanese music represents the exact opposite: the old-fashioned and uncultured. It should be tolerated and perhaps preserved, but certainly not appreciated as serious music.
>
> (ibid.:88–89)

Instruments once again become crucial foci through which to explore the shifting nature of music in Japan. As we have seen, centuries ago, many instruments were imported into Japan along the Silk Road through China and Korea; these are firmly considered Japanese today, including the *koto*. Similarly, the Meiji period saw the influx of numerous instruments of Western origin such as the violin, piano and later the guitar, which are so pervasive it no longer seems appropriate to label them indeed as "Western" (see Figure 2.4).

The piano was a particularly potent marker of identity in the early part of the twentieth century (Tokita 2013), spreading even further following World War II, as the Japanese became more affluent. Kitagawa notes:

> From the mid-1950s, music lesson venues operated by musical instrument retailers such as Yamaha and Kawai were widely established, and the piano became the dominant instrument for *keiko-goto* [lessons for cultural enrichment]. To have an upright piano in the living room became the target of middle-class aspirations. These dreams became reality as the diffusion ratio of pianos, about 3% in 1964, grew to about 19% in 1985 and to 24% in 2003 . . . From the end of the [twentieth] century, furthermore, learners of the piano have begun to emerge from among the middle-aged and elderly, including men.
>
> (2009:266)

According to the *Yearbook of Current Production Statistics* produced by the Ministry of Economy, Trade and Industry, in 2013 nearly 40,000 pianos, 175,000 electric pianos

Figure 2.4 Hardcore girl on guitar

and organs, and another 125,000 electronic keyboards were sold in Japan (Ministry of Economy 2013).

As noted above, guitars similarly impacted music making after World War II, first through the *ereki būmu* of the 1960s (Bourdaghs 2012). Kitagawa observes:

> The permeation of the guitar prompted young amateurs to form bands. The beginning of the [twenty-first] century has seen moves by middle-aged and older male amateur musicians with previous experience in bands to form bands once more.
>
> (2009:266)

The *Yearbook of Current Production Statistics* in 2013 reports that over 200,000 guitars were sold in Japan. Today, on certain trains that run to sections of cities with numerous well-known "livehouses" (*raibuhausu*, establishments devoted to the performance of live music), it is as common to see guitar gig bags as it is to see umbrellas during the rainy season, no doubt enhanced by the instruments' versatility and portability (Coldwell 1997; Hughes 2008).

In 2002, the Ministry of Education, Culture, Sports, Science and Technology (*Monbukagakushō*) (a new ministry formed in 2001 by merging the pre-existing Ministry of Education, Science and Culture and other ministries), recognizing that Japanese youth had grown increasingly distant from Japanese traditional music, mandated its return in public schools, including folksongs (*min'yō*) and instruction on Japanese instruments (*wagakki*). Over ten years later, it still remains to be seen, however, if this will have any real effect on Japanese awareness and interest in traditional musics. Blasdel, nonetheless, notes "hopefully in the not-too-distant future, Japanese children will be able to look at their own culture and discover a rich heritage of traditional arts and develop a natural, spontaneous musical identity" (2005:93; see also Kitagawa 2009:264).

The point here is not to argue for the return of Japanese instruments to their former glory—that is, that Japan should abandon all things Western as inauthentic—but rather to maintain the legitimacy and value of *all* musics within Japan; to once again render Japanese traditional music meaningful. The *Monbukagakushō* mandate ultimately may allow this happen.

Locating Japaneseness in Music

The same institutions that initiated the assimilation of Western music into Japanese cultural identity are now working to bring Japanese music back into the fold. This strategy resembles conclusions Mathews draws about Japanese musicians' perceptions of Japaneseness, and we move now from problematizing Japanese cultural identity with instruments to the musicians who use them through the metaphors of "fence," "flavor," or "phantasm" (2004). He found some musicians, for example, understand "Japaneseness as a fence separating Japanese and non-Japanese; some characterized this as a matter of 'blood' and others as a matter of 'culture'" (ibid.:339). In this way, Japaneseness in music "is something Japanese possess as their birthright, from which other people are excluded" (ibid.). This view is of course complicated by the extreme hybridity of Japanese culture; where exactly is the Japanese music they possess? Nonetheless, this "fence" may have both positive and negative effects. On the one side, the belief that the Japanese, by birth or socialization, have a special connection with traditional musics can foster great pride in their performance and preservation. A similar attitude may be motivating the Ministry of Education, Culture, Sports, Science and Technology move to insert traditional Japanese music back into education. The drawback here is that this view simultaneously may lead to exclusionary ideas: that *only* Japanese people can truly understand and perform Japanese music and in turn assert some unique Japanese identity in the face of Western cultural domination.

Even though the evidence thus far suggests that Western music is well established and fully integrated in Japan, there are some musicians who feel their identity as Japanese actually limits them from authentically playing non-Japanese music. And to be sure, much of the literature on music of the modern era, regardless of genre, explores the ways in which Japanese negotiated their ability to express a unique and therefore authentic Japanese identity through performing "someone else's music" (Atkins 2000 and 2001; Condry 2000 and 2006). Clearly, Japanese people have been doing so for centuries, even if one may argue that the historical circulation of goods, religion, language and instruments within East Asia did not lead to the same dramatic transformation that resulted from Japan's sudden contact with the West. And just as Japanese modernity as a whole continues to fascinate, so too does Japan's abrupt and complicated engagement with Western music, generating much debate amongst musicians and scholars alike. The experience is immediate and fresh, and compelling given the extensive adoption and continued dominance of predominantly Western-style musics.

This process is encapsulated in Atkins's seminal study of how Japanese musicians struggled to find an authentic voice through the performance of jazz, a process made all the more difficult given jazz's racialized history in the United States (2001):

> Japanese jazz artists and aficionados have concocted a variety of authenticating strategies to cope with their unique conundrum. From a broad historical perspective, such strategies include attempts to replicate the exact sounds of American jazz; study abroad in exotic locales such as Shanghai or the United States; apprenticeships in foreign bands; efforts to recreate the social and cultural contexts (for example, the 'hipster scene') in which jazz is produced; assertions of the basic affinity of the 'colored races', and efforts to 'indigenize' or 'nationalize' jazz by incorporating textures, instruments, or aesthetic principles from traditional musics and creating a national style of jazz, 'which foreigners cannot imitate.
>
> (Atkins 2000:37)

Japanese musicians brought Japanese and Western instruments together in fusion styles such as "jazzified Japanese folk music," while other musicians focused on originality, which was perceived as truly authentic to the genre's core (Atkins 2001:243; Wade 2005:156).

The vision of a national Japanese jazz was never realized, yet "even those who scoff at the idea feel that jazz as played by Japanese is subtly different, with the added implication that it is ultimately inferior to the American product" (Atkins 2000:42). Although we may want to celebrate music's ability to stand on its own—to be judged by individual, subjective aesthetic qualities—the fact is many aficionados still position jazz produced in Japan as somehow lacking. Atkins's exploration of jazz reveals that while some Japanese musicians long to perform blues, jazz, or other imported musics, "they can't climb the fence that separates them from these foreign forms, but can only peer over the fence from within their ineradicable Japaneseness" (Mathews 2004:340).

There are more flexible approaches to understanding Japanese cultural identity, however, including Mathews's second metaphor of identity as a "flavor," that can be understood and enjoyed by anyone, whether ethnically Japanese or not. Within this view of Japaneseness, foreigners can excel at Japanese musics and Japanese at foreign musics. However, Mathews asks if all musics are available to everyone globally, what does "culture" mean? Does our ethnic, cultural and national identity matter at all or are we all simply global citizens? Again, the fear of losing something uniquely Japanese looms and some people in response choose to learn instruments and genres more immediately "Japanese"—to preserve those traditions and assert them as representing Japanese cultural identity—while others try to insert instruments and musical elements that are clearly understood as Japanese into otherwise foreign musical vehicles, as illustrated in the "authenticating strategies" of jazz discussed above. Mathews explores whether one can "evoke a Japanese flavor" without resolving to self-exoticization, such as quoting Japanese folk songs or traditional musical elements that have little to do with the lives of current musicians (ibid.:344). This approach raises interesting possibilities about the flexibility of music—and is perhaps what allows foreigners access to Japanese music and vice versa—but also locates Japanese identity very much in the *sound* of music alone, rather than in the *performing* of music, an issue that will be further discussed below.

At the end of Atkins's study of jazz in Japan, he ultimately argues that authenticity should be determined by creative expression and not based on ethnic associations, however difficult this may be to do. This is surprising in that he takes jazz back down to an absolute music—devoid of cultural attachments—in turn connecting with Mathews' third metaphor for understanding Japaneseness as a "phantasm." In this approach, Japaneseness is irrelevant: "the very idea of Japan as a distinct musical culture is an illusion" (2004:344). Music is just music. Some of Mathews' informants do, however, acknowledge the importance of the social framework in which music is performed for assessing its meaning. Assigning the adjective "Japanese" to qualify a musical practice may be obsolete—it is just jazz or rock—but this understanding does not take into consideration the "Japanese social world that conditions [the] music" (ibid.:345); that being Japanese informs the social production of music.

The search for Japaneseness in music may seem unnecessary, even futile, particularly as styles and instruments that once had firm grounding in a specific cultural identity become increasingly displaced and global fusions proliferate. Music as a cultural possession may no longer be tenable—and as Mathews states "all the world's musics belongs to all the world" (ibid.:346). On the other hand, these global forms may be enacted uniquely in each location. And what these similar music forms mean to people in different cultural contexts still varies greatly. They may "sound" global but "mean" local (Milioto Matsue 2008a, 2008b).

"Ways of Doing"

Indeed, Japaneseness may be better understood as generated through "ways of doing" rather than "ways of sounding." In my own work with underground (*angura*) rock musicians in Tokyo in the late 1990s, I found the sound of hardcore—the instrumentation, song structure, vocal styles—rather common globally, while what these sounds mean and the ways in which this sound was produced, from the livehouse system of Tokyo and rehearsal spaces to the use of stickers and fliers, was very much located in broader Japanese cultural practices and therefore expressing local identity (Milioto Matsue 2008a, 2008b).

Keister similarly looks at the ways in which Japanese cultural identity may be created through "ways of doing," but within the context of traditional music. Specifically within the formal lesson environment (*okeiko*) of Japan, there is a strict adherence to master-disciple training which

> ... has long been considered indispensable in learning the way of Japanese arts. Found in arts as wide-ranging as *kendō* (way of swords), *sadō* (way of tea) and *kadō* (way of flowers), to name just a few, this method of training by imitative formula serves individual purposes of self-cultivation for amateurs and career development for professionals, while also serving the institutional purposes of maintaining the artistic "way" of a given school.
>
> (2008:240)

It is in fact "the *doing* of tradition [that] carries greater importance than the content of creative works. In other words, the form, appearance and style of a tradition are consistently valued over meanings or messages in creative works" (ibid.). The emphasis is placed on the action, captured in the suffix of all these arts—"*dō*"—which literally means the "way of doing." The greater meaning is therefore in the cultural work rather than the product.

Keister explores this idea in three different sites, ranging from the most traditional to more modern lessons at culture centers and public schools in Japan, as well as sites for learning outside of Japan, such as in North American university settings. Despite the variety of contexts, and degrees to which they each adhere to the following characteristics, Keister argues:

> ... there is a self-conscious and reflexive sense of tradition that is present in all three sites ... Each site is 'traditional' in its own way because of foundational values such as ownership, continuity, loyalty, imitation, and self-development that emerged out of the development of

a system for the transmission of arts (*iemoto*) that developed in the Edo period (ibid.:241; see further discussion in Chapters 3 and 6). By maintaining the values that came to characterize the teaching of Japanese traditional arts, rather than the content, Japanese cultural identity is invoked.

This is true even amongst students of traditional Japanese music beyond the borders of Japan. By engaging in traditional music training, students embrace and embody

Figure 2.5 Urban cherry blossoms

Japaneseness through the preservation of lineages of traditional music, the marking of one's artistic territory and claims to repertoire—all acts that are connected with long-established "ways of doing" traditional music in Japan rather than necessarily "sounding" Japaneseness (Keister 2013). Drawing on Mathews's idea of "phantasm," Japaneseness here is rendered an "exotic essence" that has spread globally, as evident in the North American lesson environment, evoking "another time and place for all who view it" (ibid.:2). This of course allows any and all to embody Japanese cultural identity. And students in North America often gravitate to world music ensembles, whether South Asian dance, *gamelan*, *taiko*, African drumming, etc., because of the exotic clothing, decorations on the stage—the opportunity to play dress-up in another culture's costume. Like moths to a bright light, they come to play with markers of cultural identity in ethno-drag.

Nostalgia

Within Japan, another "way of doing" Japanese cultural identity may be located in the emphasis on nostalgia in much music making. The rapid engagement with modernization, Westernization and urbanization has left Japanese longing to maintain a connection with not only a Japanese identity grounded in tradition, as suggested above, but also with a rural, pristine community encapsulated in the idea of the *furusato*—the "hometown" that assumes so much importance not only in *min'yō*, but numerous other musical practices in contemporary Japan (see Figure 2.5). Yano argues that within the context of one such music, *enka*, "the cultural logic of 'Japaneseness' builds upon processes of nostalgically framed expression and desire" as Japanese passionately search for an imagined bucolic past (2002:14). *Enka*, as noted above, is a popular music form that first emerged in the early twentieth century and was formalized in the 1960s, fusing elements of Western and Japanese music together. Although the ways this was accomplished will be further considered in Chapter 4, it is important to note the centrality of nostalgia in *enka* here and its role in building a collective national identity. Yano explains:

> The enticement of *enka* is that it suggests a forum for collective nostalgia, which actively appropriates and shapes the past, thereby building the group together. *Enka* encodes within nostalgia a historical moment of self-reflexivity, establishing a particular relationship with the temporal past that distances it from, while also placing it firmly in, the present.
>
> (Ibid.:15)

As such, *enka* invokes an "internal exoticism" with past or remote settings, marginalized characters, and "traditional" themes. *Enka*, which is heard on the radio, is regularly featured on television and is a common choice among older patrons of *karaoke*, is omnipresent in Japan and thus has played a major role in spreading ideas of the mythical *furusato* in the modern era.

In the context of *enka*, the *furusato* "has retained both the specific meaning of one's family's rootedness to a particular place and the more generalized sense of 'national family' rootedness" in Japan as a whole, creating an intimate relationship between people and their homeland (ibid.:18). As people yearn to maintain a local cultural identity in the twenty-first century, the need to preserve a connection with a bounded and identifiable national homeland may increase. Yano argues that in order to do so

> ... in contemporary Japan, the meanings given to place through the concept of *furusato* have transformed the local into the national. Regional spaces, once individuated through sometimes minute differences, have been incorporated into the national project of homogeneity and majority making.
>
> (ibid.)

This idea was illustrated in the discussion of Okinawan music, in which the unique identity of the islands came to embody a national Japan for Japanese looking for something both exotic and familiar to express who they are; through nostalgia for a distant yet accessible past and place. Nostalgia for the simpler life fuels the continued performance of *enka*, which in turn further exoticizes Japan's traditional identity.

Ironically, however, Japanese cultural identity is also constructed through nostalgia for musics beyond Japan's borders. The need for nostalgia thus may be Japanese, but the music that generates these feelings does not have to be of Japanese origin. According to Williams, Irish music is enthusiastically consumed by "a small number of dedicated Japanese enthusiasts" (2010:126), through sold-out major performances and intimate pub gatherings, festivals, singing lessons and dance workshops. She argues "Ireland's musical culture engages with the important Japanese value of nostalgia, to the point that Japanese people recognize Irish music as belonging, in part, to themselves" (ibid.:126). As noted above, one of the ways that Western music first entered Japan was through school songs. In the 1880s

> ... an American music teacher—Luther Whiting Mason—worked together with Japanese scholar Isawa Shuji to import, translate and disseminate an array of Irish, British and American songs to schoolchildren all over Japan. These songs then became so familiar to Japanese schoolchildren over the next fifty years that the sound of an Irish melody elicits fond remembrances of one's (rural or semi-rural, or merely idealized) Japanese childhood (Williams 2006:101–119). In particular, it is a sense of unrequited longing for a fictive Irish homeland that appeals so deeply to some of the Irish-music enthusiasts in Japan.
>
> (Ibid.:126)

This nostalgia for an idealized Ireland no doubt accounts for the numerous Irish pubs and proud St. Patrick's Day celebrations in Tokyo and other urban centers throughout Japan.

Japanese people similarly may be connecting with a distant *furusato* through nostalgia for Bolivian music. They enjoy Bolivian music performed by South American musicians touring Japan, who market a traditional image, and they study the music themselves, often sojourning to Bolivia to pursue their interest in situ. Bigenho argues that through these practices "the Japanese might be seen as playing Indian as they long for a traditional utopia perceived to be lost within modern life" (2012:95), but because they are not themselves Bolivian they yearn for something both intimate (the idea of a rural homeland), but distant (Bolivia):

> Andean folklore is uniquely linked to expressions of nostalgia for an unspecified ancient indigenous world, for old solidarity politics, and for a world imagined to exist before the advent of unfettered consumer capitalism. In these ways, even though Bolivian music is foreign ... its meaning may resemble the symbolic readings of *enka*. If *enka* develops a nostalgia around an internal exotic of the past, Andean music develops its nostalgia from an external exotic also located in a past.
>
> (Ibid.:115)

It is the *act* of feeling nostalgic that marks Japaneseness more than what people are nostalgic *for*. In order to legitimate these feelings of nostalgia, Japanese people may claim to "share ancient indigenous connections" with Bolivians (ibid.:122), invoking musical evidence, such as similar pentatonic scales, to support this claim (ibid.:123).

In all these cases, the nostalgia for a rural past results from Japanese people's confrontation with modernity and the increasingly impersonal and complicated lives that we lead. Bigenho summarizes:

> The Japanese fascination with Bolivians is tied to both an imagined indigenous world and a nostalgia for a bucolic life where social contacts are perceived as easier to make and more meaningful, particularly when set in contrast with the fast-paced life the Japanese see themselves as forced to live in their own country.
> (Ibid.:144)

And life in contemporary Japan is nothing short of exhausting, with its overcrowded cities, packed public transportation, and expensive albeit tiny living spaces. Despite the fact that rural areas within Japan have also modernized, and that both Ireland and Bolivia have thriving urban centers and modern citizens, only a pastoral and pristine past is imagined and desired. And thus this arguably universal emotional need can be fulfilled with diverse musics, perhaps even more so through those from a great distance.

The Japanese may look far away for musics to satisfy their individual needs, at least in part as a result of the influence of *nihonjinron*, which created and perpetuated an idea of a homogenous Japan with a common shared past. Thus "the Japanese sense of intimate distance ... tends to look beyond the nation for difference" (Bigenho 2012:142); to find musics that express a distant past, one must move beyond the shared history of Japan encapsulated in indigenous musical practice. And this in turn inspires Japanese people's active participation in all kinds of music, from the jazz discussed above to Jamaican reggae (Sterling 2010).

This nostalgia for difference may also account for the Japanese penchant throughout the twentieth century to "authentically" replicate imported musics. Drawing on Hosokawa (1999) Wade argues performers of so-called "niche musics" "choose to play the style as authentically as possible, that is, to reproduce an authentic sound, seldom interjecting any Japanese features" (2005:137). The widely celebrated and critically acclaimed Japanese salsa group Orquestra de la Luz, for example, sang exclusively in Spanish and strived to maintain an authentic salsa sound, staying number one for eleven weeks on the Billboard Latin chart in the 1990s. In considering their popularity in Japan, Hosokawa

> ... takes the perspective of consumers, urbanites who are experiencing a sense of rootlessness as a result of the inexorable process of modernizing. Being alienated from the continuity of the indigenous tradition evokes in them a nostalgia for "roots music," music that is closely attached to the "heart" of the people. Having lost their own traditions, they search for the roots of the Other.
> (Wade 2005:137–138)

Both the band and their fans are nostalgic for an authentic Latin sound with little reference to Japan (see further discussion in Chapter 4).

The ability to find one's roots in an Other's music holds true only for some imported musics, those that are perceived as "ethnically exotic" in some way, such as Bolivian, Latin, even Irish, but not other imported musics, such as jazz and European art music. In the case of the latter two, according to Atkins and Wade again, there is a privileging of musics by those people perceived as more authentic; Americans, as regarding jazz, and Europeans, in the case of Western art music (Wade 2005:139–140). This assessment results in some Japanese musicians of these genres, despite high technical proficiency, being excluded from recording and touring opportunities, an exclusion solely based on race.

But Wade rightly asks "Why do Japanese fans seek roots music of others, rather than turning to their own music?," given that *hōgaku* for most people is already exotic. For whatever reason, some may be looking farther afield for this sense of connectedness with who they are as a person—to the musicians in the hills of Bolivia and the pubs of Ireland.

Gendered Performance

Modernization obviously has deeply informed the sense of who the Japanese are as individuals and as a nation. To this point, however, we have not explored how expectations of appropriate male and female behavior, both in society in general and more specifically within musical performance, also express changing values and transforming gendered conceptions of Japanese cultural identity. Although the musical examples in this text were selected for the specific characteristics illustrated within and the overall quality of each performance, rather than gender of the performers, there is, nevertheless, representation of both male and female musicians throughout, just as there are men and women actively performing all varieties of music in contemporary Japan. This does not mean, however, that their pursuits have enjoyed the same public presence throughout the history of music, nor that their products are equally valued in the present day.

During the Edo period, for example, public female performance was banned from *kabuki*, despite the fact that the origins of the art form are attributed to the female dancer Izumo no Okuni. According to Oshio,

> The ban was deemed necessary because musicians and dancers of the rapidly proliferating female troupes were thought to have corrupted public morals by, in many cases, also being prostitutes ... The shogunate's policy made public venues the exclusive domain of male performers.
>
> (2002:764)

In the Edo period, men thus came to dominate public, professional spaces, while women remained active as students, historically learning "music appropriate to their social class," such as merchants' daughters mastering *shamisen*, while *samurai* daughters learned *koto* (ibid.:764). Women also composed music (often publishing under a male pseudonym) and became teachers of these art forms to men who could perform professionally (Fujie 2002:347). Women consequently served a crucial role transmitting these traditions, while also supporting professional male performers, roles they eagerly continue to fulfill.

Today most professional musicians who perform regularly on stage must also support themselves through teaching, with the vast number of their students comprising women who have the leisure time and expendable income necessary to pursue such activities. Many of these women obtain extremely high levels of skill and are completely devoted to their studies and to their instructors (see further discussion in Chapter 6). Oshio agrees that "Without these devotees, who form an enthusiastic audience at concerts, professional musicians and teachers would not be able to maintain their musical activities" (2002:765).

Women thus have long served an essential role in the private sphere of traditional Japanese music. But a similar gendered division of labor marked the production of an underground (*angura*) hardcore rock music scene in western Tokyo in the late 1990s, in which there were a surprising number of active female performers (Milioto 1998; Milioto Matsue 2008b). The sheer numbers, as well as apparent creative autonomy enjoyed by women in the underground, suggests that they were experiencing great freedom. They had access to instruments, production equipment and other music technology that had been reserved for men in the past. In some cases, they even felt that their gender was no longer used to qualify their musical talents; gone is the label "*female* musician." But while this may seem liberating for these artists, as well as for women in society at large, this perceived "freedom" requires additional critique.

Prevailing social systems that limit women's opportunities publicly once again partially explain the liberty that they enjoy in the underground. Historically, women labored in numerous public professions, but in the late nineteenth century, through the discourse of "good wife, wise mother" (*ryōsai kenbo*), adult women were positioned "primarily as the dependent caretakers of the home"; thus a women's place became firmly situated within the private sphere in the modern era (Aoyagi 2005:95). Aoyagi explains:

> ... officials in the Ministry of Education differentiated women from men in the 1890s and universalized the image of women as homebound agents of biological and social reproduction. Ever since, women have been simultaneously typified as "protectorates" (so to speak) of the patriarchal rule—a characterization that continues to influence the public imagination of womanhood in Japan today.
> (Ibid.:91)

This understanding of appropriate female behavior, for example, affects how women are portrayed in mainstream popular culture, which predominantly perpetuates a conservative reading of their roles as rulers of the home, keeping life in order so that husbands can work long hours and children prosper at school. Aoyagi goes so far as to argue that "Starting from birth, girls are treated differently from boys: they are nurtured to be gentle, quiet, meek, accommodating, and self-sacrificing" (ibid.). Even though this interpretation undervalues the power women exert through management of all aspects of domestic life, women in Japan today continue to negotiate individual identity within the context of this dominant social discourse, either behaving as expected or resisting in various ways, including playing in a hardcore rock band.

Most men and women in bands in the underground must necessarily work part-time jobs, supporting themselves while leaving room in their schedule for time-consuming rehearsals and public performances. In the late 1990s, for example, Kimura Kaori and Chiba Megu, two female members of a then well-known underground hardcore rock band the Berotecs, both held part-time jobs: Kimura at one of the livehouses, and Chiba in a guitar shop, earning approximately 900 yen (US$8.00) an hour. The same social restrictions that have prevented many women from pursuing full-time work outside the home (largely a result of the discourse of *ryōsai kenbo*), concomitantly pressure men into professional careers, and they no longer have the leisure time to perform in bands as a hobby. Since many women still feel that these types of career employment are unavailable to them, they have the time to continue pursuing their musical interests. This socioeconomic situation also leaves more space for these women to assume jobs as mixers and stagehands; positions dominated by men in other more mainstream levels of music making. Women are usually not employed in such positions at larger clubs, for example, and such opportunities are only available at the underground, or "underpaid," level.

If the underground is considered a private sphere, with its absence of labels and market attention and limited audience attendance, the prominence of female musicians is not so surprising. In more prominent and public levels of the popular music system in Japan, however, the numbers of women enjoying such creative autonomy begins to dwindle. Women are more often seen as mainstream popular musicians, singing and dancing as idols (*aidoru*) and under the control of men, or as singer-songwriters performing in a non-aggressive style. All-female rock bands rarely if ever attract major label attention, and usually the members make no money from performing in a band. While women are able to enjoy creative freedom, only a small following are able to share in the music. Nonetheless, these women take music making very seriously. Thus women clearly are able to explore artistic avenues in their lives through making music in the underground, while at the same time, it is precisely the systems of inequality in place in mainstream Japanese culture that allow this to happen.

Patriarchal social, political and economic structures have long shaped such alternative spaces for women to pursue a variety of arts, whether in early forms of Japanese literature, studying traditional music in contemporary Japan, or performing hardcore rock. And much of Japan's richest art has indeed emerged through women working in the socially acceptable private sphere, gaining limited attention for their efforts, or large-scale recognition only through a process of historicization and retrieval of their work from the margins.

Gendered conceptions of performance continue to permeate both traditional and popular musics in myriad ways. The ban on public female performance established in the Edo period was lifted in 1877; nevertheless, men still dominate the public performance of theatrical forms, including *kabuki*. The results of these gender-based restrictions are not all negative of course, as such limitations inspired the creation of the *onnagata*, an idealized female character performed exclusively by male actors with mesmerizing results. Similarly, Takarazuka Revue, a fascinating form of all-female theater that developed in the early twentieth century, relies on *otokoyaku*, female actors to present an idealized and romantic version of masculinity (Robertson 1998; Watanabe 2013).

Women also have developed ways to perform musics of the traditional male-dominated theater, and in doing so reveal how understandings of gender invade not only the spaces where music is performed, but also the sounds themselves. There are, for example, female versions of previously all-male theatrical forms, including *gidayū-bushi* (narration for the puppet theater) (referred to as *joryū gidayū* when performed by women) (Coaldrake 1997), and now there are occasional performances of *noh* by women. Women also perform musics from the *kabuki* theater as absolute music, removed from the public stage and placed in a more private chamber setting. However, in all these examples,

> ...women play the same repertoire as men, and they follow male aesthetic standards. There is no distinction concerning vocal parts: men and women sing

in almost the same register (without any octave difference), and female singers try to imitate men's voice color.

(Oshio 2002:765)

This shared aesthetic standard results "in a general tendency to regard male performance as 'authentic' whereas women 'learn' and follow," which results in a lack of "feminine" expression in art music (ibid.). With few historical exceptions, the "masculine" is upheld as the ideal. As a result, today "female *gidayū-bushi* (*joryū gidayū*) performers prefer to abandon feminine expression in favor of an 'authentic' masculine performance" (ibid.).

Once again we see a similar gendered understanding of vocal production in hardcore rock in the late 1990s, which privileged an arduous style amongst both men and women that could be understood as "masculine." A particular combination of thick hardcore instrumentation and deep, intense screaming (*sakebi*) were tropes common in the underground, but the quality of the female voice added a certain dimension, actually privileging the girls who sang like boys; a slightly different interpretation than in the case of traditional Japanese music.

Female performance, however, has come to dominate some traditional genres, such as *koto* music (*sōkyoku*). According to Oshio, "although only men could become authorized *sōkyoku* musicians during the Edo period, female musicians are now evaluated according to an equal musical standard and have also exceeded men in numbers" (ibid.). Oshio argues this change occurred as the instrumental parts were emphasized over the vocal "and it is the vocal aspects that are more naturally connected with gender differences, because of innate voice color and registers" (ibid.). Thus male vocals became privileged and idealized as authentic, but women have excelled in instrumental music, which lacked the same gendered association. Once again, limitations seem to present opportunities.

Since the economic bubble burst in the early 1990s, a woman's primary role as "wife" and "mother" has been challenged. With the sluggish economy, for example, increasing numbers of women have entered the labor force, albeit often in underpaid and underappreciated part-time positions. Young adults today are delaying marriage and family, or deciding not to have children at all, leading to an alarmingly low birthrate in Japan. In 2014, the number of children per family averaged 1.4, compared to 1.8 in the United States (World Bank 2014). The population of Japan is actually decreasing—from a peak of 128,000,000 in 2008 to 127,500,00 in 2012, and is projected to be less than 100,000,000 by 2050 (Ministry of Internal Affairs and Communications 2014). This is not an argument to return to bans on female public performance or the gendered boxing-in of *ryōsai kenbo*, but rather a comment on the struggles Japan faces today as women's roles change. And as both men and women confront new social concerns in the twenty-first century, no doubt gendered performance practices will transform as well.

Summary

The proceeding discussion explores how the Japanese have created, embraced and embodied Japanese cultural identity in diverse musical practices. Although modernity complicated this process, one thing is absolutely clear—Japaneseness is not located exclusively in musics of purely Japanese origin solely performed by Japanese people kneeling on *tatami* mats in tea houses, an assumption that in turn would require that musicians who are Japanese by birth to somehow necessarily *sound* Japanese. The access to information and the exchange of ideas throughout the world increased dramatically throughout the twentieth century and exploded in recent decades with the expansion of the Internet. Now one can sit in their living room in icy upstate New York and take a lesson with their *shakuhachi* teacher in Kyoto. And certainly today it seems preposterous to claim a music must be performed in Japan by Japanese to express Japaneseness.

This is further complicated by the movement of Japanese people beyond the borders of Japan, performing in Japanese diasporas in Brazil (Olsen 2004) or Hawaii (Odo 2013), or even completely removed from any ethnically unified communities (Keister 2008 and 2013). And how do we define Japanese ethnicity and national identity anyway, when Japanese are second-, third-, or fourth-generation abroad? Or claim interracial heritage and possess dual passports? There are also many non-ethnically Japanese, perhaps even that *shakuhachi* player in New York, performing musics that are still easily understood as Japanese. Clearly, ethnic identity and geographical location are not the primary factors determining Japaneseness. What do these categories even mean in a progressively borderless and interconnected world?

With musics performed throughout the world, mixing and melding numerous styles, what constitutes Japanese music seems to be becoming increasingly complex, even calling into question whether we can still identify *any* musics as uniquely Japanese (Novak 2013:130). Though musical identity and by extension cultural identity is fluid—both are a performance in a constant state of flux—we nonetheless often describe something as somehow "Japanese," "American," "Spanish," connecting artistic expression with ethnic and national associations as a way of ordering our world. It may in fact be impossible to move away from such generic labels. This in turn may suggest that there still are qualities that we can identify as undeniably Japanese about Japanese music; as expressing Japaneseness either through sound or the activities involved in the production of that sound.

Precisely because of Japan's history of shaping its own identity through the hybridization of the cultural products of Others, the Japanese are both long-practiced at considering just such questions (evidenced by the perpetual *nihonjinron* debate) and quite adept at doing so. These are not new questions to Japanese—and not likely to go away—and it is this search for that Japaneseness which motivates the exploration of music in Japan that follows.

References

Aoyagi, Hiroshi. 2005. *Islands of Eight Million Smiles: Idol Performance and Symbolic Production in Contemporary Japan*. Cambridge, MA: Harvard University Press.
Atkins, Everett T. 2000. "Can Japanese Sing the Blues? 'Japanese Jazz' and the Problem of Authenticity." In T. Craig, ed., *Japan Pop!: Inside the World of Japanese Popular Culture*, pp. 27–59. New York: M.E. Sharpe.
——. 2001. *Blue Nippon: Authenticating Jazz in Japan*. Durham, NC: Duke University Press.
Bakan, Michael B. 2012. *World Music: Traditions and Transformations*. New York: McGraw-Hill.
Befu, Harumi. 2001. *Hegemony of Homogeneity: An Anthropological Analysis of Nihonjinron*. Melbourne: Trans Pacific.
Bigenho, Michelle. 2012. *Intimate Distance: Andean Music in Japan*. Durham, NC: Duke University Press.
Blasdel, Christopher Y. 2005. *The Single Tone: A Personal Journey into Shakuhachi Music*. Tokyo: Printed Matter Press.
Bourdaghs, Michael K. 2012. *Sayonara Amerika, Sayonara Nippon: A Geopolitical Prehistory of J-Pop*. New York: Columbia University Press.

Chun, Allen, Ned Rossiter and Brian Shoesmith. 2004. *Refashioning Pop Music in Asia: Cosmopolitan Flows, Political Tempos and Aesthetic Industries.* New York/London: Routledge.

Coaldrake, Kimi A. 1997. *Women's Gidayū and the Japanese Theatre Tradition.* New York/London: Routledge.

Coldwell, Robert. 1997. "Introduction to the History of the Guitar in Japan." *Guitar and Lute Issues* (1997): http://www.guitarandluteissues.com/j-intro.htm (accessed August 14, 2014).

Condry, Ian. 2000. "The Social Production of Difference Imitation and Authenticity in Japanese Rap Music." In H. Fehrenbach and U. Poiger, eds., *Transactions, Transgressions, Transformations: American Culture in Western Europe and Japan*, pp. 166–84. New York/Oxford: Berghahn Books.

——. 2006. *Hip-Hop Japan: Rap and the Paths of Cultural Globalization.* Durham, NC: Duke University Press.

Cook, Lisa M. 2014. "Venerable Traditions, Modern Manifestations: Understanding Mayuzumi's Bunraku for Cello." *Asian Music* 45(1):99–131.

Craig, Timothy J. and Richard King. 2002. *Global Goes Local: Popular Culture in Asia.* Honolulu: University of Hawaii Press.

de Ferranti, Hugh. 2002. "Japanese Music can be Popular." *Popular Music* 21(2):195–208.

—— and Alison Tokita, eds. 2013. *Music, Modernity and Locality in Prewar Japan: Osaka and Beyond.* Farnham: Ashgate.

Fujie, Linda. 2002. "East Asia – Japan." In J. Titon, ed., *Worlds of Music: An Introduction to the Music of the World's Peoples 4th Edn.*, pp. 331–384. Belmont, CA: Schirmer/Thomson Learning.

Goto-Jones, Christopher. 2009. *Modern Japan: A Very Short Introduction.* Oxford: Oxford University Press.

Hebert, David G. 2012. *Wind Bands and Cultural Identity in Japanese Schools.* New York/London: Springer.

Hosokawa, Shūhei. 1994. *Japanese Popular Music of the Past Twenty Years: Its Mainstream and Underground.* Tokyo: Japan Foundation.

——. 1999. "Salsa no Tiene Frontera: Orquesta de la Luz and the Globalization of Popular Music." *Cultural Studies* 13(3):509–34.

Hughes, David. 2008. *Traditional Folk Song in Modern Japan: Sources, Sentiment and Society.* Folkestone: Global Oriental.

IASPM-Japan. 1990. *A Guide to Popular Music in Japan.* Takarazuka: IASPM-Japan.

Iwabuchi, Koichi. 2002. *Recentering Globalization: Popular Culture and Japanese Transnationalism.* Durham, NC: Duke University Press.

Jaffe, Jerry C. and Henry Johnson. 2008. "Introduction." In J. Jaffe and H Johnson, eds., *Performing Japan-Contemporary Expressions of Cultural Identity*, pp. 1–10. Folkestone: Global Oriental.

Keister, Jay. 2008. "Okeikoba: Lesson Places as Sites for Negotiating Tradition in Japanese Music." *Ethnomusicology* 52(2):239–269.

——. 2013 "Exotic Essence and Contested Boundaries: Traditional Music and Being Japanese in Colorado," Paper Presentation, Society of Ethnomusicology National Conference in Indiana.

Kitagawa, Junko. 2009. "Music Culture." In Y. Sugimoto, ed., *The Cambridge Companion to Modern Japanese Culture*, pp. 261–280. Cambridge: Cambridge University Press.

Malm, William P. 2000. *Traditional Japanese Music and Musical Instruments.* Tokyo: Kodansha.

Mathews, Gordon. 2004. "Fence, Flavor, and Phantasm: Japanese Musicians and the Meanings of 'Japaneseness'." *Japanese Studies* 24(3):335–350.

McClimon, Sarah J. 2011. "Music, Politics and Memory: Japanese Military Songs in War and Peace." Ph.D. Dissertation, University of Hawaii.

Milioto, Jennifer. 1998. "Women in Japanese Popular Music: Setting the Subcultural Scene." In T. Mitsui, ed., *Popular Music: Intercultural Interpretations*, pp. 485–498. Kanazawa, Japan: Kanazawa University

Milioto Matsue, Jennifer M. 2008a. "The Local Performance of Global Sound: More than the Musical in Japanese Hardcore Rock." In J. Jaffe and H. Johnson. eds., *Performing Japan: Contemporary Expressions of Cultural Identity*, pp. 221–238. Folkestone: Global Oriental Press.

——. 2008b. *Making Music in Japan's Underground: The Tokyo Hardcore Scene.* New York/London: Routledge.

Ministry of Economy. 2013. "The Yearbook of Current Production Statistics." *The Ministry of Economy* (2013): http://www.meti.go.jp/statistics/tyo/seidou/result/gaiyo/resourceData/05_seni/nenpo/h2dff2013k.pdf (accessed November 3, 2014).

Ministry of Internal Affairs and Communications. 2014. "Population of Japan." *Ministry of Internal Affairs and Communications* (2014): http://www.stat.go.jp/data/nihon/02.htm (accessed November 22, 2014).

Minoru, Miki. 2008. *Composing for Japanese Instruments*. Translated by M. Regan, P. Flavin, ed. Rochester, NY: University of Rochester Press.

Novak, David. 2013. *Japanoise: Music at the Edge of Circulation*. Durham, NC: Duke University Press.

Odo, Franklin. 2013. *Voices from the Canefields: Folksongs from Japanese Immigrant Workers in Hawai'i*. Oxford: Oxford University Press.

Olsen, Dale. 2004. *The Chrysanthemum and the Song: Music, Memory, and Identity in the South American Japanese Diaspora*. Gainesville: University of Florida Press.

Oshio, Satomi. 2002. "Gender roles in the performing arts in Japan." In R. Provine, Y. Tokumaru and J. Witzleben, eds., *East Asia: China, Japan and Korea. The Garland Encyclopedia of World Music Vol. 7*, pp. 763–766. New York/London: Routledge.

Peluse, Michael S. 2005. "Not Your Grandfather's Music: Tsugaru Shamisen Blurs the Lines Between 'Folk,' 'Traditional,' and 'Pop'." *Asian Music* 36(2):57–80.

Robertson, Jennifer. 1998. *Takarazuka: Sexual Politics and Popular Culture in Modern Japan*. Berkeley: University of California Press.

Sakai, Naoki. 2002. "Nihonjinron." In S. Buckley, ed., *Encyclopedia of Contemporary Japanese Culture*, pp. 356–357. New York/London: Routledge.

Spiller, Henry. 2008. *Focus: Gamelan Music of Indonesia*. New York: Routledge.

Sterling, Marvin D. 2010. *Babylon East: Performing Dancehall, Roots Reggae, and Rastafari in Japan*. Durham, NC: Duke University Press.

Stevens, Carolyn S. 2008. *Japanese Popular Music: Culture, Authenticity, and Power*. New York/London: Routledge.

Sugimoto Yoshio. 2010. *An Introduction to Japanese Society*, 3rd Edn. Cambridge: Cambridge University Press.

Tierney, Kenji R. 2007. "From Popular Performance to National Sport (*Kokugi*): The 'Nationalization' of Sumo." In W. Kelly, ed., *This Sporting Life: Sports and Body Culture in Modern Japan*, pp. 67–89. New Haven, CT: Yale CEAS Occasional Publications.

Tokita, Alison M. and David W. Hughes, eds. 2008. *The Ashgate Research Companion to Japanese Music*. Farnham: Ashgate.

Tokita, Alison. 2013. "The Piano as a Symbol of Modernity in Prewar Kansai." In H. de Ferranti and A. Tokita, eds., *Music, Modernity and Locality in Prewar Japan: Osaka and Beyond*, pp. 93–122. Farnham: Ashgate.

Wade, Bonnie C. 2005. *Music in Japan: Expressing Music, Expressing Culture*. Oxford: Oxford University Press.

Waswo, Ann. 2007. "Modernism and Cultural Identity in Japan." *Asian Affairs* 20(1):45–56.

Watanabe, Hiroshi. 2013. "Takarazuka and Japanese Modernity" In H. de Ferranti and A. Tokita, eds., *Music, Modernity and Locality in Prewar Japan: Osaka and Beyond*, pp. 193–210. Farnham: Ashgate.

Williams, Sean. 2006. "Irish Music and the Experience of Nostalgia in Japan." *Asian Music* 37(1):101–119.

——. 2010. *Focus: Irish Traditional Music*. New York/London: Routledge.

World Bank. 2014. "Fertility rate, total (births per woman)." *The World Bank* (2014): http://data.worldbank.org/indicator/SP.DYN.TFRT.IN (accessed November 22, 2014).

Yano, Christine R. 2002. *Tears of Longing: Nostalgia and the Nation in Japanese Popular Song*. Cambridge, MA: Harvard University Press.

—— and Shūhei Hosokawa. 2008. "Popular Music in Modern Japan" In A. McQueen Tokita and D. Hughes, eds., *The Ashgate Research Companion to Japanese Music*, pp. 345–362. Farnham: Ashgate.

PART II
Sounding Japan

Part II, "Sounding Japan," explores the ways in which music "sounds" Japanese, both in the sense of sonic attributes and a view of broader cultural characteristics. The chapters are separated roughly by musics that originate in the pre-modern era comprising predominantly traditional music and those that have developed in the modern era, reflecting the influx of Western musical sounds, instruments and ideas.

CHAPTER 3

Performing Music of Pre-modern Japan

Like a brushstroke painting, there is space, but here created through silence broken by the plaintive tones of a flute, approached, sustained, and trailing away to silence again. Slowly, intermittently percussive sounds drip from the edges, increasing in rhythmic intensity as the flute begins to explore higher pitches of shorter duration, often returning to the same starting point, dipping the brush in yet more ink. The canvas begins to fill as the percussion establishes a firm pulse and regular rhythms; the flute still hovers above the driving beat, rising in emotional intensity in higher registers, building through row after row of rapid ascending motifs. The brushstrokes quicken, like a leaf scurrying across a wind-blown plain, as the flute becomes increasingly frenetic, buzzing and blurring pitches in a most demanding manner, drawing in the listener. The flute maintains the breathy tone, returning to opening sustained pitches, and inviting the listener into the moments of silence that follow while the percussion quiets to circular strokes on the drums. The painting is complete when silence again descends on the hushed audience which has just been taken along on the journey as well.

"Duet" by Kenny Endo and Kaoru Watanabe (Website Example 5), illustrates the Japanese aesthetic focus on simplicity and space. But there is also liveliness and rhythmic intensity as Watanabe's flute (*fue*) fills the space through increasing variation, flutters, trills and even buzzing of pitch until Endo swishes the normally quite loud drums (*taiko*), taking us back to nothingness.

I used this video to illustrate basic ideas of Japanese music to an introductory course on Japanese visual arts—likening the musical expansion and use of space to a brushstroke painting (*sumie*). I would later learn in an interview with Watanabe that he was studying *sumie* at the time he and Endo performed this largely improvisational piece at the club rRed Elephant in Hawaii in 2007 (interview May 5, 2014). This visual reference may not be obvious to every listener, but the musical ideas presented here nonetheless begin to illustrate sounds that may be understood as characteristic of Japan—from the timbre of the instruments themselves to more broad conceptual aesthetics. Endo and Watanabe also clearly explore improvisation, although the practice is not typically found in much traditional Japanese music. Rather Endo and Watanabe bring their experiences in jazz and avant-garde art musics to Japan. This performance thus illustrates the intersection of musics that originate in pre-modern Japan with modern musical practices, a topic that will be further considered at the end of Part II when we return to both of these musicians to frame this discussion.

The proceeding section introduced the diversity of musics that can be heard in contemporary Japan, highlighting the historical melding of styles, between "old" and "new," indigenous and borrowed, that has taken place throughout Japanese music history. However, many of the arts that we have come to think of as representing unique Japanese aesthetic ideals flourished in Japan during the Edo period—the era of mythical isolation—even though they may enjoy origins dating farther back. The following discussion is thus focused primarily on the general characteristics of these pre-modern musics, on traditional Japanese music (*hōgaku*) that "sounds Japanese." The ways in which these musical elements confront or conform to Western music in the Meiji period and beyond will be further explored in Chapter 4.

Overviews of *hōgaku* typically begin with *gagaku*, *shōmyō* and *min'yō*. The order in which these are introduced might depend on the emphasis one wants to place on *min'yō* and indigenousness—that is, the idea that folk music comes first and then the importation of music from China begins. Typically, accounts next move through the great theatrical genres, numerous solo instrumental repertoires that blossom through the Edo period, and finally the rapid transformation of musical practice in general, and more specifically, the development of popular music in the modern era (Malm 1959; Kishibe 1984; Malm 2000; Fujie 2002; Alves 2013).

Many of the so-called "major genres" of Japanese music have already been introduced in the proceeding pages. *Kagura* of Shintō and Buddhist *shōmyō*, for example, were already mentioned in Chapter 1 as a way to bring religion to life through song and dance, and certainly represent some of the oldest forms of music still heard in contemporary Japan. The regional *min'yō* of east and west Japan, as well as the Ryūkyū islands, also introduced in Chapter 1, highlights the historical regionalism of Japan that is once again in resurgence. These genres of course also introduced some of the characteristics of music that sound particularly Japanese, such as vocal ornamentation and scale types. The following sections take a closer look at several additional genres within *hōgaku* to deepen this understanding. As with some other recent texts on Japanese music (Wade 2005), I move away from the typical overview in historical order, rather using other frameworks to organize these materials.

The goal of the ensuing discussion is therefore not to include a summary of *all* elements, aesthetic principles and styles, but to introduce tools for listening positioned within some key genres of traditional Japanese music in an efficient and approachable format. Neither is this presented as a survey of genres, but rather a "focusing in" on the specifics necessary to explain the character of the sound—particularly as it expresses Japaneseness. Thus my intention is to explore why Japanese music indeed sounds Japanese—what makes Japanese music distinct. Each musical example therefore highlights a particular aesthetic issue or, in some cases, several issues. As we progress through these pages, and the reader increases their knowledge, the analysis builds upon elements already introduced.

One of the potentially alienating features of *hōgaku* is that pieces can either sound quite similar or be hard to follow, particularly if grounded in a free rhythm. The same of course could be said for much Western art music produced from the early twentieth century onwards. Understanding some basic principles that characterize Japanese traditional music will undoubtedly lead to a better connection with what one is hearing. And with repeated listening, the qualities that make Japanese music so fantastic become visceral. Hopefully, these moments of deeper reflection collectively paint a vivid picture of music in contemporary Japan.

Terminology

Japanese musical culture abounds with seemingly limitless terms to describe every level of music making, from broad general categorizations to labels for numerous sub-genres, with at times complicated and obscure nuances. Given that every instrumental tradition has its own theoretical system, not surprisingly there are also extensive terms for describing the specific elements associated with each, down to the minutest details of formal organization or gesture. Although the following pages try to focus on the labels most necessary to navigate the world of traditional Japanese music—some terminology is necessary to better understand how Japanese cultural identity is constructed and contested through musical performance—much terminology, even though important, is not included.

Elements of Japanese Traditional Music

Ma

Much is often made of the poetic concept of "*ma*" within Japanese music—on the surface typically defined as the space between things. *Ma* is recognized in numerous traditional Japanese arts, such as flower arrangement (*kadō*), where the absence of flowers highlight those that are there, a technique similarly employed in traditional garden design. In the traditional Japanese tea ceremony (*sadō*), the tearoom is precisely designed and decorated to make the practitioner aware of the spaces and objects that fill them, while the preparation and pouring of the tea itself uses measured and precise movements to create a particular rhythm with moments of repose, inviting reflection. The opening piece of this chapter, "Duet," sonically interprets the visuals of *sumie*, illustrating well the idea of *ma*.

As a musical concept, *ma* "refers to the overall timing of a piece—not just the pauses and rests but also the relationship between sound and silence on which all music is fundamentally based. It embraces the idea that sound enhances silence and silence enhances sound" (Fujie 2002:343). Grounded in Zen Buddhist philosophies, *ma* stresses the importance of emptiness, asking performers to be aware of the silences surrounding notes as much as the notes themselves. There certainly are "spaces" in musics found throughout the world; however, within Japanese music, the concept of *ma* has been highly theorized by scholars, composers and performers to encompass much more than a rest between notes.

Famed twentieth-century art composer Takemitsu Tōru, for example, became fascinated with *ma*, writing extensively on the topic in *Confronting Silence* (1995). Here Takemitsu envisions *ma* as an "intense silence" proceeding and therefore enhancing a strong sound, but elaborates that

> ...there is a metaphysical continuity that defies analysis...It is here that sound and silence confront each other, balancing each other in a relationship beyond any objective measurement. In its complexity and its integrity this single sound can stand alone. To the sensitive Japanese listener who appreciates this refined sound, the unique idea of *ma*—the unsounded part of this experience—has at the same time a deep, powerful, and rich resonance that can stand up to the sound. In short, this *ma*, this powerful silence, is that which gives life to the sound and removes it from its position of primacy. So it is that sound, confronting the silence of *ma*, yields supremacy in the final expression.
> (1995:51)

Galliano applies the concept of *ma* to other aspects of performance beyond sound:

> It is the time between events, the space between objects, the relationship between people, or that moment in a person's mind between thoughts. It is the white space in a pen-and-ink drawing, the pause between notes, or the moment in a *shite* dance in the last section of a [*noh*] play when all movement is frozen...In other words, *ma* describes neither space nor time, but the tension in the silence and in the space surrounding sounds and objects.
> (2002:14)

Takemitsu takes this even further explaining that "The concept of *ma* is one special form of recognition in the universe, in the cosmos. *Ma* is the big universe, and man is very little, small. We feel the big space—*ma*. This is most primary. Man is part of nature—no less, no more" (Takemitsu, Cronin and Tann 1989:213). Ultimately, even Takemitsu acknowledges that *ma* is a difficult concept to isolate and describe (ibid.:212). Perhaps it is in fact the indefinable quality of *ma* that has made it a most attractive aesthetic idea, resulting in some over-romanticizing in regards to Japanese music. Nonetheless, the idea of *ma* permeates the performance of *noh* theater (see further discussion below), as well as the repertoire and performance techniques of the *shakuhachi*, one of the most iconic instruments of Japan.

Constructed from a slightly curved bamboo stalk complete with the root, *shakuhachi* are end-blown flutes of varying sizes; the standard is about 54 centimeters, with a range of approximately two-and-a-half octaves. The most common *shakuhachi* has four holes on the front and one in the back. A deceptively simple-looking instrument, the *shakuhachi* is actually extremely difficult to play. The player blows across an oblique cut, called the *utaguchi* (song mouth), inlaid with ivory, or buffalo or deer horn (Gunji and Johnson 2012:230); no easy feat as the player rests one's chin on the near side and blows across the opposite. One is able to slightly vary the intonation through changing

Performing Music of Pre-modern Japan • 71

the angle of the chin (Kishibe 1984:80). The interior may be left plain or lacquered, the latter producing what some consider a better sound (ibid.).

The *shakuhachi* is an incredibly versatile instrument, capable of producing an array of microtones through strong breaths and fingering in a variety of qualities ranging from "'pure' (with few overtones) to quite breathy, sounding almost like white noise" (Fujie 2002:338), thus inspiring musicians to explore its sonic possibilities in a wide range of genres beyond traditional Japanese music, including jazz. There are numerous techniques that create the *shakuhachi*'s characteristic melodic patterns, wide vibrato and deep pitch bends.

The *shakuhachi* is believed to have originated in China and first appeared in Japanese court music, although the instrument was likely formalized during the Edo period. The solo repertoire of the *shakuhachi* is similarly believed to have entered Japan with the Fuke sect of Zen Buddhism, introduced from China by the Zen priest Kakushin (1207–98) in the Kamakura period (Gunji and Johnson 2012:232). Some hermits of the Fuke sect—known as *komusō*, "monks of nothingness or emptiness"—began soliciting alms while playing *shakuhachi* during the Muromachi period (ibid.:230). During the Edo period, many master-less *samurai* (*rōnin*) found themselves essentially without work during the long period of relative peace, and with few options, given the strict limitations imposed by the hierarchical social system of the day. Some of these aimless *samurai* took religious orders, and played the *shakuhachi* while begging as *komusō* on the streets (Fujie 2002:339; Wade 2005:49):

> In 1614, Ieyasu, the founder of the Tokugawa shogunate, bestowed a special charter upon the *komusō* that in effect gave that military government a means of controlling a large group of *rōnin*. The charter granted them unique privileges, including a monopoly over the playing of the *shakuhachi*, and also the right of wearing an identity-obscuring basket hat over the face—in Buddhist terms, a sign of humility, but if misused, an opportunity to hide or spy.
> (Wade 2005:50)

Some scholars argue that the Fuke sect in fact needed to legitimate itself with the Tokugawa government and in exchange became spies (Malm 2000:168; Blasdel 2005:38–39). Today, such basket-wearing itinerant beggars can still be spotted in front of the occasional train station, though some are suspected of being imposters and not actually practicing Buddhist humility.

In the early Edo period, the *shakuhachi* became strongly associated with the ritual practices of the Fuke sect and was seen as a spiritual tool towards enlightenment—an aid in mediation referred to as *sui zen* ("blowing Zen") (Gunji and Johnson 2012:232). When necessary the *komusō* may also have wielded the *shakuhachi* as a club in self-defense. The Fuke sect was abolished in the Meiji period and since then the *shakuhachi* has become "a solo and ensemble instrument . . . as well as an accompanying instrument in folk song" (Gunji and Johnson 232), nevertheless retaining these strong associations with Zen Buddhism in general.

Shakuhachi pieces are roughly divided into *honkyoku*, the original solo pieces, and *gaikyoku*, outside pieces, first written for *koto* or *shamisen*, and later adapted. Blasdel explains that

> The beginner is expected to learn seventy-four *gaikyoku*, a commitment of about six years. It is only after the student has mastered these pieces that he or

> she can proceed to the heart of *shakuhachi* music: the lofty Zen-inspired solo *honkyoku* pieces.
>
> (2005:21)

Though players new to *shakuhachi* may find this a daunting task, Blasdel argues the *gaikyoku* teach both technique and teamwork, as one performs in ensemble settings. It is the *honkyoku*, with their meditative Zen qualities, that have captured the imagination of both Japanese and foreigners alike (see further discussion below). And the *shakuhachi* remains a powerful tool in the quest for spirituality. With the *shakuhachi*:

> Each single tone is a mystery, and the awareness of tone (including mundane sounds) becomes a vehicle for heightening consciousness. The idea of sound as spiritual exercise may seem strange in modern commercial urban cultures where endless, abrasive noises bombard the senses and create considerable stress. Nonetheless, one only needs to consider the noble sounds still used in various religious ceremonies around the world to understand how deeply they affect the heart and mind.
>
> The fabric of natural sounds is intricately woven and richly connected, and by listening we place ourselves into its weave. The act of listening brings the world of outer sounds inside, and thereby we become an active participant in their transmission. The further we allow sounds to enter the consciousness, the deeper glimpse we get of ourselves. A point is eventually reached when the listener becomes aware of the necessity of each sound. It is at such times the world whispers its most intimate secrets through sound. All we must do is listen.
>
> (Ibid.:42)

The *shakuhachi* requires great concentration and focus on one's natural breathing pattern to create these sounds, which in turn bring the performer into a heightened state of awareness:

> The exhaling of breath is heard in the dynamic level and tone quality of a pitch; at the same time, it carries the possibility of instant spiritual enlightenment. Thus, each moment of 'performance,' whether the intake of breath or its slow release, whether the subtle, delicate shading of a tone or the explosion of air through the instrument, can be interpreted in the context of a larger spiritual life.
>
> (Fujie 2002:340)

Thus sound and spirituality come together in the *shakuhachi*. And it is this intensity of sound that so attracted North American *shakuhachi* player James Nyoraku Schlefer to the instrument.

Schlefer explains that as a graduate student in musicology in the 1980s, he was exposed to the *shakuhachi* and was immediately drawn to the sound of "the bamboo." He became increasingly interested in this sound, took a course on Asian music, and began to study *shakuhachi*. He feels that although much Japanese traditional music sounds distinctly Japanese, for him the *honkyoku* of *shakuhachi* actually have

> ... a universal sound, a non-specific Japaneseness quality, unlike the *sankyoku* [pieces for *koto* and *shamisen*], which sounds distinctly Japanese, particularly because of lyrics in the vocal tradition. But the *shakuhachi*, because it is not melodic or rhythmic in traditional ways and it is really just focused on sound and the sound is so penetrating it is the kind of thing anybody can relate to because of the abstractness and non-musicalness

which perhaps accounts for its "appeal to non-Japanese more than any other instruments." Schlefer continues, saying that while

> There is something about the rigor of the study, which is kind of Japanese in a way because it is disciplined, the music itself rises above and is its own kind of world. That being said, the sound immediately draws one to the hills of Japan, though these can be hills anywhere ... Shakuhachi is increasing in popularity around the world, even as traditional music declines. This same thing is not happening with *koto* for example. It is portable and so sound focused—rather than place focused.
>
> (interview May 4, 2014)

The *shakuhachi*'s plaintive tone, expressiveness and potential as a spiritual tool, all feed into its increasing popularity with foreign practitioners (Keister 2004).

Foreign Practitioners of Japanese Music

The inclusion of non-Japanese professional performers acknowledges the increasingly prominent position and importance of foreign practitioners for supporting and maintaining Japanese traditions (Trimillos 2004). The active performance of Japanese traditional music by both amateurs and professionals also affirms that Japaneseness does not reside in the nationality or ethnicity of the performer (see further discussion in Chapter 2). Schlefer claims he never met with resistance as a foreign player, in fact only encouragement. He finds "Japanese can actually be more interested seeing a foreigner playing this instrument they may know little about," thus foreigners may be attracting Japanese to their own traditional music. (interview May 4, 2014).

Takemitsu beautifully summarizes:

> In performance, sound transcends the realm of the personal. Now we can see how the master *shakuhachi* player, striving in performance to re-create the sound of wind in a decaying bamboo grove, reveals the Japanese sound ideal: sound, in its ultimate expressiveness, being constantly refined, approaches the nothingness of that wind in the bamboo grove [bringing us back to *ma*].
>
> (1995: 51)

Both the meditative quality of the *shakuhachi*, in large part created through the controlled Zen breath, as well as the expansiveness of *ma* are exemplified in "Choshi" (Website Example 6), featuring James Nyoraku Schlefer (see Figure 3.1).

Figure 3.1 James Nyoraku Schlefer at Columbia University (photo by Lenny Pridatko)

This short piece is intended to establish pitch and center the musician as he or she prepares to play a longer *honkyoku*. There are many versions of "Choshi," as there are of most *shakuhachi* pieces, each belonging to a different school, such as the well-known *Kinko* school established by monk Kurosawa Kinko (1710–71), and are even more specifically associated with numerous temples throughout Japan. This version of "Choshi" is associated with the Futaiken temple in northern Honshū and is considered part of the broader *Meian* repertoire. Composer Hilary Tann, who embarked on a journey with the *shakuhachi* herself, argues that although sometimes referred to as a school of *shakuhachi* "[m]ore accurately, the term *Meian* denotes a style of playing which is modeled closely on the original Fuke aesthetic . . . Together *mei* (brightness) and *an* (darkness) represent all of the opposites found in nature" (1989:53). The style of *Meian shakuhachi* came to be associated with as many as 140 temples (ibid.:54), resulting in the numerous versions of essentially the same pieces.

Of course individual players bring their own interpretation—their own breath—to these pieces as well. And here Schlefer draws the listener into the studio apartment in Brooklyn where this recording was made. While it is difficult to capture the actual moment, listen for the sounds of the neighborhood outside to invade the space—my son talking, people walking on a nearby street, even the ticking clock on a side table and the hum of the refrigerator in the next room come into focus. As Schlefer plays, *all* the sound comes into focus. Schlefer considers this *ma*—"it is the silence and then the awareness of what is happening around you when nothing is happening. It is not just emptiness. It is that space. It is not that space and not that sound, it is the awareness of that sound. That is what *ma* brings." He continues to explain that *ma* is "also how you feel—anxious, hungry, hot—you become more aware of that because there is nothing really going on . . . So when I play that opening phrase, as the sound dies away you hear the other sounds coming in" (interview May 4, 2014).

It is difficult to transcribe *shakuhachi* music into Western notation, given its unique timbral qualities and microtonal pitches; however, Schlefer provided the following scores of "Choshi" to illustrate how these pieces are rendered in Japanese fashion, and then translated onto the Western staff (see Figures 3.2 and 3.3).

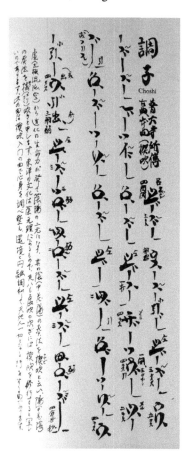

Figure 3.2 "Choshi" (Japanese score)

76 • Sounding Japan

The Japanese version, written by Jin Nyodo, who collected many *honkyoku* from *Meian* temples throughout the twentieth century (Sawyer n.d.), reads from top to bottom and right to left, in Japanese fashion. Although performances differ from school to school, teacher to teacher, and even performer to performer, the basic outline of the piece is presented. The characters correspond to pitches on the instrument, with additional pictographs to indicate microtonal inflections, flats and sharps, and deep pitch bends. Pitches may appear to be the "same," but there are many timbral choices. Breath, which directs the rhythmic feel of the music, is indicated with horizontal lines, while strong brush strokes sometimes mark intense gestures. Dynamics can also be determined by fingering. Schlefer translates these elements into the Western staff example below.

Such transcriptions, however, cannot replicate the expressiveness of the *shakuhachi*. And neither the Japanese nor Western versions are intended for students to learn to play on their own. Rather, Japanese traditional music has long been transmitted orally, from

Figure 3.3 "Choshi" (Western score) (provided by James Nyoraku Schlefer)

teacher to student, with written notation only developing fairly recently (see further discussion below). These two scores nevertheless do assist with one's ability to "hear" how this piece moves, bringing *ma* to life.

Ma creates a spacious quality in music that feels somehow distinctly Japanese, while inspiring similar explorations of sound and silence around the world. *Ma* will no doubt be evident in many of the examples that follow; however, be careful not to assume that *all* Japanese traditional music embraces such meditative principles. The folk music of the proceeding chapters, for example, offers an explosive alternative to the stoicism and meditative quality of much traditional music.

Timbre

The *shakuhachi* also illustrates another striking element of Japanese music: the deep appreciation for a breadth of sound and varied tone qualities, including indeterminate pitch. Fujie explains that in Japanese music

> ... "unpitched" sounds are commonly heard in the middle of instrumental melodies. When we hear a sound wave with a stable frequency, it is easy for us to distinguish pitch. But if the frequency varies too quickly, we do not hear a pitch. A cymbal, for example, is unpitched compared with an oboe. In Japanese music, examples of unpitched sound include the breathy sound made on the *shakuhachi* bamboo flute and the hard twang produced when the plectrum strikes the *shamisen* lute. Just as Japanese poetry is full of appreciation for unpitched sounds of nature such as water flowing or trees whispering in the wind, Japanese music recreates such sounds for the enjoyment of their listeners.
> (2002:335)

Thus sounds that may be interpreted as auxiliary in some cultural contexts are seen as essential in Japanese music and instruments are therefore designed with the ability to imitate nature sounds (Minoru 2008:3). Minoru further describes how the "materials unique to Asia—bamboo, paulownia wood, mulberry wood, cat skin (which replaced python skin)—are decisive in determining the timbre of Japanese instruments" (ibid.). And these materials therefore exert a great influence on how these instruments sound, so much so that "When substitute materials are used, approximating the original timbre to the greatest possible extent is always of primary importance" (ibid.). Even today, when modified materials must be used, such as synthetic skins on *shamisen* or resin bodies for drums, every attempt is made to maintain the desired timbre of the original instrument.

The voice, of course common throughout the world, is a most potent instrument in Japan, expressing varied timbre, numerous unique ornamental techniques and emotional qualities (ibid.). We have already seen the voice in *shōmyō* move through elongated melismatic singing, or within *min'yō* employ ornaments (*kobushi*), including wide vibrato, and shouted emphatic words of support (*hayashi-kotoba*). The voice is also essential in traditional Japanese drumming with dramatic swooping calls between performers (*kakegoe*) and similar calls of encouragement as in *min'yō*, which motivates performers (*kiai*). Even popular musics have emphasized wide timbre in the voice, with the female performers of male characters in the all-female Takarazuka Revue singing in deep "masculine" voices, or women in hardcore bands employing a vocal technique akin to screaming (*sakebi*), both sometimes chain-smoking to crush their voices to achieve the desired husky effect. Minoru even suggests varied vocal techniques developed historically as a result of the dominance of vocal music in Japan, noting that with the exception of *gagaku*, instrumental repertoires developed in conjunction with vocals (ibid.).

This appreciation for varied timbre and indeterminate pitches is already well illustrated in the flutes and percussion of the proceeding examples, but "Kasuga Sanbasō" (Track 4) further highlights the voice and strings. "Kasuga Sanbasō" is an example of a *kouta*, or "short song" for voice and *shamisen*. The performance here features vocals by Kasuga Toyoeishiba, with Kasuga Toyokisen playing the main *shamisen* line (*honte*) and Kasuga Toyoshibashu playing another *shamisen* part (*kaede*). The two *shamisen* are clearly discernable mid-way through the piece and again at the end.

> ### *Intertextuality in Japanese Performing Arts*
>
> In *Music in Japan* (2005), Bonnie Wade explores the ways in which Japanese performing arts borrow from each other "intertextually" across genres and over time. "Kasuga Sanbasō" reveals this intertextual dialogue. There are in fact many different versions of "Sanbasō," which literally translates as "third one" in a set of pieces that can be traced back to *noh*. At the time of writing, a performance of "Sanbasō" from *noh* featuring well-known actor Nomura Mansai (in part made famous by his regular appearances on the beloved children's program *Nihongo de Asobō* (Let's Play in Japanese!)) could be viewed at http://www.youtube.com/watch?v=aZDgfm88unE. The "Kasuga" refers to the particular school of *kouta* in which the version of "Sanbasō" discussed here was created, while the connections with the much earlier *noh* version are vague at best.

Figure 3.4 Stanley Jiang (Union College '16) and the author on *nagauta shamisen*

The *shamisen* is one of the most versatile of the traditional Japanese instruments found in the theatrical forms of *bunraku* and *kabuki*, chamber music performances of the same music that originates in these theatrical genres, including *nagauta* (literally "long song") (see Figure 3.4), the *kouta* of teahouses of the *geisha* and numerous styles of *min'yō*. The *shamisen* typically accompanies singing in all these contexts.

Shamisen come in many varieties depending on the specific genre in which they are found; some have thicker necks and larger bodies, such as the instrument used in the flashy folk genre *tsugaru-jamisen* (see Figure 3.5). In general, the body of the instrument is positioned on the right thigh. The right forearm rests on top and the wrist bends at nearly a 90 degree angle downwards allowing the performer to strike the body, referred to as a "drum" (*taiko*), with a large plectrum (*bachi*) made of different materials also depending on the genre; in *nagauta*, for example, performers use a wooden or plastic plectrum for practice and ivory in performance, or more recently plastic that resembles ivory (see Figure 3.4) while *tsugaru-jamisen* uses an even larger tortoise-shell plectrum (see Figure 3.5).

Figure 3.5 Yamauchi Reach on *tsugaru-jamisen*

Fujie notes, however, that in "*kouta*... the bare fingers or fingernails pluck the strings, producing a lighter, less percussive sound" than in some of the other *shamisen* genres (2002:346). Historically, silk strings were used, although today nylon is common; the strings pass over a small bridge near the bottom of the instrument.

The left hand, fitted with a small strip of knitted fabric between the thumb and forefinger (*yubikake*), can slide easily up and down the neck of the *shamisen*, pluck or strike hard on the neck producing a tone, while the right hand uses the plectrum to strum, flutter in a tremolo, slap down on the strings and strike the body, or snap upwards, thus creating numerous timbral variances. The *shamisen* overall has a unique quality created by an small indentation underneath the lowest string at the top of the neck, just below the tuning pegs, while the two upper strings rest on a nut or bridge, creating what Kishibe describes as a "trailing sound together with a slight noise" called *sawari* (1984:74). This modification allows the lowest string to rattle, creating the buzzy sound heard in this example. As noted above, such a sound would be avoided in Western instrument construction, but it is an essential component of Japanese aesthetics. Alves argues that "imperfections" such as these in instrument construction that create obstacles for players are deliberate (as "perfection" would in fact be "an affront to the divine"), while also inspiring great creativity (2013:321).

Although the *shamisen* has been highlighted thus far, this version of "Kasuga Sanbasō" features a tremendous vocal performance by Kasuga Toyoeishiba, the current head of the Kasuga school, full of restrained emotion.

Ryū, Ie and Iemoto

Japanese traditional music is organized within a *ryū*, literally translated as "way of doing," but commonly referring to schools; or *ie*, which translates as "house" or "guilds." Within art worlds, historically such guilds emerged in the Edo period both as part of the rigidification of the social system and to secure the transmission and protection of particular musical practices (Surak 2013:91–118). These guilds (*ie*) or schools (*ryū*) of a certain art are headed by an "*iemoto*," a role often acquired by a combination of skill and birth into the family. After typically years of study, a student (*deshi*) may be granted the title of "*natori*," somewhat equivalent to "master," and receive a performing name from their teacher, thus creating important connections and building lineages within a specific practice. As we have seen already in the case of the *shakuhachi*, there are many styles of performance related to any one instrument or genre, each belonging to one of many *ie* or *ryū*.

Notation is a fairly modern convention, with the specific types that developed in part delineating different schools. See, for example, the difference between the notation for the *nagauta* piece "Echigojishi" ("The Echigo Lion") in Appendix A and B. The score for voice and *shamisen* from the Yoshizumi school of *nagauta* is included in Appendix A. Referred to as *Yoshizumi Kojūrō-fu*, this type of score reads from top to bottom and right to left in typical Japanese fashion. The numbers refer to pitch names with other characters indicating specific durations and techniques. The same piece is rendered for the Kineya school of *nagauta* in Appendix B. Referred to as *Kineya bunkafu*, this score is a bit more Westernized, reading from left to right and top to bottom. The melody is basically the same, but rather than indicate pitch names, the numbers here refer to position on the instrument—taking a slightly different approach than in the Yoshizumi school (see further discussion in Chapter 6; see also Track 16). Other differences between the two schools are conveyed through one-on-one instruction in the lesson.

In fact, notation limits the flexibility of Japanese traditional music and does not accurately portray the nuances of performance transmitted from teacher to student. Rather, notation is often used simply as a tool to aid in memorization or to show in general how a piece should sound. This is due in part to the difficulty in capturing the free rhythm of much traditional music (see further discussion below). Composition is not as fixed a concept as in the West, and often composer's names are not known. Pieces instead are passed from teacher to student. Once a piece is fixed though, it remains relatively unchanged within a school.

Japanese students are free to take anything from a teacher, to imitate and transmit to future students. Indeed, traditional music is marked by imitation rather than innovation, but this should not be dismissed as therefore inferior—it can be extremely difficult to master the work of another, so well that the work becomes one's own. And originality can only spring forth from internalizing the common practice. Zen Buddhist monk and educator Muchaku Seikyō (1927–) once said "You need to know the box (*kata*) to think outside the box (*kata yaburi*), and if you don't have the box to begin with, what you are doing is no-box (*kata nashi*)."

Since the Edo period, *kouta* have been strongly associated with the world of *geisha* and the teahouses in which they perform. Dalby argues these short songs express the idea of *iroke*, a difficult concept to precisely translate, but somewhat equivalent to the idea of "eroticism," though not as sexually charged as in the Western use of this term (2000:10). She explains:

> *Iroke* is sensuality; it is evoked by images, which appeal to senses. It denotes attraction felt between the sexes in the passing glance or the swish of a trailing *kimono*. The essence of *iroke* is understatement. The minute it becomes obvious it ceases to be *iroke*. It is a subtle atmosphere created by the contact of two people. It cannot exist in the abstract, and it is not as blatant as "sex appeal." It implies intimacy in that it becomes lost in an impersonal situation . . . The *geisha* probably best understand and embody *iroke*. It is a middle state between the elegant, refined, but somewhat unapproachable "proper lady," and the obvious come-on of the rather loud, conventionally "sexy" bar hostess.
>
> (Ibid.:11).

Many of the texts of *kouta* reflect the atmosphere of the world of the *geisha* and this *iroke* spirit, ranging from comments on the seasons to more overtly erotic tales of love. They are informed by Japanese poetic styles and the texts of *noh* plays, and therefore are written with lines typically of five and seven syllables in length.

The lyrics of the *kouta* "Kasuga Sanbasō" are highly poetic, even vague, and therefore difficult to translate. According to Kurokawauchi Shigeru (member of the Kasuga *kouta* school), in 1950, Kasuga Toyo, the founder of the Kasuga *kouta* school, commissioned Hirayama Rokō to write a "*sanbasō mono*," essentially a "celebratory" song to commemorate her seventieth birthday, but which continues to be performed today (e-mail correspondence, October 7, 2014). Listen to "Kasuga Sanbasō," as the *shamisen* weaves in and out of the vocal part in a most intimate dialogue here (this relationship between different parts will be further discussed below), while both voice and instrument express *iroke*.

春日三番叟
"Kasuga Sanbasō"
("Kasuga Sanbasō")

(:24)
おうさえおうさえ
ōsae ōsae
Big happiness, big happiness
(Also means stamping the ground hard to ensure a good harvest.)

(:30)
よろこびありや
yorokobi ari ya
Here comes the happiness

(:35)
わがよろこびは
wa ga yorokobi wa
My happiness is

(:42)
春の日を
haru no hi o
(Reading) A spring day

(1:12)
春日と読んだ
kasuga to yonda
As a spring day
(There is play on words here—"*haru no hi*" literally translates as a spring day, but uses the same characters as in "Kasuga.")

(1:18)
とよの秋
Toyo no aki
Toyo's fall
(This is a reference to Kasuga Toyo's birthday, which is September 15th.)

(1:35)
十たびを七つ
tō tabi o nanatsu
(Living) 10 by 7

(1:48)
くりかえす
kuri kaesu
times
(The proceeding two stanzas combine as "10 by 7 times" referring to Kasuga Toyo's age, 70.)

(2:08)
袖にかざせば
sode ni kazase ba
Seeing through the kimono sleeves

(2:18)
鶴の舞
tsuru no mai
A crane's dance

(Instrumental interlude featuring *honde* and *kaede shamisen*)

(3:58)
小唄ぢらしの盃に
kouta jirashi no sakazuki ni
In the *sake* cup sprinkled with *kouta*

(4:32)
とうとうたらりと
tōtō tarari to
(A famous line found in different versions of "Sanbasō" but the meaning is debated)

(4:42)
酌む酒を
kumu sake o
pouring *sake*

(4:52)
うけておさえて
ukete osaete
receiving and touching

(5:05)
口紅はのこしたままの
kuchibeni wa nokoshita mama no
leaving a trace of lipstick

(5:21)
思いさし
omoi zashi
my feelings
(This line is written "*sashi*" but is pronounced "*zashi*" in this recording; the meaning does not significantly change either way.)

(5:26)
はずかしながら
hazukashi nagara
even though shy

(5:50)
ほかえはやらぬエー
hokae wa yaranuē
I will not let you go (to someone else)

Japanese Traditional Dance

From the court to folk festivals, and theaters to teahouses, dance is an integral part of many of the performing arts of Japan. Just as with the instrumental and vocal genres, Japanese classical dance (*nihon buyō*) also has its own schools of performers—both amateur and professional—who bring great enthusiasm and commitment to their study. Tomie Hahn in *Sensational Knowledge* (2007) explores the ways in which *nihon buyō* allows one to better understand both culture and self through bodily sensation in the dance lesson (see also Gunji 1970). "Musume Shirasagi" ("The Young Girl—White Heron") (Website Example 7) features Hanayagi Michikaoru performing a newly composed piece for classical dance, based on the *nagauta* work "Sagi Musume" ("Heron—Young Girl"). The main character is a heron that transforms into a young girl only to tragically perish from unrequited love. This example highlights the ways in which dancing, singing and *shamisen* combine to create a powerful performance.

Just as with music, in the modern era, dance forms developed that combined elements of *nihon buyō* with European styles. *Butoh*, a type of Japanese dance theater that developed after World War II, for example,

(continued)

> *(continued)*
>
> ... draws upon the traditional Japanese dance forms of *kabuki* and *noh*, even as it seems to repudiate them, and it also travels back to the foundations of Expressionism in the Western modern dance of the early twentieth century. In so doing, *butoh* retrieves something essentially Japanese. (Fraleigh 2010:3)
>
> *Butoh* then, like other theatrical and musical forms, is Japanese in its conflagration of styles and ideologies to produce something unique. But at the same time "*Butoh* ... is fast becoming a borderless art for a borderless century" (ibid.:1).

Pitch and Scales

The importance of the *Ryūkyū* scale for marking Okinawan identity was introduced in Chapter 1, but let us step back and look at conceptions of pitch and scales more broadly in mainland Japan. Japanese music is based on twelve possible tones, equivalent to an untempered Western chromatic scale, with the smallest interval of a semitone. Not surprisingly however, Japanese pitch and scales are derived from Chinese models, first introduced through *shōmyō*, as heard in Chapter 1, and further formalized in *gagaku* (see further discussion below). Just as with the tuning of the *koto*, the inclusion of semitones actually differentiates Japanese music from its Chinese progenitor. When compared to Western concepts, there is a certain flexibility to pitch and much potential confusion about scales in Japan. For example, as raised in the proceeding discussion of timbre, not all pitch has to be absolute, evidenced through instruments and techniques that produce indeterminate pitch, as well as an appreciation for the bending of pitch and wide vibrato.

Even when there is an understanding of formalized scales in place, "intervals between notes still differ in traditional music according to genre, school, the piece performed, and the individual performer" (Koizumi 1974:73, quoted in Fujie 2002:334). For example, the *koto* can be tuned to any pitch to suit a particular vocalist's range that one may accompany. And in my experience playing *nagauta shamisen*, although staying in tune with a group of musicians is important, what pitch everyone tunes to is much less so. *Shamisen* are temperamental creatures and go flat quickly, which is acceptable as along as everyone goes down together. And teachers can be seen scurrying behind pupils, frantically tuning *shamisen* in mid-song during recitals to ensure this happens.

As there is no single, common set of pitches or scales used in all genres by all musicians, making broad generalizations is quite complicated and indeed, a review of literature in English reveals remarkably different ways of interpreting and explaining Japanese conceptions of scales to a Western audience. In general though, Japanese scales are understood as pentatonic, thus containing five primary pitches. Many musics have been influenced by the theatrical genre *noh*, which is typically understood as focused on three pitch centers organized in relation to each other as high, medium and low, plus a pitch a perfect fourth higher than the highest tone, and another pitch a perfect fourth lower than the lowest tone. Additional tones of course can be used well, but this way of organizing pitch also resembles a pentatonic scale (Kishibe 1984:52).

Pentatonic scales in Japanese music, however, also contain two additional tones. This can cause some confusion as Japanese scales therefore are often rendered as seven tones, with these two additional tones depicted within parenthesis, as solid noteheads (as opposed to open to represent primary pitches), or simply assumed in Western interpretations. These two "auxiliary tones," known as *hen'on* (literally, "changing tones"), are primarily used for modulation or in other transitory and supporting roles; thus there still are five primary tones comprising the majority of Japanese scales. Hughes argues that the great flexibility of pitch in Japanese traditional music is in part possible because of the greater distance between intervals in pentatonic scales than in a Western chromatic scale. As a result, "even considerable latitude in intonation does not imperil the recognition or identity of a melody" (Hughes 2008:37).

It is important to remember that these are scale *types*, just as major and minor are types in Western music that determine intervallic relationships (the names of these scale types can be followed by the suffix "*sen*" in Japanese). These scale types then generate modes that start on different pitches (these are typically followed by the suffix "*chōshi*" in Japanese), even though there are rules for which pitches may be used to begin the scale depending on the genre. For example, *gagaku* uses two basic scale types—the *ryo* and *ritsu* depicted below—which generate three modes each, for a total of six possible modes, each of which of course has its own specific name (Kishibe 1984; Malm 2000).

The scale types in this text predominantly are rendered with a starting pitch of C for ease of comparison and understanding intervallic relationships for readers used to the Western system. But in no way should this suggest that scales in Japan regularly start on or emphasize C—to be sure, they do not—and often scale types will be depicted starting on other pitches more suitable to the genre under consideration.

The *ryo* and *ritsu* scales dominated from the Nara through the Heian periods. Their general qualities are illustrated in the example of *shōmyō* "Rishukyō" (Track 1) and *gagaku* "Etenraku" (Track 9).

Much traditional Japanese music, however, is based on either the *in* or the *yō* scale types, which emerged in the Edo period. As with *ryo* and *ritsu*, these scales are comprised of five primary pitches, and hence are considered pentatonic; the *in* contains semitones while the *yō* does not, as seen below. Here the tones differ ascending and descending, something akin to the melodic minor in Western contexts (see Figure 3.7).

Ryo Scale

Ritsu Scale

Figure 3.6 *Ryo* and *ritsu* scales

In Scale

Yō Scale

Figure 3.7 *In* and *yō* scales

Just as with the *ryo* and *ritsu*, these scale types can start on different pitches that differ by genre resulting in numerous modes each with their own name.

Twentieth-century Japanese ethnomusicologist Koizumi Fumio, influenced by Western comparative musicology, focused on tetrachords in developing a theory for understanding how Japanese scales work in the context of distinct musical forms (see Figures 3.8 and 3.9). Technically a tetrachord is "a perfect fourth and the set of four diatonic, chromatic, or enharmonic notes encased within" (One Music Dictionary n.d.). Koizumi took

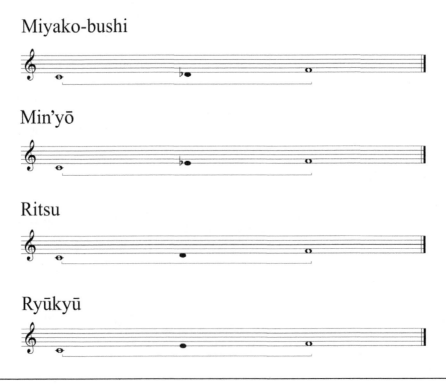

Figure 3.8 Koizumi's tetrachords

this concept and identified a tetrachord with two stable nuclear tones spaced a perfect fourth (*kakuon*) and one "indeterminate" tone within (*chūkan'on*), similar to the way pitch relationships are conceived in *noh*, that varies depending on the genre and geographical location in Japan (Kawase 2013; Gillan 2012:40; Hughes 2008:36). These tetrachord relationships are indicated in Figures 3.8 and 3.9 with the bar below the note heads, but do remember the *hen'on* tone is not included, but can be understood to be part of the four-pitch tone row, thus fitting with the technical definition of a tetrachord.

Combinations of two identical types of tetrachords with a whole tone between generate scales named after the tetrachord type (see Figure 3.9).

The nuclear tones are typically emphasized in melodic passages, including serving as the final, concluding tone, with the infixes as leading tones or in other supporting roles. Within this model, the most popular scale, and therefore most characteristically Japanese, *in*, becomes known as *miyako-bushi* (where "*miyako*" means capital and "*bushi*" song), the *yō*, with its strong association with folk music as the *min'yō*, while the *ritsu* keeps the name and its association with Chinese court music. The *Ryūkyū* scale from Okinawa is of course also included as one of Koizumi's primary scale types.

There clearly is an emphasis on the fourth in these conceptions of scale, and "much melodic movement tends to emphasize this interval" as well (Fujie 2002: 335). Of course variants do exist, especially within different instrument traditions, and Hughes reminds us that Koizumi's way of approaching Japanese scales works well for the majority of

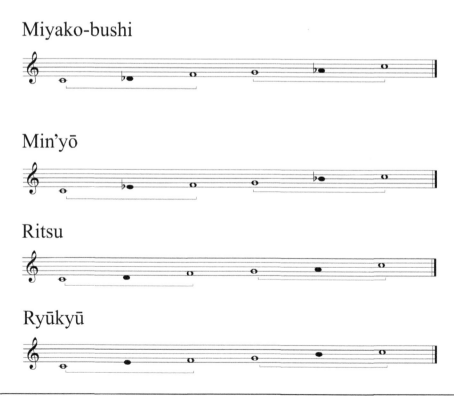

Figure 3.9 Koizumi's scales

traditional music, but is by no means flawless (2008:35). His tetrachord theory, while dominant, offers only an "approximation" of which pitches may assume dominance in melodic constructions. And other theorists have continued to explore ways of understanding scale types in Japan (see twentieth-century theorist Seiichi Tokawa). Nonetheless, these scales provide a sense of the building blocks used to create much Japanese music, and thus are an extremely important way that Japanese cultural identity is created through sound.

Stevens suggests that what is more important than details of the scales is "their aesthetic and psychological interpretations" (2008:18) as all these general scale types and individual modes have emotional qualities associated with them that listeners recognize. Hughes explains, for example, that

> *In and yō* are the Japanese pronunciations of the Chinese philosophical concepts *yin* and *yang*; the names reflect the perception by some scholars that these two scales are respectively "*dark*" and "*light*" in mood, although this contention is hard to demonstrate.
>
> (2008:35)

The *in* scale is commonly found in music for *shamisen*, *koto* and *shakuhachi*. James Nyoraku Schlefer demonstrates this scale type on the *shakuhachi* in Website Example 8. Numerous musical examples discussed are in this scale type including "Rokudan" (Track 8) and "(Futaiken) Tsuru no Sugomori" (Track 6), while the *yō*, which is perceived as brighter and soft in comparison, is found in folk songs, such as in "Kagoshima Ohara Bushi" (Track 3) and "The Hack-Driver's Song of Hakone" (Track 2), introduced in Chapter 1, and not surprisingly in early forms of popular song. Hughes thus believes

> The alternative names preferred by Koizumi are more enlightening: *miyako-bushi*, "urban/Capital melody" is indeed most common in the urban musics of the seventeenth century and after, whereas folk song more often uses the scale appropriately named *inaka-bushi*, "rural melody", or *min'yō*
>
> (Hughes 2008:35–36)

capturing not only mood but place through sound.

Melody and Harmony

Of course scales are not the only musical elements that create connections to national and ethnic identity, as the ways in which these pitches are put together in melody is also culturally based. Melodies are brought to life through dynamics, timbral variety and ornamentation, as opposed to rapid movement through pitches, and therefore may seem quite slow in much traditional music. Once again, we want to be careful about such generalizations as of course much *min'yō*, *shamisen*, *koto*, *taiko* and other musics are amazingly fast-paced. The emphasis on the interval of a fourth has already been noted, but larger leaps are of course also possible in instrumental music, and "In vocal music, both syllabic and melismatic treatment of text can be found" (Fujie 2002:336), depending on what the genre or individual performer wants to stress. Listen again to the melodic qualities of the voice and *shamisen* in "Kasuga Sanbasō," as Kasuga Toyoeishiba stretches the text across the beat. The vocal music introduced thus far leans towards such melismatic treatment; however, genres that must convey a story quickly may rely on syllabic delivery.

The Western construction of harmony—that is, chords organized in hierarchical relationships with each other (for example, I IV V I) that in turn motivate musical movement from melody to modulation—does not exist in Japanese traditional music; in fact, the introduction of harmony became a clear marker of Western identity in the Meiji period. Although the simultaneous sounding of pitches on the *shamisen* in "Kasuga Sanbasō" may sound "harmonious," these combinations of pitches should not be understood as harmony. Within Japanese traditional music, melodic contour therefore is not motivated by harmony, but rather pitches have controlled or patterned movement that is unique to specific genres. And just as with pitch sets and scales, melodic styles vary greatly, making generalizations difficult.

However, repetition of short motifs is quite common, or repetition of longer phrases at the beginning and end of a section or entire piece to create a sense of conclusion, as is quoting melodies from other well-known pieces to evoke a mood or character (Fujie 2002:336). Cadences, for example, are created through melodic patterns rather than harmonic in traditional Japanese music. Cadential moments can be heard throughout "Kasuga Sanbasō" (Track 4); the vocal line cadences on the first statement of text with an extended, bending pitch around 0:51 and the *shamisen* cadences approaching 1:10, before the vocal line enters again. Similar cadential moments can be felt as the voice and *shamisen* approach 1:58, and then the *shamisen* moves on to a new phrase. Continue listening for these moments of completion until the final vocal cadence from 5:50, as the tempo slows and the pitch bends again from 6:00. The *shamisen* performs a final solo conclusion from 7:13 through the end.

Texture

Traditional Japanese music is often monophonic, a single voice or instrument, or a group of voices or instruments playing together in unison, or heterophonic, a group of voices playing simultaneous variations on a single melody. Polyphony also involves multiple voices sounding together, each with their own melody that harmonizes with the others, but this is distinct, as heterophony is not organized by the rules of Western harmony that inform polyphony. It is also important to keep in mind that there is intentionality behind heterophony, meaning the composer or performer *chooses* to create these variations; they are not accidental discrepancies that may occur when a multi-voiced piece is intended to sound in unison, but some parts stray. Heterophony can be a difficult concept to understand, as it is not the most common voicing in many Western contexts, although it is found in Irish music and other parts of Asia. Williams offers useful imagery to understand heterophony in the following:

> An image that might help clarify the practice of heterophony is that of a small marching band. Picture the scene: eight players all headed in the same direction, but on eight separate trails running roughly parallel. Some players have to negotiate the equivalent of tree stumps, children on tricycles, or possibly a slip-n-slide! Others march on paving stones with guardrails; their steps are easy to follow. Everyone arrives at the street corner at the right time (ideally), free of injuries (ideally), and they all start marching on the next block. An Irish music session could include a handful of musicians, all 'marching' (or reeling, or jigging) on the same well-known trails, but the player of each instrument has an individual trail to negotiate.
>
> (2010:10)

In Japanese music, heterophony is created when each part intentionally varies pitches, inserts ornaments, or highlights rhythmic differences, even delaying the melody. Malm identified what he called the "sliding door" (*fusuma*) effect to help visualize one way this heterophony is created—just as traditional Japanese sliding doors of the same size slide back and forth within a single frame, musical phrases of the same duration on various parts can start in different places (Malm 2000:60). This can be heard most easily in musics featuring voice and an accompanying instrument, such as *koto* or *shamisen*, but also in larger ensemble works, including *gagaku*, and theatrical genres, such as *noh* (see further discussion below).

Kouta performer and ethnomusicologist Yuko Eguchi explains:

> In *kouta* song, the voice melody and the *shamisen* melody sound pretty different at first hearing, but when I learned both parts and transcribed it carefully, I found that the *shamisen* actually plays the same notes as the singer's melody, so there is a core melody that both performers share. The *shamisen* part actually comes in slightly before the voice so that it plays as a "cue" for the singer to simply notify which note to land in and when she/he should come in.
>
> (E-mail correspondence February 17, 2014)

Fujie, in her analysis of another *kouta* piece, "Hakusen no," found that

> Rather than sounding simultaneously on the same beat, the two parts tend to weave in and out; sometimes the voice precedes the *shamisen* in presenting the melody and sometimes the *shamisen* plays the notes first. The result of this constant staggering and shifting is a duet in which both voice and instrument share and enhance the melody.
>
> (2002:351)

The interpretations vary slightly here, but both nevertheless result in heterophonic voicing.

This type of texture, as well as the other elements introduced thus far, are well demonstrated in "Ōgi no Mato" ("The Folding Fan as a Target") for voice and *biwa* (Track 5). This piece, performed in 1976 by Handa Ayako (now Handa Junko), is a well-known example of narrative singing with *biwa*, made all the more familiar to audiences around the world by its inclusion in the classic film *Blade Runner* (1982).

The *biwa* is another instrument which entered Japan from China, where it is known as the *pipa*, likely during the Nara period. This pear-shaped lute features "a fixed pegbox, which is joined to the end of the neck at nearly a right angle" (Gunji and Johnson 2012:17) and usually four strings, which may rest close to the neck or sit on high frets depending on the style. The construction of the *biwa* depends on the genre in which it appears, however in general:

> The instrument's neck is held in the player's left hand, which manipulates the strings to adjust their length. In performance, the instrument rests just above the player's right knee, and the right hand holds a [large] plectrum, which plucks the strings. Depending on the genre, players traditionally kneel or sit cross-legged.
>
> (ibid.:17)

The earliest *biwa* is found in *gagaku*, then *Heike-biwa*, a style that emerged in the Kamakura period to accompany the singing of the great *Heike Monogatari* (*The Tale of the Heike*), an epic relaying the war between the Heike and Genji clans at the end of the twelfth century. Later regional styles performed by blind priests (*mōsō*) in Satsuma and Chikuzen developed as well. The example here actually features the *Satsuma-biwa* used to accompany a scene from *Heike Monogatari*. The singer tells a tale "similar to that of William Tell, in which a folding fan, instead of the famous Swiss apple, serves as the target" (Anon. 1976).

The narrator passionately relates when the two families, who have been at war for a long time, find themselves resting at sunset. A beautiful woman appears on the ocean in a boat, holding a fan on a pole. Munetaka, a member of the Genji clan, assumes this is a challenge from the Heike clan to shoot an arrow at the fan (see Figure 3.10), at which point this piece begins. The arrow Munetaka uses—a *kaburaya*—is a special type that resonates as it pierces the air from a specific bow called a *shigetō* (see the film *Sukiyaki and Chips* introduced in Chapter 1, which goes into some detail about the sound of the arrow). A discussion of the interplay between the vocal and *biwa* parts follows:

扇の的
"Ōgi no Mato"
("The Folding Fan as a Target")

(:52)
入り日傾く屋島潟　さっと乗り入る海の面
irihi katamuku Yashimagata   satto nori iru umi no omo
The sun is setting at Yashima beach. [Munetaka] rides into the ocean on a horse.

Figure 3.10 *Yabusame* (archery on horseback) at Shimogamo-jinja in Kyoto

(2:15)
渡る潮風いと強く　打ち込む波の高ければ
駒の足掻きの定まらず
wataru shiokaze ito tsuyoku　uchikomu nami no takakereba
koma no agaki no sadamarazu
The waves and the wind are very strong. The waves are high; even the horse struggles to stand still.

(2:54)
扇も風にたまらねば　くるりくるりと打ち回り
狙い定むる術もなし
ōgi mo kaze ni tamaraneba　kururi kururi to uchimawari
nerai sadamuru sube mo nashi
A fan is turning round and round in the wind. There is no way to focus on the fan.

(4:50)
崇高じっと目を閉じて　この波風を打ち沈め
扇を射落とさせ給えやと　一心込めてぞ祈りける
Munetaka jitto me o tojite　kono namikaze o uchishizume
ōgi o iotosase tamaeya to　isshin kometezo inorikeru
Munetaka closes his eyes. He prays hard for the waves and wind to calm down so that he may hit the fan successfully. [If he misses, he will be a disgrace to his lord and must kill himself.]

(6:41)
念じ終わって眼をば　開けばさても不思議やな
波風はたと静まりぬ　崇高心勇み立ち
nenji owatte manako o ba　hirakeba sate mo fushigi yana
namikaze hata to shizumarinu　Munetaka kokoro isamitachi
Surprisingly, when he opens his eyes after his prayer, the waves and wind have quieted down. Munetaka's heart fills with bravery.

(7:40)
十二束三伏の鏑矢を　爪繰りしてぞ抜き出し
握り太なる重藤の　弓に食わせて弾き固め
狙いをきいっと定めしが　日の丸射ては畏れあり
要の点をと志し　ひょぉと放ちし命矢は
はしっと射切って　矢は海に扇を空へ舞い上がり
jūni soku mitsu buse no kaburaya o　tsumaguri shitezo nukidashi
nigiri buto naru shigetō no　yumi ni kuwasete hiki katame
nerai o kītto sadameshi ga　hinomaru ite wa osore ari
kaname no ten o to kokorozashi　hiyō to hanachishi inochiya wa
hashi to ikitte　ya wa umi ni ōgi o sora e mai agari
He takes out a special arrow that makes sound when released in the air, places it on the bow and pulls. He looks to the target, knowing not to aim at the center of the image of the rising sun on the fan, instead shooting for the bottom. The arrow makes a "*hiyō...*" sound as it flies through the air. He hits the target as the arrow falls into the water and the fan flies in the sky.

(9:14)
暫しは宙にひらめいて　海へさっとぉぞ落ちにけり
shibashi wa chū ni hirameite　umi e sattōzo ochi ni keri
The fan flutters in the air for a while, slowly falling into the ocean.

The piece opens with the *biwa* strumming briefly before sliding across the strings. The audience is invited into the extensive use of space before the voice enters at 0:52, sustains and immediately bends the pitch. The female voice is low and thick, leading the rest of the piece, which of course is not surprising given that this is a narrative genre and therefore the words are of paramount importance. At times, the *biwa* can be heard mimicking the voice, for example, through the vocal pitch bend and slide at 1:15, while at other times the two parts seem quite separate. At 1:24, the *biwa* begins to strum, increasing rhythmic intensity and establishing a pulse (and displaying the different tonal qualities possible through varying gestures). The voice and *biwa* reach a high point—both in terms of register and emotional intensity—together at 2:15, as the *biwa* continues to support the melismatic and melodramatic quality of the voice through rapid strumming.

At 2:54, the *biwa* moves to a lower register, changing the emotional quality of the song, at times following the melodic contour of the voice through 3:00–3:23. The *biwa* next provides an extended instrumental interlude, quieting before the voice enters again at 4:50. From here, the *biwa* only comments on the vocal part with brief articulations, even tags after each vocal phrase, creating quite a contrasting effect to the preceding freneticism. These instrumental comments occasionally extend through 6:23–6:44. The *biwa* enters full force momentarily at different points beginning at 7:33, though brief, each time enhancing the emotional intensity of the vocal line once again. The characteristic strumming reappears from 8:55. A final melodic line in the voice starts at approximately 9:45 moving through 10:05, the cadential gesture extended until 10:20, when a momentary dip creates the sense of conclusion. The voice finishes with a melodic movement common in much Japanese music that signals a cadence, and the *biwa* adds a final comment, punctuating the narrative.

The heterophonic play between the voice and *biwa* is all the more remarkable when one remembers that a single person performs this piece. "Ōgi no Mato" thus demonstrates the ability in Japanese music to create tremendously powerful and engaging music with relatively few tools—only the *biwa* and voice—through timbral variation (created through different means of stroking and strumming the strings, plucking and sliding and with the *Satsuma-biwa*, even striking the body) and the powerful, thick and emotive vocals. If the preceding "Kasuga Sanbasō" is reserved and elegant, "Ōgi no Mato" is dramatic and overt. Much of the emotion is lost in translation, yet one can still feel the build-up of tension—this is "Japanese Rock" full of drama and passion.

Free Rhythm

Those accustomed to Western music may have some difficulty listening to traditional Japanese music at first, because of its elastic sense of rhythm or even the lack of a distinct pulse or beat. But this quality of Japanese music also "conveys a powerful expression of feeling because of its freedom and flexibility" (Fujie 2002:336). "(Futaiken) Tsuru no Sugomori" ("Nesting Cranes") (Track 6), with the *shakuhachi*'s required meditative breathing, exemplifies the potential emotional impact of such "beatless music."

Performed here once again by James Nyoraku Schlefer, this is a well-known *honkyoku* piece with many variations by school and temple association. This version, as with "Choshi" (Website Example 6), is from the Futaiken temple in northern Honshū (see further discussion above).

Here the *shakuhachi* paints a vivid picture of the cycle of life, as male and female cranes call to each other, meet and mate for life. They proceed to build a nest, brood their chicks and watch as these youngsters take their first flight. The chicks grow to adulthood, and their parents age and pass away, knowing that during their time on earth they fulfilled their role as good parents. "This unconditional love between parent and child is a Buddhist idea" (interview with James Nyoraku Schlefer, May 5, 2014). The story of the cranes embodies well the Buddhist ideals of familial duty and love, as well as acknowledging the cycle of life, as the young adults presumably go on to have children of their own. Life is ephemeral in the story of the cranes, but all the more poignant as a result.

Schlefer's school plays three pieces from the Futaiken temple including "Reibo," "San'ya," and of course "Tsuru no Sugomori." He finds the Futaiken version of "Tsuru no Sugomori" particularly interesting because of the extensive use of a technique called *tamane*, or "flutter tongue," despite the fact that the tongue is not actually used to create this sound on the *shakuhachi*. He explains "almost the whole piece uses this technique, which is unusual in all these versions" creating clear, but dramatic imagery. The powerful trills extend to sustained pitches evoking the image of birds fluttering their wings and calling to each other (interview May 4, 2014). The *tamane* can be heard throughout the piece, as compared to "Choshi," which does not highlight this gesture, therefore making its presence and effect all the more apparent and dramatic in "(Futaiken) Tsuru no Sugomori."

The piece of course invokes many of the elements of Japanese music introduced thus far with its extensive use of *ma*—moments of repose as Schlefer's breath fades before the next phrase begins—varied timbral qualities created through different fingering and head positions; manipulations of pitch through wide vibrato, or bending and swooping; repetitive melodic motifs as lines flow one from the other seemingly without form, and of course the free rhythm under discussion in this section specifically. Drama is not created through rhythmic intensity and fast tempos, but rather the absence of both. So while free rhythm can be alienating for some, it is this meditative, atmospheric quality that draws in listeners and attracts others to Japanese traditional music.

Although the free and flexible rhythm of the *shakuhachi* often enthralls listeners, one should not assume that traditional Japanese music is characterized exclusively by this quality. We have already seen examples when one part, the voice for example, performs a relaxed, free rhythm, while an accompanying instrument maintains a strong beat ("Ōgi no Mato," Track 5). There is much music organized into groups of two, four, or eight beats, but even this can be flexible, akin to an extreme *parlando rubato* style, and in general Japanese music is not understood as metered.

Organized Time

Nonetheless, there are moments when underlying rhythmic patterns organize music in time—as found in *noh*, the oldest of the so-called "great theatrical traditions" of Japan. Grounded in earlier forms of dance, music and theater, *noh* was formalized as a style through the work of father and son playwrights—Kan'ami Kiyotsugu (1333–84) and his son Zeami Motokiyo (1363–1443), the latter of whom developed highly sophisticated theoretical ideas that continue to resonate in Japanese music today. With support of then *shōgun* Ashikaga Yoshimitsu (1358–1408), *noh* came to express many Zen Buddhist ideals, while also becoming associated with the elite, and continues to be viewed as a highly sophisticated art form. Alves eloquently captures the essence of *noh* in the following:

> Like much Japanese fine art, it is highly refined, stylized, and reserved; to those unfamiliar with its conventions, it may seem inaccessible. Props and settings, reflecting that sparsity of the *ma* principle, are represented only symbolically, if at all. Similarly, the slow, weightless movements of the actors create spaces during which only the hollow sound of the *nohkan* flute pierces the silence. Like the weightless mountains of Japanese landscape paintings, the experience of *noh* can surround the audience with a floating timelessness.
>
> (2013:324)

Noh creates "maximum effect from a minimum of means" (Wade 2005:80; Kishibe 1984:49), relying on abstract and symbolic staging, with little to no props, often slow and deliberate movement by the actors, and stories with at times obscure and conceptual themes. The music of *noh* may on the surface initially appear particularly random and abstract, but is actually highly theorized and organized.

Noh features the *noh-hayashi*, an ensemble comprised of the *nohkan*, a transverse bamboo flute, a *taiko*, a double-headed drum placed on a stand and struck with sticks (*bachi*), and a pair of drums struck by hand: the *ō-tsuzumi*, a large double-headed hourglass-shaped drum with two heads, and the *ko-tsuzumi*, a small double-headed hourglass-shaped drum, both with skins affixed with rope. The method of playing these two drums is quite distinct, as the *ō-tsuzumi* is positioned to the left of the performer and is struck with the middle finger of the right hand covered with a thimble made of leather or papier-mâché (*yubikawa*) (Kishibe 1984:54), while the *ko-tsuzumi* is held on the right shoulder and is struck with bare fingers (see further discussion below and in Chapter 6). These two drums work in partnership with each other, the *ō-tsuzumi* providing the downbeat to the *ko-tsuzumi*'s upbeat—the two becoming one balanced whole embodying the concept of *yin* and *yang* (Shimosako 2002:546). Although not usually listed as one of the instruments of the *noh-hayashi*, the vocal calls of the drummers (*kakegoe*) truly distinguish *noh*.

Noh performances include *maigoto*, or long instrumental dances featuring the *noh-hayashi*. There are eight types of these *maigoto*, each of which can be performed as the main dance in a number of the some 200–250 *noh* plays that still exist today: "One of these, the 'Chū-no-Mai,' literally the 'middle' or 'medium' tempo 'dance,' can be considered the most basic dance, and is usually the first dance that is taught to either instrumental or dance students" (Emmert 1983:6). I had the opportunity to study *noh-hayashi* with master performer Tosha Rōetsu in 2010 (see further discussion in Part III) and in my last few lessons, he began to introduce a rhythmic pattern from a "Chū no Mai" dance piece (see Figure 3.11). He explained that once I mastered this eight-beat underlying rhythmic organization, or perhaps better put, *feeling* this rhythm, I could play many variations. I am not sure about the latter claim in my case, but I did work diligently in my last few lessons to come to terms with this pattern (Website Example 9 and Website Example 10).

Chū no Mai

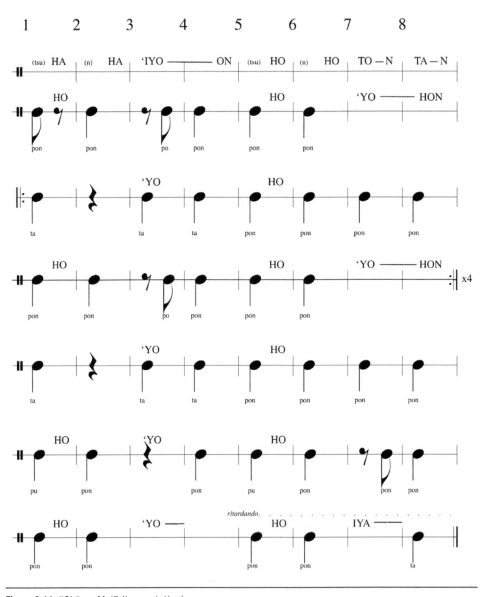

Figure 3.11 "Chū no Mai" (transcription)

The first line contains the mnemonic (*kuchishōka*) for the underlying eight-beat rhythmic pattern, as heard in Website Example 9. The text in parentheses assists a performer to keep time internally, but should not be spoken aloud in performance. The "IYO" comes in slightly after the beat, indicated with an apostrophe. In the recorded excerpt from one of my lessons, Tosha can be heard teaching me the underlying pattern orally, as I call out the mnemonics "HA HA'IYON HO HO TON TAN" as indicated in the first line of the transcription. This pattern should be sung without accent, however, I found this extremely difficult to do.

Kuchishōka

Kuchishōka, or *kuchishōga*, mnemonics similar to Western solfége, are a common tool to learn new pieces. Unlike solfége however, *kuchishōka* are instrument-specific and contain various information. Minoru explains:

> The melodic lines for the instruments are realized through syllables assigned to different techniques or fingerings. The mnemonics for the *shinobue* and *koto*, for example, represent the actual melodic line, and they provide a means of understanding musical nuances. There is, however, no indication of fingerings or string numbers. Mnemonics for the *shakuhachi*, on the other hand, indicate fingerings, and *shamisen* mnemonics indicate both string number and performance technique.
>
> (2008:3)

In my experience, *kuchishōka* can vary by not only the instrument, but the teacher as well. (See Hughes 1989 and 2000 for further consideration of the use of mnemonics.)

To understand this pattern, begin clapping for eight beats. Note that the downbeat falls before the first "HA" with the *taiko*. All the mnemonics, with the exception of "TON" and "TAN" fall slightly after the beat. Listen to this example repeatedly until you have a *feel* for how the pattern moves.

The remainder of the above transcription contains several lines of the actual rhythm on the *ko-tsuzumi*, the small hourglass-shaped drum of the *noh-hayashi,* as heard in Website Example 10. The mnemonic for the *ko-tsuzumi* appears below the noteheads, while the vocal calls (that now should be performed aloud) appear above, in alignment with their placement in the first line of the transcription. Note that the "HO" you hear can be rendered as "HA" in written interpretations; however, Tosha writes both "HO" and "HA" in his notes. I choose therefore to include the *kakegoe* as "HO," as this is the pronunciation. Nonetheless, such notation, as with all notation in Japanese traditional music, represents only an approximation of the sound of both the voice and *ko-tsuzumi*.

Again listen repeatedly now to Website Example 10, in which Tosha continues to indicate the unifying rhythmic pattern, while I attempt the *kakegoe* and to complete the rhythmic pattern on *ko-tsuzumi*. The timbre of the *ko-tsuzumi* can be controlled by squeezing the ropes used to tie on the skins and the placement of strikes, which combined create the sounds "*po*," open if you will, and struck in the middle of the drum, "*pu*," struck in the middle while tightening the strings slightly, and "*ta*," a sharper, tighter sound made by striking towards the edge of the drum primarily with the ring finger. In the recording, I cannot yet clearly articulate these differences and falter near the end, but regain some composure for the cadence created through a decrease in tempo. The point here is not to present a perfect performance, but rather to illustrate the ways in which the rhythm of *noh* may be organized.

There are reasons, nonetheless, for why *noh* sounds so "unstructured." According to *noh* performer and scholar Emmert, the rhythms I was learning here, for example, only inform certain pieces, while other, much more complex, rhythms are found in other types of music of *noh*—even within these eight-beat phrases there is freedom and elasticity of the beat, as the *noh-hayashi* follows the vocal part (e-mail correspondence, September 24, 2014).

The music is further complicated by the fact that there are some 200 rhythmic patterns for each of the instruments within the *noh-hayashi*, each of which of course has its own name, and what can be understood as the downbeat of these phrases does not fall together (Malm 1959:91; Malm 2000:286–290). Malm argues that *noh* rhythm is oriented away from the first beat, as the opening pattern exercise with Tosha here illustrates:

> The effect, musically speaking, is to keep the flow of the rhythm always "off balance." Patterns never seem to lose their dynamism but continue to push forward . . . If the *hayashi* parts are played separately, their natural phrase accent seems to fall elsewhere; when they are played together, this simultaneous combination of varying rhythmic phrases produces one of the most distinctive qualities of *noh* music—the "sliding door'" effect [mentioned earlier in regards to melody].
> (Malm 2000:289)

This rhythmic sense is apparent in the *noh* piece "Kagura," another type of *maigoto*, or dance piece (Track 10). "Kagura" refers to Shintō music, and the piece "with its overtones of purity and gravity, certainly is derived from such a religious source. In the plays *Muwa* and *Makiginu* the composition accompanies dances by divine women offering consolation to a god" (Anon. 1994). The vocal style is derived from *shōmyō*, as discussed in Chapter 1. The inclusion of Shintō into a predominantly Zen Buddhist art form again reveals the fluid blending of these religious practices within Japan, as well as the intertextuality that Wade highlights (2005). There may be a discernible connection with the rhythmic exercise discussed above, as one begins to recognize eight-beat units; remember, however, that with so many to choose from, you might not hear the exact same rhythmic patterns.

From noh to nori

Nori (literally "riding") is another important aesthetic idea related to rhythm in *noh* that has influenced not only other Japanese traditional music, but also popular music. De Ferranti explains:

> In historical genres it denotes the relationship between vocalized text lines and temporal frameworks established by percussion in music of [*noh*] drama, the recitation of text with a marked rhythm in *gidayū-bushi* music of the classical puppet theatre, and degrees of tempo in some other Edo period *shamisen* genres; but it has also been used in modern popular music to refer to the way melody or overall ensemble sound "rides" a beat, as well as a general condition of musical efficacy, in the sense of a live or recorded performance's ability to transport audience or listeners".
> (2002:203–204)

Nori thus corresponds to the Western, jazz-based idea of "groove" and is an important part of making diverse styles of Japanese music. The sensation of *nori* can be subjective, but the "groove" should be discernible in the underlying rhythm in *noh-hayashi*, as illustrated above.

The idea of *nori* is also essential in much secular ensemble drumming (*taiko*) (see further discussion in Chapter 4 and Part III). It can, however, be difficult to isolate whether this rhythmic sensation is actually grounded in Japanese practice, as *taiko* traces its origins at least in part to jazz drumming. And indeed, this ability to "ride the beat" may be a musical universal. Nonetheless, "Yaraiya," composed by Yamauchi Reach (see further discussion in Part III) and performed here by his group Wakana (Track 7) beautifully illustrates the *feeling* of riding a rhythmic wave. The piece in its basic form contains one main melody that repeats throughout. The group passes through a number of other sections and moments of improvisation, always returning to this main melody. Both the fast tempo and swinging rhythm, reminiscent of big band jazz, feeds the *nori* and propels the piece forward, despite a minimum of materials and much repetition. When I taught this piece to my college group Zakuro-Daiko, I found that the whole work only came together for us at a fast clip that facilitates this groove. And that those students with experience in jazz quickly captured the swinging feeling of the piece.

Nori thus can happen in the slow tempos of *noh*, or the fast tempos of *taiko*. And tempo obviously varies greatly in Japanese music in general. Even within the same piece, tempo is flexible as there are no fixed tempo markings. Just as with scales and melodic motifs, tempo is determined by genres, schools within genres, and even individual performers. Fast tempos are common in lively folk music and of course swinging pieces, like the one we've just heard, although *noh* too grooves, even at a slower tempo.

Form

The form of several of the proceeding pieces may be obvious while in others less so; but much traditional Japanese music is organized in a form called *jo-ha-kyū*. Originally imported from China, *jo-ha-kyū* comprises three parts in a convenient tripartite structure. In the simplest terms, the "*jo*" serves as an introduction, "*ha*" a "breaking apart" with increasing tempo, and the "*kyū*" rushes to a climax until slowing again, providing a sense of cadence and conclusion. *Jo-ha-kyū* can be articulated through increasing rhythmic density, rather than melodic conventions and may inform an entire piece of music, or a single section within. This basic structure may also be understood as moving from simplicity through increasing complexity. Therefore *jo-ha-kyū* may be better understood as a process than as a fixed form, in the Western sense. *Jo-ha-kyū* also differs from Western ternary forms, such as sonata form, that are motivated by harmonic relationships through an introduction, development and recapitulation of earlier material.

Despite the simplicity of this basic explanation, movement through the form can actually be difficult to discern without knowledge of how it works within specific styles, and of course interpretations of *jo-ha-kyū* and its importance differ by genre. The ability to comprehend *jo-ha-kyū* is further complicated as the movement from one section to the next is not always clearly understood through musical markers and organizational boundaries. *Shakuhachi* scholar Bruno Deschênes notes his "impression is that it is something that must be intuitively, so to speak, grasped not intellectualized or rationalized." He continues:

> My Japanese *shakuhachi sensei* would tell me that a single sound must start softly, coming out of silence, go into a kind of climax (crescendo and decrescendo), and then go back to silence, and this within one breath. I knew he was

talking about *jo-ha-kyū*, but did not answer my question about it . . . Although it is obviously a structural concept, it appears that it is more something to be felt than to be structurally understood.

(E-mail correspondence January 30, 2014)

Jo-ha-kyū thus is expressed in far more than the music. *Jo-ha-kyū* is most often mapped in *gagaku*, where the idea initially emerged, *noh*, in which Zeami further established key Japanese aesthetic principles, and subsequently its influence in later instrumental genres. The following discussion explores *jo-ha-kyū*, moving from the concrete to the most conceptual understandings, in the end, however, debating some of the mysticism circling around the form.

Jo-ha-kyū as a structural concept is perhaps most easily (in the context of this discussion at least) distinguishable in the well-known piece for *koto* "Rokudan" (Track 8). The *koto*, introduced in Chapter 2, is of course one of the iconic instruments of Japan, easily recognized around the world. Imported from China in an early form as one of the string instruments of *gagaku* (see further discussion below), the instrument and its repertoire transformed from its role in the orchestra through the years into a sophisticated solo form by the Meiji period, practiced by young women in particular as a mark of refinement and elegance. Many pieces still performed today, known as *sōkyoku* (music for *koto*), including "Rokudan" by Yatsuhashi Kengyō (1614–85), were composed during the Edo period (Kengyō is actually a title indicating high rank, rather than a name) (Wade 2005:69; e-mail correspondence with Anne Prescott, February 11, 2014). Yatsuhashi adopted the *in* scale to *koto* music, helping promote its unique emotional quality as most Japanese in character (ibid.).

"Rokudan" is considered a *danmono* (sectional piece) for solo *koto*. The "*roku*" translates as six, while "*dan*" refers to sections. Thus the piece at its most basic level contains six sections. *Dan* are another common sectional organization, but not created by tonal or thematic content, such as with key areas in Western music. Each *dan* in this piece contains 26 units, which sound essentially like 26 measures in common time, or 104 beats. Each repeats with increasing variation of the first *dan*.

Wade argues, however, that this music should not be understood as fitting rigidly within Western meter:

> The non metric rhythmic flow of traditional *koto* music—a big factor in that "flowing ongoingness"—is probably the one element of style that is being most affected by Western music enculturation. To my hearing, most *koto* players now unconsciously fall into the trap of stressing first counts in those notated boxes, coming perilously close to turning this into metered music.
>
> (2005:76)

This may account for why some sections of the recording of "Rokudan" included here are easily counted, while others, particularly at faster tempos, are more difficult to follow in such strict terms.

This version of "Rokudan" features Iseki Kazuhiro and Nishi Yoko on *koto*, each playing different parts; the original "Rokudan" and a second part, "Kumoi Rokudan," although it is unclear who composed the second part. There are in fact many pieces, which continue to be written even today, to accompany "Rokudan" (e-mail correspondence with Anne Prescott, February 11, 2014). Interestingly, both parts in this version are in the *in* scale type, but different modes (*chōshi*).

The piece opens with a short, four-beat introduction consisting of a long note at a slow tempo, followed by a note a fourth below and then a brief pitch is heard approaching the simultaneous sounding of two pitches a fifth apart. Try to find the beat by counting the latter three sounds as "3 and 4 and" then the first *dan* begins on the moment of silence following. This motif will repeat throughout the piece as a cadence, signaling the start of the next variation (Fujie 2002:345; Wade 2005:72; Alves 2013:325) and is easily heard at the end of the first and second *dan* here. However, there is no single melody to follow, rather patterns that may reoccur with great variation. The piece will gradually increase in tempo, making each *dan* more difficult to identify, but there are some distinct moments nevertheless.

The first *dan* begins at :08 and presents the melodic material at a relatively slow, even elegant tempo until the return to the opening four-beat motive, followed by the moment of silence that signals the beginning of the second *dan* at 2:40. The tempo gradually, almost imperceptibly increases as the piece continues along until the beginning of the third *dan* at 4:42. This is marked with a specific gesture on the *koto* called *sararin*—a mnemonic representing a tremolo followed by a sweep across the strings. The tempo and tension increase as the *koto* moves towards the fourth *dan*, which begins at 6:26, marked by decidedly more frenetic, rhythmically dense patterns. The divisions between *dan* becomes increasingly difficult to discern given the rapid tempo, but the fifth begins at 7:20 and moves quickly to the sixth at 8:06. This will slow down considerably from 8:45, returning to the original slow tempo. The piece concludes with another *sararin* tremolo and sweep.

There is some debate in how the *dan* are viewed in relation to *jo-ha-kyū*. Fujie claims the *jo* comprises the first two *dan*, the *ha* the second set of two *dan*, and the *kyū* the last two (2002:345). Others place the first *dan* at the beginning of the *jo*, while the fourth begins the *ha*, and the *kyū* is the sixth. Given the dramatic change in mood with the fourth *dan* in this version, it seems likely the *ha* begins here. However, these changes are understood more as a "feeling" "rather than designation of musical form in an empirical or objective sense." In other words, the precise points of *jo-ha-kyū* are subjective even within this structure, accounting for the different assessment (e-mail correspondence with David Locke, February 6, 2014).

Tamaki Hikaru and Kimura Yoko, of Duo-YUMENO, emphasize that

> ... *jo-ha-kyū* is found at what we might call multiple architectonic levels in the music, from a single note, to a short motif, to a phrase, to a passage, to an entire piece, and to an entire performance. Thus it is a general aesthetic "practice," as well as a dimension of performance technique. They often mention a three-note rhythmic figure identified in "*kuchi-shamisen*" mnemonics as "*ko-ra-rin*" that is roughly equivalent to dotted eighth-note, sixteenth-note, quarter-note in a 2/4 time signature. The three notes should be "phrased" with a *jo-ha-kyū* "sensibility."
> (E-mail correspondence with David Locke, February 5, 2014)

And certainly within each of the *dan* we can hear *jo-ha-kyū* expansion and increasing tension.

Jo-ha-kyū spills forth primarily through ideas of texture in "Etenraku" ("Music of Divinity"), a classic piece in the *gagaku* repertoire "especially associated with New Year celebrations and other symbols of new beginnings, and Shintō rituals" (Alves 2013:317)

(Track 9). As previously noted, *gagaku*, or "elegant music," was imported to Japan from China and Korea during the Nara period and therefore is broadly considered the oldest orchestral music in the world. *Gagaku* as we know it today consists of four categories: music for instrumental ensemble (*kangen*), which is heard here performing "Etenraku," instrumental music to accompany dance (*bugaku*) (see Figure 3.12), vocal songs, and music for Shintō rituals. In the latter case, the actual instruments are often replaced with a recording during various Shintō rites today.

Large *gagaku* works develop through *jo-ha-kyū* with the entrance of different instruments including winds, strings and percussion. The version of "Etenraku" here performed by the Kyoto Imperial Court Orchestra illustrates the way these parts enter one by one, building upon each other and expanding the texture. The order of instruments is standardized by piece and "Etenraku" opens with a solo on the *ryūteki*, a transverse bamboo flute, until the *kakko* enters, a small double-headed barrel drum that sets the tempo and directs the ensemble in *tōgaku* repertoire (imported from China and India, as opposed to *komagaku* from Korea). The *shōko* is next heard in most versions of the piece, a bronze gong suspended in a stand that "punctuates the melody just after the beginning of every four-beat metrical unit" (Alves 2013:316), followed by *gagaku taiko* or *tsuri-daiko*, a large double-headed drum suspended in a stand which enters with a resounding thud. Next enters the *shō*, a mouth organ with 17 bamboo pipes, which can be manipulated to play five to seven pitches simultaneously. However, these "chords" do not function in quite the same way as Western harmony. Instead, "The lowest note of each chord on the [s]*hō* follows the important point of the main melody. This means the chords hang over the melody" and are thus distinct from

Figure 3.12 *Bugaku* performance at Shiramine-jingū in Kyoto

Western music "in which the melodic element is supported by the chord" (Kishibe 1984:39). The *hichiriki* follows, a small double-reed oboe made with bamboo, which has a distinctive nasal quality that is quite clear in the ensemble. The *hichiriki* supplies the main melody. Finally, strings appear: first the *biwa* enters with a thwack, and last, the *koto*. The strings "underline the melody by sounding strategic pitches at rhythmically important points. In effect, they function as a bridge between the melodic parts and the percussion instruments" (Wade 2005:30). This version of the piece is particularly sparse, performed without the clear metallic sound of the *shōko* typically found in other performances, and the thud of the *taiko* is muffled.

The piece comprises three repeating melodic phrases consisting of 32 beats each; however, the tempo is so slow and flexible at first that these can be difficult, if not impossible to hear, but become increasingly apparent as the piece accelerates. It is possible to map these three movements through their melodic patterns (that is, labeling A, B and C sections) (Alves 2013:317–319; Malm 2000: 117–118): however, *nagauta* scholar and performer Keister cautions

> ... analyzing *jo-ha-kyū* with such precision (ABC etc.) perhaps misses the point as it is meant to be a more flexible concept rooted in the cycles of nature. Unless you're talking about [*noh*] drama, which actually does label movements as *jo-ha-kyū* (*gagaku* also has multi-part pieces labeled as such), identifying *jo-ha-kyū* can't really be broken into discrete sections in an analytical fashion in most traditional Japanese music. So to my mind "Etenraku" demonstrates *jo-ha-kyū* by progressing from low rhythmic density and sparse instrumental texture in the beginning to higher rhythmic density and full instrumental texture by the time the piece concludes. This cannot be mapped precisely onto the AABBCC structure because ensembles choose ahead of time how long they want to play each repetition of the parts. What does happen in every performance, however, is the gradual build-up of instrumental texture (for example, *biwa* and *koto* appear last) and a rhythmic density that doubles at one point in the piece (you can hear the *taiko* play twice as fast) at some point in any performance.
> (E-mail correspondence, February 1, 2014)

This piece clearly flows, even if it is difficult to identify exactly where the *ha* and *kyū* begin, and I make no attempt to do so. However, the point is to listen to how the piece passes through *jo-ha-kyū*, gradually increasing in rhythmic density before breaking apart at the very end with the melody fading out on the *biwa* and a final pluck of the *koto*. This may require repeated deep listening.

As Keister notes above, within *noh*, movements are actually marked *jo-ha-kyū*, and this expansion can be heard in the *maigoto* "Kagura" introduced before (Track 10). Again, repeated listening may be necessary to "feel" the piece progress through *jo-ha-kyū*, with increasing tempo in places that seems to break apart midway through. It is difficult once again to identify exact points when *jo-ha-kyū* is executed, nevertheless some moments do stand out, such as a noticeable deceleration from 5:45 to the sudden intensification at 6:00 and final denouement.

But with *noh*, the idea of *jo-ha-kyū* is most expansive, referring to essentially all aspects of the performance. Emmert beautifully explains how the concept is used in *noh*, taking us to quite a conceptual level:

In *noh, jo-ha-kyū* is in practical use. It is the one concept that all my teachers of *noh*, musicians and dancers, could always relate to. While it doesn't make much sense to say, "let's try that again but with a bit more *yugen* [an aesthetic ideal developed by Zeami roughly corresponding to the idea of "courtliness"]," it makes a lot of sense to say "let's try that again with more *jo-ha-kyū*."

In its musical use, while it can describe the tempo progression of an entire piece, in individual phrases it is . . . very related to the term "*ma*." It is clearly a part of how one should express a phrase of a line . . . where the drum pattern of the *ō-tsuzumi* at the beginning of the phrase is expansive and the singing is too, but then the second half of the phrase tends to speed up along with the consecutive strokes of the *ko-tsuzumi*. So each phrase has an individual sense of *jo-ha-kyū* over just the several seconds of the phrase. And that is brought about both by the sense of *jo-ha-kyū* in the drum patterns, particularly the drum calls, and in the chant of the chorus.

Similarly, in terms of movement, one can describe movement in the course of an entire segment or scene as having a *jo-ha-kyū* sense to it. Practically one can talk about how to express an individual movement pattern or how one slides one's feet forward in a line of movement: both have a sense of holding back or resistance at the beginning of the movement before one finally breaks free to move forward. That sense of resistance is, to me at least, musical in nature— a sense of expansion and then contraction as one rushes forward—although "rushing forward" might not be generally used to describe movement in *noh*. . .

What gets even more complicated in *noh* is when *jo-ha-kyū* is used to explain pretty much everything else, from how individual lines within phrases are expressed, how phrases within segments are expressed, how segments within scenes are expressed, how scenes within acts are expressed, how acts within full plays are expressed, and how plays within a full day's program of plays are expressed. And I dare say, in those special instances when there are several days of programs, such as when the National Noh Theatre first opened in 1983 and when it celebrated its 30th anniversary last year, those days in combination would have been put together with an awareness of *jo-ha-kyū*.

. . . it is more an expression of appropriateness: what is an appropriate beginning, what is an appropriate middle, and what is an appropriate ending. And that perhaps is worthy of even more discussion.

(E-mail correspondence, January 31, 2014)

Like the idea of *ma*, *jo-ha-kyū* is often referenced as a characteristic element of Japanese traditional music, but not without some debate. The vagueness of the concept is only enhanced by the fact that different genres embrace it in myriad ways. Emmert in particular paints a powerful, even romantic, picture of the ways in which *jo-ha-kyū* is invoked in *noh*. But its significance as a marker of Japanese musical identity is arguable. Tripartite or ternary forms are extremely common in much music throughout the world. We can understand the literary narrative—which introduces characters, expands the storyline, contains a penultimate moment, and denouement—as moving along a similar path of expansion. The ubiquity of the concept calls into question whether it can in fact be understood as somehow Japanese. Indeed, *jo-ha-kyū* may be an oversimplification of the ways in which much Japanese traditional music is conceived, or on the flip side, is broad enough to cover a great variety of forms, and therefore should not be seen as any more unusual than other forms and organizing principles found in Western art music, such as rondo or sonata.

Keister adds that, although he agrees

> ... we have to avoid reducing everything down to tidy labels such as *jo-ha-kyū* and *ma*, these concepts nevertheless have proven to be historically significant, in spite of their overuse bordering on cliché and regardless of whether they seem to be Japanese, pan-Asian or even universal forms.
> (E-mail correspondence, January 31, 2014)

He continues to reflect:

> The more I think about *jo-ha-kyū* and *ma* the more I feel that these are not really unique to Japan. They're just Japanese explanations of an observation of nature that seems particularly Taoist to me; and the Japanese built their artistic tradition around it. Now it has led to our intellectual agonizing over how to make sense of it all. As any *sensei* would say: "just play your instrument."
> (E-mail correspondence, February 1, 2014)

Whether these ideas are uniquely Japanese is not the point. The concept exists in Japan as *jo-ha-kyū*—a similar structural process may exist elsewhere, if not everywhere, but this does not undermine the fact that the idea has clearly taken on much import historically within Japanese music. It is important to remember that not all Japanese traditional music expresses this formal structure, just as it is not all in free rhythm or permeated with *ma*. Whether these processes actually do express a unique Japaneseness, perhaps through their association with nature, the ideas have come to be associated with Japanese musical aesthetics and continue to inspire contemporary composers to explore interesting performative possibilities. Clearly, the concept of *jo-ha-kyū*, even if perhaps overly romanticized, is still intriguing to some scholars and artists alike.

Coming Together in Endo's "The Calling"

We conclude this exploration of the elements of Japanese music with Kenny Endo's "Yobikake" ("The Calling") (Track 11). This piece illustrates many of the ideas above—from *ma* to *kakegoe*—in a modern composition that brings numerous traditions together. The piece features four eminent musicians: Tosha Kiyonari (*shime-daiko*), Okura Shonosuke (*ō-tsuzumi*), Suzuki Kyosuke (*nohkan, shinobue*), and Kenny Endo (*ō-daiko*).

The piece opens with a large, low-pitched *taiko*, called an *ō-daiko*, deeply resounding, as the *nohkan*, the flute of the *noh-hayashi* introduced earlier, pierces the open space. The *kakegoe*, emotive vocal calling of the drummers invoked in the title of the piece, signals the entrance at 0:27 of the *ō-tsuzumi*, the larger of the hourglass-shaped drums of the *noh-hayashi*, with its characteristic "clacking" sound produced by the thick finger cover striking the drum head. The distinctive timbre continues through a solo, which makes great use of space, at times resembling the sounds of intermittent raindrops at the end of a storm. The concept of *ma* is powerfully demonstrated between 0:59 and 1:06 as the listener is invited into the emptiness between the gentle drops. Restrained patters continue to seemingly enter at random until the *kakegoe* signals a change at 1:30, increasing intensity until 1:52, dramatically establishing another moment of silence before the *shime-daiko*, another drum of the *noh-hayashi* as well as festival (*matsuri*) musics, with a duller timbre than the *ō-tsuzumi*, enters at 1:58. The powerful *ō-daiko* returns at 2:07, moving in dynamic waves as the sticks (*bachi*) are passed from the center to the edge of the skin, revealing the potential of the *ō-daiko* to perform quietly as well as the more expected constant loudness. The full percussive ensemble enters at 2:50 and performs in highly energetic styles derived from *noh* and *kabuki*, the *kakegoe* and *nohkan* floating above the churning percussive grounding, the *ō-tsuzumi* improvising. At 6:07, the two vocalists (Okura and Endo) take center stage improvising based on traditional patterns from *noh*, until the *ō-tsuzumi* indicates the transition to the next section at 7:05. Here the *shime-daiko* and *ō-daiko* improvise, as the *ō-tsuzumi* occasionally interjects. The *shinobue*, another transverse bamboo flute found in *matsuri*, solos from 8:21. The piece reaches a frenetic state punctuated with groaning, plaintive vocal calls from 9:30 before a brief return of the theatrical music, with the *nohkan*, and then moving directly into the final conclusion:

> "Yobikake" ("The Calling") was created for a concert held in October 1997 in Tokyo. Sponsored by Miyamoto Unosuke Shoten (a famous *taiko* maker and producer), this concert was a recital for *taiko* artist, Kenny Endo, and featured some of the top musicians in Japan:

> "Yobikake" was meant to bring together four musicians from four distinct traditions who were all open to collaborating and improvising ... The concept was to create an open base for free expression within each of the traditions and allow as much improvisation as the music called for. This was a piece made possible by the skill, flexibility, and creativity of the four musicians.
> (E-mail correspondence with Kenny Endo, September 18, 2014)

This piece, although grounded in Japanese tradition and performed by renowned musicians trained in *hōgaku*, brings us back to an element briefly introduced in the opening of this chapter—improvisation—that again is not a musical practice common in the majority of traditional Japanese music. It is, however, primary in contemporary *taiko* performance (see further discussion in Chapter 4 and Part III). As such, this piece transitions us from the musics that originated in pre-modern Japan to the modern era—the topic of the next chapter.

References

Alves, William. 2013. "Japan." In *Music of the Peoples of the World*, 3rd Edn., pp. 309–333. Stamford, CT: Cengage Learning.

Anon. 1976. "Liner Notes" to *Japan: Traditional Vocal & Instrumental Music*. Nonesuch Records 9-72072-2.

—— 1994. "Liner Notes" to *Japanese Noh Music: The Kyoto Nohgaku Kai*. Lyrcd 7137.

Blasdel, Christopher Y. 2005. *The Single Tone: A Personal Journey into Shakuhachi Music*. Tokyo: Printed Matter Press.

Dalby, Liza. 2000. *Little Songs of the Geisha: Traditional Japanese Ko-Uta*. Rutland, VT: Tuttle.

de Ferranti, Hugh. 2002. "Japanese Music Can be Popular." *Popular Music* 21(2):195–208.

Emmert, Richard. 1983. "The Maigoto of Nō: A Musical Analysis of the Chu-no-mai." *Yearbook for Traditional Music* 15:5–13.

Fraleigh, Sondra. 2010. *Butoh: Metamorphic Dance and Global Alchemy*. Urbana-Champaign: University of Illinois Press.
Fujie, Linda. 2002. "East Asia – Japan" In J. Titon, ed., *Worlds of Music: An Introduction to the Music of the World's Peoples 4th Edn.*, pp. 331–384. Belmont, CA: Schirmer/Thomson Learning.
Galliano, Luciana. 2002. *Yōgaku: Japanese Music in the Twentieth Century*. Lanham, MD: Scarecrow Press.
Gillan, Matthew. 2012a. *Songs From the Edge of Japan: Music-Making in Yaeyama and Okinawa*. Farnham: Ashgate.
Gunji, Masakatsu. 1970. *Buyō, The Classical Dance, Performing Arts of Japan III*. New York: Walker/Weatherhill.
Gunji, Sumi and Henry Johnson. 2012. *A Dictionary of Traditional Japanese Musical Instruments: From Prehistory to the Edo Period*. Tokyo: Eideru Kenkyujo.
Hahn, Tomie. 2007. *Sensational Knowledge: Embodying Culture through Japanese Dance*. Middletown, CT: Wesleyan University Press.
Hughes, David. 1989. "The Historical Uses of Nonsense; Vowel-Pitch Solfège from Scotland to Japan." In M. Philipp, ed., *Ethnomusicology and the Historical Dimension*, pp. 3–18. Beuzlen: Philipp Verlag.
——. 2000. "No Nonsense: The Logic and Power of Acoustic-Iconic Mnemonic Systems." *British Journal of Ethnomusicology* 9(2):93–120.
——. 2008. *Traditional Folk Song in Modern Japan: Sources, Sentiment and Society*. Folkestone: Global Oriental.
Kawase, Akihiro. 2013. "Scales Theory in Japanese Music." *Akihiko Kawase's Website* (April 30, 2013): http://blog.a-kawase.net/blog/2013/04/30/jpn-scale/ (accessed June 14, 2014).
Keister, Jay. 2004. *Shaped by Japanese Music: Kikuoka Hiroaki and Nagauta Shamisen in Tokyo*. New York/London: Routledge.
Kishibe, Shigeo. 1984. *The Traditional Music of Japan*. Tokyo: The Japan Foundation.
Koizumi, Fumio. 1974. *Nihon no Ongaku (Japanese Music)*. Tokyo: National Theater of Japan.
Malm, William P. 1959. *Japanese Music and Musical Instruments, 1st Edn*. Rutland, VT: Tuttle.
——. 2000. *Traditional Japanese Music and Musical Instruments*. Tokyo: Kodansha.
Minoru, Miki. 2008. *Composing for Japanese Instruments*. Translated by M. Regan, P. Flavin, ed., Rochester, NY: University of Rochester Press.
On Music Dictionary. n.d. *On Music Dictionary* (n.d.): http://dictionary.onmusic.org (accessed May 14, 2014).
Sawyer, David. n.d. "The life and work of Jin Nyodo – A short history of a great *shakuhachi* player." *Japanshakuhachi* (n.d.): http://www.japanshakuhachi.com/jinnyodo.html (accessed June 9, 2014).
Shimosako, Mari. 2002. "Philosophy and Aesthetics." In R. Provine, Y. Tokumaru and J. Witzleben, eds., *East Asia: China, Japan and Korea. The Garland Encyclopedia of World Music Vol. 7*, pp. 554–55. New York/London: Routledge.
Stevens, Carolyn S. 2008. *Japanese Popular Music: Culture, Authenticity, and Power*. New York/London: Routledge.
Surak, Kristin. 2013. *Making Tea, Making Japan: Cultural Nationalism in Practice*. Stanford, CA: Stanford University Press.
Takemitsu, Tōru. 1995. *Confronting Silence: Selected Writings*. Translated and edited by T. Kakudo and G. Glasgow. Berkeley, CA: Fallen Leaf Press.
—— with Tania Cronin and Hilary Tann. 1989. "Afterward." *Perspectives of New Music* 27(2):206–214.
Tann, Hilary. 1989. "Coming to Terms: (Futaiken) Reibo." *Perspectives of New Music* 27(2):52–77.
Trimillos, Ricardo D. 2004. "Subject, Object, and the Ethnomusicology Ensemble: The Ethnomusicological 'We' and 'Them.'" In T. Solis, ed., *Performing Ethnomusicology*, pp. 23–52. Berkeley: University of California Press.
Wade, Bonnie C. 2005. *Music in Japan: Expressing Music, Expressing Culture*. Oxford: Oxford University Press.
Williams, Sean. 2010. *Focus: Irish Traditional Music*. New York/London: Routledge.

CHAPTER 4

Making Music in the Modern Era

Team Kozan's cover of Lady Gaga's "Telephone featuring Beyoncé" (Website Example 11) opens with a lovely image of a woman in a kimono *playing the* koto, *soon joined by an older gentleman on* shakuhachi, *both seated on a raised platform with golden Japanese folding screens framing them from behind. As the camera pans to a wider shot, two young women are seen demurely seated traditionally on the floor (seiza), bowing to the viewer in proper Japanese fashion. Although some may immediately recognize the melody as* not *belonging to sounds of the traditional music introduced in the proceeding chapter, the performance context clearly is, at least until approximately 25 seconds into the song. At that point, a drum machine enters the mix, with additional synthesized instrumentation; the young ladies leap up and begin to dance in a fashion more akin to the choreographed back-up dancers of J-Pop, a term coined in the late 1980s to refer to the mainstream, mass-produced, and immensely popular style of music that continues to dominate the Japanese music industry today. The conflation of stylistic and national references continues.*

Team Kozan's cover of Lady Gaga's "Telephone featuring Beyoncé" opens with sounds similar to those highlighted in the previous chapter, but quickly moves us out of the traditional world of Japan and its music to contemporary popular music. The original video opens in a prison ("Lady Gaga—Telephone ft. Beyoncé" released in 2010. At the time of writing, the official video is available at http://www.youtube.com/watch?v=EVBsypHzF3U); however, Team Kozan's version is set in traditional Japanese rooms (*washitsu*) at Suga shrine in Tokyo. The behind-the-scenes black and white shots could be a reference to the black and white shots in the original video viewed through a security monitor in the prison in which we find Lady Gaga doing time.

The dancers in Lady Gaga's version appear in nothing but bras and panties, while in Team Kozan's Japanized interpretation the dancers are in shiny modernized summer cotton robes (*yukata*), hiked-up to allow some freedom of movement, yet still more suitable for the formal context of the Japanese-style room. The dancers are yukata-clad foreign in the Lady Gaga song, but very Japanese within the context of the Japanese idol industry in which their dance moves no doubt originate. Even Ishikura Kōzan drops the *shakuhachi* (worn on a strap akin to an alto-saxophone) to his side and joins the exuberant dance. Sakamoto Sayuri retains her composure throughout, supplying the melody of the Western harp in the original now on the Japanese equivalent—the *koto*.

The group explains that they covered this song to show their gratitude to Lady Gaga for her assistance to Japan following the earthquake and tsunami in 2011. Their official website asks "Have you ever heard beautiful Japanese traditional music?" (Team Kozan 2013). The point seems to be to bring *hōgaku* to the youth of today through a more palatable, or at least familiar vehicle: Lady Gaga. And in the first two months alone, this cover video received 400,000 hits on the Internet and continues to garner much media attention (Faith 2013).

Whether intentional or not, ultimately there appears to be a self-conscious rendering of Japanese identity here. The setting of the video in a shrine, either actually wearing or playing with traditional clothing, glimpses of a Shintō wedding, and ending with the cliché of cherry blossoms all reinforce typical markers of Japaneseness. The melding of Western and Japanese musical elements into fantastic new mixes is of course another common Japanese practice.

To this point we have explored genres with origins dating prior to the Meiji period in the pre-modern era, including religious, folk, art and music for entertainment. When Japan entered the modern era, they actively engaged with art and popular musics of the West, resulting in dramatic changes. Chapter 2 introduced the immediate and intense influence of Western ideas on Japanese modern identity and some of the ways in which this was implemented through musical practice. Here we take a closer look at how this actually *sounded* in music of the time.

This chapter therefore now turns to consider music composed in the style of European art music in the early twentieth-century (*kindai ongaku*) (Kotobank n.d.b), through more contemporary art music from the late twentieth century (*gendai ongaku*) (Kotobank n.d.a), several popular musics including *enka*, *angura* and *aidoru*, and finally the recent proliferation of musics that combine elements of traditional Japanese music and popular music, and subsequently inspired a so-called *hōgaku būmu* (boom), and modern secular ensemble drumming (*taiko*). Just as with the preceding chapter, this exploration is in no way intended to present the breadth of music making in the modern era, but rather to introduce some interesting themes, key genres and notable composers and performers. The musical examples hopefully capture the different ways that the Japanese have come to express a unique cultural identity in the twentieth- and twenty-first centuries.

Encounters with European Art Music

In the late nineteenth- and early twentieth centuries, numerous Japanese composers began to engage with European art musics, at times purposefully developing compositional techniques that integrated characteristics of Japanese music with European-based compositional practices, while at other times creating works devoid of any noticeable markers of Japaneseness, such as including the traditional instruments or musical elements discussed in the proceeding chapter. Wade rightly cautions that expecting a unique Japanese sound in such works would be inappropriate and artificially exoticizing. She reminds us:

The lines along which musical modernity in Japan has developed are different from those of Europe and the Americas, but only to a certain extent. Nor does most of the music created by Japanese composers "sound Japanese" (i.e., sound different in traditional Japanese musical ways). Indeed, why should it? After all, 141 years have passed since the decision was made to systematically introduce the music of Europe and America in order to create a shared cultural space for all the people of the new nation.

(2014:5)

We want to be careful therefore not to presume that all Japanese artists must somehow "sound Japanese," and yet the following discussion explores some of the ways composers have engaged with European compositional ideas, while conveying elements of Japanese cultural identity, through comparison of the well-known children's song (*dōyō*), "Akatonbo," from the early twentieth century, and an instrumental piece for piano and flute, "Lied," composed nearly a hundred years later.

In the early twentieth century, for example, Pacun argues specific compositional tropes emerged that came to be seen as Japanese. This involved modifying standard rules of Western harmonization and phrasing to fit the modal qualities of Japanese melodies, while remaining within the realms of possibility dictated by Romantic music sensibilities (2012:11–13). Such conventions came to represent Japaneseness in European-style art composition and appeared in early popular song in Japan as well, becoming a "mode of expression that contemporary Japanese listeners embraced as their own and valued as an authentic expression of modern Japanese life" (ibid.:16). Japanese composers also experimented with texture, "with a special focus given to the inclusion of quasi-heterophonic textures and non-triadic harmonies" in line with the musicality of traditional Japanese music (ibid.:17). Composers of this era had to consciously choose to make their music sound "Japanese," so much so that "by 1914, there had arisen a reasonably concise set of musical parameters that were or could be sonically identified as 'Japanese' [which] eventually became a conscious music style" (ibid.:10). Even if providing a method of expressing one's identity in another's language, such tropes have the potential to exoticize and limit Japanese composers as well.

Throughout the twentieth century, however, Japanese composers explored increasingly abstract modes of expressing concepts of Japanese cultural identity in music. In a talk delivered to the Japan Society in 1988, Takemitsu Tōru describes such shifts within his own compositional projects:

> All of us have been deeply influenced by the traditions of Japanese classical music [here meaning *hōgaku*], but I think we've each transcended these traditions in finding new and personally unique forms of expression—forms that are now reaching a global level of appreciation, a music that can communicate to people everywhere.
>
> (1989:203)

He continues:

> I wouldn't want you to think that this music is "Japanesey" in any way. The instruments are not traditional Japanese instruments by any stretch of the imagination. Yet I can be equally definite in saying that all the pieces in the repertory of Sound Space ARK [one of his projects at the time] are based on, influenced by, immersed in the Japanese musical tradition. Again, what I and my fellow composers are *not*

doing is simply, in a facile way, adapting Japanese tradition to Western form. What we're trying to do is to study very deeply, and very carefully, the essence of traditional music, to explore unknown worlds, and to recreate, or reelucidate, in new, modern forms, what we've learned from our traditions.

(Ibid.:203)

Thus Takemitsu Tōru is an example of someone offering new means of expressing local cultural identity in global sounds.

"Akatonbo" by Yamada Kōsaku

The merger of Japanese and Western ideological and musical ideas in the beginning of the twentieth century is apparent in "Akatonbo" ("Red Dragonfly"), composed by Yamada Kōsaku (1886–1965) in 1927, the lyrics being a poem by Miki Rōfu (1889–1964) written in 1921 (Track 12). Yamada was a prolific and highly active composer, who left an indelible mark on the musical life of modern Japan. Galliano explains that Yamada was exposed to Western music, including naval bands and English hymns from early childhood; he studied piano and organ at a young age, and later attended the Tokyo School of Music, earning a degree in vocal music in 1908 (2002:43). He also studied cello, theory and of course composition, earning a degree in Germany in 1912; he was the first Japanese person to compose a symphony, *"Kachidoki to Heiwa"* ("Victory and Peace"). Yamada wrote several more orchestral works and songs for voice and piano during this period. Strauss influenced Yamada's work while he was in Berlin, and would continue to do so throughout his life. In 1913, he returned to Japan, producing an opera, symphonic poems, and pieces for piano. Between 1917 and 1919, Yamada toured America, and his pieces were performed at numerous venues, including Carnegie Hall. Prompted by interview questions on this tour, Yamada began to question the connection between new music in Japan and Japanese traditional music (ibid.:48). He became incredibly active in the 1920s composing for film, conducting, and touring. It is believed he wrote some of his best music at this time, including collections of songs for children (*dōyō*).

Yamada composed many *dōyō*:

> ... lyrical tonal songs for children (with piano accompaniment), many of which are included in the series *Yamada Kōsaku dōyō hyakkyoku shū* (*100 Children's Songs by Kōsaku Yamada*), published in 1927 ... The style of text setting is consistent from one piece to the next, and the music is very accessible. Calling for proper, natural pronunciation of carefully selected texts, lyrical melody, and simple manipulations of tonal materials, the songs of Kōsaku Yamada established a style of Japanese song that would endure.
>
> (Wade 2014:193–194)

Wade further describes the inspiration for the creation of *dōyō* in the following:

> In the early years of the twentieth-century there was a reaction on the part of individual composers against the pedantic quality of the primary-school songs and against the use of texts (patriotic and Meiji-moralistic) so far removed from the children's world. A countermovement gathered outside of the school system on behalf of "good music" for children.
>
> (Ibid.:192)

A number of respected composers, including Yamada, and poets were part of this movement: "They wanted to compose and offer to children more beautiful and emotional songs than the popular and school songs" (ibid.:193). The earlier Ministry of Education, Science and Culture school songs (*Monbushō shōka*) were not considered to be of great artistic quality. Drawing on the work of Naka Mamiko, Wade describes Yamada's desire to compose songs that would speak to the Japanese and thus he turned to "Japanese poetic expressiveness in his choice of song texts," such as the poem by Miki here, and musical settings that privileged this text (ibid.:193). Naka continues:

> Already here, we can see his endeavor to make his works intelligible to common Japanese audience. As a matter of fact, his associations with contemporary poets helped change his creative attitude into something Japanese or ethnic, thus resulting in the simplistic manipulation of the tonal materials. Perhaps for this reason, he became involved in composing new songs for children's appreciation.
> (Naka 1991:564, quoted in Wade 2014:193)

Dōyō, however, are not just "songs for children," but are appropriately sung in art music contexts by adults. And indeed, Wade argues that although they are "no longer popular with children, *dōyō* are still appreciated by older Japanese" (ibid.:194). Wade found in her work with Itoh Miki, the director of the *Nihon Dōyō Kyōkai* (The Association of Children's Song Writers in Japan), that *dōyō* continue to speak to adults in part because new compositions are "conceived of as music for mothers of young children," who need to learn songs to sing to them (ibid.). And Yamada's songs remain popular amongst young women soloists and choruses. The performance here, featuring Yamada's wife Tsuji Teruko on vocals, beautifully illustrates these points.

"Akatonbo" also reveals the ways in which Yamada brought Japanese sensibility to Western song settings. The piece is written in a pentatonic scale type—known as *yonanuki*—that became an important marker of modern Japanese cultural identity in the early twentieth century. In simplest terms, the *yonanuki* scale is based on the Western major or minor diatonic scale types with degrees 4 and 7 removed ("*yo*" means 4, "*na*" means 7, and "*nuki*" means "without"), resulting in a pentatonic major scale type and pentatonic minor scale type (see Figure 4.1).

Yonanuki Pentatonic Major Scale

Yonanuki Pentatonic Minor Scale

Figure 4.1 *Yonanuki* pentatonic scales

The *yonanuki* scale type was "deliberately created" to bring Japanese melodic qualities that rested on predominantly pentatonic scales together with Western diatonic modal sensibilities (Yano 1998:248; Stevens 2008:19). The *yonanuki* scale types, and especially the minor form, have been readily used in Japanese popular music as well.

"Akatonbo" was originally written in F pentatonic major and later changed to E♭ pentatonic major, as seen in the vocal melody below (see Figure 4.2).

Typically performed in a gentle ¾ time, the dynamics for the most part swaying between *piano* and *mezzo-forte*, the vocal melody is quite simple but emotive, built as an eight-measure melody consisting of a four-measure antecedent phrase and corresponding four-measure consequent phrase. The antecedent phrase opens with an ascending leap of a perfect fourth from the B♭ below middle C to E♭, or from the dominant to the tonic in Western contexts. This leap is repeated an octave above in the second measure of the antecedent phrase. The consequent phrase opens with another leap of a perfect fourth from G above middle C to the upper C. The scale type combined with the emphasis on leaps of perfect fourths, which Koizumi identified as a characteristic of Japanese scales in his tetrachord theory, and in turn are stressed in melodic patterns in much traditional music, create a decidedly Japanese quality to this modern melody.

Galliano argues that Yamada established "a personal musical language" through which he avoided the pitfall of other composers of the time, who made "all too often hybrid works that were weakened by personal quests to bridge the gap between two different musical worlds" (2002:50). He did so in part by avoiding "the formal structural relationships of Western harmony in order to create a music that was closer to Japanese melodic ideas and his use of harmony as a color" (ibid.:50). And to be sure, the harmonization on the piano in "Akatonbo" is simple and unobtrusive, supporting the elegant lyrical line.

These eight measures are repeated with four stanzas of poetic text as seen below. One line is included in Figure 4.2 to illustrate where the text falls with the melody.

赤とんぼ
"Akatonbo"
("Red Dragonfly") (JASRAC 出1414514–401)

夕やけ小やけの　赤とんぼ　負われて見たのは　いつの日か
yūyake koyake no akatonbo owarete mitano wa itsu no hi ka
Red dragonfly at dusk, I saw you while carried as a baby on my nanny's back

山の畑の　桑の実を　小籠に摘んだは　まぼろしか
yama no hatake no kuwa no mi o kokago ni tsunda ha maborohi ka
Placing mulberry fruit into a basket, at the garden in the mountain
Was this just a dream?

Figure 4.2 "Akatonbo" (vocal melody) (JASRAC 出 1414514–401)

十五で姐やは　嫁に行き　お里のたよりも　絶えはてた
jūgo de nēya wa   yome ni iki   osato no tayori mo   taehateta
At 15, nanny married, and letters from the countryside
No longer arrived

夕やけ小やけの　赤とんぼ　とまっているよ　竿の先
yūyake koyake no   akatonbo   tomatte iruyo   sao no saki
Red dragonfly at dusk, resting on the tip of the bamboo reed.

The song uses the imagery of red dragonflies to evoke nostalgic feelings of the past and of course for the old country home of the *furusato*. The red dragonflies also connect with the seasons, as they typically appear at the end of summer as autumn approaches and the nights grow cool. Imoto claims that "In this song, [Miki, the author of the text,] whose mother died when he was only seven years old, sings about his childhood memories and a nostalgia for the past" (1997:32). The lyrics are actually a bit unclear, still we envision a mother, a sister, a nanny, who carried the narrator on her back years ago, but then married and moved away. Over the years the narrator lost contact with her, but the memory of these events is triggered by the sight of the red dragonfly—and in turn prompts longing feelings for all "mothers" in all our childhoods. These lines similarly capture the loss felt when loved ones move away, an increasingly common occurrence in the rapid urbanization of modern Japan in the early twentieth century.

"Akatonbo" is still one of the best-known songs in all of Japan. And despite Wade's claims that *dōyō* are no longer popular amongst children, in Osaka in fall 2014, my son sang this every day at kindergarten. Perhaps the song will become all the more poignant as the population of red dragonflies dwindles. One day, red dragonflies may no longer exist, but "Akatonbo" no doubt will still survive.

"Lied" by Hosokawa Toshio

"Lied," composed by Hosokawa Toshio in 2007, offers a more recent example of how composers, in line with Takemitsu's conceptual approach noted above, have explored expressions of Japaneseness (Track 13). Hosokawa (b. 1955), a prolific and versatile composer of operas, orchestral works and chamber music, studied with Korean composer Yun Isang at the Berlin University of the Arts in 1976, and from 1983 to 1986 with Klaus Huber and Brian Ferneyhough in Freiberg (Wade 2005:158); he has served as composer-in-residence with the Tokyo Symphony Orchestra since 1998. Hosokawa was born in Hiroshima and is now based in Berlin, regularly returning to Japan. He is in fact greatly concerned with Japanese composers' ability to find a new Japanese voice in compositional styles not based purely on the assimilation of Western music that marked the early years of the twentieth century (ibid.). He has composed for Japanese instruments, including those of the *gagaku* orchestra, as well as coaxing the sounds of Japanese instruments from Western counterparts.

According to Galliano,

> . . . it was during his period of study abroad with Isang Yun, namely that he became truly aware of his cultural identity, of his Japanese roots, and of his own oriental approach to life. It was Klaus Huber who encouraged Hosokawa

Making Music in the Modern Era • 115

to study Japanese court music and it was this that led him to reelaborate his complex compositional ideas on a Japanese basis.

(2002:303)

Several compositions from this period, for example, explore the concept of *jo-ha-kyū* (see previous discussion in Chapter 3): "Then in the mid-1980s Hosokawa changed his musical language, as to the structural logic he had learned in Europe he began to apply a concept of sound inspired by Japanese aesthetics" (ibid.:303). He became particularly interested in concepts of time and space, and like Takemitsu, with silence—*ma*—and wide timbres. Galliano feels that "the words *tension* and *spiritual* are key . . . for describing Hosokawa's musical language" (ibid.:305). She continues:

> Hosokawa's deep aesthetic awareness has often led him to compose in such a way that it seems as if his thoughts about the music he is about to write spring from within the birth of the first sound, as if composing were an act of unveiling sound itself.
>
> (ibid.:306)

Hosokawa, like Takemitsu, often analyzes his own compositional inspiration and intentions. He describes his approach to "Lied" in the following:

> I have continued to compose musical works, conceiving of music as a calligraphy of space and time. What I mean here by "calligraphy" is the form of a musical note. You could also call it the shape of a song, the shape of its core melody. The idea that the melodic shape of Eastern music has a calligraphic form was suggested to me by my composition teacher, Isang Yun. Without seizing hold of the melody as a structural element in a combination of several notes, like the brickwork of Western architecture, just one single note is born beyond the space-time of silence, grows like a plant and decays, like the form of an oriental writing brush. The glissando, the various forms of vibrato, the tone color changes often used and seen in the melody of Eastern songs are the means of keeping alive the flow of life of this one single note.
>
> In one stroke of the writing brush appears the breath of life, the power and depth of the person who draws the stroke. It is an expression of the original power of life, and it is proof that the person lives.
>
> Japanese calligraphy places value not only on the subject being drawn but also on the blank space behind it, the power of the places where nothing is drawn. The appearance of the visible brush stroke is improved by means of the blank space in its background where nothing is drawn. In musical terms, the musical note is given greater expressive power by means of the inaudible blank space, or silence.
>
> (Hosokawa n.d.)

The National Flute Association, Inc. commissioned "Lied" in 2007 for use in the semi-finals of their annual Young Artist Contest. Hosokawa explains that the flute is a particularly powerful instrument for expressing the expansiveness he desires in the following:

> The flute is the instrument, which can most deeply realize my musical ideas. The flute can produce a sound by means of the breath, and can be a vehicle by which the breath transmits the sound's life-power.

In Japan from ancient times we have had a tradition of various flutes such as the *ryūteki* of *gagaku, noh* wind instruments, and the bamboo *shakuhachi*. My flute music no doubt is influenced by various forms of this tradition. The breath noise you sometimes hear in it, which sounds just like the wind of the natural world, is a noise that was until the nineteenth century forbidden in Western flute music. In the Japanese tradition, however, this noise is something used positively as a way to approach a more natural breath.

(Ibid.)

Hosokawa further describes this piece specifically as a "'song without words', a prototype for the form of my songs, sung with the flute. The flute can be taken as the prolongation of the voice. The piano symbolizes the universe which spreads out in the background of the song" (ibid.).

The recording included here features Kolbeinn Bjarnason, an accomplished flautist who also studied *shakuhachi*, and thus is capable of bridging the instrumental styles, with members of Caput Ensemble. Hosokawa transforms the Western flute into the *shakuhachi* through sustained, breathy tones, slow and large vibrato, trills, the use of microtones, bends and multiphonic fingering (all described in the key to the score). The piano provides expansive, atonal cushioning—it is indeed the universe spreading in the background—the piano and flute appearing through the fog in the beginning, increasing emotional intensity, peaking, before fading into nothingness together at the end. Hosokawa does not directly invoke elements of traditional Japanese music, but nonetheless captures a conceptual essence of Japanese cultural identity in his work.

Enka, Angura (Underground) and *Aidoru* (Idols)

Enka and Markers of Traditional Japan

Popular musics in the modern era went through a similar process of negotiating Western influences as Japanese struggled to assert a unique voice. One of the most interesting of these, without a doubt, is *enka*. Originally a politically charged song in the Meiji era, *enka* eventually was formalized into a sentimental ballad style, following World War II (Fujie 2002; Yano 2002). *Enka* as we know it today emerged and solidified in response to increasing proliferation of Anglo-American popular music, such as guitar-based rock and folk song (see the previous discussion in Chapter 2). Drawing on pre-war popular song styles, "*Enka* arose in reaction to Japanese pop, and perhaps also as a reaction to the wider Western presence in popular culture, as symbolized not only by the electric guitar but also by fashion such as long hair and miniskirts" (Yano 2002:41; Stevens 2008:45). *Enka* was created to sound Japanese and somehow old, and despite Western stylistic components, came to represent Japanese tradition. *Enka*'s popularity concomitantly would grow amongst an older generation as more musics developed for young people. *Enka* thus met the needs of audiences looking for something Japanese, but not necessarily the traditionalism of actual *hōgaku*.

The Japaneseness of *enka* is created through the use of Japanese-sounding scales, especially the *yonanuki* pentatonic minor introduced above, which produces a particular plaintive quality, melodic style, and vocal ornamentation (*kobushi*), including a characteristic wide vibrato (*yuri*). Although *enka* was initially accompanied by the *shamisen*, Western instrumentation quickly became common—first with the violin, and later the saxophone, trumpet, electric guitar, electric bass, piano—all supporting the vocal melody. Later, *enka* would include simple chordal harmonization, consistent with most popular music in general, with sweeping orchestral accompaniment. Form is typically verse-chorus, with instrumental sections in between the stanzas and to support the voice with a steady beat and gentle rhythm (Fujie 2000:373–374; Yano 2002:42; Stevens 2008:45). Broader aspects of *enka* performance are also characterized by specific markers of Japanese cultural identity, such as wearing *kimono*, moving in particular prescribed ways (*kata*), and the thematic content of the songs (Yano 2002:29–31).

As considered in Chapter 2, *enka* typically expresses themes of "love, loss, and yearning" (ibid.:3), that speak to Japanese people looking for an imagined collective past and connection with the rural identity of the *furusato*; the nostalgia for a country home, inspired by the increased urbanization of the modern era. *Enka* is a "direct," "simple" expression of simpler times in a period of economic, social, and political upheaval (ibid.:6), through which the Japanese consume a glorified past. Lyrics evoke "images of *sake* bars, with the ubiquitous red lantern hanging outside, port towns (the site of many sad farewells), and foggy or rainy, lonely evenings" (Fujie 2000:374). Snow often falls in the *furusato* as well, which is often in the north, cold and somehow depressed (Yano 2002:19–22; Stevens 2008:45).

Yano further describes *enka* as "music to make you cry," which expresses the heart of Japan, but not intended for global consumption. Rather, the Japan of *enka* is "vulnerable"—a "Japan in tears." She elaborates:

> These songs are small performances of the heart meant to play primarily, although not exclusively, to a home audience. Through a wash of tears, *enka* contradicts official international cultural images: not Japan as number one, but Japan as vulnerable to the subtlest affront; not Japan as cute or smiling, but Japan in tears and by its own definition (*nihonjin no kokoro*, "heart/soul of Japanese") at its most Japanese. This construction may be interpreted as a kind of "self-orientalism": Japan exoticized for its own consumption, synopticized in its own stereotype.
>
> (Yano 2002:9)

Japanese people tend to turn to *enka* as they age, while many young people reject the music, themes and broader performative elements as old-fashioned (ibid.:8). Nonetheless, despite low sales and critiques of the type of Japan that is purported in *enka*, it is still predominantly recognized as "symbolic of Japanese cultural identity" (Stevens 2008:46). *Enka*'s ability to express idealized characteristics of an idealized Japan is exemplified through comparison of three current *enka* performers: Ishikawa Sayuri, Hikawa Kiyoshi and Jero.

Ishikawa Sayuri was born in Kumamoto on Kyūshū in 1959 and debuted at the tender age of 14 in 1973. Since then, she has released a hundred albums (including compilations) and 115 singles, and continues to actively record and perform live. She enjoys a beloved place in the imagination of *enka*, having released a song so well-known that a single vocal gesture invokes the entire piece in the minds and hearts of Japanese. She first appeared in 1977 on the annual New Year's broadcast of "The Red and White Song Contest" (*Kōhaku Uta Gassen*) (the New Year's Eve program featuring well-known performers "competing," men against women); in the same year, she released her signature hit song "Tsugarukaikyō-Fuyugeshiki" ("Winter Scenery along the Tsugaru Channel"). This song sold 727,000 units and ranks as the 34th best-selling *enka* single of all time (Nendai-Ryūkō n.d.).

The song opens with a dramatic instrumental section featuring strings, percussion and synthesizer on repetitive chords. A saxophone and then clarinet supply the melody and establish the mood before the vocalist enters (please note that the background instrumentals of *enka* vary with performances, thus these observations are based on the versions I viewed, but was not able to include in the accompanying audio-visual materials). The lyrics express the quintessential ethos of *enka*, which no doubt feeds its long-standing popularity. This song illustrates *mūdo* ("mood) *enka*, a subgenre

> ...concerned with the heartbreak of romance. Often written in the *yonanuki* minor scale to express sadness, these songs tend to be slow, pensive ballads. Singers of *mūdo enka* employ traditional vocal techniques, especially *yuri* and *kobushi*, the vibrato-like ornamentation that can produce an effect much like stylized crying. Women's *mūdo enka* are more common than men's.
> (Yano 2002:43)

The narrator alights from a night train from Tokyo in the snowy cold of Aomori, a hush in the air with the exception of the sound of the ocean in the distance—thus capturing the idea of leaving the urban metropolis and returning home to the *furusato*. The winter imagery continues as she gazes at freezing seagulls and we hear Sayuri cry a sound equivalent to "Oh"– the penultimate vocal gesture in the piece before she sings the hook and title "Tsugarukaikyo-Fuyugeshiki"—as a ferry travels along the Tsugaru channel. As she tries to look through a foggy window, she can see nothing but vague images in the distance. The narrator calls farewell to a lover perhaps, announcing she is going home, and cries with the wind. And the Japanese cry with her, again and again. "Tsugarukaikyo-Fuyugeshiki" is still so popular that she has performed this song eight times out of her 36 appearances on *Kōhaku Uta Gassen*; the most recent in 2013.

But the idea of "popularity" must be put in perspective here. *Enka* sales were never really very high, compared to other popular genres, peaking in the 1970s and 1980s, and they have been seen as in decline since the late 1990s. Japanese people in general are aware of *enka*, but there is concern in the industry about the future health and relevance of the genre. *Enka* received a noticeable lift, however, with the debut of Hikawa Kiyoshi.

Born in 1977 in Fukuoka on Kyūshū, Hikawa Kiyoshi voices many of the characteristics of *enka*. Adoringly referred to as "*Enkakai no Kikōshi*" ("The Prince of Enka") because of his immense popularity and young age, Hikawa discovered the joy of singing—and his particular skills with traditional vocal techniques—while in high school. He traveled to Tokyo to properly train and debuted as an *enka* singer in 2000, receiving the Japan Records Award for Best New Artist that same year.

Hikawa released his first number one hit on the Oricon weekly single chart (equivalent to the Billboard charts) in 2005 and has since released two more number one hits, "making him the first solo *enka* singer to make three number-one singles in Oricon history" (Nippon Columbia 2014). He also won the Grand Prix award, a significant recognition of his talents, at the Japan Record Awards in 2006. His charming style, youthful looks, and powerful vocal abilities bridged the gap between the younger and the more typically mature audiences, reminding Japanese listeners in the 2000s of the continued relevance of *enka*.

Although not one of his number one songs, "Shigin Shunbō—Hakuun no Shiro" ("Recitation of Spring View—Castle of White Clouds") illustrates his style well, while also highlighting one of the other subgenres of *enka*, "real *enka*" (*do-enka*), so named as this is considered the most traditional style. *Do-enka* "songs focus on themes of *giri-ninjō* (duty vs. human feelings), morality, and hardship" (Yano 2002:42–43). They typically employ the *yonanuki* scale, relatively slow tempos and often include

> ... a dramatic spoken *serifu* (recitative) between verses. The singing technique for these songs relies on narrative inflections and extra-musical vocalizations such as grunts and growls ... Men's *do-enka*—songs expressing a male point of view—tend to be more common than women's.
>
> (Ibid.:43)

One can clearly hear the wide vibrato, emotional outpouring and surprising intimacy created through grandness in this piece. "Shigin Shunbō—Hakuun no Shiro" opens with the sound of a thunderstorm, rain beating down, as a *shakuhachi* pierces the air and fades away. This is quickly followed by Hikawa's distinctive voice fabulously reciting the first few lines of the famous Chinese poem "Shigin Shunbō" by Du Fu (again, these observations are based on a specific version). The poem decries the futility of war and ephemeral existence of mankind, while nature is eternal, describing this world as full of dreams, an illusion like a floating cloud. The narrator, looking at the moth-filled stone walls of a long-ago abandoned castle, thinks about an earlier time. The poem establishes the tone of the lyrics of the song "Hakuun no Shiro" ("Castle of White Clouds"), separated by a brief interlude on guitar. The song beautifully expresses the same idea as in the opening narration, as Hikawa evocatively executes the *kobushi*, the vocal ornaments of *enka*, at one point interjecting a *serifu*, the recitative of *do-enka*. He further reflects on the castle that once thrived and teemed with life, which is now dormant and decaying as a result of war; the song builds in emotional intensity, supported by lush instrumental accompaniment on orchestral strings, the acoustic guitar of the opening, flutes and other sound effects.

Hikawa continues to deliver powerful performances as he matures in the music industry. But even though he has toured outside Japan, he has not garnered the international attention of Jero, another recent male *enka* star.

Born Jerome Charles White, Jr. in 1981 in Pittsburgh, Pennsylvania, White is recognized as the first black *enka* singer. He now simply goes by the name "Jero" "a nickname his Japanese friends gave him and which, perhaps by sounding more Japanese, gave him a deeper sense of Japanese-ness" (Fellezs 2012:338). He became interested in *enka* through his Japanese grandmother, who exerted a great influence in his early years. After graduating from the University of Pittsburgh in 2003, he moved to Japan and soon thereafter appeared on the popular song-contest program "Proud of My Voice" (*Nodo Jiman*). He underwent five years of training before releasing his first single "Umiyuki" ("Ocean Snow") in 2008, reaching number four in the Oricon charts. That same year, he won the Japan Records Award for Best New Artist. Since then he has released several more singles and albums and toured internationally (Jero n.d.).

Non-ethnically Japanese singers, including Koreans and Taiwanese, have long performed *enka*; however, Jero's position as a foreigner has drawn particular attention. His heritage allows him to perform *enka* for both Japanese and Japanese-Americans alike, but in turn complicates the reading of *enka* as expressing a uniquely Japanese national sensibility. Fellezs explains:

> Jero actively contests a long history of positioning *enka* as a distinctly Japanese musical idiom by challenging its construction as the sound of a pre-modern,

pre-Western-influenced Japan (despite its blatant use of Western instrumentation and reliance on modern production techniques and technologies). Yet Jero's performative displays of Japanese-ness—his bowing low before elderly Japanese for example—reinforce rather than challenge Japanese cultural norms.
(2012:334)

Jero at once both challenges and affirms conceptions of Japaneseness. But his "polycultural" identity as both Japanese and African-American—as Fellezs comments, his "black body" (ibid.)—expands understandings of Japanese musical identity as located in racial and national identity; that only Japanese can authentically perform *enka* (ibid.). Jero disputes the idea that race is necessary to express Japanese cultural identity, but the irony here is that he relates his Japanese grandmother as the source of inspiration for becoming an *enka* singer, which actually serves as a racial legitimator for him to do so. Whether he intends this or not, his grandmother becomes a marker of his racial authenticity. His Japaneseness is further expressed through his obvious love and respect for Japanese people and culture, which allow his "black body" to perform *enka* for a predominantly middle-aged female audience. And although his body language and emotional expression is all *enka*, we never forget his "black body," his racial distance from Japan (ibid.:338).

Jero's ability to sing Japanese *enka* with a foreign "black body" is illustrated in the official video for "Umiyuki" ("Ocean Snow") (https://www.youtube.com/watch?v=KFdUGs6qIuw), which has a similar feel as "Tsugarukaikyō-Fuyugeshiki." The lyrics are in the tone of *mūdo enka* and seem to be written from the perspective of a female narrator, who, after describing a cold winter scene of snow falling on the ocean near Izumozaki (a town located in Niigata on the west coast of Japan), bemoans her inability to join her lover, and ponders whether it would be better to cast herself into the freezing sea.

The official video for the song brings two worlds together, as Jero appears in a party hip-hop style clothing, complete with two Japanese back-up dancers sporting similar fashion. Other than the costumes and the dance sequences, however, the piece is predominantly performed in a rather standard *enka* style. Fellezs elaborates in the following:

> In truth, little else in the audio track itself signifies blackness or points to Jero's blackness apart from the brief introductory material. His singing is in the traditional male *enka* mode, emotionally charged yet (barely) contained as dictated by the style for male singers [in contrast to the feminine nature of the lyrics]. In addition, his bodily stance and posture throughout the majority of the video for the song assumes the still, resolute body positioning of traditional *enka* male performers, and is meant to convey an emotional control that might only be betrayed by a single tear or by a wide vibrato in the voice. Jero's video, however, cannot help but make visible his black presence and its foreign-ness.
> (2012:339)

Thus "Umiyuki" juxtaposes hip-hop style with its strong association with "blackness" to *enka*'s stereotypical expression of a constructed "Japaneseness." This may actually be a most authentic way for Jero to express his own blended heritage—he is both African-American and Japanese. He claims that the hip-hop references early in his career are true to himself, while wearing *kimono* for example, like so many Japanese male *enka* singers, would be odd, even a parody of *enka* (Japan Society New York 2012). Rather, Jero does not want to re-invent *enka*, but wants to express his own unique identity through *enka*. But this is complicated by the expectation of *enka* to express a stereotyped idea of homogenous Japan that does not allow for racial diversity. Jero's performances, however, may in fact be challenging those very assumptions, in turn expanding ideas of Japanese racial identity. Enka nevertheless continues to represent the ways in which Japanese construct a unique cultural identity *vis-à-vis* the West in a well-known popular music, steeped with markers of traditional Japan (even if constructed).

Language, Technology and the Angura (Underground)

There are, of course, numerous genres of music that exist beneath the glossy and stylized world of mainstream Japan, existing both literally and figuratively underground (*angura*). I use "underground" to refer to both the physical spaces where such music is performed, in the livehouses (*raibuhausu*) often buried deep below the streets in the basements of buildings, and the production and circulation of recordings and other marketing materials through independent labels or "indies" (*indīzu*) (Milioto Matsue 2008a and 2008b). *Angura*, as an extremely broad category here, traces its history back to the birth of independent and rebellious music making that emerged in Japan in the late 1970s (Hosokawa 1994:17; see previous discussion in Chapter 2). And more recent underground music making also reveals ideas of Japaneseness, particularly through play with language (meaning the choice for lyrics and similar modes of expression), as well as the complicated relationship the Japanese have with the technology of modernity.

As Japanese people imported popular musics from the West, decisions were constantly being made as to which language to perform them in: the original "foreign" language, even if incomprehensible and not understood by the new Japanese audience; or in Japanese, which may not fit either sonically nor ideologically with the musical fabric. This concern inspired much debate amongst Japanese musicians throughout the twentieth century.

The importance of language as a marker of shifting cultural identity is well-illustrated in the much-discussed work of the Japanese rock band "Happy End," who successfully melded the rock aesthetic to Japanese language. Hosokawa explains:

> The rock of the early seventies was divided mainly into two opposing camps. The hard-rock school (sometimes called the English-language faction, since they sang mainly in English) was thought to be the first to establish itself musically. The folk-rock school, consisting of composers who wanted to sing their own words to a rock beat, sang exclusively in Japanese.
>
> (1994:5)

The general belief was that English was better suited to the rebellious rock aesthetic, while Japanese was of course necessary to convey the meaning of folk songs. Drawing on Hosokawa, Bourdaghs argues the group "Happy End" successfully "linked rock music melodies to the rhythms of spoken Japanese" (2012:164) and paved the way for future syncretizations. Stevens adds, "Their self-titled debut album represents a sophisticated assimilation of Western rock with Japanese sentiment and cultural symbolism" that extends beyond language alone" (2008:46). "Haru Yo Koi" ("Come, Spring!"), for example

> ... melds the two cultural sources into a hybrid piece. The instrumentation is pure bluesy folk-rock, à la Crosby, Stills, Nash and Young. The title is a classic Japanese phrase, and the lyrics tell of a young man's loneliness during the New Year holiday, the most important event in the Japanese ritual calendar. As he hears the temple bell ring (and we do as well, in the background), his thoughts stray to his family, celebrating without him.
>
> (Ibid.:46)

In this way, Happy End "intellectualized expressions of urban angst and alienation" in their lyrics at a time when other genres, including *enka*, were re-visioning a romantic past rather than commenting on and connecting with current social ills (Bourdaghs 2012:169).

Bourdaghs argues these "gesture[s] can be read as a form of resistance to U.S. cultural hegemony—and yet this resistance was couched in the genre of rock music, a genre generally identified as arising out of American culture" (ibid.:164).

The group released three albums, all containing original songs (also unusual at the time) in Japanese. Singing in Japanese thus can be perceived as a way to return to Japan—as a clear marker of Japanese cultural identity. Ultimately, they did not fit in either the United States or Japan, but successfully sidestepped boundaries by singing American music in the Japanese language (ibid.:169).

Artists and audiences have continued to explore which languages are best to use to create an authentic Japanese expression. There are times when the sound alone takes precedence and meaning is much less significant, if necessary at all. After World War II, Japanese musicians sang country music in English, without really understanding the lyrics, rather memorizing and mimicking them, with the simple and short texts of many country songs facilitating this process (Mitsui 1993; Furmanovsky 2008). There are also cases when lyrics in a foreign language become a timbral inflection. To lose the quality of that specific language would affect the overall characteristic instrumentation. Such is arguably the case with the use of Spanish by the highly successful Japanese salsa band Orquesta de la Luz. As noted in Chapter 2, they regularly recorded and performed in Spanish, nevertheless creating lyrics that spoke to Japanese audiences, for example, about food (Hosokawa 1999). To sing in Japanese, although perhaps allowing the lyrics to reach a greater Japanese audience, would ultimately have changed the Latin character of their music.

In other cases, the ability to convey meaning in a native language, such as with the popular folk music of the 1960s and 1970s, is paramount. This need similarly informed the adaptation of hip-hop into Japan, as artists developed ways to maintain the potency of the genre by commenting on troubling social issues, but localized to the immediate context of Japan. Drawing on Condry (2000 and 2006), Wade notes:

> Texts comment on the problems of Japanese culture—the stress on seniority, for instance, worrying over the effects of the worst economic situation Japan has experienced since World War II with their fathers out of work and themselves unable to find a job, commenting on the problems of contemporary life.
>
> (2005:141)

Japanese rappers went through a similar process with hip-hop as earlier Japanese musicians had done with jazz, experimenting with so-called "authenticating" strategies in order to express a unique identity. While larger performative elements were certainly part of this process, the language of rap was a particularly contentious point. And rappers experimented with the language to deliver these messages—English, to maintain the "authentic sound" of the original; Japanese, which was particularly problematic as it does not easily rhyme, or finally, modifying Japanese to convey meaning but function aesthetically (Condry:2000), much like Happy End's work in rock.

Groups in the underground continue to explore which language best conveys both individual and broader understandings of identity, even opting to not use any at all. In the late 1990s, for example, I found that musicians in the underground hardcore rock scene of western Tokyo (see Figure 4.3) continued to consciously engage in debates about the language in lyrics Milioto Matsue 2008a and 2008b). The majority of bands in this scene sang in garbled "*Japanglish*"—a unique Japanized English—that distanced this musical practice from mainstream Japanese popular music, which is dominated by Japanese lyrics. In this way, cultural identity *within* Japan—here between the mainstream and the underground—is marked by language as well. The all-male band Sports, however, who self-identified as a specific subgenre of hardcore known as "emo-core" (an "emotional" style), sang in Japanese, claiming a particular need to convey a message to their audience, even if obfuscated through the screaming style that characterized their performance. At the other extreme, the female-fronted group the Berotecs, introduced in Chapter 2, captured the creative freedom possible by singing minimalist English lyrics, for example, with the song "Go To Garage," in which the vocalist screams those three simple words over and over to great effect. In this case, vocalizing in a foreign language allowed greater freedom to explore sound.

The group Demi Semi Quaver plays with musical possibilities in similar ways, but uses the voice as an instrument, with no lyrics in any *real* language. I first encountered

Figure 4.3 Hardcore band Jug

Demi Semi Quaver in the late 1990s, but they are still active in diverse artistic endeavors, such as in fashion, as writers, and performing in other bands, and they still play live together once or twice a year. Demi Semi Quaver move one step beyond the Berotecs, who used minimalist English essentially as a vocable, by actually employing vocables to make their own language: "*Emi-go*" (literally "Emi language"), named after the lead singer Eleonola Emi. According to Eleonola, she has been experimenting with *Emi-go* since she was two, humming and singing along with the piano. She does sing in English and Japanese, but Eleonola also brought *Emi-go* to Demi Semi Quaver (e-mail correspondence, October 11, 2014).

In past interviews, she has explained that she wanted her voice to be perceived as an instrument, and Demi Semi Quaver's music therefore instrumental music (*kigaku*). But at the same time, she feels that all the instrumentalists in Demi Semi Quaver perform like vocalists (in the way they create melody or "sing" with their instruments). Singing in an actual language would actually inhibit the ability of the instruments (including voice) to convey the group's real message. She therefore sings freely, as if playing an instrument, but includes the lyrics to their songs in the liner notes to the recordings. However, she really doesn't think about the lyrics in terms of meaning when performing, instead concentrating on the sound. Interestingly, she is not improvising, as she sets the *Emi-go* for each song and does not stray once fixed. When asked why she does this, she explains "it is like writing the melody for an instrument, there is something poetic about the way the syllables come together," although she only came to understand this ideological and aesthetic approach to making music later in her career. When Demi Semi Quaver first debuted, she employed *Emi-go* rather naturally, without a lot of thought. The leader Yokoyama Hidenori found it most powerful and encouraged her to continue with this distinctive vocal style (e-mail correspondence, October 11, 2014).

Producer Kamiyama "Hoppy" feels that there are a number of bands that don't use real language, or artists that use vocables, and what he calls "voice performers":

> The language that emerges naturally from one's body without thinking, one's internal spirit is stronger and there is greater impact than if singing meaningful lyrics. The use of made-up language is essential for free expression and improvisation, and it widens the freedom of musicality. The expression, which is not restricted to the lyrics and breadth of the image—Emi Eleonola's vocal style in this way pours forth like water from a spring.
> (E-mail correspondence with Kamiyama, October 8, 2014)

This use of *Emi-go* is well-demonstrated in "Love Maniac" (Track 14) produced by Kamiyama and released in 1994 featuring Eleonola Emi on vocals and accordion, Yokoyama Hidenori on bass, Terashi Toru on guitar, Naka Koichiro on drums, Eto Steve on percussion and metals, and Kuwajima Genya on keyboards:

> The song came together as improvisation in the studio. At one point during a break, Kamiyama encouraged [Eleonola] to say something in *Emi-go*, at which point she repeated '*iridīan*' five times, which really pops in the recording, even if it doesn't mean anything. The song reflects the member's talents and Kamiyama's vision.
> (E-mail correspondence with Eleonola Emi, October 11, 2014)

The lyrics are included below, but again Eleonola does not actually sing them in the recording.

"Love Maniac"

セ．ク．ス　セ．　　セクス．ス．セ．
「マニア　ハ　途中デ　死ニハシナイ」
se. ku. su se. sekusu. su. se. (vocables)
Maniacs won't die in the middle

クス．クス．セ．ク．ス．　ク．セス．♥
トケル　ソビエタツ　見タクナル
kusu. kusu. se. ku. su. ku. sesu. ♥
melt, loom, desire to see

「とびきり見たくなる　その箱の中です」
"Desire to see very much inside that box"

SAY OPEN SESAMI　　　さあ　開いて！
Say "Open Sesami!"　　Go ahead and open!

マニアは信じられる
マニアは　夜になっても眠らない
マニアは　スターエッセンス　飲み込んで
自動的な　夢を画面に映し出す
スターシロップ　最初から最後まで　なめて　恋をする
Maniacs are believable
Maniacs won't sleep at night
Maniacs drink the essence of stars
Showing automatic dreams on a display
Star syrup, from beginning to the end, lick and falling in love

クス．クス．セクス．クス．セ．ク．ク．ス
kusu. kusu. sekusu. kusu. se. ku. ku. su

「マニアは途中で死にはしない」
Maniacs won't die in the middle

Although Kamiyama rightly notes that vocables are a part of much popular and world music, and of course jazz in the form of scat singing, there is something very Japanese about *Emi-go*. This is especially true when heard in conjunction with pieces such as Endo's "Yobikake" (Track 11), which highlights the fantastic vocal calls of the *noh-hayashi*, as well as the ability to make the most with minimal materials that characterizes much Japanese traditional music. Eleonola might not draw such a connection herself, and some may argue that *Emi-go* connects more with global popular music practices than Japanese. But I still contend that these sounds take on unique meaning in the local context.

Kamiyama also produced another important underground band from the 1990s, Kirihito, who, like Demi Semi Quaver, are still active today. Kirihito, a duo from Tokyo featuring Hayakawa Shunsuke on percussion and Takehisa Ken on guitar and keyboard, however, often forgo the use of vocals at all. They do sing, but vocal melodies and the associated lyrics are not the primary focus of this group. Rather Hayakawa's driving, pounding, exuberant drumming and Takehisa's distorted guitar take center stage. Indeed, vocals may obscure the real stars here. "Sai-bo" (Website Example 12) from 2009, Kirihito's first release in nine years, illustrates their instrumental focus. Takehisa does call out "Sai-bo," processed even when live, but the line does not easily translate to English, and in fact seems to once again only expand the instrumental tapestry, rather than serving as a vocal conveying any meaning. Hayakawa's precise drumming dominates the recording. It is, however, difficult to assess how this song expresses Japaneseness based on sound alone; the mixture of styles may represent contemporary hybridization, but then again, this now is so common globally that the process here may have more to do with global flows than local practices.

The song does sound vaguely reminiscent of early electronic music by Japanese pioneers Yellow Magic Orchestra (YMO) (see previous discussion in Chapter 2). Hayakawa became interested in electronica when he broke his arm and could not play his regular drums, instead turning to an electric drum pad (Anon. 2009). The emphasis on sound, particularly as the piece progresses from 3:00 with the inclusion of an excruciatingly high pitch, and again from 4:00 with additional sound effects and Hayakawa's fantastic drumming taking us home, may connect with Japanese aesthetic ideas—to the Japanese appreciation for a breadth of timbre, even pitch-bending—but again, it may not. And it is highly unlikely these musicians would draw such conclusions themselves.

An argument could also be made for Japaneseness in the play with technology, a theme not covered to this point, but a major component of Japanese cultural identity in other realms of popular culture—such as *anime* and *manga*. As noted in Chapter 1, the Japanese have a complicated relationship with technology, as massive consumers of the latest technological gadgets but also uniquely wary of the dangers of technology as the only country devastated by nuclear weaponry, reinforced by the 2011 post-tsunami Fukushima nuclear reactor meltdown. The official video for the song, created by Mizuhiro Savini and included here, features not Kirihito, at least not directly, but rather bright graphics at play with technology—a throwback to the emergence of early video games, 1970s disco, or a bad acid trip. Hayakawa and Takehisa are seen as colorful silhouettes, at times resembling the pink elephants on parade from Walt Disney's *Dumbo* (1941). The overall effect is frenzied.

Where Kirihito's controlled craziness remains positive and upbeat, taking the listener along for the ride, the genres of noise (*noizu*) and *onkyō* employ a similar play with technology, but are arguably combative, challenging conceptions of music itself in the process.

Drawing on Novak (2006), Plourde defines noise as "a genre in which sound is produced through the extreme distortion, manipulation, and often deliberate misuse of technology, including guitar pedals, microphones and, more recently, laptop computers" (2008:276). First appearing in the 1970s, noise became increasingly recognized as a genre in the 1980s:

> ... a period when avant-garde music and art flourished in Japan's thriving bubble economy. During the 1990s, Japanese experimental music more generally,

including noise music, was circulated and consumed on a transnational level throughout the US and Europe"

(ibid.:276)

Thus noise became an important sound of Japan within broader global markets (Wade 2005:154). But this sound, produced through the distortion of feedback loops, is not easily definable as *music*.

The qualities of noise, nonetheless, necessitate intensive listening—this is not music one puts on in the background while cleaning the house or running errands in the car. Noise certainly challenges traditional ideas of music, and in this way arguably illustrates the Japanese characteristic appreciation for a breadth of sound—both natural and technological. Novak in fact argues noise is perceived as a genre of music in part because of the use of equipment associated with live music, such as pedals and turntables, and even more importantly in the way it is circulated as a recording and in livehouses, but not as a result of some identifiable shared sonic qualities (2013).

There is no single sound of noise; nevertheless, its general qualities are illustrated in the work "Woodpecker No. 1," released in 1995 by famed performer Merzbow (aka Akita Masami) (Track 15). According to Novak, Akita, a true renaissance man involved in a range of art forms in contemporary Japan, began producing noise in the 1970s and has released over three hundred recordings since. His name has become synonymous with the noise genre, even as he personally rejects the generic label (2013:132–136). In interviews with Novak, Akita explained his view of noise "as a project that could help unravel the social effects of Japanese consumerism . . . Merzbow became Akita's way of making audible these excesses of Japan's self-destructive capitalism" (ibid.:192). Noise, he told Novak, "could sound out the frozen modern landscape of Japanese consumption" (ibid.). For Novak, Merzbow therefore embodies "creative destruction" (ibid.:194) clearly audible in "Woodpecker No. 1."

Although this example may at first sound completely random (and to be sure, the technologies employed in the production of noise produce unpredictable sounds), with deep listening, one may begin to hear this "creative destruction." There is a conscious breakdown of traditional conceptions of music and simultaneous commentary on the destructive potential of technology, both of which feel very Japanese in character.

Connections to Japanese musical ideas and broader philosophies may be more immediate in *onkyō*, a genre of performance that emerged in the mid- to late 1990s, and became closely associated with one particular performance space in Tokyo, Off Site, before it closed in 2005. Plourde describes *onkyō* as

> . . . an extremely minimal, improvisatory musical style and performance approach that pays particular attention to sound texture, gaps, and silences. One of *onkyō*'s most distinctive characteristics is its seemingly utter lack of any discernible musical structure—rhythmic, harmonic, or otherwise—which is often performed at barely audible levels.
>
> (2008: 270)

Even more so than noise, this is a "style in which the primary emphasis has shifted from producing and performing sound, to that of concentrated and attentive listening" (ibid.:273), which is exacerbated by the need to strain to hear the incredibly low volume of the sounds of *onkyō*. While noise is cacophony and chaos, *onkyō* is introspection and space. Plourde explains "In noisemusic the listener is assaulted by excessive volume, while in *onkyō*, which draws on often barely audible sounds and silences between them, the listener is assaulted by the virtual absence of sound" (ibid.:277), which requires tremendous concentration.

Plourde draws connections with the early twentieth-century Western avant-garde's exploration of modernism, technology and sound to understand the aesthetic philosophy behind the at times painful listening experience; nevertheless, can we find connections with Japanese aesthetic philosophies as well? Ideas of *ma*, for example, permeate both genres, but are perhaps most obvious in *onkyō*, which draws the listener into the moments of silence, until the next electric jolt snaps them back to attention:

> The audience member becomes aware of his/her own body and the demands placed on it. Listeners are expected to concentrate and listen carefully to the performance as well as the outside sounds, yet they themselves must not outwardly react to the music to the point that they give up any self-control. The atmosphere and subtleties of the performance become oppressive to the point that it produces a heightened awareness of space and the sensation of time.
>
> (Ibid.:286)

Thus Tokyo's urban soundscape invades the space of Off Site, just as the sounds of Brooklyn invaded the *shakuhachi* performance of "Choshi," described in Chapter 3. And perhaps the chaos of noise represents the most extreme heterophony. Both genres are an "aural assault," although they ask different things of the audience.

We want to be careful here, however, in looking for expressions of Japaneseness, not to force intersections where none may exist between traditional and popular music. And it is highly unlikely these performers of noise or *onkyō* sit around discussing their intended use of *ma* while having drinks. But that does not mean they have not absorbed some of these ideas through passive listening, nor that we cannot hypothesize about such potential understandings. The point in referencing elements of traditional Japanese music is by no means an attempt to "legitimate" other musical expressions, whether popular or not. Rather, the purpose here is to challenge the reader to reflect on such possible connections to further our exploration of how Japan *sounds* in all these examples. Ideas of Japaneseness may of course be expressed in elements completely unrelated to sound as well.

Both noise and *onkyō*, for example, mirror Japan's complicated negotiation with modern technologies, revealing a deep respect for the power of technology, but also an innate awareness of its destructive potential. Novak beautifully summarizes the dilemma:

> ... electronic feedback embodies a human-machine relationship that is uncertain, excessive, and out of control. Noisicians forced their listeners to witness the technological overload of individual consciousness in consumer societies. The millennial narratives of Japanoise [Novak's way of locating noise in Japan] extended the aesthetic modernisms of futurism and surrealism to the symbolic power of 1980s industrial music and post apocalyptic *anime*. This technocultural critique fused noise to Japanese culture through a global imaginary in which postwar Japan has become iconic of the destructive impact of modern technologies.
>
> (2013:23)

Noise, by distorting and destroying the very technology that allows its creation, serves as a critique of the identification of Japan as a "technoculture" (ibid.:173), feelings that only increased in the post-bubble recession, as Japanese became increasingly disillusioned, individually oriented and skeptical of technology (ibid.:89):

> Japanoise tells a John Henry story. Like that tale of a man bound in a fatal contest with a machine, it relates a moral narrative of crisis, in which modern industry endlessly triumphs over the individual subject. Humanity is thrown under the bullet train of technology; the man becomes a man-machine and dies with his hammer in his hand. By acting out this failure over and over again, Noisicians expose the ruse that technology can free humanity. Instead, they show how a mechanical society feeds human energy back into the machine and measure just how deeply creative subjectivity has become embedded in this cycle.
>
> (Ibid.:197)

Noise ironically uses technology to remind us all, perhaps especially the Japanese, of our humanity. However, the Japanese engagement with technology through popular music is not always antagonistic, as is the case of worldwide virtual idol star Hatsune Miku, who exists *as* technology.

Intertextuality and Japanese Aidoru *(Idols)*

On October 8, 2014, Hatsune Miku made her television debut on *The Late Show with David Letterman*, a well-known American evening talk show. The screen went dark, with

Figure 4.4 Hatsune Miku (Illustration by KEI (C) Crypton Future Media, INC. www.piapro.net)

only a soft light illuminating her back-up band of guitar, bass, drums and keyboard. The center of the stage remained dark until Hatsune Miku, in her jazzed-up schoolgirl uniform and nearly floor-length turquoise pigtails suddenly appeared in a burst of radiant blue flame. She sang "Sharing the World," an energetic pop song with a good dance beat, swishing her hips, tapping her foot, gesturing to the audience, and midway through the song twirling amidst multi-colored bursts of swirling light. David Letterman appears on stage as the song comes to a close and Hatsune Miku bows and waves, vaporizing before our eyes. He quickly quips "Like being on Willy Nelson's Bus," likening Hatsune Miku's performance to a marijuana-induced hallucination.

No performer captures the modern if not post-modern ethos of contemporary Japan than Hatsune Miku (see Figure 4.4). She sits firmly at the forefront of hundreds of years of music history, embracing everything from the wide timbral possibilities of traditional music in her synthesized voice, to the fascination with technology we've seen in the preceding discussion of *angura*. She is the most popular Japanese performer ever, releasing over a hundred thousand recordings, including the song "World is Mine," which reached number 7 on the US iTunes charts, and opening for Lady Gaga's 2014 spring tour. These accomplishments are all the more amazing when one remembers that she does not even exist. Hatsune Miku is actually a type of vocal synthesizer software developed by Crypton Future Media, Inc. using "Vocaloid" technology produced by the Yamaha Corporation. Other vocal synthesizer softwares had come before, but none have enjoyed the same success as Hatsune Miku.

Based on samples of Japanese voice actress Saki Fujita, Hatsune Miku, or simply "Miku," is the personification of Crypton's Vocaloid 2 (Japanese) and Vocaloid 3 (Japanese and English) software, initially depicted on the product packaging in the style of a *manga* character that continues to resonate with fans today. According to Hiroyuki Itoh, CEO of Crypton, fans actually use Miku as a "collaborative hub" for their creativity (Condry 2009, 2011 and 2013), resulting in the copious amounts of songs and video posted on "Piapro" (http://piapro.jp/), a website Crypton developed precisely to allow the creative chain of shared work to continue to flourish (Itoh 2013). It was her ever-increasing popularity and global presence that inspired Crypton to project her image as a 3D-holographic "live" in concert, and as seen on David Letterman.

But despite her global presence, Miku still remains uniquely Japanese, resulting primarily from the ways in which she exemplifies how idols (*aidoru*) function as intertextual media within Japanese popular culture. *Aidoru* developed as a term in the 1960s, referring to young performers who sing, dance, pose for photographs and appear in diverse media (Galbraith and Karlin 2012). As noted in Chapter 2, idols boomed in the 1970s and 1980s as Japan enjoyed unprecedented economic prosperity, then suffered briefly in the 1990s in the aftermath of the bubble bursting, but soon surged once again; today, they dominate not just popular music, but the popular culture industry as a whole in Japan. Managed by agencies known as *jimusho* who control all creative output and collect the majority of profits (Marx 2012), female idols appear as soloists, groups, or even huge teams, such as the extremely successful girl-group AKB48 comprising more than sixty girls, while male idols are dominated by one agency, Johnny's, and almost always appear as part of a group, such as SMAP or Arashi (Darling-Wolf 2004; Nagaike 2012).

Galbraith and Karlin argue that although idols are an important category in the contemporary production of popular music, they are often dismissed because of a noticeable lack of musical talent, and inability to translate to outside Japan, given the intensive intertextual construction of idol identity. Idols, whose primary purpose is to sell products, appear on television on variety shows, in dramas, and on commercials, as well as in print media through magazine spreads, advertisements, and news coverage. Idols thus do not exist in one frame only, as a singer *or* actor *or* television personality; instead, an idol's identity is constructed simultaneously through appearances in all these mediums. Within these distinct platforms, idols may appear in both fictional and non-fictional contexts, confusing their existence as real or fictional characters. They may appear on one show to promote another program or a product, and often make references to a past only known by Japanese viewers, once again using nostalgia, in Japanese fashion, to captivate and connect with an audience. This complex intertextuality of the Japanese media system makes it difficult for idols to translate cross-culturally (2012:12). Galbraith and Karlin further explain:

> With their cross-platform media ubiquity, an idol group like AKB48 or Arashi is integrated into everyday life in Japan today. On a morning "wide show," a news report discusses Arashi's recent concert. Billboards in train stations feature the members of AKB48 in advertisements for everything from computers to coffee. The magazine racks of convenience stores and kiosks are crowded with magazines featuring members of these groups on their covers. On the subway, a hanging advertisement for a tabloid magazine features gossip about the groups' members. On television, they star in dramas, host variety shows, and appear in commercials. Altogether, with no effort or intention, one might easily encounter countless images of AKB48 or Arashi in the course of a day. The frequency with which they and other idols and celebrities present themselves within Japan's media-saturated culture makes them not only identifiable but familiar. In the daily routine of life in contemporary Japan, one might have more contact with a particular idol or celebrity than with one's own family.
>
> (Ibid.:9)

This creates a particularly intimate relationship with Japanese audiences, but alienates others:

> Without the intertextual knowledge that comes from a shared understanding of the cultural codes that circulate across media forms within Japan, the idol is reduced merely to his or her ability as a singer, dancer, or actor, which is limited. As a result, Japanese popular culture does not translate well cross-culturally, since its forms are over-determined by the self-referential structures of the domestic media landscape.
>
> (Ibid.:2)

The play between real and imagined persona by idols—between the public and private—may be possible because of the ideologies of *tatemae* and *honne*, a pervasive understanding in Japanese culture where one assumes a public persona or front (*tatemae*), while maintaining a private version of one's self for family and close friends (*honne*). The Japanese therefore may be quite accepting of the idol system, grounded in a constructed identity, but which is so often critiqued by outsiders. Idols as intertextual images—fictional characters—may not even require a human body to exist, as in the case of the virtual idol, Eguchi Aimi, who was fashioned from features of members of AKB48 and appeared in a commercial in 2011 alongside her human colleagues (Galbraith 2012:193).

Her fans consumed Eguchi Aimi as an image, with no consideration of her talents as a singer. And to be sure, the music of idols is rarely if ever discussed in academic or popular literature beyond a passing comment on a hit song's album cover and lyrics; this is a result no doubt of the general perception that idols are invented characters whose primary purpose is to market goods and be marketed themselves, rather than singers. In fact, a successful idol typically cannot possess any great talent for singing as this may actually undermine one's ability to remain accessible to fans. Idols therefore cannot be too talented nor too attractive, as this may distance them; while lacking certain attributes or skills in turn rallies fans behind a particular idol, encouraging him or her to succeed (ibid.:192). Thus the music of idols, albeit catchy, is not the primary source of their immense popularity.

Nonetheless, despite the emphasis on intertextual identity, idols are still expected to release songs and sell CDs. And while other music industries around the world are suffering from low sales, Japan is actually in an upswing. Galbraith and Karlin explain idol groups such as AKB48 and Arashi are remarkably successful at selling recordings because of the intimate relationship they build with their fans. In the case of AKB48, fans are given opportunities to meet their favorite members, but only if one first purchases a CD to gain access. Fans were also able to vote for favorite members, but had to purchase a CD to acquire vouchers to do so. Thus some bought the same CD multiple times to sway the vote, causing dissension amongst fan groups, and pushing up sales. Such marketing strategies for AKB48, even if coming under increasing criticism, are nothing short of brilliant, as the fans actively participate in supporting favorite performers, thus feeling involved and intimately connected, while the management agency and record company clean up on CD sales and related goods (Galbraith and Karlin 2012:20–23). These groups have become so popular that when AKB48 member Iwasa Misaki released the *enka* song "Tomo no Ura Bojō" ("Tomo no Ura Love") in January 2014, it debuted at number one on the Oricon charts, the first time for an *enka* song to attain such success in over four years.

Hatsune Miku is similarly an extremely adept idol (Milioto Matsue (forthcoming)). She *is* intertextual media, but unlike the human idols of Japan who are unable to succeed in cross-cultural contexts, she is immensely popular globally. She easily moves between fan-produced videos and professionally organized live performances, appearing on the computer screen of a teenage boy in Tokyo as easily as going on tour with Lady Gaga and television with David Letterman in the United States. Hatsune Miku's lack of any body of course facilitates her ability to smoothly work in intertextual media. She has no personality to interfere with fan desires, and thus anyone can generate whatever traits they want, controlling her every move, and creating a tremendous sense of intimacy with her image. Human idols must hide their personal lives from fans to maintain the illusion of their fantasy persona—they must separate the *honne* from the *tatemae*—but Hatsune Miku cannot cause trouble and draw negative media attention to her—there is no *honne*.

As with other idols, musicianship seems secondary and in reality, her popularity is grounded in the fact that anyone, even without any musical training, can create songs and express himself or herself through her persona, generating the creative collaboration celebrated by Crypton. And as a result, fans eagerly consume not only the primary software package, but also additional add-ons, as well as all the goods created with her image, which has appeared on everything from dolls to racecars. So not only does she market other goods, but she herself is marketed brilliantly by Crypton.

Hatsune Miku thus is without place, completely global, connecting a cyber-world with vanishing geographical, ethnic and national boundaries, yet she somehow still feels entirely "Japanese," and not just because she is rendered with wide *anime* eyes. She resembles the dolls of *bunraku*; "Writing for Vocaloid Software is a bit like pulling strings of a puppet. Miku does what a composer wants, albeit a little jerkily," observes Rao (2014). She was born in Japan, but also connects to something beyond the borders of the country. With idol culture, therefore, we may have a uniquely Japanese expression, no longer in contention with Western ideologies and musical sounds. Thus we find the Japanese popular industry is no longer looking to the West to speak the language of popular music, but instead is speaking fluently in Japanese. The following section explores in more detail how this influx of Western popular music in particular impacted Japanese traditional music.

Taiko and the *Hōgaku Nyū Wēbu* (New Wave)

> Many Japanese musicians have experimented with new forms of expression while playing traditional Japanese instruments, in addition to performing classic pieces. Until [the] 1990s, much of this activity was centered on contemporary music as an extension of Western classical music ... This situation, however, has changed over the last 15 years. The classics and contemporary music, of course, still exist, but in addition to these genres, musicians have drawn on their favorite grammars—pop, rock, jazz, folk music, etc.—to create music that transcends boundaries and borders ... The accomplishments of young musicians not constrained by the exclusive institutions of traditional music as well as the current ethos geared to reinventing Japan have underpinned this movement. The current era bridges two centuries.
>
> (Tanaka et al. 2005:4)

Contemporary works that combine traditional instruments and musical elements with popular styles are informed by both a similar synthesis of Japanese and Western sources in art musics and the overwhelming presence of both Japanese and Western-produced popular musics in Japan. The Ministry of Education, Culture, Sports, Science and Technology mandate requiring Japanese instruments be added to the music curriculum perhaps will further inspire even more hybrid styles to emerge in the coming years. New terms already have appeared to grapple with such ever-evolving trends—such as *"hōgaku nyū wēbu"* ("new wave")—coined by the music industry in the late 1990s to label "new traditional" musics, even though the term has not caught on in general discourse.

Nonetheless, the adaptation of Lady Gaga's "Telephone ft. Beyoncé" for *shakuhachi* and *koto* that opens this chapter is one example of this "new tradition," as are the globally recognized hybrid forms that have developed with Okinawan *sanshin* and *tsugaru-jamisen*. Tanaka suggests the quality of the music of the *sanshin* and *tsugaru-jamisen* in their respective traditional contexts has actually fostered interesting syncretizations with popular music:

> Okinawa *sanshin* and *tsugaru-jamisen* are both rooted in folk songs, so they have a good groove and the flexibility to incorporate just about any type of music. In that respect, they have a slightly different character than other instruments based in traditional music.
>
> (Ibid.:5)

The ability to fuse well with new popular styles fed the Okinawan boom of the 1970s, launched by performers such as Kina Shokichi, and the more recent success of *tsugaru-jamisen* performers Agatsuma Hiromitsu and the Yoshida Brothers (an actual pair of brothers: Yoshida Ryōichirō and Yoshida Kenji).

Successful hybrids tend to feature performers with great skill in the original *hōgaku* or *min'yō* genre. For example, in 1990, Ishikura Kōzan of Team Kozan was the youngest ever to receive his grandmaster license in the Tozan school of *shakuhachi*, a demonstration of his exceptional talent and dedication. Agatsuma Hiromitsu and the Yoshida Brothers are also award-winning musicians in *tsugaru-jamisen*, respected for their musicianship, but also for their ability to bring a new younger audience to these "older" styles. They do so both through their musical choices, which blend traditional techniques with synthesized grooves and rock rhythms, to their costuming; men's formal pants (*hakama*) and spiky red hair in the case of the Yoshida brothers (Domo Music Group. n.d.; Peluse 2005; Hughes 2008:280–282). The *tsugaru-jamisen*'s flexibility, especially its ability to function in the same way as a lead guitar, makes it particularly adaptable in these types of fusions (Hughes 2008:281).

Peluse states that these performers

> . . . freely [mix] old and new sounds on their records. Yet they have not turned their backs on the past, and it is possible that if they did, they would not be considered *tsugaru[-j]amisen* musicians at all. If they experiment too much, they risk losing their older audience, but if they are not "pop" enough they also risk losing younger fans. They must maintain a balance between inventiveness and tradition to keep their core audience and to continue to gain new admirers.
> (2005:69)

They are very aware of how they package themselves to reach these audience members, combining traditional iconography with snappy cool hairstyles, staging, or clothing (ibid.:71). They seem to know how far they can push the limits while generating fans, in turn changing audience expectations about folk music (ibid.:72–73). And in doing so, they have successfully melded folk and popular idioms, in turn launching a new "*hōgaku* boom," as described by Tanaka above, where artists with serious skills as traditional and folk musicians play in new styles. Such fusions do risk becoming bland, however, lacking any cultural identity and with no personality; it is much more difficult to effectively merge such grammars than one might first imagine.

Nonetheless, this movement between traditional, folk and popular styles of course results in the hybridization that defines Japanese culture, especially where "popular" is often still read as "foreign." Peluse goes so far as to argue this type of *tsugaru-jamisen* actually "defies classification; indeed a strict designation is not appropriate, for such a definition would undoubtedly ignore either the music's folk heritage or its pop traits" (ibid.:59). Peluse clearly reveals the existence of musical practices that flow between the genres of folk, traditional and popular to the degree that they actually resist modes of classification at all, and would in fact be limited if forced into categories. He introduces *taiko* (here referring to modern ensemble drumming as a genre) as a similar hybrid form of music that "remains in an ambiguous position" in contemporary Japan (ibid.:76). But unlike *tsugaru-jamisen*, where performers had to prove themselves first within a specific performance tradition, *taiko* is not grounded in any single well-defined musical style.

Up to this point, percussion has remained largely in the background, providing the rhythmic framework and propelling numerous musics forward, with the notable exception of examples featuring Kenny Endo, Kaoru Watanabe and Kirihito. Clearly, in the modern era, percussion moves to the front of the stage. Japanese ensemble drumming is commonly referred to simply as *taiko* or *wadaiko* (I choose to use *taiko* to refer to the genre as a whole, as this was the term I encountered most often in my research on the subject in Kyoto; *kumidaiko* refers to a specific type of ensemble drumming within this broader category). *Taiko* has exploded in popularity on a global scale with groups now numbering well over four thousand in Japan and hundreds more in North America alone (Pachter 2013:34). We now find rapid growth in community groups and college clubs, to ever-increasing numbers of professional performers throughout the world. Tanaka agrees:

> Of all of Japan's instruments, the *taiko* (drum) is the most prominent on the world stage. Amateur and professional *taiko* groups of various sizes are prevalent both in Japan and in various countries around the world. The instrument's appeal lies in the entertaining performances given with it and the sounds produced by it—sounds from bass tones to high-pitched rhythms that reverberate through the body. Like the *tsugaru[-j]amisen*, *kumidaiko* (ensemble-drumming practiced by modern *taiko* groups) as a genre of music is new, but it is regarded as being the most expressive of Japanese tradition.
> (Tanaka et al. 2005:6)

Taiko's development encapsulates many of the points raised thus far in this exploration of Japanese music and identity—beautifully bridging the pre-modern and modern eras, and in reflecting the processes involved in Japan's adaptation of both foreign forms and the refashioning of musics from within into new performance contexts. Rooted in religious practice, essential to folk and festival performances, and distinctive on the theater stages and in related chamber musics (de Ferranti 2000:40–54), *taiko* emerged after World War II as its own performance style, which continues to blossom today. By definition, *taiko* is a genre that both expresses global flows and local identities, cosmopolitan, constantly innovating, and stressing active and creative exploration.

Taiko clearly has taken not only Japan, but also the world by storm, crossing both genre and national borders. No game center is complete now in Japan without the NAMCO *taiko* game (*Taiko no Tatsujin*) as children and adults line up to take a turn, and compete for a high score (see Figure 4.5). There is a similar game featuring the *shamisen*, but it never developed the same appeal as *Taiko no Tatsujin*. The immense popularity of *taiko* is rooted in its ability at once to capture elements of Japaneseness, while being malleable to different musical languages.

Nonetheless, contemporary enthusiasts are not always aware of *taiko*'s history, often viewing it as a so-called "traditional" and therefore "ancient" art of Japan, when in fact it is actually a fairly modern creation. Several scholars (Varian 2005; Bender 2012; Pachter 2013), however, have standardized the story of *taiko*'s early development, and in the process credit specific artists with originating the secular style in post-World War II Japan. Osuwa Daiko, Sukeroku Daiko, Ondekoza and Kodō are typically considered the four main groups who established key characteristics that continue to resonate in *taiko* today, and which will be discussed further below.

Figure 4.5 NAMCO "*Taiko no Tatsujin*" (©BANDAI NAMCO Games Inc.)

The History of Taiko

> The word taiko in general conjures up images of beautiful barrel-shaped drums of various sizes in warm chestnut to deep mahogany lining a stage; muscular, sweaty bodies on display in colorful costumes clearly at play with traditional Japanese festival wear as the performers raise their arms in unified, choreographed moves, joyful though intense expressions on each face, drum sticks flying. The sound spreads

infectiously through the audience as each person's chest reverberates, feet tapping along with the driving beat as one connects with the heart of traditional Japan.

This description captures the stereotypical image of live *taiko* performance, even as it belies the diversity of styles present in even the earliest manifestations of the style in the 1950s. Rather, Bender argues contributors to the development of *taiko* were inspired by different motivations and involved performers with diverse musical skills, resulting in distinct performance styles and social implications. Today, however, it is difficult for the novice to identify the precise influences that remain from each group (2012:48). The following discussion therefore highlights the distinctive qualities of the originators that came to constitute modern ensemble drumming as a whole.

Osuwa Daiko's founder, Oguchi Daihachi, for example, is

> ... widely credited with inventing the modern style of ensemble performance [in the mid-1950s] in which *taiko* of different pitches are combined in a drum set-like setup ... and *taiko* of different sizes, shapes, and pitches are arranged on stage as in an orchestral rhythm section.
> (Bender 2012:49)

He also included the use of arm movements (*furi*) and call-and-response vocal gestures (*kakegoe*). Nonetheless, it would be incorrect to say he invented these gestures, as they of course have roots in other Japanese folk and classical musical practices (see previous discussion in Chapter 3). They continue to be standard amongst *taiko* performers globally today. Trained as a jazz percussionist, Oguchi became interested in rhythms associated with rural or folk Japan, such as those found in Nagano prefecture where he established Osuwa Daiko, but Oguchi "increased the speed of the drumming to 'match that of the times' and integrated rhythmic patterns more characteristic of jazz drumming than of festival *taiko* performance" (ibid.:51), thus mixing regional folk styles with global jazz technique. Yet Oguchi virtually denied the Western elements that were present in his innovative style of ensemble *taiko* from the beginning, instead incorporating "Western rhythms and instrumental composition in a manner that appears entirely indigenous" (ibid.:52), and ultimately feeding the interpretation of *taiko* as a uniquely traditional art of Japan.

The original members of Sukeroku Daiko—Kobayashi Seidō, Onozato Motoe, Ishizuka Yutaka, and Ishikura Yoshihisa—in contrast, found their way to *taiko* through festival music (*bon-daiko*) in the 1960s in Tokyo. But rather than performing the inherited rhythms in strict imitation and in the typical supporting role of percussionists, they developed a flashier style of play which favored innovation to the point that "thrilling performance was desired more than ritual practice" (ibid.:54). Bender further argues

> ... without the dictates of local custom casting a shadow of authority over their performance, young *taiko* players in Tokyo were able to experiment and innovate in a manner that reflected the dynamism and cosmopolitanism of their city.
> (Ibid.)

In order to do so, the group emphasized what they called "'free solo' or 'freestyle': building on the basic rhythm common to all kinds of [b]*on-daiko* by adding one's own mallet twirls and acrobatic movements" (ibid.:56). Thus lively group performance "provided a backdrop for highly individual display" (ibid.), another trait that remains consistent through much contemporary *taiko* performance.

Sukeroku's energetic and flashy style influenced subsequent Japanese groups, particularly in Tokyo as they performed in cafés and clubs, as well as arguably exerting the greatest influence in North America through the work of such performers as Tanaka Seiichi and Kenny Endo, both of whom studied with them and are credited as being two of the first major *taiko* performers and teachers in the United States (Varian 2005). The Sukeroku "slant stand" style of play is especially ubiquitous in North America.

Originally located on the now well-known Sado Island, Ondekoza was the first group to elevate *taiko* performance to an art form intended for stage performance in Japan. Den Tagayasu (born Tajiri Kōzō) created the group in 1971 "with the primary aim of reinvesting desiccated regional folk entertainments with youthful vigor and style" (Bender 2012:60). Kodō later emerged from Ondekoza when some of the performers split with manager Den, but combined both groups contributed greatly to the artistic development of *taiko* as we know it today. One of the most influential aspects of both groups is their position as "new folk" artists. Bender argues Ondekoza and later Kodō attempted to recreate folk culture. Den, informed by Marxist-Maoist beliefs, saw artistic vigor in the "authentic" work of the so-called peasants and a connection between "proletarian labor and the performing arts" (ibid.:65).

This vision informed all aspects of the group. For example, even though they trained with classical masters (including Tosha Rōetsu of Kyoto, who will be discussed further in Part III), they only learned technique, while the content of their pieces continued to be from folk performing traditions (ibid.:70) as Den's communist leanings privileged folk over classical art forms. Ondekoza thus presented an interesting combination of elements of folk and classical Japanese styles. But they necessarily had to modify original folk forms to fit the larger instrumentation necessary for grand public stages and arranged the music to suit the new performance contexts. As with Oguchi and Osuwa Daiko, Ondekoza also had to increase tempo, in part to make performances more interesting as they were not the most skilled drummers at the time.

Den would eventually grow increasingly interested in film, causing a rift between him and the young players he had recruited, until he abruptly left the group. Hayashi Eitetsu renamed the remaining members "Kodō" in 1981 (Kodō n.d.), and since then the group has become the "rock stars" of the *taiko* world, maintaining their commitment to folk arts, while transforming under the leadership of each new artistic director as they expand their repertoire.

Kodō's approach to transforming folk music for the big stage is illustrated in their adaptation of "Miyake" (Website Example 13). This performance opens with "Kiyari," a song for working with logs, possibly referring to the lumber used to rebuild the Ise shrine (Kotobank n.d.c): "Today, even though Kiyari's origin as a work song is very evident in its structure and rhythm, it has become an almost purely ritual song, sung on festive occasions, especially by groups of traditional firefighters" (Columbia Music Entertainment n.d.). The song features a strong lead, here provided by Mitome Tomohiro, and choral response. As *min'yō*, the vocals are highly melismatic and ornamented:

木遣り
"Kiyari"
("Kiyari")
今日のめでたさ　　これは伊勢へ
kyō no medetasa　　kore wa Ise e
Today is very celebratory　　This will go to Ise [shrine]

これから打ち込みます　　これは伊勢へ
kore kara uchikomimasu　　kore wa Ise e
We will start hitting now　　This will go to Ise [shrine]
[The "hitting" could refer to the striking of wood, as well as the striking of *taiko* about to begin.]

The folk song opening focuses the audience's attention, preparing them for the entrance of the *taiko*. The underlying rhythmic pattern (*ji*), a seemingly simple "do DON" in mnemonics (*kuchishōka*) for *taiko*, is well established before Funabashi Yuichiro takes the lead solo. The accents in this rhythm are subtle and can easily shift, changing the entire feel of the piece, so even if the basic supporting rhythm and skeleton of the main melody may appear relatively easy, the nuances are quite difficult to articulate and sustain.

Kaoru Watanabe explains that Kodō are arranging the original piece, which they learned from the Tsumura family on Miyake Island, who are similarly "popularizing the traditional way" (this too is complicated as there are numerous versions of the piece even on Miyake Island). But since Kodō has a much broader audience, their version, which added more drums, became well known. Kodō also encourage people to learn the original version and do not teach the piece any more, deferring to the Tsumura family. Watanabe explains "Kodō has always been very good about getting permission" to perform pieces they learn from different local communities throughout Japan, or modifying their versions so much that the originators are not concerned that their cultural property has been misappropriated. The version of "Miyake" that Kodō performs is decidedly their own, and to the members of the Tsumura family, easily distinguishable in the nuance of the *ji* and movement of the hips Watanabe likens this to "speaking with an accent" (interview, May 5, 2014).

Today Kodō may enjoy the greatest global recognition, but by the 1980s, all of the above groups shared particular performative tropes that constitute what has come to be perceived as the unified genre known as "*taiko*." For example, they all placed Japanese drumming techniques and instruments drawn from traditional and folk musics into new performative contexts, foregrounding percussion as a solo, virtuosic instrument, rather than serving primarily a supporting role. They also secularized religious works, simplified complicated folk rhythms for playability, and combined foreign, at times Western, musical elements. These performers also added sweeping arm movements and choreography to highlight healthy, muscular bodies, thus at times emphasizing the visual over the rhythmic, with a strong focus on audience appeal. Indeed, one of the critiques of *taiko* is the use of excessive arm gestures and artificial choreography, which at times can be quite inefficient as opposed to playing closer to the drum.

The discipline that has been assigned to the practice of *taiko*, which in some situations can be likened to the physical demands of a martial art, may also feel artificial outside of the context of Japan, but perhaps is actually a way that *taiko* is similar to other musics discussed in Chapter 3. American percussionist Marty Bracey, who lives and teaches in Kyoto (see further discussion in Chapter 5), is critical of these aspects of *taiko*, but nonetheless acknowledges that excessive discipline and the use of stylized gestures is very Japanese. He equates this to how one is supposed to hand things over with two hands in Japan, facing the person head-on, with great ceremony, as opposed to casually tossing the item (interview, April 22, 2010). Higashi Munenori, founder of the Taiko Center, a school of *taiko* located in Kyoto (see further discussion in Part III) compares the grand arm movements to the poses (*mie*) that signal penultimate moments in *kabuki*; the slow movement as one deliberately raises an arm is full of *ma*. In these ways, he feels *taiko* expresses Japanese cultural identity. And just as *kabuki* developed from a local entertainment in Kyoto centuries ago into a *national* art form, he would like to see *taiko* become a *national* art of Japan in the future (interview, June 23, 2010).

As introduced in Chapter 2, hybridity itself may define *taiko* as Japanese, and performers continue to meld different styles together, moving farther away from the folk forms that inspired the genre's progenitors. The group Gocoo, for example, almost immediately lend themselves to being called popular by style, through their costuming, instrumentation, and performance contexts. Gocoo is listed in the Japan Foundation booklet *Performing Arts in Japan: Traditional Music Today* (Tanaka et al. 2005) as part of "new tradition," though their leader Asano Kaoly refers to them as a band (e-mail correspondence, November 20, 2014) and as "The Tokyo Tribal Groove Orchestra" on their official website (Gocoo 2014). They perform at raves and rock concerts, have recorded with techno superstars Juno Reactor, and made a cameo appearance, as the humans of Zion danced in preparation for battle, in the second installment of the well-known *Matrix* film series (2003). Given the group's close association with the trance-techno scene in the late 1990s and early 2000s, it is not surprising that they often wore bright, psychedelic clothing; both men and women sport long hair, sometimes in braids or dreads, adorned with ethnic beads and other "world beat" accessories.

"DKN," filmed during their European tour in 2012, captures well Gocoo's continued hybridization of *taiko* (Website Example 14). Gocoo comprises twelve professional

Figure 4.6 Asano Kaoly, leader of Gocoo with additional members (photo by Mark Dozadzillo)

members, but they also maintain a studio called Tawoo where anyone can come and play *taiko* (see Figure 4.6). "DKN" is the first song that was created by Gocoo and regular attendees at Tawoo, DaiKen and J Suzuki. Gocoo combine the *taiko* with other world instruments, such as the *didgeridoo*, and Western gong, cymbals, and tambourine as heard throughout this piece. Their staging features elaborate lights, glowing in bright green to purple, or an eye-grabbing checkerboard pattern of black-and-white and hyperactive blue squares. Huge monitors to each side of the stage show the details of what is happening to those not lucky enough to find a spot up front. The audience is large, excited, dancing and cheering with the group as they perform. This is clearly not the *taiko* of *min'yō* or *matsuri-bayashi* (traditional festival music).

This performance opens with immense energy right from the top, with the rhythmic guttural cries of the group—"fu" "ha"—that will periodically resurface throughout the piece. Immediately a strong groove is established in the lead *taiko* that propels the group and audience forward. The unbridled excitement of the performers is expressed in the spontaneous *kakegoe* and *kiai*, their enthusiasm apparent on their smiling faces and in their flapping hair. They dance and jump, creating a real party atmosphere on the stage. The exuberance is momentarily subdued from 1:35, as the *taiko* quiet down and the flute is highlighted. But this repose does not last long, as the *taiko* quickly take the melodic lead once again, driving the piece to even higher levels of intensity. A new rhythm enters from 3:16, expanding the texture even further, punctuated by the crashing of a Western gong and near-moaning by one of the members. The musical freneticism and collective emotional energy are more in line with a peak moment at a techno event than perhaps a typical *taiko* concert, before Gocoo suddenly breaks down for the final statement on the drums, accompanied by the constant shimmer of the gong, framing the piece.

This performance begs us to ask: is this even *taiko*? Is this even Japanese? To be sure, there are numerous instruments not of Japanese origin here, but they nevertheless assume similar functions as in a more traditional ensemble. For example, there are wind instruments (the *didgeridoo* and a type of transverse flute, although it is difficult to tell if this is Japanese in origin or not), just as one would find in many *taiko* ensembles around the world. Gocoo often use unexpected mallets and sticks, but the *taiko* still are lined up at the front of the stage and supply the main melody of the piece. Meanwhile, metallic percussion, supplied by *atarigane* (a small brass gong) or *chappa* (cymbals) in a typical *matsuri-bayashi*, is performed on a Western gong and on other types of percussion.

Gocoo engage with media and practices that are firmly grounded in popular culture, taking the traditional instrument *taiko* and placing it firmly within a popular idiom; other groups are following suit. This may lead to new hybrids that will eventually be codified into unique genres. Tanaka "firmly believe[s] that close, cross-border interactions will continue to increase and develop as the traditions of Japan are utilized in modernity" (Tanaka et al. 2005:6).

Summary

It seems most appropriate to close Part II of this volume with another performance by Kenny Endo and Kaoru Watanabe, the performers who first introduced elements of Japanese music in "Duet" (Website Example 5). Website Example 15 differs from the preceding, as it moves through snippets of various styles from their performance together at the Metropolitan Museum of Art on May 16, 2009, from the classical flute of *noh* theater to highly improvisatory-sounding modern works. The opening two minutes revisits the wide timbre of the *shinobue* in what feels like an improvisatory exchange, establishing the mood; Watanabe slowly strolls across the stage while Endo interjects on the *ko-tsuzumi*, manipulating the pitch, punctuated by his distinctive *kakegoe*. Endo then swishes the skins on the *nagado-daiko*, a barrel-shaped drum, clacking the sides with his *bachi*. From approximately 2:20, the style is immediately distinct, drawing on festival flute melodies and rhythms. Endo and Watanabe deftly reveal the types of timbre and rhythmic sophistication possible on the various *taiko* clearly at 3:00, as they share the drum set comprised of a *hira-daiko*, small *nagado-daiko*, large *nagado-daiko* and a *shime-daiko* (all different types of *taiko*). Watanabe returns to the flute again at 4:00, but now the *nohkan*. The concert concludes with an excerpt of "Miyake," with the accent on the supporting rhythm clear, but the piece is modified yet again as Watanabe supplies the *ji* at breakneck speed on the *nagado-daiko* and Endo improvises on the kit. At 8:00 the tables turn again and Watanabe takes the lead, soloing with the large and fluid arm gestures characteristic of Kodō's adaptation of this piece. This video collage thus takes the viewer through a wide range of folk and classical Japanese styles, modern compositions which draw on traditional elements, and newly emerging techniques from two of North America's most respected *taiko* performers.

The background of these performers captures the difficulty of locating Japaneseness in ethnicity or nationality. California-born Kenny Endo, for example, originally trained as a jazz musician and then began learning *taiko* in the US, before spending a decade in Japan studying classical Japanese drumming, festival music and the ensemble drumming so popular today (see Figure 4.7). Endo is considered one of the most versatile

Figure 4.7 Kenny Endo on *ō-daiko* (photo by Raymond Yuen)

musicians in *taiko*—working as easily with classically trained Japanese artists as Latin and Indian percussionists (Endo 2014). Watanabe is also of Japanese heritage, but born in St. Louis, Missouri. He initially studied Western classical flute and saxophone before moving to Japan, where he pursued different flute traditions and *taiko*. Watanabe apprenticed with Kodō for two years before becoming a full performing member from 2000 to 2006. He returned to New York and has since been incredibly active performing in numerous collaborations with various musicians including Kenny Endo, and teaching in his Brooklyn-based studio (Watanabe 2014).

Both Endo and Watanabe are of Japanese heritage, but were born and raised in the United States; trained first in Western forms (jazz, classical flute) and then studied *hōgaku* and *taiko* in Japan. Their backgrounds thus perfectly capture the complexity of musical identity. Even the costumes in this video (which have become signature for each of them) express this blending and blurring—clearly drawing on traditional Japanese style, but modified by modernity.

Part III will further focus on the performance of classical Japanese drumming and *taiko* in Kyoto, a city that encapsulates the continued negotiation of tradition and modernity.

References

Anon. 2009."Kirihito collaborating with PV Maker for Okuda Tamio." *Searchina* (June 11, 2009): http://news.searchina.ne.jp/disp.cgi?y=2009&d=0611&f=entertainment_0611_018.shtml (accessed October 15, 2014).

Bender, Shawn. 2012. *Taiko Boom: Japanese Drumming in Place and Motion*. Berkeley: University of California Press.

Bourdaghs, Michael K. 2012. *Sayonara Amerika, Sayonara Nippon: A Geopolitical Prehistory of J-Pop*. New York: Columbia University Press.

Columbia Music Entertainment. n.d. "Kiyari." *Columbia Music Entertainment* (n.d.): http://jtrad.columbia.jp/eng/o_kiyari.html (accessed on July 13, 2014).

Condry, Ian. 2000. "The Social Production of Difference Imitation and Authenticity in Japanese Rap Music." In H. Fehrenbach and U. Poiger, eds., *Transactions, Transgressions, Transformations: American Culture in Western Europe and Japan*, pp. 166–184. New York/Oxford: Berghahn Books.

———. 2006. *Hip-Hop Japan: Rap and the Paths of Cultural Globalization*. Durham, NC: Duke University Press.

———. 2009. "Anime Creativity Characters and Premises in the Quest for Cool Japan." *Theory, Culture & Society* 26(2–3):139–163.

———. 2011. "Post-3/11 Japan and the Radical Recontextualization of Value: Music, Social Media, and End-Around Strategies for Cultural Action." *International Journal of Japanese Sociology* 20:4–17.

———. 2013. *The Soul of Anime: Collaborative Creativity and Japan's Media Success Story*. Durham, NC: Duke University Press.

Darling-Wolf, Fabienne. 2004. "SMAP, Sex, and Masculinity: Constructing the Perfect Female Fantasy in Japanese Popular Music." *Popular Music and Society* 27(3):357–370.

de Ferranti, Hugh. 2000. *Japanese Musical Instruments*. Oxford: Oxford University Press.

Domo Music Group. n.d. "Yoshida Brothers." *Domo Music Group* (n.d.): http://www.domomusicgroup.com/yoshidabrothers/ (accessed September 8, 2014).

Endo, Kenny. 2014. "About Kenny Endo." *Kenny Endo* (2014): http://www.kennyendo.com/about (accessed October 21, 2014).

Faith Aquino. 2013. "Lady Gaga and Beyonce's 'Telephone' remade with traditional Japanese instruments." *Japan Daily Press* (May 29, 2013): http://japandailypress.com/lady-gaga-and-beyonces-telephone-remade-with-traditional-japanese-instruments-2929673 (accessed November 22, 2014).

Fellezs, Kevin. 2012. "'This is Who I Am': Jero, Young, Gifted, Polycultural." *Journal of Popular Music Studies* 24(3):333–356.

Fujie, Linda. 2002. "East Asia – Japan" In J. Titon, ed., *Worlds of Music: An Introduction to the Music of the World's Peoples 4th Edn.*, pp. 331–384. Belmont, CA: Schirmer/Thomson Learning.

Furmanovsky, Michael. 2008. "American Country Music in Japan: Lost Piece in the Popular Music History Puzzle." *Popular Music and Society* 31(3):357–372.

Galbraith, Patrick W. 2012. "Idols: The Image of Desire in Japanese Consumer Capitalism." In P. Galbraith and J. Karlin, eds., *Idols and Celebrity in Japanese Media Culture*, pp. 185–208. Hampshire: Palgrave Macmillan.

Galbraith, Patrick W. and Jason G. Karlin, eds. 2012. *Idols and Celebrity in Japanese Media Culture*. Hampshire: Palgrave Macmillan.

Galliano, Luciana. 2002. *Yōgaku: Japanese Music in the Twentieth Century*. Lanham, MD: Scarecrow Press.

Gocoo. 2014. "The Tokyo Tribal Groove Orchestra GOCOO." *Gocoo* (2014): http://www.gocoo.de (accessed July 13, 2014).

Hosokawa, Shūhei. 1994. *Japanese Popular Music of the Past Twenty Years: Its Mainstream and Underground*. Tokyo: Japan Foundation.

——. 1999. "Salsa no Tiene Frontera: Orquesta de la Luz and the Globalization of Popular Music." *Cultural Studies* 13(3):509–34.

Hosokawa, Toshio. n.d. "About this Recording." *Naxos* (n.d.): http://www.naxos.com/mainsite/blurbs_reviews.asp?item_code=8.572479&catNum=572479&filetype=About%20this%20Recording&language=English# (accessed August 15, 2014).

Hughes, David. 2008. *Traditional Folk Song in Modern Japan: Sources, Sentiment and Society*. Folkestone: Global Oriental.

Itoh, Hiroyuki. 2013. Public Lecture at the Japan Foundation in New York City on October 8, 2013.

Imoto, Yoko. 1997. *Best-Loved Children's Songs from Japan*. Tokyo: Heian.

Japan Society New York. 2012. "Nihon NY Episode 30 Jero." *Japan Society New York* (June 18, 2012): http://www.japansociety.org/webcast/nihon-ny-episode-30-jero (accessed October 15, 2014).

Jero. n.d. "Biography." *Jero Official Website* (n.d.): http://jero.jp/pc/bio.jsp (accessed October 15, 2014).

Kodō. n.d. "Kodō Official Website."*Kodō* (n.d.): http://www.kodo.or.jp/index_en.html (accessed September 8, 2014).

Koizumi, Fumio. 1974. *Nihon no Ongaku (Japanese Music)*. Tokyo: National Theater of Japan.

Kotobank n.d.a "Gendai Ongaku." *Kotobank* (n.d.): https://kotobank.jp/word/現代音楽-60823 (accessed August 30, 2014).

Kotobank n.d.b "Kindai Ongaku." *Kotobank* (n.d.): https://kotobank.jp/word/近代音楽-248211 (accessed August 30, 2014).

Kotobank n.d.c "Kiyari." *Kotobank* (n.d.): https://kotobank.jp/word/木遣り (accessed October 29, 2014).

Marx, David W. 2012. "The Jimusho System: Understanding the Production Logic of the Japanese Entertainment Industry." In P. Galbraith and J. Karlin, eds., *Idols and Celebrity in Japanese Media Culture*, pp. 35–55. Hampshire: Palgrave Macmillan.

Milioto Matsue, Jennifer M. 2008a. "The Local Performance of Global Sound: More than the Musical in Japanese Hardcore Rock." In J. Jaffe and H. Johnson. eds., *Performing Japan: Contemporary Expressions of Cultural Identity*, pp. 221–238. Folkestone: Global Oriental Press.

——. 2008b. *Making Music in Japan's Underground: The Tokyo Hardcore Scene*. New York/London: Routledge.

——. 2015, forthcoming. "The Ideal Idol: Making Music with Hatsuen Miku."

Mitsui, Toru. 1993. "The Reception of the Music of American Southern Whites in Japan." In N. Rosenberg, ed., *Transforming Tradition: Folk Music Revivals Examined*, pp. 275–293. Urbana: Urbana-Champaign: University of Illinois Press.

Nagaike, Kazumi. 2012. "Johnny's Idols as Icons: Female Desires to Fantazise and Consume Male Idol Images." In P. Galbraith and J. Karlin, eds., *Idols and Celebrity in Japanese Media Culture*, pp. 97–112. Hampshire: Palgrave Macmillan.

Naka, Mamiko. 1991. "Polarity in Acculturation Process: A Composer Yamada Kōsaku." In M. Kanazawa, M. Ohmiya, M. Shimosako, A. Takamatsu, Y. Tokumaru, T. Tsukitani, and O. Yamaguchi, eds., *Tradition and Its Future in Music: Report of SIMS Osaka 1990*, pp. 563–566. Tokyo and Osaka: Mita Press.

Nendai-Ryūkō. n.d. "List of Most Enka CD Sold and Artists." *Nendai-Ryūkō* (n.d.): http://nendai-ryuukou.com/article/016.html (accessed August 15, 2014).

Nippon Columbia. 2014. "Profile of Hikawa Tsuyoshi." *Nippon Columbia* (2014): http://columbia.jp/hikawa/prof.html (accessed October 15, 2014).

Novak, David. 2006. "Japan Noise: Global Media Circulation and the Transpacific Circuits of Experimental Music." Ph.D. dissertation, Columbia University.

———. 2013. *Japanoise: Music at the Edge of Circulation*. Durham, NC: Duke University Press.

Pachter, Benjamin. 2013. "Wadaiko in Japan and the United States: The Intercultural History of a Music Genre." Ph.D. dissertation, University of Pittsburgh.

Pacun, David. 2012. "Nationalism and Musical Style in Interwar Yōgaku: A Reappraisal." *Asian Music* 43(2):3–46.

Peluse, Michael S. 2005. "Not Your Grandfather's Music: Tsugaru Shamisen Blurs the Lines Between 'Folk,' 'Traditional,' and 'Pop'." *Asian Music* 36(2):57–80.

Plourde, Lorraine. 2008. "Disciplined Listening in Tokyo: Onkyō and Non-Intentional Sounds." *Ethnomusicology* 52(2):270–295.

Rao, Mallika. 2014. "Meet Hatsune Miku, The Sensational Japanese Pop Star Who Doesn't Really Exist." *Huffington Post* (October 8, 2014): http://www.huffingtonpost.com/2014/10/08/hatsune-miku-letterman_n_5956420.html (accessed November 5, 2014).

Stevens, Carolyn S. 2008. *Japanese Popular Music: Culture, Authenticity, and Power*. New York/London: Routledge.

Takemitsu, Tōru. 1989. "Contemporary Music in Japan," text adapted for publication by H. Tann, *Perspectives of New Music* 27(2):198–205.

Tanaka, Takafumi, Mayusa Oda, Kimiko Iwashita, Kiyo Furusaki and Mariko Okeda. 2005. *Performing Arts in Japan: Traditional Music Today*. Translated by ALAYA INC. Tokyo: The Japan Foundation.

Team Kozan. 2013. "Lady Gaga Telephone cover/TEAM KOZAN (Shakuhachi, Koto)." *YouTube* (May 9 2013): https://www.youtube.com/watch?v=ZZ06aVZpGYA (accessed September 3, 2014).

Varian, Heidi. 2005. *The Way of Taiko*. Berkeley, CA: Stone Bridge Press.

Wade, Bonnie C. 2014. *Composing Japanese Musical Modernity*. Chicago, IL: University of Chicago Press.

Watanabe, Kaoru. 2014. "Kaoru Watanabe Biography." *Kaoru Watanabe* (2014): http://www.watanabekaoru.com/e/biography (accessed October 21, 2014).

Yano, Christine R. 1998. "Refining the Modern Nation in Japanese Popular Song." In S. Minichiello ed., *Japan's Competing Modernities*, pp. 247–264. Honolulu: University of Hawaii Press.

———. 2002. *Tears of Longing: Nostalgia and the Nation in Japanese Popular Song*. Cambridge, MA: Harvard University Press.

PART III
Focusing In: Identity, Meaning and Japanese Drumming in Kyoto

Part III, "Focusing In: Identity, Meaning and Japanese Drumming in Kyoto," takes a closer look first at the identity of one of Japan's most iconic cities, Kyoto, which itself highlights the complex negotiation of modernity and tradition that characterizes Japan as a whole. This provides the cultural context for the ensuing ethnographic-based case studies that explore how people perform Japanese drumming within this urban space, followed by some conclusions.

CHAPTER 5

Taiko and the Marketing of Tradition in Kyoto

The energy is palpable in the air as we walk through the crowded streets of Kyoto, blocked off for pedestrian use only, viewing the brightly lit and elaborate floats that will parade through the city tomorrow. The smells of competing food stalls, colorful items for sale at numerous shops, and jostle of the immense crowd is accompanied by the repetitive, even monotonous music of multiple percussion ensembles; each group's sound melding into the next as we push forward against the crowd, like fish swimming upstream. The city thus teems with the hustle and bustle of festive feelings generated by the Gion Matsuri.

The *Gion Matsuri* is believed to have originated in 869 C.E.

> . . . while Kyoto was in the grip of a horrible plague. At the behest of the emperor, a priest from Yasaka[-jinja (shrine)] led a procession through the streets to pray for mercy from the god who was the source of the disease. The pestilence subsided but the ritual continued, gradually evolving through the years to its modern form.
> (Kyoto City Official Travel Guide n.d.)

Now recognized as a Nationally Important Intangible Folk Cultural Property (Iguchi 2008:251), *Gion Matsuri* is the largest annual festival in Kyoto. Lasting a month, the merriment begins on July 2nd when a representative from each community that wants to enter an elaborate tapestry-covered float (generally known as *dashi*, more specifically *yamaboko* in this festival) draws to find their position in the parade, the festival's highlight, that will occur several weeks later. Although it can sometimes be easy to forget that this festival, as with most in Japan, has religious origins, the *Gion Matsuri* makes clear its foundation in Shintoism. Elaborate portable Shintō shrines, in which the gods temporarily dwell (*mikoshi*), are removed from their place of residence at Yasaka-jinja; they are cleaned and paraded around Kyoto on July 10th, accompanied by the sounds of *Gion-bayashi* (the music of the *Gion Matsuri*) practiced in the background, creating quite a festive atmosphere. The three *mikoshi* will remain prominently on display on one of the busiest shopping streets in Kyoto throughout the month, until they are safely returned to their home to wait for their spin around town the following year (see Figure 5.1).

From July 14th through the 16th, the floats, adorned with traditional Japanese lanterns (*chōchin*), cast a romantic glow on the hordes of people who have gathered, and "During the height of the festival, streets bustle late into the night with crowds of people in traditional dress and with booths selling barbequed chicken skewers, traditional Japanese sweets and many other culinary delights" (Kyoto City Official Travel Guide n.d.).

The communities supporting each float erect tents fronted by large barrels of *sake*, waiting to be drunk, while local shops sell traditional Japanese summer cotton robes (*yukata*), and numerous other goods at massive discounts, as the city gears up for the big party to come. People tour around the floats, purchasing unique souvenirs and talismans for protection at each, the collective summer-happy spirit apparent amongst the crowd (see Figure 5.2).

Figure 5.1 *Mikoshi* from Yasaka-jinja on display

Taiko and the Marketing of Tradition • 151

Figure 5.2 Crowds at *Gion Matsuri*

Yasaka-jinja holds numerous types of performances for the gods (*kagura*) on July 16th, the day the *yamaboko* are placed in their appropriate position, ready for tomorrow's procession through Kyoto (see Figure 5.3). The parade proper attracts thousands of viewers who cram the crowded streets. Towering two stories into the air, the 32 floats, the oldest of these types in Japan, are pulled by hand through the city by a group of community members, dramatically pivoting around corners on their two large wheels. Some contain dolls on the upper level, while others have room for musicians—performing the *Gion-bayashi* that has been wafting through the air for the past two weeks, as neighborhood associations of men practice the music unique to each float.

In the weeks leading up to this main event, male musicians throughout the city can be seen practicing in the evening hours as they prepare to accompany twelve of the floats in the parade, either riding on the top or walking alongside, offering a wonderful opportunity for fathers and sons, elders and youngsters, to bond while practicing for and performing in the actual *matsuri*. On one evening in July 2010, while strolling through the streets with my family, I came upon a brightly lit outdoor staircase that had been constructed to temporarily lead up to the second floor of the building where a community group was practicing, with the windows wide open, inviting and enticing passersby to ascend for a closer look. The group of men and boys, dressed in matching blue and white *yukata*, sat on three benches facing a large Shintō altar (*kami-dana*). Most lovely to see was the way young boys were initiated into the playing: an older man waving a boy (maybe seven or eight years old) over to sit in front of him, then guiding him through the pattern on the hand-gong (*kane*). Two or three other slightly older boys were similarly

Figure 5.3 *Gion Matsuri yamaboko*

being taught the same core rhythm. Adult men played the flute (*shinobue* or *nohkan*) and small double-headed drum (*shime-daiko*). The whole experience walking through the area and hearing different *Gion-bayashi* reminded me much of the competing *gamelans* one hears in Bali, as did the teaching of the young boy seated in the elder's lap.

Lancashire summarizes the scene:

> This music is regarded as an accompaniment to the parade of floats, providing a musical offering to the gods of the Yasaka shrine, to whom the festival is dedicated. Until the day of the parade, the musicians perform nightly at each "town house" ... and on a float reconstructed and stationed beside it. For the residents in the vicinity and the tourists who swamp the city during the period, the sound of their music floating from wide-open windows to the street outside is an essential part of the Gion festival experience.
>
> (2011:251)

Each float features its own repertoire, which was formalized in the middle of the sixteenth century under the influence of *noh* (Tsuchiyama n.d.). On the surface, the *Gion-bayashi* all sound similar, even plodding and repetitive, but actually possess subtle differences in the details, which are passed down through the community association (Tai 2005).

The *Gion-bayashi*, and by extension the festival as a whole, thus builds local community spirit, while attracting both domestic and foreign tourists who've come to absorb the atmosphere of Kyoto—just as I did when I looked through the window that evening several years ago.

Kyoto: A *Machi* of *Matsuri*

During 2009–10, while conducting research on Japanese drumming in Kyoto, I often heard people refer to the area as a "*matsuri no machi*," or a "town of festivals." Kyoto is home to several major festivals, including the *Gion Matsuri*, the *Aoi Matsuri*, with its origins in the Heian period, and the *Jidai Matsuri*, invented in the Meiji period, as well as countless, more intimate gatherings in specific neighborhoods.

On June 30th, for example, numerous small shrines throughout Kyoto conduct a purification ritual in which visitors write their name and age on pieces of paper and throw them into a river to wash away their sins. At Ichihime-jinja, a shrine dedicated primarily to women, after paying 3000 yen (US$31.50) and writing one's wishes on these strips of white paper, the priest gives a speech before a group of young teenage girls in *yukata* lead the participants through a round gate of straw and then around the gate

Figure 5.4 *Matsuri* at Ichihime-jinja in Kyoto

to the shrine (*torii*) three times (see Figure 5.4). Prayers and blessings from the priest continue as the white papers are thrown over one's shoulders. Another group of teenagers perform live on *gagaku* instruments, the *shō*, *hichiriki*, and *ryūteki*, introduced in Chapter 3. Soon after, they all march over to the nearby Takase-gawa (river) into which the little paper slips inscribed with wishes are thrown, flowing down in between candlelit *chōchin* to the next major bridge where a group of young people frantically gather them up, presumably to take them back to the shrine to be burned. The event in 2010 was mainly attended by the young men and women described already, a handful of older men and women from the neighborhood, and a few random foreigners, including myself, who stopped to watch. This was clearly a *matsuri* localized to this specific neighborhood (*chiiki*). Similar festivals occur throughout the year, bringing together the local community through ritual, which are often supported by music and dance (see Figure 5.5).

Figure 5.5 *Matsuri* at Genbu-jinja in Kyoto

Even the farmers outside the city of Kyoto proper still walk through their rice fields during planting season to a steady drum beat (supplied by a small hand-held drum), offering prayers for a successful crop, and driving pests away.

Both the large and the small festivals help maintain strong connections amongst the local community. Gillan elaborates that such events and rituals "also serve an important social function as a context through which social cohesion is achieved and identities are constructed" (2012:82) and "for the formation and delineation of social relationships within society" (ibid.: 83). As such, "Festivals are also an important way in which societies themselves are constructed and imagined" (ibid.:84), in what they portray and the community involvement necessary to bring them to life. Festivals therefore are an essential means through which identity is formed, even, if not especially, in modern metropolises, as neighborhood communities come together to enact them. But festivals also attract countless tourists, ultimately commoditizing the city.

Even though the *Gion Matsuri* brings communities together, and in turn informs the identity of the city, it is also big business for Kyoto, as permanent residents as well as domestic and foreign tourists pour into the streets, consuming food, alcohol, trinkets and other goods. Various people I spoke with in Kyoto felt that as a result the *Gion Matsuri* has lost its neighborhood feel (see further discussion below); but the excitement was still palpable the night we strolled through the floats, all lined and lit up, waiting for the parade the following day. The connection with neighborhood identity may be diminishing with increased commercialism; nevertheless, the grandness of the *Gion Matsuri* definitely feeds the image of Kyoto as a *"matsuri no machi."* The *matsuri* thus are both community builders and commodities themselves, to be avidly consumed. And through that consumption, an identity of Kyoto as steeped in tradition is actively created.

The Traditional Image of Kyoto

> From the moss garden at Saihō-ji to the shining apparition that is Kinkaku-ji, Kyoto is home to the most beautiful temples in all Japan, and most of them are surrounded by sublime gardens. You've probably got an image of the perfect Japan in your mind—if it exists anywhere, it's probably somewhere in Kyoto waiting for you to discover it
>
> (Rowthorn et al. 2007:4)

And indeed, in the 2007 edition of the well-known travel guide *Lonely Planet*, quoted above, Kyoto's temples and gardens are listed as the number one attraction in all of Japan. Kyoto holds a special position in the global imagination as a bastion of tradition (see Figure 5.6). First settled in the seventh century and serving as the imperial capital of Japan from 794–1868, and based on the capital of China during the Tang dynasty, the city was organized in a grid pattern much like Manhattan's. Located in the central Kansai region of western Japan, within easy distance of Nara, Osaka and Kobe, Kyoto is nestled in a valley enclosed by mountains on the eastern and western borders, and divided within by the famed Kamo-gawa (river) (see Figure 5.7).

Kyoto's geographical position in a valley results in oppressive heat in the summer and bitter cold in the winter, but lovely autumns with magnificent foliage in the mountains, and spectacular springs with its explosion of cherry blossoms—both spring and autumn attracting thousands of domestic and foreign tourists.

Figure 5.6 Kiyomizu-dera in Kyoto

Figure 5.7 Kamo-gawa

Although once the seat of the government, political power shifted, settling eventually in Tokyo where it remains today, and Kyoto's population of approximately 1.5 million is tiny in comparison to Tokyo's estimated 13.4 million. Kyoto, nonetheless, assumes a special place within the identity of Japan as a whole. Much of Kyoto was destroyed during war in the fifteenth century, and was subsequently rebuilt during the Edo period, at which point the city blossomed as a center of culture and religion. Kyoto remains home to more than 1,600 Buddhist temples (*otera* or *jiin*) and 400 Shintō shrines (*jinja*) and 17 UNESCO World Heritage sites (City of Kyoto n.d.). The recognition of the historical significance of these many temples and shrines, as well as artworks within, is one of the reasons Kyoto was removed from consideration for bombing in World War II.

Kyoto continues to maintain its image as the former *miyako*, or "courtly capital," where the emperor resided for over a thousand years, and the sprawling home and grounds of the imperial family is still there even today (even if it is no longer the primary residence, which is now in Tokyo). A male staff member in his late fifties to early sixties at the Kyoto Tourist Center for Japanese tourists described Kyoto's culture as first and foremost *kyūtei bunka* (court culture), second *kuge bunka* (royal family culture), and third, *otera bunka* (temple culture) (interview, March 20, 2010). Kyoto is a city steeped in historical references, imperial associations and religious iconography—the protector of Japan's traditional culture.

As the cultural capital of Japan, Kyoto relies a great deal on tourism for its economic survival. Therefore the image preserved and presented through the tourist industry, as illustrated in the comments above, is important to understanding Kyoto's identity. The *Lonely Planet* guide, which is produced for an English-speaking visitor to Japan, describes Kyoto as

> ... where you will find the Japan of your imagination: raked pebble gardens, poets' huts hidden amid bamboo groves, arcades of vermillion shrine gates, *geisha* disappearing into the doorways of traditional restaurants, golden temples floating above tranquil waters. Indeed, most of the sites that make up the popular image of Japan probably originated in Kyoto.
> (Rowthorn et al. 2007:309)

Thus the traditionalism of Kyoto has become synonymous with the identity of Japan as a whole for many foreign tourists.

Yet this association also holds true for Japanese people, who similarly flock to Kyoto to experience Japan's traditional past. Kyoto's culture is perceived as "classy"—a place where people do things right—which of course means following tradition. From *kaiseki*, an elaborate traditional cuisine involving many elegantly displayed, seasonally appropriate dishes, to the subtle color and sophisticated patterns of *kimono*, the Japanese turn to Kyoto when looking for artistic expression that captures the essence of an old, traditional, and therefore superior Japanese aesthetic. Kyoto practices, for example, are the standard by which tea ceremony (*sadō*) is judged throughout Japan, so much so, that the timeline to recognize seasonal changes within this art form follows the Kyoto calendar even in other parts of the country (Surak 2013:38–39). In other words, spring blooms in the images of artwork, utensils, flowers and *kimono* that are associated with *sadō* when the cherry blossoms appear in Kyoto, even if it is still snowing in Hokkaidō where the tea is actually being made.

With its central position in Kansai, the general area dialect (*Kansai-ben*) can be heard. But the specific dialect of Kyoto—often referred to as *Kyo-kotoba* or literally

"Kyoto words"—affirms the elegant, sophisticated and softer image of Kyoto's inhabitants, as opposed to their immediate neighbors in Osaka and Kobe, who speak harsher dialects in comparison. *Kyo-kotoba* also distinguishes the character of Kyoto from the ever-looming presence of Tokyo, expressed in *Tokyo-ben*, the dominant language of Japan, heard in the mainstream mass media and disseminated through education (Kano 1994; Mori 1995; Horii 2009).

The Geiko of Kyoto

There is a lesser acknowledged, yet nonetheless pervasive identity of Kyoto as "erotic," in a romantic sense rather than an overtly sexual connotation. From Prince Genji, in *Genji Monogatari* (*The Tale of Genji*), catching a glimpse of the tip of a woman's *kimono* sleeve and falling madly in love during the height of court culture in Heian-period Kyoto, to the *geisha* strolling through Gion (a particular district within Kyoto) today, Kyoto's identity is steeped in erotic imagery. Both this refined sexuality and the importance of tradition in the creation of Kyoto's unique character are captured in the arts of the *geiko* (another term for *geisha*, commonly used in Kyoto). And the subtle eroticism known as *iroke* in the *shamisen*-accompanied song form *kouta* of the *geisha* was already noted in Chapter 3.

Yet *geisha*, one of the great markers of Japanese traditional identity as a whole, are often misunderstood by Japanese and foreigners alike as prostitutes. Originating as entertainers in the eighteenth century, "*gei*" refers to arts, and "*sha*" or "*ko*" to the people who pursue them. The *geiko* of Kyoto devote incredible amounts of time to develop the artistic skills necessary to perform in both private and public settings (see further discussion in Chapter 6). The profession in fact has long offered women a rare opportunity to pursue the arts professionally and maintain independent lives, even if perhaps problematically so. All the same, the emphasis on prostitution has been grossly overplayed in popular renderings, such as books and films that depict the lives of these women. *Geiko* have a need for customers and sponsors that is increasingly difficult to maintain, but a *geiko* no longer requires a specific patron (*danna*), and instead *geiko* support themselves (Downer 2006:226). As such, the world of *geiko* offers opportunities for women to run businesses, such as the teahouses where they entertain, specialize in and transmit music, dance, and become skilled conversationalists. *Geiko* are in fact "unique in the context of the traditional arts in Japan because they are multidisciplinary artists in contrast to highly specialized professional musicians, dancers, or actors" (Foreman 2008:1). With the ban of women from *kabuki* in 1645, *geiko* came to perform dances and music from the theater in a more private parlor setting. The dances they learn are accompanied by music featuring the *shamisen* and singing. They also learn the hourglass drums *ko-tsuzumi* and *ō-tsuzumi*, the small drum *taiko* and the flute (*nohkan* or *shinobue*) that accompanies so much traditional music. The *geiko* also support other related businesses, which often involve women as well; these include hairdressers, *kimono* makers, and the artisans who create the elaborate wigs and hairpieces; all of which combine to create the *geisha*'s allure:

> Everything about a *geisha*—her makeup, the louche way in which she wears her *kimono*, her dance—offers the promise of the erotic. But it is a promise that is very seldom kept, at least among city *geisha*. It is about enticement and desire, not about realization. It is a game, a flirtation—but it takes place only within the

bounds of the teahouse; it has no reality outside. For a *geisha* to make herself any more accessible would be to decrease her own high value.

(Downer 2006:239)

Nonetheless, the association of *geisha* with prostitution gained strength after the end of World War II, as a result of the ratification of the anti-prostitution law in 1948. Women who were actually prostitutes started calling themselves "*geisha*," since "prostitution" was not part of the *geisha* job description and therefore one could legally pursue this profession (Foreman 2008:7). Unfortunately, this solidified the association of *geisha* with prostitution. The image of the *geisha* also came to embody the imagined, ideal subservient Asian woman and ultimately to present "generic passivity and servitude" (ibid.:11). The idea of the *geisha* thus becomes a way to present Asian women as oppressed, as opposed to Western women who are liberated by comparison (ibid.:12–14); a stereotype women in Japan continue to struggle against. The *geisha* hold a controversial position in contemporary Japan, more likely reviled and seen as anachronistic, than respected as artisans, and their numbers are dwindling.

Geisha practice their arts during the day, but come dusk they emerge from the hairdressers to head to teahouses to entertain. So much so, that the streets of *geiko* districts in Kyoto belong to the women during the day, scurrying here and there before heading to work, while at night the streets are the domain of the predominantly male clientele who come to enjoy the fruits of the women's labor (Dalby 1998). *Geisha* can be found within specific districts in several cities including Tokyo, Fukuoka, Kanazawa and, of course, Kyoto. And even within these urban areas there are distinguishable *geiko* communities, such as Gion or Pontochō, the area where Tosha Rōetsu (with whom I studied in 2009–10) maintains a studio. And to be sure, the atmosphere of his lessons was deeply influenced by the constant presence of *geiko* or *maiko*, the young women in training unique to Kyoto (see further discussion in Chapter 6).

As with many other arts, such as *sadō*, in which the way of doings things in Kyoto becomes the highest standard, the *geiko* of Kyoto are often lauded as superior:

> Kyoto, everyone told [Downer] in tones of unquestionable superiority, was the only place where the flower and willow world [a reference to the 'pleasure quarters' of traditional Japan] survived. Here there was still a community where people preserved the *shikitari*—the proper ways of doing things. In other cities the so-called *geisha* might cycle to work and put on their *kimonos* when they got there. But in Kyoto *geisha* lived the lifestyle twenty-four hours a day.
>
> (Downer 2000:296)

Downer worked with *geisha* in Tokyo who she feels were worthy of the same accolades, while I saw *geiko* in Kyoto regularly making appointments and texting on cellphones popped open during breaks at a lesson, taking full advantage of the convenience of modern technology. These impressions combined might dispel some of the romanticization of the superiority of Kyoto *geiko*, but for Downer

> ... the essence of Kyoto was that sense of innate superiority. It was a bit like being among the British aristocracy. They did not claim to be more virtuous, cleverer or richer than anyone else. They just felt themselves to be indisputably classier. There was no way one could challenge it.
>
> (Ibid.)

And, despite some negative associations, often tourist materials proudly display images of *geiko* and *maiko* as emblematic of the traditionalism of Kyoto.

However, as younger generations lose interest in either joining or partaking of the world of the *geisha*, their existence may be in jeopardy. And "If *geisha* disappear, they will take with them much of Japan's traditional culture, of which they have become custodians" (ibid.:241). The erotic mystic of *geisha* may be necessary for their very survival: "Indeed, if *geisha* are to survive, they need to remain both anomaly and artistes" (ibid.). The world of the *geisha* remains purposefully wrapped in mystery.

Modernity Wrapped in Traditional Garb

Despite the fact that Kyoto consciously constructs an image of tradition—as the depository of Japanese culture, fine arts and sophistication—there are other sides to this story. And without a doubt, there is no better place in Japan than Kyoto to explore cultural identity grounded in the contested negotiation of tradition and modernity.

At the Kyoto Tourist Center for Foreign Tourists (as opposed the Kyoto Tourist Center for *Japanese* Tourists noted above), a female staff member in her late twenties

Figure 5.8 Kyoto Tower

first affirmed the typical image of Kyoto as steeped in tradition, describing the city as old, with a large river running in the middle (Kamo-gawa), wide, and calm, captured in the specific dialect *Kyo-kotoba* (interview, March 20, 2010). She elaborated that Kyoto is a perfect size, noting that a person can go anywhere by bicycle, making it easy to navigate the city. She further described Kyoto's culture as similar to that of Paris or other cities in Europe—perhaps a more attractive image for the foreign tourist than the Japanese—with numerous cafés everywhere, clearly positioning Kyoto as a cosmopolitan city center within a global context. In contrast to the older gentleman (mentioned above) who kept to the script and presented only the traditional Kyoto, this young woman stressed that there is actually a mix of the "old" and the "new."

Kyoto actually sits on the cusp of cutting-edge culture, home to technological giants Kyocera and Nintendo, iconic Kyoto Tower (see Figure 5.8) and the ultra-modern Kyoto train station; the second-largest station building in Japan, which opened in 1997, complete with a shopping mall, hotel, theater and more. Another major shopping center opened in 2010 just behind this station, and more recently the huge electronics and home-product store Yodobashi Camera moved in shortly thereafter. For families, there is a new aquarium and the Kyoto Zoo was recently upgraded—all these measures both increase tourism while further modernizing the city.

There is a playful recognition of tradition in much modern design within Kyoto, expressed in everything from food to fashion. Young people may wear *kimono*, but bring in bright patterns and bold hairstyles. Several of my older informants dismiss such modernizing techniques as garish, exclaiming that these types of *kimono* are actually rentals worn by tourists from Tokyo and elsewhere, thus upholding the refined image of Kyoto aesthetic sensibilities. The traditional and the modern are often at odds with each other in Kyoto.

When asked what music best characterizes the city, both interviewees at the Kyoto Tourist Center, not surprisingly, immediately highlighted the *Gion-bayashi* of the *Gion Matsuri* introduced above. But then their perceptions differed, confirming that tradition and modernity are at play in the contemporary music of Kyoto as well. The older gentleman elaborated that traditional music, such as *gagaku* and *noh*, with a connection to the Heian period and the history of Kyoto, is an important marker of Kyoto's musical identity. He therefore sends tourists to Gion Corner to experience traditional Japanese music and Kyoto culture.

The Gion Corner is an establishment that offers the tourist a conveniently commoditized taste of traditional Japanese culture. The brochure invites one to "Experience All About Traditional Kyoto!" through demonstrations of *kadō* (flower arranging), *gagaku* (court music), *bunraku* (puppet play), *kyōmai* (Kyoto-style dance), *koto* (Japanese harp), *sadō* (tea ceremony), and *kyōgen* (traditional comic play), all within one building and the span of a few hours. This approach to consuming culture is of course problematic. And to be sure, when asked about Gion Corner, the younger staff member looked reluctant explaining that Europeans (and Japanese too for that matter) "don't like it because it is too touristy"—presenting Kyoto culture in ten-minute snippets of lots of styles: "Europeans [she never mentioned Americans] understand what an authentic atmosphere would be, even if they don't really understand the music, and they know this is strange."

The younger staff member instead suggested the first livehouse developed in Kyoto, called "Takutaku"; although there are not a lot of nightclubs for dancing, she continued to recommend some other livehouses (see Novak 2013 for further discussion of livehouses and *jazu kissa*—establishments where people gather to listen to recordings—in Kyoto). She quickly added that there are *koto* and *shakuhachi* concerts, and there is music at the temples of course, never losing sight of the traditional music of Japan and image of Kyoto. She came to an important observation here, namely that there are few performance spaces suitable for live music making in Kyoto. And to be sure, the number and quality of these locations becomes important for understanding the musical life of the city more broadly.

Mapping the Musical Life of Kyoto

One might expect an active and vibrant musical life in this cosmopolitan city; upon closer look, however, there actually is limited music in Kyoto in general, largely due to the lack of performance spaces. *Kabuki*, which originated on the riverbank of Kamo-gawa, is still performed at a large theater (Minami-za) and selections of *noh*, as well the comic stories of *kyōgen*, are performed at shrines. At the temples, you might also find traditional instrumental music in autumn and spring (I performed in one such "fall festival" on *shamisen* in 2004), which are the major tourist seasons, but there is little music programmed in the winter or summer. Traditional instrumental genres including *shakuhachi* or *koto* may be performed in smaller spaces, but these are rare and quite expensive events. There is the larger Kyoto Prefectural Center for Arts and Culture, which programs a variety of events from *bunraku* to Korean dance to *taiko* (all of which I saw at this hall during my fieldwork stay—http://www.bungei.jp/index.shtml). And the Kyoto Concert Hall—featuring a large main hall with two floors of seating and regular performances of Western orchestral music—is modern, elaborate and impressive (http://www.kyoto-ongeibun.jp/kyotoconcerthall). Access to these latter spaces, which no doubt charge high fees, is limited to professional performers.

It is similarly difficult to find suitable rehearsal spaces not just in Kyoto, but also throughout Japan, due to the close proximity of Japanese homes to each other, thin walls, and limited interior space. In Kyoto, people could often be seen practicing along the riverbanks of Kamo-gawa, harkening back to the days of *kabuki*, but more often they resorted to renting rehearsal space in expensive studios. Studio Rag (http://www.studiorag.com), for example, rents rooms ranging from 800–1000 yen (U.S.$8.50–10.50) an hour. Studio Rag maintains a number of establishments around Kyoto, all of which typically offer rooms of various sizes on multiple floors. Studios normally include a drum kit and amps, so people only need to bring their wind, string, or smaller percussive instrument. I frequented Studio Rag myself in 2009–10, but never saw anyone with Japanese instruments (*wagakki*). And the staff confirmed that rarely does anyone practice traditional Japanese music (*hōgaku*).

Those unfamiliar with *hōgaku* often made the false assumption that there were numerous opportunities to enjoy traditional music in Kyoto, including the staff at the Kyoto Tourist Center. The general expectation for an abundance of traditional music again speaks to the image of Kyoto—as one steeped in tradition—and therefore also presumably traditional music. Musicians in this world, however, had a decidedly different impression, regularly noting the lack of music in general in Kyoto. The disparity here may lie in one's definition of "a lot"—what may seem like "a lot" for the casual audience member may not be so for the professional musician trying to make a living from teaching opportunities and live performance fees.

Professional classical Japanese drummer Tosha Rōetsu and his wife and *shamisen* player Imafuji Misuzu (both their professional names) agree that given the classic image of the city, one would think there would be a great deal of classical Japanese music (interview, June 29, 2010). Both explained, however, that with the exception of the *geiko* community, there are not many opportunities to perform and therefore most teachers have moved to Tokyo, with only a few left in Kyoto. Even their son, a professional *fue* performer, went to Tokyo University of the Arts (Tokyo Geijutsu Daigaku, Tokyo's premiere arts college) and has stayed in Tokyo ever since. There is a much larger population in Tokyo, and therefore, even though Tokyo's image is wrapped up with the height of modernity and technology, more people can be found who are interested in traditional arts.

Kenny Endo first suggested I contact Tosha Rōetsu to pursue the study of traditional percussion before departing for Japan. However, once in Kyoto, I quickly became anxious about establishing relationships with teachers and locating various research sites. As I had some trouble reaching Tosha at first, I searched for other classical percussion teachers with little success. I did find one teacher who traveled to Kyoto once a month and offered lessons on Saturday afternoons in a small, rental studio in a residential area. Finally making contact with Tosha, I never attended these classes, but this experience affirms both his and Imafuji's impressions of the state of *hōgaku*.

Tosha bemoans the lack of quality performers in Kyoto, and claims therefore that "it is difficult to express Kyoto's heart through the music anymore. Whenever one wants to perform publicly, performers must be invited from Tokyo." Imafuji does not feel the *geiko* are affecting the lack of performance of *hōgaku* elsewhere in the city; instead, other issues seem to be at play. Professional *nagauta shamisen* player Kineya Hiroki agrees that there isn't much *hōgaku* in Kyoto, but he thinks that today Japanese people just don't connect with traditional music—literally because "the tempo is too slow." He explained this with the image of trains clarifying that "the tempo of *hōgaku* does not match the speed of today's fast trains . . . the speed of life . . . " (interview, June 22, 2010).

As discussed in Chapter 2, young people simply do not feel connected to *hōgaku* and know very little about Japanese instruments because they learn Western instruments in school. With the change in the Ministry of Education, Culture, Sports, Science and Technology policy perhaps this awareness of *hōgaku* will change. The particular percussion that Tosha teaches, however, including the *ko-tsuzmi*, *ō-tsuzumi* and *taiko* of the *noh-hayashi*, although included in this new curriculum, are prohibitively expensive for most schools to afford (see Yamaha's (n.d.) website for an idea of the immense cost) and there are few teachers available and willing to instruct even those that have the means to acquire the necessary equipment. Though the numbers are low, nevertheless some people do find their way to Japanese classical drumming, and Tosha Rōetsu specifically, through the more mainstream and accessible world of *taiko* (here referring to the ensemble drumming introduced in Chapter 4), just as I did.

Finding My Way to Taiko

I too falsely assumed that Kyoto would contain a great deal of *hōgaku* and, given my belief that *taiko* was in fact a traditional music originating centuries ago, that there must be an abundance of *taiko* performers in Kyoto as well. Through fieldwork in 2009–10 in Kyoto with numerous musicians of both traditional percussion and the more modern *taiko*, both assumptions were of course proven false. Once on the ground in Kyoto, my enthusiastic plans to study *taiko* were temporarily derailed when I found it extremely difficult at first to locate any groups or teachers. The one exception was the widely publicized Taiko Center, a large school actively teaching *taiko*, which would become a central focus in my research (see further discussion below).

Through various conversations with *taiko* enthusiasts in Kansai, several people indicated there are lots of *taiko* groups in Osaka and Nagoya because of the presence of *taiko* makers (Bender 2012), but few groups in Kyoto. Opinions varied about Kobe, some finding even less than Kyoto, while others noted several prominent professional groups. Much of this data is speculation, as it is extremely difficult to track the exact numbers of groups and to precisely differentiate between amateur, semi-professional, and professional practitioners.

In fall 2009, for example, the National Taiko Database (Kuni n.d.), a database of registered *taiko* groups throughout Japan, included only 26 groups in Kyoto prefecture and twelve in Kyoto proper, with none in Shimogyō-ku, the specific area where we were living inside the city at the time. Even amongst those listed, several of the groups were no longer active when I contacted them. And one of the main groups I did form a relationship with, Murasaki Daiko, was not listed at all. As I contacted performers recommended by colleagues in North America, or on both the National Taiko Database and Taiko Resource: Japanese Taiko Group Listing (Leong n.d.), I developed a clearer understanding of what constituted the broad category of *taiko* in Kyoto. This data did reveal that performers ranged from professionals to college teams and community groups, nursery school teachers and parents.

Without question, the numbers are relatively low in Kyoto, but the very fact that I had such a difficult time locating performers to work with, despite my initial expectations, actually became one of the main theoretical interests motivating the entire project. I tried to understand this dearth of *taiko*, which in the end may have made the project more doable. If I were in Tokyo, for example, sifting through all the opportunities to find a "way in" would have been nothing short of overwhelming. I certainly could not claim after only one year of fieldwork that I had a thorough grasp of *taiko* in all of Tokyo, while I feel somewhat confident saying this about Kyoto.

As I wanted to develop my own skills as a *taiko* player and in the process expand my repertoire to bring to my burgeoning ensemble, Zakuro-Daiko, back home, I decided to kill two birds with one stone and focus my attention primarily on groups with which I could play myself. This narrowed my research considerably and created advantages when collecting interviews. The nature of my fieldwork, which involved taking both private and group lessons, participating in long rehearsals, and regularly practicing on my own, involved numerous ways of both participating and observing; nevertheless, interviewing became a central means of collecting data. Sharing so much time with fellow practitioners increased intimacy and inspired questions. Interviewing can be nerve-wracking for anyone, especially when the two people involved do not speak the same native language, but talking when you've just worked together through a new piece for the past four hours—sweating, counting, tapping—can put everyone at ease. My perception is that people came to know me, recognize my sincerity, and were willing to work through the tricky bits. I simply became much less interested in pursuing interviews with people with whom I did not share this intimacy, concerned I would not gain as much from the experience.

Shortly after I arrived in Kyoto, for example, I became extremely interested in the group Bachi Holic, who beautifully combine elements of folk music through song and dance with *taiko*. At the time of research, their name dominated initial Internet searches, further distinguished by the most professional looking promotional materials (posters, fliers, etc.). I went to see them perform in a small livehouse called Chicken George in Kobe in fall 2009 and enjoyed their performance immensely, made all the more interesting as they invited a Korean *janngu* (an hourglass-shaped drum) player on stage, hinting at new intercultural exchanges. I immediately made contact, but was disappointed to learn that they do not teach and therefore I had to put my interest in them on the back burner. Nearly a year later as my time in the field came to a close, I would visit their main office and have the opportunity to interview their creative director Nakajima Hiroyuki, expanding my understanding of *taiko* in general. But such difficult choices must be made as any ethnographic project develops.

Aesthetic preferences also informed my decisions about who to explore in more detail. One cannot devote endless hours to rehearsal and practice—navigating at times complicated discussions in Japanese—of a music one does not connect with on some level. The music must motivate the research. There was one group in Kyoto, for example, who did offer classes, and I went to see them perform live in fall 2009 at a large auditorium on a campus. They exhibited great enthusiasm, possessed wonderful equipment, and maintained a high level of professionalism, but performed a style of *taiko* which, while impressive in the performer's exuberance and stamina, did not speak to me personally. I thus decided it best to place my efforts elsewhere, and I wish this group well.

There were also performances by smaller or less well-known groups, often comprising members of other larger groups I was working with, students at the large Taiko Center, or other amateur groups I located on the Internet. But they either were not in Kyoto proper or too far removed from the central research, landing both literally and figuratively on the periphery. Collectively, the information gathered while exploring all these groups and attending numerous events throughout the year painted a broad picture of *taiko* in Kyoto, which certainly helps contextualize the specific groups that motivate the remainder of this study. It would be presumptuous, however, to claim the following presents an exhaustive study of Kyoto drumming practices in every neighborhood. Nonetheless, given the relatively small number of groups in total, this restricted pool is fairly representative of what was actually happening at the time.

My research therefore focused on specific "sites"—encompassing the individuals, groups and institutions where I found myself taking lessons or participating in rehearsals—one of course being Kyoto as a whole. With a relatively small population, and encompassing 320 square miles and eleven wards, Kyoto and its distinctive culture become a pervasive background informing the musical practices within; some people reject while others completely embrace the classical image. More specific sites include the world of *hōgaku* and the intensive lessons of master performer Tosha Rōetsu, whose prominent position in both the musical life of Kyoto and the history of *taiko* has already been noted. *Taiko* takes on many faces within even the relatively small city of Kyoto, though all the groups that I focused on express the cosmopolitan characteristics established by the originating performers as described in Chapter 4. These additional sites in which I encountered the diversity of *taiko* circulated around the semi-professional group Basara, who rehearsed in a one-room schoolhouse just outside of Kyoto, and who consider their melodically focused aesthetic as "unusual"; the centralized Taiko Center, and by extension Matsuri-shū, the professional group associated with the school, who prize challenging rhythmic grooves; and the all-female professional group Murasaki Daiko, who are trying to assert tradition, but at the same time intensely focus on the marketability of their creation.

The specific stories of the performers, teachers and students in each of these sites will be told in the Case Studies of Chapter 6. What I learned in interviews with them all, however, first feeds the understanding of the position of both the Taiko Center and the lack of *taiko* in general in Kyoto to be considered below.

Family and Fieldwork

Once I established relationships with teachers at the Taiko Center, Basara and Murasaki Daiko, I was either in lesson or rehearsal well over 15 hours a week, and even more when Tosha Rōetsu held his traditional lessons, lasting all day long in some cases. I also spent considerable time practicing, at least two hours a day, and memorizing music, which naturally differed with each group. This all took quite a toll on my middle-aged body and mental health, but also resulted in my musical transformation; rarely as adults do we have such time to devote to our development as musicians.

Much is often made of the cut muscles and aggressive playing style often seen as characteristic of *taiko*—but there is another side to this physicality—as one must "persevere with patience" (*gaman suru*) through the pain. As a novice, I often had blisters on my hands and even feet, especially when switching sticks (*bachi*) or practicing new pieces with unfamiliar choreography. I came to see these blisters as a badge of courage, displayed proudly as evidence of my commitment to the art.

The stress on my body was both further exacerbated by the presence of my family, including one very active toddler. Having children in the field can impede one's research plans as unexpected family demands take precedence over fieldwork possibilities. Already having several lessons a week that kept me out at dinner, bath and bedtime, I did not feel I could schedule extensive interviews in the evening hours. And with informants working or in school during the day, particularly at the Taiko Center, this seriously effected the way that I collected my data—biking, busing, or taking the train throughout the city, meeting people at coffee shops at their convenience—while making it home in time to tuck in my little one in bed whenever possible. The trick was constantly trying to find a balance between family and an unstructured work schedule. On the positive side, having my son with me exposed me to sides of Japanese culture and an understanding of everyday life in Japan that I never experienced before (see Bestor, Steinhoff and Bestor (2003) for further consideration of fieldwork in Japan with and without family in tow).

The Kyoto Taiko Center

The Kyoto Taiko Center has arguably done more than any other institution in Japan to disseminate *taiko* to the masses and popularize the musical practice, even if at times problematically so. The Center presents a conveyor-belt approach to the study of *taiko*, offering large hour-long weekly classes, with little social interaction outside the classroom, thus requiring minimal commitment from participants, while easily spreading the joy of *taiko* to large numbers of interested parties. This approach to teaching Japanese ensemble drumming is definitely removed from the traditional Japanese music lesson, during which one sits patiently on the floor listening to other students while waiting for one's turn (see further discussion in Chapter 6). The classes are generally perceived as expensive, but nevertheless, the Taiko Center, which now has branches from Tokyo to Kyūshū, consistently fills all weekly courses and daily workshops.

Higashi Munenori, founder of the Taiko Center, has strong motivations and a clear vision for the school (interview, June 23, 2010). Originally from Nagano prefecture, Higashi graduated from Ritsumeikan University, where he first learned to play *taiko* in a traditional music and dance circle. Higashi first established the Taiko Center in 1988 in Kyoto; then people he knew opened centers in other cities including Fukuoka and Hiroshima, but not all these were successful and several have closed.

Higashi established the Taiko Center so that people with an interest in *taiko* could gather and have a good time, equating the practice to pursuing a martial arts (*budō*), where students can systematically pursue the art in the classroom. Higashi also established the Taiko Center with people's health in mind, to release stress and improve physical and mental well-being. To play *taiko* requires "good ears" and great concentration, all while providing significant physical stimulation. He finds that when striking the drum you hear the rhythm but also feel the vibrations in the stomach, which is a powerful experience. Higashi in fact believes that compared to other instruments "*taiko* produces the greatest reverberation or resonance in the body (*shindō*)," and not surprisingly, a number of people I interviewed mention the sheer power of these vibrations as a main attraction.

In 2010, there were in total eleven studios in Kantō (eastern Japan, including Tokyo) and Kansai (Kyoto, Osaka, and Hyogo prefectures), offering a range of weekly classes, which run for three months, divided into beginning, intermediate and advanced levels, and one-day workshops. At the time of research, there were 18 instructors in Kyoto (as compared to 36 in Tokyo). The instructors are either professionals or have "graduated" from classes, with whom Higashi makes a "loose agreement" to teach, but in the future he would like to develop a "*taiko gakkō*" (taiko school) to train Taiko Center instructors, "granting licenses" to people in order for them to do so. According to Higashi, the studios in Kansai service some 3,000 students (others I interviewed thought there are more likely 1,500 students in Kansai and 3,000 in total in Kantō and Kansai). There are approximately five to twelve students in the classes at the Kyoto center, and more at the Osaka center, which is a larger space and therefore can accommodate bigger groups.

In the past, both Higashi and Kawarazaki Yoshihiro (long-time instructor at the Taiko Center, former member of Matsuri-shū, and one of the central people to be discussed in Chapter 6's case studies) found that most of the students were actually primary school teachers, learning *taiko* to bring back to children in their own classes, but things are changing and there are more housewives and seniors (interview with Kawarazaki Yoshihiro, April 27, 2007). The vast majority of students at the Taiko Center are now women over 40, whose children are grown and have the time to pursue a hobby. One female student interviewee thinks that women want to have fun and the Taiko Center suits this purpose. She explained that

> ... men don't as easily join a group and make new friends. Women are more likely to look at something and say I would like to try that and join a class. Also men, for the most part, are company workers so they don't have the time to do these things at night ...

an impression shared by many. One male interviewee in his forties however, believed that even though men his age are rare at the center, as they are too busy working, since everyone is there to learn *taiko*, he doesn't feel "out of place."

More subjective assessment of the students in general at the school depended on the goals and level of the specific student I questioned. Students in the beginner classes are more likely there for "fun," while, even if there are not a lot of classes to meet the needs of intermediate and advanced students, those who really want to improve their skills in these classes are perceived as "committed" and "serious." But regardless of level and motivations, students and instructors referred to the typical student at the Taiko Center as "positive," "bright", "active," "energetic," "healthy," "people who enjoy life"—but also as people who "work hard." Just as Higashi envisioned, some may be there primarily for musical reasons or mental health—to "refresh" from the stress of the day—while others are there for exercise.

I first took beginner-level classes at the Taiko Center in 2004, at which time there were a number of other foreigners attending. In the more advanced-level courses in 2009–10, I never encountered foreigners. This disparity could result from the fact that foreigners, with some exceptions, are in Japan only for a short time. They often come to Japan with little to no previous training in *taiko*, and do not stay long enough to build up the skills necessary to proceed to more advanced classes. With the ever-increasing popularity of *taiko*, this is changing of course, and foreigners may not be as common at the Taiko Center because they have found other avenues to study while in Japan.

Higashi finds that amongst the Japanese students that there are lots of "teams" or groups in the areas surrounding Kyoto, including Osaka, Mie and Shiga whose members come to the Taiko Center and take classes, especially the one-day workshops, bringing pieces back home. In Kyoto proper, there are many festivals that require drummers, who then belong to a team associated with the neighborhood, which may or may not perform the repertoire learned in Taiko Center classes in their local groups.

Taiko Groups: Pros, Teams, Clubs and Circles

Taiko is performed by a variety of types of groups in Japan, each with a slightly different designation, albeit difficult to distinguish at times. The term "pros" typically refers to performers who make a living teaching and performing *taiko*. Although opinions varied, there was general agreement that Matsuri-shū were professionals, possibly Bachi Holic, and to a lesser extent another group called Shien. "Group" and "team" refers to serious amateurs who typically meet weekly to practice, or have a specific performance for which they are preparing. "Circles" are common at colleges, are student-run and offer an opportunity to do everything from playing tennis to practicing *taiko*, but the primary purpose is for fun, and more time can be spent sitting around and chatting than actually performing. "Clubs" in junior high school or high school are school-sponsored, and therefore a bit more regulated. Most *taiko* practitioners share these basic conceptions; however, one group could be called any of these terms at different times.

At a one-day workshop on the piece "Buchiawase Daiko" taught by Kawarazaki on January 24, 2010, for example, the students (all women of various ages, the youngest a teenager and the oldest late middle-aged) came from as far as Osaka and had different backgrounds; one knew the piece well and was very confident, another, a high school music teacher, was learning *taiko* so she could teach her students while the 13-year-old girl, affectionately referred to as "daughter" (*musume*) by Kawarazaki, was playing with her club at junior high school. Both Kawarazaki's comments and the goals these students shared during breaks made clear it was understood by all that this piece could be brought back to their respective groups. Kawarazaki continually stressed the flexibility of the piece, noting places where each particular individual could make changes. The Taiko Center produces notation and supporting video of many of the pieces they transmit, a process that problematizes their position in the broader *taiko* community (see further discussion below), but the published notation differed from the interpretation Kawarazaki shared with the class, and just as with scores in *hōgaku*, was only a loose map for all to follow.

Whether one is learning pieces to take back to perform with their group, to maintain health, or to improve mental acuity, the Taiko Center is there to service these needs. Ultimately it is a business, one that Higashi feels—as the only organization in Kyoto to offer systematized classes (*kyōshitsu*) in *taiko*—serves an important function nevertheless. Several students described the school in similar terms—as a business that supports people's hobbies, or literally a "company for drumming" (*tataku kaisha*). As a business, the Taiko Center promotes itself through its welcoming website (http://www.taiko-center.co.jp), regular newsletters, numerous glossy fliers, its biannual recitals, and the professional group Matsuri-shū (comprising teachers from the school); the center also runs a shop selling instruments, clothing and accessories, and of course the scores, recordings and instructional materials which they produce. The Taiko Center certainly has collected numerous interesting pieces for people to play, described by one student as "fun and catchy," with equally enjoyable choreography. This approach increases the music's accessibility and in turn marketability—an indication of Higashi's good business sense.

Indeed, one of the critiques of the Taiko Center's work is that they have taken regional pieces without permission, simplified them, and distributed them through DVDs, VHS, and scores, clearly commoditizing *taiko*. Higashi defends his approach, however, explaining years ago while teaching at a cultural-music center (Nagaoka Ongaku Center) both youngsters and adults were "really excited but did not know much about *taiko*." He realized there was no information, such as videos and written data, available about the style. As he taught at these cultural centers, more and more people wanted to learn *taiko*, so he made videos, arranging well-known pieces like "Raijin Daiko" and "Buchiawase Daiko" so children could learn them, and thus began to spread *taiko* awareness. According to Higashi, people had some understanding of other *wagakki* (*shakuhachi*, etc.), but these are "difficult to teach children . . . whereas *taiko* is teachable—accessible."

The Taiko Center has continued this centralizing work by producing a section in the Ministry of Education, Culture, Sports, Science and Technology instructional guide on Japanese music to introduce *taiko* to the masses through junior high school education programs (Urata et al. 2006). Higashi thinks that 80 percent of schools in Japan are using this guide, which includes a large section on *taiko*, featuring pictures of Kawarazaki on the barrel-shaped drum common to the genre (*nagado-daiko*). And according to Kawarazaki, children in fact regularly ask for his autograph. But scholars and performers look at the inclusion of *taiko* in schools with some skepticism, both because of the standardization and ultimate canonization of a limited repertoire, as well as the fact that *taiko* may be seen as an "easy" traditional music (Tokita and Hughes 2008:16). It is possible that through *taiko*, which is accessible and visceral, people may find their way to other traditional musics that require a greater commitment to master even the most basic of skills. And certainly both the Ministry of Education, Culture, Sports, Science, and Technology and organizations that promote Japanese culture, such as the Japan Foundation, may strategically be using *taiko*'s "coolness" as a conduit to other traditional musics that consumers may otherwise ignore. But the resistance to the approach of the Taiko Center I have experienced (based on casual conversation with professional *taiko* players) suggests that this work does not represent the feelings of everyone.

Nonetheless, the Taiko Center has successfully introduced *taiko* to numerous people who might not otherwise have the opportunity to drum—including women and children. This is especially important in a city like Kyoto, which offers limited opportunities to pursue music in general. But this comes at a high cost. As a business, the center is commonly critiqued as being expensive. The biannual student recitals (*Wadaiko Ongakusai*), for example, at which students perform the pieces they have worked on in the proceeding months, run for three days with up to a hundred performances, interspersed with "guest artists." Tickets to simply view the marathon cost 800 yen (U.S.$8.50) for a single day or 2,000 yen (U.S.$21.00) for all three days. But students who wish to perform on stage have to pay a 7,000 yen (U.S.$73.50) participation fee, with subsequent family members receiving a 50 percent discount. Despite the high costs, these events are so well attended they regularly sell out.

The recital not only provides an important goal for the students in the classes, but also attracts new members to the Taiko Center. One interviewee explains, "people come to the recital to watch friends and family and are surprised by what they see and take the classes." They don't know anything about *taiko* beforehand, but become interested at the recital, decide to try classes and the number of students increase—so in this way the recital has a positive affect on the *taiko* world. However, she went on to complain that the recital now combines classes from all over Kansai; in the past, Kyoto, Osaka, etc. all used to have separate recitals. Now that all the Kansai locations are combined, "there is no time to practice, everything is rushed and pressured." She was uneasy about only having five minutes to rehearse on stage before performing later in the day. She also agreed that it is expensive, and "feels too much like a business," a concern shared by other students as well. The emcees constantly encourage audience members to come take a class themselves, drawing attention away from the students actually performing that day and making the event more about the business than their accomplishments.

There is no doubt that the Taiko Center is expensive, especially for the younger students in college and on tight budgets, but older working adults are willing to pay for the convenience. One informant described the Taiko Center as handy for mature students—no fuss, no muss—"the staff is polite, everything is well managed, classes are scheduled at convenient times, with lots to choose from, with regular goals in the recital. Participating in a team, in contrast, can be quite demanding time wise. . . ."

Whether one approves or not of the approach of the Taiko Center—that standardizes *taiko* through its operation as a business—its prominent position in Kyoto cannot be denied. And although *taiko* is found throughout Japan now, before Higashi established the Taiko Center, he feels that beyond the neighborhood *matsuri* or *Gion Matsuri*, there were few opportunities for the average person in Kyoto to play, and therefore he is really responsible for starting *taiko* in Kyoto. This perception was confirmed by comments of both instructors and a number of students in interviews. Even though one might expect the work of the Taiko Center to actually be inspiring the promulgation of *taiko* in Kyoto, its dominance may in fact have the opposite effect, as people can pick or choose courses at ease without committing to the regular work of a group. But there are of course numerous reasons for the lack of *taiko* in Kyoto.

Taiko within Kyoto

Given the prominent position of the *Gion Matsuri*, for example, I had initially wondered if the percussive music of the *Gion-bayashi* dominated Kyoto, therefore accounting for the lack of *taiko* as its own ensemble style. In interviews, when asked about this festival several informants even hummed the rhythm of *Gion-bayashi*, affirming its ubiquitous presence. But others felt the festival was geared more for tourists now and engaged only a small portion of Kyoto residents who are actually involved in the maintenance of the *yamaboko* and performance of the music. Even amongst these neighborhood groups, some felt the festival has lost its thrill.

Kawarazaki, a proud native of Kyoto, shared the story of a well-known musician of *Gion-bayashi*, Yoshida. He explains that Yoshida was very enthusiastic about *Gion Matsuri* and used to be invited to come to the Taiko Center to teach. People thought the music involved just a simple "konchiki chin" (mnemonic on the brass-gong (*atarigane*)) rhythm but Yoshida played this with great passion. Kawarazaki thinks there must have been really more intense *Gion-bayashi* within the *Gion Matsuri* in the past, and Yoshida apparently agreed "*Gion-bayashi* used to be the kind of music that would make your blood boil." Since the *Gion Matsuri* has become one of the best-known festivals in all of Japan, Kawarazaki bemoans that "it has become elegant (*miyabi*) but has lost its heart."

The rhythms of *Gion-bayashi*, albeit catchy, do not allow the same type of excitement that one expects from *taiko*. The instrumentation includes smaller *shime-daiko*, but not the large *nagado-daiko* drums that similarly draw people to *taiko*. Since rehearsals for the *Gion Matsuri* only last a few weeks in the summer, and involve men who belong to specific community groups, the *Gion-bayashi* therefore are not keeping the drummers busy all year round. Some feel that the presence of the *Gion Matsuri*, just like the Taiko Center, should inspire more *taiko* performance in Kyoto, but this does not seem to be the case.

There is a general perception that there must be a great deal of drumming associated with the smaller *matsuri* attached with the many temples and shrines that inhabit the city, since these groups have strong associations with the neighborhood (*chiiki*). However, newcomers to the city have no connection, no "way in" to these drumming groups. As a result, it is highly likely that there are numerous neighborhood groups that I just never encountered as I am not a member of those communities—there may be additional research to be done to more thoroughly map the musical life of Kyoto.

Kawarazaki nevertheless feels that even at temples and shrines, there are fewer and fewer *matsuri*. Such festivals "used to be a part of everyday life," but a lot of people from other areas of Japan are moving into Kyoto, who do not feel connected to their neighborhood, and therefore are less interested in continuing such traditions. Since there are fewer festivals being organized, "the festival itself becomes something detached from everyday life," which in circular fashion furthers the festival's decline. *Gion Matsuri* is no longer something you "*participate in,*" instead becoming something that you "*watch.*" Several other informants agreed that the festivals have become so elegant that even the drumming of *matsuri* no longer connects with residents in Kyoto. In neighboring Shiga prefecture, in comparison, agriculture is important, so there are lots of festivals related in particular to the rice harvest—from asking for rain to fruitful crops. The need for groups to supply music for these festivals results in a thriving *taiko* community.

The association of drumming with such "working-class" activities actually may prevent its proliferation within Kyoto. Frankly, the reality of *taiko* performance does not fit the overall image of the city as refined and classical (*kotenteki*). Yamauchi Reach (another teacher at the Taiko Center and member of Matsuri-shū, who will be further considered in Chapter 6's case studies), when asked his opinion on the reasons for the low number of professional groups in Kyoto simply answered "Because it is Kyoto" (*Kyoto da kara*) (interview, May 9, 2010). Kyoto people do not play drums because they feel it is something "lower-class" people do; Kyoto people are too refined, too attached to the image of the court, and do not want to be associated with such an activity. This image may be exacerbated by the association of drum makers with Japan's "untouchable" class (*burakumin*), the caste of people allowed to work with leather (see the documentary *Angry Drummers* (2010) for more information on *taiko* amongst *burakumin* in Osaka).

As noted earlier, there is a perception that there are prolific performances of fine arts and numerous people who study and/or like traditional music, such as *shamisen*, *noh* or *kyōgen*. Yamauchi argues "This does not leave space for *taiko,*" implying that most people feel that if you are going to learn music in Kyoto, you learn traditional music instead. Yamauchi, who has also studied Western and classical Japanese percussion as well, explains that amongst established, traditional Japanese teachers, there is a pervasive belief that "one does not mix classical styles with folk and/or modern styles"—one does not play both *nagauta shamisen* and *tsugaru-jamisen*, classical percussion and *taiko*.

Whether *hōgaku* is actually widely practiced in Kyoto is not the point, rather the "idea" that it is may affect ensemble drumming, which is too modern and unrefined in comparison. Anything "new" is incongruous with the powerful historic image of the city, and therefore modern ensemble drumming does not fit with the concept of traditionalism that seems to be so supported and prized by Kyoto people. And this belief extends to the music itself, as one informant explained "Kyoto people cannot connect with the rhythms of *taiko,*" which have no history: "Unchanging things are important in Kyoto ... Old things [are] important ... so contemporary things don't fit so well."

One informant, however, a Kyoto native, recognizing the mixture of old and new that actually characterizes both *taiko* (with its melding of old instruments and modern musical elements and performance practice) and Kyoto (with the *miyako* image and modernity of companies like Kyocera and Nintendo) are actually well suited to each other. But this recognition was rare amongst *taiko* performers I interviewed. Kawarazaki suggests that even if the style were to "fit," the very fact that *taiko* is popular would prompt Kyoto people to turn away; the "personality of Kyoto people" leads them to resist jumping on the latest bandwagon. If we accept Kyoto culture as in fact "classier" than all the rest of Japan, is there any wonder that *taiko*, with its bare and sweaty bodies, has been slow to blossom?

There are more practical reasons inhibiting the widespread enjoyment of *taiko* in the city as well. With the lack of suitable rehearsal and performance spaces for both traditional Japanese music and European art musics, it is no surprise there are even fewer performances of *taiko*—with its large instruments and deafening volume. Locations can be found, but they are expensive and often awkward to access. Rehearsal space can be rented at the Taiko Center; for example, on weekends, one person costs 1,500 yen (U.S.$16.00) per hour and four people 5,000 yen (U.S.$52.50) per hour, though this includes the use of the drums as well. Even if spaces can be found to rehearse within the city, drums must be muted, or rooms soundproofed with double doors to dampen the sound, sending many groups outside the city proper to find suitable spaces, and therefore discouraging new groups from forming.

Even for the few well-known professional performers, there similarly are few spaces for public performances, and many professionals must perform in livehouses, perhaps harkening back to Sukeroku playing in cafés and cabarets in Tokyo in the 1960s (Pachter 2013). In Kyoto, this means carrying heavy equipment up and down narrow stairs, and performing on small stages with low ceilings. Matsuri-shū only performed at the larger Kyoto Cultural Center twice in 2009–10. Many informants feel *taiko* should be performed outside, but not everyone enjoys its booming qualities, and therefore even these opportunities are limited. At the time of research, in Kyoto there were still no *taiko* festivals, gatherings bringing multiple *taiko* enthusiasts together, as is common in other cities in Japan and North America. The lack of numerous *taiko* performances in Kyoto can lead to healthy, enthusiastic crowds and filled seats at these rare events, ultimately presenting a false idea that this is a well-supported and received music, but which in reality is not the case.

Marty Bracey is an American percussionist who has lived in Japan for over 35 years spending ten years in Tokyo, ten years in Kanazawa, and ten years in Kyoto working with different musicians and students along the way (interview, February 3, 2010). He feels that there is so little *taiko* in Kyoto because of a lack of financial support from both local and broader governing and artistic organizations; a result of *taiko*'s lack of "roots" in a tradition of drumming in Kyoto. He stresses that he doesn't see a single "Kyoto drumming style," rather he finds "everyone is just doing his or her personal thing." Bracey credits Kodō and Ondekoza as creating ensemble drumming, but in Kyoto there are actually a lot of "personal styles" in *taiko*, rather than groups that trace a lineage to either of these significant figures, or any other tradition for that matter. Performers may claim a "Kyoto connection" consciously as a way to be recognized as a cultural representative of the city, and thus gain municipal support (financial and otherwise), but, as Bracey jokingly says, "don't believe the hype."

The lack of "common roots" that Bracey identifies leads to the tremendous diversity of performance practices that will be explored in more detail in the four case studies to follow.

References

Angry Drummers: A Taiko Group from Osaka Japan. 2010. 85 minutes.
Bender, Shawn. 2012. *Taiko Boom: Japanese Drumming in Place and Motion*. Berkeley: University of California Press.
Bestor, Theodore C., Patricia G. Steinhoff and Victoria Lyon Bestor, eds. 2003. *Doing Fieldwork in Japan*. Honolulu: University of Hawaii Press.
City of Kyoto. n.d. "World Heritage Historic Monuments of Ancient Kyoto." *City of Kyoto* (n.d.): http://www.city.kyoto.jp/bunshi/bunkazai/sekaiisan-e.htm (accessed November 25, 2014).
Dalby, Liza. 1998. *Geisha*. Berkeley/Los Angeles: University of California Press.

Downer, Lesley. 2000. *Geisha: The Secret History of a Vanishing World*. London: Headline.
——. 2006. "The City Geisha and Their Role in Modern Japan: Anomaly or Artistes?" In M. Feldman and B. Gordon, eds., *The Courtesan's Arts: Cross-Cultural Perspectives*, pp. 223–242. Oxford: Oxford University Press.
Foreman, Kelly M. 2008. *The Gei of Geisha: Music, Identity and Meaning*. Burlington, VT: Ashgate.
Gillan, Matthew. 2012. *Songs From the Edge of Japan: Music-Making in Yaeyama and Okinawa*. Farnham: Ashgate.
Horii, Reiichi. 2009. *Oriori no Kyō Kotoba [Everyday Kyoto Dialect]*. Kyoto: Kyoto Shimbun Publishing Center.
Iguchi, Kawori. 2008. "Reading/Playing Music: The Musical Notations of the Kyoto Gion Festival and the Noh Flute." *Ethnomusicology Forum* 17(2):249–268.
Kano, Shin. 1994. *Kyō Kotoba Mame Jiten [Kyoto Dialect Small Dictionary]*. Kyoto: Kyoto no Shiseki o Tazunerukai.
Kuni. n.d. "The National Taiko Database." *Kuni-net* (n.d.): http://www.kuni-net.com/cgi/database/main.html (accessed September 11, 2009).
Kyoto City Official Travel Guide. n.d. "Gion Matsuri Festival." *Kyoto City Official Travel Guide* (n.d.): http://www.kyoto.travel/events/gionmatsuri_festival/ (accessed November 13, 2009).
Lancashire, Terence. 2011. *An Introduction to Japanese Folk Performing Arts*. Farnham: Ashgate.
Leong, David. n.d. "Resource: Japanese Taiko Group" *Rolling Thunder* (n.d.): http://www.taiko.com/taiko_resource/groups_j.html (accessed September 11, 2009).
Mori, Ken. 1995. *Kyō Kotoba Kyō Zaikyō Ei Jiten [Kyoto Dialect Phrasebook]*. Kyoto: Uni Plan.
Novak, David. 2013. *Japanoise: Music at the Edge of Circulation*. Durham, NC: Duke University Press.
Pachter, Benjamin. 2013. "Wadaiko in Japan and the United States: The Intercultural History of a Music Genre." Ph.D. dissertation, University of Pittsburgh.
Rowthorn, Chris, et al. 2007. *Lonely Planet: Japan, 10th Edn*. Oakland, CA: Lonely Planet Publications.
Surak, Kristin. 2013. *Making Tea, Making Japan: Cultural Nationalism in Practice*. Stanford, CA: Stanford University Press.
Tai, Ryūichi and Takeshi Masuda. 2005. "Gion Matsuri." *Research Centre for Japanese Traditional Music* (March 31, 2005): http://w3.kcua.ac.jp/jtm/archives/resarc/gionbayashi/kikusuiboko/english.html (accessed May 14, 2014).
Tokita, Alison M. and David W. Hughes, eds. 2008. *The Ashgate Research Companion to Japanese Music*. Farnham: Ashgate.
Tsuchiyama, Yukiko. n.d. "Brief summary of Gion Matsuri." *Kyoto Mirahouse* (n.d.): http://kyoto.mirahouse.jp/gion/gion_matsuri_e.html (accessed November 13, 2014).
Urata, Kenjiro, et. al. 2006. *Chūgakusei no Kigaku. [Junior High School Instrumental Music]*. Tokyo: Kyoiku Geijitsu Sha.
Yamaha. n.d. "Wagakki." *Yamaha* (n.d.): http://jp.yamaha.com/products/musical-instruments/educational_equipments/download/images/09.pdf (accessed November 25, 2014).

CHAPTER 6

Four Case Studies and Some Conclusions

The following case studies explore in ethnographic detail classical Japanese percussion, and the world of *hōgaku*, and ensemble *taiko* performance in contemporary Kyoto. My methodological approach leans towards "performative ethnography" (Wong 2008:88), in which I often find myself performing as well, opening up lines of communication through music making that would not be possible otherwise (see previous discussion in Chapter 5). Performative ethnography moreover "shows" rather than "tells" how an event occurs. As Wong explains "This is central to the methodology of performative ethnography: you circle around particularities and skirt the conceit of the typical, the normative, the generalized, the characteristic, the archetypal" (ibid.:85), but still provide analytical potential, however, any one experience can provide many conclusions: "It may fracture a given moment into mirrored possibilities, but I am not using it to shut down the necessity of arrival points" (ibid.:87).

The following stories are therefore intended to show rather than tell, while I will draw some conclusions and connect with broader themes of the text in the end. Each site presents unique practices, asking varied questions of the data, and therefore the discussion is organized slightly differently throughout. However, each case study seeks to understand the pedagogical philosophy of teachers, motivations of students, and vision of performers, captured in illustrative musical examples.

Each one paints its own picture but collectively provides an overview of how both Japanese classical percussion and *taiko* inhabit Kyoto. Despite the fact that in the proceeding discussion most people see no connection between *taiko* and its immediate context, the following case studies show the ways in which the performance of percussion within each of these sites is at play with Kyoto's cultural identity. In doing so, these case studies also reveal the extreme diversity of performance styles even within a relatively small urban space and limited musical and, more specifically, *taiko* scene.

More broadly, these case studies expand our understanding of processes at play in the performance of a broad range of musics in contemporary Japan. They reflect the regionalism and diversity that actually characterizes Japanese culture, as well as the effects of modernization—the melding of the traditional and the modern—Japanese and foreign—that occurred in the twentieth-century and continues to occur.

Tosha Rōetsu and the *Pontochō Okeiko* (Lesson)

There may be some question at first as to why I include Tosha Rōetsu who, strictly speaking, is not an ensemble *taiko* performer in a study of the genre in Kyoto. But as will be seen in the discussion below, he assumed an important position not only in my imagination of *taiko* in Kyoto, and the performance of *hōgaku* more importantly, but also in the experiences of *taiko* performers around the world.

Figure 6.1 Tosha Rōetsu

Tosha Rōetsu is originally from Yokohama, but moved to Osaka when a child, and then to Kyoto about fifty years ago (see Figure 6.1). He initially became interested in traditional Japanese arts through his mother, a Japanese classical dance (*nihon buyō*) teacher, and went to study with Tosha Rosen, the former head (*iemoto*) of this particular school of classical percussion, which includes *taiko*, *ko-tsuzumi*, and *ō-tsuzumi*—the drums and styles of the *noh-hayashi*. These are used in numerous other genres including *kabuki* and the narrative dance form *nagauta*, which is performed both in the theater and as a chamber music on its own. He is an active performer and much in demand, despite the limited opportunities in Kyoto, and his vocal calls (*kakegoe*) are considered by many to be some of the best in Japan, and were even featured in a television commercial. For Kineya Hiroki, when employed in *shamisen* performance, the *kakegoe* conduct or manage the group, but in *noh-hayashi*, and especially with Tosha, *kakegoe* "are music" themselves. Another one of Tosha's students describes his *kakegoe* as "the best," full of incredible nuance as he moves through timbres and pitches. But he is also known for his role in the early development of *taiko* as an ensemble style.

The Ideal Sound of Hōgaku and Ō-daiko

Tosha Rōetsu and his wife, Imafuji Misuzu, explain how rare it is for a *hōgaku* performer to also play what he calls *ō-daiko* (*ō-daiko* refers to a specific large drum in *kabuki* but Tosha applies the term to the type of ensemble drumming under consideration more broadly here as *taiko*), which is one of the reasons he became interested in the first place (interview, June 29, 2010). He claims he did not learn *ō-daiko* (ensemble) from a teacher, explaining one "doesn't have to learn *ō-daiko* from anybody" (implying that anyone can study on their own, through imitation, which is not the case with classical percussion). As a percussionist in *kabuki*

> ... you have to strike the *ō-daiko* (specific drum) to create atmospheric sound effects, such as when people are near a river for which you make a '*don don don don don*' sound, or for the ocean '*don don don don don tsu do don*'
> (mnemonics for larger-sized drums)

Originally the *ō-daiko* was never placed on stage, but was kept behind the curtain or wall that blocks these musicians from the audience's view (*kuromisu*). *Ō-daiko* were just instruments to create "artificial sound" (*gion*). He further explains: "in certain scenes in *kabuki*—the dawn, the mountain, the river, etc.—there is a specific way of playing the *ō-daiko* as artificial sound," which informs how he believes *ō-daiko* here meaning *taiko* as an ensemble should function musically.

He was first introduced to Ondekoza in the 1970s, traveling to work with them now and then over a period of about ten years. He thus holds an important position in the historical development of *taiko* as we know it today, a "fact" he is not shy to share. Since then he feels he has worked with approximately 200–250 people within the *taiko* world; however, it is unclear if he is primarily referring to professionals. He also established the amateur *taiko* group Kaze, who are associated with a specific Buddhist temple in Kyoto, and continue to perform his pieces. Despite his influence, he feels that *taiko* is rooted in the musics of *matsuri*, Shintō festivals, prayers for rain, or the gods, etc., confirming Bender's claim that early *taiko* performers took primarily technique from *hōgaku* and not rhythms or pieces (2012). And today the performance styles vary greatly between ensemble drumming and classical percussion—"the music is distinct, movements distinct, and audiences distinct." Nonetheless, numerous well-known performers, including Kenny Endo, have formally studied with not only Tosha, but also other masters of classical percussion.

Even if he does not articulate this directly aloud, he revealed his attitude that he does not see the instruments of the ensemble *taiko* as in fact "instruments" in the same way he views the *taiko*, *ko-tsuzumi* and *ō-tsuzumi* of *hōgaku*. He does explain that for him the business of *hōgaku* is just that: "business"; it is hard work and his profession, while *taiko* is a hobby and enormous fun. He is able to combine his interests because they are both grounded in rhythm and Japanese instruments, but this is where the similarities end for him.

Not surprisingly, Tosha stresses the ability to create the best sound as the most important quality in a performer, whether in *hōgaku* or *taiko*, with proper form and movement necessary to attain this goal in both. For him, the sound-color (*neiro*) is paramount. I mentioned that some performers focus on exciting the crowd, to which he replied, with his typical sense of humor, "if you want that you can just drink!" He continued to stress that improving the quality of the sound (*onshitsu*) should be a performer's primary goal. If one focuses just on "excitement," their skills never really improve. Both he and his wife, Imafuji, do feel that arm gestures and how people look is important in *hōgaku*. But when they compare *hōgaku* to *taiko*, *hōgaku* automatically appears more "polished because people are in proper *hakama* (formal Japanese clothing), while with *taiko*, people can perform in a t-shirt or *fundoshi* (a type of Japanese underwear) and nothing else."

The two worlds actually vary so greatly for them that comparisons are problematic. In regards to the way of striking the drum, for example, Tosha explains "in *hōgaku* it is really difficult to keep the body still and face expressionless, while moving only the striking hand, while in *ō-daiko* you move your entire body." The attitude of the performer is different, resulting in varying levels of musicality or sophistication (*kaku*), which is of course grounded in the sound: "*Ō-daiko* doesn't have that much color in the sound (*neiro*)—you can just hit the drums. Some people may just hit the *ko-tsuzumi* but the audience will grow bored; the color of sound on *ko-tsuzumi* is what draws in the audience." Although this claim may be a bit dismissive of the variety of timbre possible in contemporary *taiko* performers, Tosha's comment could be based on the fact that in *taiko* most of the drums cannot actually be tuned once skinned. The *ko-tsuzumi*, on the other hand, in comparison does not involve flashy choreography, but can produce both different timbre and numerous pitches by adjusting the tension on the cords used to affix the skins. Tosha finds some people value the immense sound of *taiko*, so much so that there is never contrasting silence, but in *hōgaku* "there is sound added to silence," creating a more harmonious balance through *ma*. Of course *taiko* groups are capable of performing "quietly," as well as taking advantage of the musicality possible through contrasting timbre, moments of repose, dynamic changes, etc.—but Tosha's comments reveal again his privileging of "the business of *hōgaku*" over "*ō-daiko* as a hobby."

Producing an image through sound is therefore quite important in his own compositions. When he creates music he usually envisions natural phenomena such as " a horse galloping, fire or wind blowing up spirally, or running water." He feels his music moves in a "circular fashion"; it can start anywhere and connect anywhere because he doesn't focus on a melody. Indeed, he prefers not to include any melodic instruments, such as *shamisen* or *shakuhachi*, as this would compete with the percussive rhythms; instead he creates drama through dynamics. After watching a documentary about Mongolia in which a large herd of running horses made a dust cloud, he was inspired to create the piece "Chonrima" for Kodō, which captures well his aesthetic vision (not included with the accompanying audio-visual materials). Tosha is an accomplished performer and composer, whose diverse interests and varied creative inclinations led him to experiment in other styles including *taiko* and even *jazz*. But his bread and butter, as with so many professional performers, is in teaching *hōgaku*.

Teaching to Make a Living

Even so, Tosha prefers to be a performer first and then a teacher. He explains, "I did not enter this profession in order to work with students"; rather he was motivated by his desire "to become a first-class musician." According to Tosha, in the National Theatre of Japan in Tokyo they actually have an advertisement to encourage new students to study classical percussion, a move of which he is quite critical. "If you place an ad like that and you acquire more students (*deshi*), then you can make more money," but he prefers to acquire students through introductions, which in turn minimizes numbers. "There are other people who have a lot of *deshi* who do not often perform publicly," but Tosha wanted to continue focusing on his own musicianship, something he felt he could not do if he had large numbers of students. Initially, he was able to survive on his income from performing, only teaching when people made a special request for him and his wife to do so. When young, he didn't like to teach all, regularly canceling classes, preferring to travel and perform, or simply "fool around in his free time," and had "no drive" to teach. This attitude reveals the difficult path professional musicians must walk, balancing the desire to perform with the need to teach for one's economic survival, which Tosha at least, feels can be at odds with each other. Over the years, he nevertheless has worked with large numbers of classical percussion students, including professionals performing in *kabuki*, and of course has a particular approach to teaching.

Tosha offers lessons (*okeiko*) once a month on four consecutive days in a small, second-floor studio on Pontochō, a charming narrow street lined with restaurants and teahouses in central Kyoto. His studio (*okeikoba*, referring to the lesson location), has an unobtrusive door with a small name plaque to the side nestled between the shops that otherwise characterize this street. The space is divided into the main room, where the lesson occurs, and a smaller room to the side that serves as a holding area while other students wait for their turn in front of the "master." The rooms are clean and sparse, except for the instruments that litter the floor and a huge painting of his son playing the flute on one of the walls (see Figure 6.2). A small alley-kitchen and bathroom to the back completes the *okeikoba*. Once a month, *deshi* slip 20,000 yen (U.S.$210) into an envelope in a box positioned discretely at the back of the side room. This fee (*ogessha*) is required whether one can attend all four days, and regardless of the length of each lesson, which can range from ten minutes to close to an hour. One instead is paying for the "privilege" of being part of this environment, to be considered amongst Tosha's *deshi*, who in turn exhibit tremendous loyalty to him (Blasdel 2005:22). His energy in lessons is visceral, palpable, and these ten minutes can be as exhausting as a full-day rehearsal with someone else.

In regards to his teaching style, Tosha claims, first and foremost, he tries to be "natural." He believes other teachers sometimes force students to do something they are not ready to attempt; introducing new material through explanations rather than demonstration, especially in cases where the teacher cannot yet properly perform the technique or rhythm themselves. He prefers to demonstrate what he wants to convey, which also teaches him, allowing him to fine-tune his musicianship even in a lesson. But the focus remains on helping students improve through mimicking what he does, rather than explaining with logic. His approach is in line with the discussion of Japanese ways of performing traditional music and aesthetic concepts in Chapter 3, in which numerous scholar-performers report being told to "just *feel*" musical ideas, such as *jo-ha-kyū*; all the theorizing in the world cannot replace the benefits of just picking up the instrument and playing. In order to facilitate this development, Tosha continues to teach in the one-on-one style that characterizes traditional Japanese pedagogy, offering comments as the student works through the section of a piece. He usually plays one of the other drums or uses a special leather-covered fan (*hariōgi*) to beat out either the same rhythm as the student or a complementary one on a large, but now-worn wooden block (see Figure 6.1).

Despite his claim that he tries to be "natural" and not pressure students, Tosha actually used to be quite strict and is still demanding with the professional *geiko* and *maiko*. His more relaxed attitude with his amateur students may be indicative of broader changes in the traditional music world, as teachers have to be more lenient to avoid losing students to less restrictive artistic pursuits, or is simply a reflection of his changing attitude towards teaching as he ages. Tosha plans to teach as long as he lives, jokingly exclaiming that he "needs the money." But in reality both he and his wife do find it gratifying to see someone improving, and become quite engaged with students in lessons. In turn, the experience "keeps them both young" and connected with the *hōgaku* world.

Enacting Japaneseness in the Okeiko

Japaneseness is enacted in numerous ways in the hierarchical and formal world of the traditional lesson (*okeiko*). For example, while one actually practices one-on-one with the teacher, the presence of others in the room fosters camaraderie amongst fellow students and group identity (Gillan 2012:100). Blasdel, in relating his experience studying *shakuhachi* in the 1970s, describes how:

> ... the actual lesson (*okeiko*) began at that moment—when I entered the house and sat down. Unlike music lessons in the West, *shakuhachi* lessons were not by appointment, but on a first-come, first-taught basis. One came, stayed as long as one liked and then left. Arriving at the teacher's house in the morning meant fewer people, less waiting and more time with the master. Arriving after work hours, when most people came, meant a longer wait but the opportunity to hear many other students play.
>
> (2005:17)

Blasdel was confused at first by this pedagogical approach (as was I when I first started studying *shamisen* in the mid-1990s) but quickly came to recognize certain advantages. "It meant that the lesson day was exactly that—a day when everything else was subordinate to the time in front of the master" (ibid.:17). In comparison, in the United States, lessons are scheduled not only on specific days, but precise times, and students brush past each other in the doorway as one finishes and the next begins. In Japan, one has the opportunity to listen to others, which becomes an important part of the lesson experience. One not only learns from other's mistakes and triumphs, but also develops a broad awareness of the repertoire so that the student already has some familiarity when one begins working on a new piece (ibid.:17–18). In my experience studying both *shamisen* years ago and more recently *ko-tsuzumi*, I often would arrive early, wait for my own lesson, and return to sit and listen to yet more students after I finished.

As with Tosha, the focus in the *okeiko* should be on "the practical act of performing, rather than through overt analysis or theoretical discourse" (Gillan 2012:100). One should just "do" and experience music through the body, and not chitchat while waiting or discussing the music with the teacher. Blasdel explains:

> Unlike the United States, learning traditional music in Japan is not considered a scholastic endeavor. The teacher is to be copied and the music to be absorbed through the body, not the head. [Previous] generations of traditional musicians did not have the kind of scholastic training necessary to verbally explain the music. They were trained by rote from childhood, and the music remains deeply connected with their bodies, internalized and fluent as their native tongue. Explanatory words and concepts just do not come easily to them. In fact, scholastic, analytical research into Japanese music by the Japanese themselves is a relatively recent phenomenon.
> (Blasdel 2005:19)

Understanding music "within the body" is further facilitated by copying the master without comment, as well as by playing through entire pieces from beginning to the end, even when struggling and not fully prepared to do so (ibid.:20) (as I clearly demonstrate in the examples of "Chu no Mai," introduced in Chapter 3). The importance of form (*kata*) takes precedence over content at such moments (Shimosako 2002). And to be sure, perseverance is appreciated in Japanese culture even if content never succeeds (ibid.:27). Thus internalizing what one learns in the *okeiko* through the body—going through the motions, as it were—is central to the learning process.

Japaneseness is even enacted in the body in the *okeiko*, through kneeling on the floor in traditional fashion (*seiza*) while both waiting and watching, as well as when working with the master. Surak explains that this way of positioning oneself

> ... is widely considered the most formal seated posture, and though Japanese may be accustomed to settling on the ground, most kneel only on particular occasions. Annual work-place parties, which often take place without chairs in the large *tatami*-floored rooms of restaurants, provide such opportunities... Children, when reprimanded, may be commanded to listen and apologize from a kneeling position, and formal requests, like a daughter's hand in marriage may be offered in *seiza*. Yet kneeling is considered not only a *formal* way of sitting, but also a *Japanese* way of sitting. Books on the Japanese body frequently contain sections describing how it is perfectly made for kneeling, how *seiza* has affected Japanese culture, and so forth.
> (Ibid.:27–28)

"Sitting *seiza*" is demanding, as one's legs tingle and go numb, but a requirement in most formal *okeiko*.

Geiko and Maiko

The *okeiko* offered quite a distinct environment for learning than I had encountered at any of the other sites where I conducted fieldwork; it was one of increased formality and elegance, incredibly focused and intense. This particular atmosphere was enhanced by the regular attendance of the *geiko* and *maiko* who comprise the majority of Tosha's students.

It actually is quite rare to sit in such an *okeiko* surrounded by *geiko* and *maiko*, all the more so as although all these women are required to dance and play *shamisen*, they do not all study percussion, only coming to the art if they are really interested. Those who do study with Tosha are quite skilled, coming from different *geiko* districts in Kyoto to work with him specifically, even leaving other schools (something one is really not supposed to do in traditional Japanese music). On the day I came equipped with a camera to take pictures of Tosha, the *geiko* seen in Figures 6.2 and 6.3 happened to come in full regalia, also fairly unusual, so I was lucky to capture this moment. Both were squeezing in lessons between formal dance performances, revealing a passion for the study of this art. Tosha, thoroughly delighted with this good fortune, clapped joyously when the first arrived; there seemed to be no question that I would want pictures of him with the *geiko* and that these should be the ones to go in the book. He was particularly thrilled when he realized one *geiko*, Gionkōbu Mamechizu, plays *ko-tsuzumi* (see Figure 6.2) and the other, Miyagawa Yachiho, *ō-tsuzumi* (see Figure 6.3). But Tosha reined himself in and put on his stoic public performance face while the camera was flashing away (see Figure 6.1).

Since most of Tosha's students are *geiko* the level of his *okeiko* is really high. And several of his amateur students that I interviewed commented on what a privilege it is to sit and listen to all the excellent professionals while waiting one's turn. And I must

Figure 6.2 *Geiko* Gionkōbu Mamechizu on *ko-tsuzumi* at *okeiko*

admit, I too was mesmerized while sitting next to this *geiko* in the holding area as she prepared for her lesson, following along to her notation with a Sony mp3 player, white headphones with sparkling pink rhinestones, in full make up, wig and purple *kimono*. Often amateur students would return to the side room and continue watching other lessons for several hours, while the professional *geiko* and *maiko* would scurry away to make preparations for evening appointments.

Imafuji Misuzu, Women, and the Atmosphere of the Okeiko

The nature of Tosha's *okeiko* was also deeply informed by the constant presence of his equally formidable wife, Imafuji Misuzu, herself an accomplished performer trained in *Imafuji-ryū nagauta shamisen* (see Figure 6.3). They met in the professional *hōgaku* world when they were both around twenty years old. She stopped performing professionally when they had children, but often supplies the *shamisen* part live during lessons, a rarity according to both of them. Indeed watching the exchange between this couple was one of the most remarkable aspects of this *okeiko*. Most percussion teachers rely on recordings as a live *shamisen* player would make the monthly fee too expensive for students. But using tapes may complicate lessons considerably as one must match the tempo of the recording and take time to find the desired spot when repeatedly practicing a specific section within a piece. But as a husband-and-wife team, they can manage at the current fee, and in fact they seemed to enjoy playing with each other immensely in this setting. Kineya Hiroki, who also specializes in *nagauta shamisen*, feels this makes their fee especially reasonable as when he does pick up the instrument, Tosha's wife

Figure 6.3 Tosha Rōetsu (with Imafuji Misuzu), instructing *geiko* Miyagawa Yachiho on *ō-tsuzumi*

instructs him as well, thus one is really working with two teachers. Tosha's wife can also play all the percussion, so she truly understands the music from both sides. The monthly *ogessha* may seem quite high at first, but many of his students, including Kineya, feel the money is well spent. Thus students may be attracted to Tosha's *okeiko* because his wife is such a fine musician as well. And her role continues the long history of women transmitting traditional Japanese music essentially "behind the scenes," as discussed in Chapter 2. Women were of course well represented at Tosha's *okeiko*.

The majority of his female students are *geiko* and *maiko*, while he does have an estimated four to six amateur female students as well; housewives, part-time workers, dance teachers, and also wealthy young women who do not work, and are perhaps studying this music as "bridal training," as they will quit when they marry and have children. But one of his students is quick to add that since everyone has the same hobby, they naturally have something in common and are collegial and supportive in the lesson setting.

Many of Tosha's students find their way to this specialized percussion through other arguably more accessible traditional arts, particularly classical dance (*nihon buyō*) and *shamisen*. The few male students I encountered regularly in class also came to Tosha through other related musics. For example, Yamauchi Reach, of the Taiko Center and Matsuri-shū, first specialized in Western percussion. Kineya Hiroki, the professional *nagauta shamisen* performer and teacher quoted several times above, wanted to study the percussion that accompanies his melodic instrument. Both were drawn to Tosha because of his reputation and high degree of musicality; Kineya even exclaimed at one point Tosha is the "best in Kyoto, the best in Japan, the best in the world"! Although these men are career musicians, they do not perform percussion professionally on the *kabuki* stage, nor (to my knowledge at least) are they seeking a professional name within Tosha's lineage, rather they are interested in expanding their artistic knowledge and musicianship.

Since most of Tosha's students are women, who still are not allowed on the *kabuki* stage, he currently only has one former student performing professionally, "Tosha Etsuho." The *geiko* and *maiko* are considered professionals, but are not part of the *kabuki* line. Tosha confirmed that for the most part amateurs don't become professionals; professionals are still usually "born" into the profession (implying they have parents who play). So despite Tosha's immense presence in the *geiko* world in Kyoto, his influence in the professional world of *kabuki* may be limited now. This situation, however, may be a result of the declining interest in the study of these instruments in general.

The Decline of Japanese Classical Percussion

Becoming a professional *hōgaku* musician requires years of study before one can perform publicly. Imafuji compares this to

> ... salarymen (businessmen)—who graduate from school, start work and earn a paycheck their first month. But in the *hōgaku* world you have to pay a monthly fee to the teacher for a long time. Additional fees are collected as students pass upwards along the hierarchy of the *ie* system, and you have to buy expensive instruments and *kimono* to perform professionally.

She continued to say that you have to have capital to provide for yourself while young, such as the support and understanding of parents (who need to be relatively wealthy in order for their children to pursue these studies). Imafuji believes it is easier to "make a living teaching *shamisen*—some company's president can learn it if they want to. But the *tsuzumi* [referring to both the *ko-* and *ō-tsuzumi*] is fairly restricted in comparison," implying that not a lot of people want to commit to learning either. *Shamisen* and *taiko* are also more familiar to people—both are seen regularly on television, neighborhood events, and professionally on the stage. But classical percussion is much less visible. Imafuji passionately intones, "You don't see your grandma or grandpa playing the *ko-tsuzumi*, nor is the instrument part of local festivals," and even in *kabuki* these instruments are hidden backstage. *Shamisen* teachers are also relatively easy to find, but percussion teachers are much less common. Most people simply do not know how to find their way into this world without an introduction and have no idea that someone of Tosha's level is even *in* Kyoto.

Another reason for the declining interest in these instruments could be the fact that one can learn and perform *shamisen* on its own, but you cannot perform *ko-tsuzumi*, *ō-tsuzumi* and classical *taiko* without *shamisen* and *fue*, in other words, the full ensemble. The increasing rarity of all of these instruments is also no doubt having a detrimental effect, despite the efforts by the Ministry of Education, Culture, Sports, Science and Technology to keep this music alive in the schools (see previous discussion in Chapter 5). The decline of *hōgaku* in general has already been noted, but this may be exacerbated with this type of classical percussion. Imafuji explains that these instruments "are extremely difficult to learn and you can't start doing so as a hobby" (even though the accounts of the female amateur students may contradict her opinion to a degree). In comparison, both Tosha and Imafuji agree that although the *shamisen* is still a difficult instrument, one can more easily create sound as a beginner.

The ko-tsuzumi

> In Japan there is a hand drum called the *tsuzumi*. One hand holds the cord and one hand beats the drum. The heart and soul of the drummer is contained in each strike. The *tsuzumi* is used in [n]oh plays, which were once beloved by the warrior class, and it is that same vigorous spirit that draws people to the *taiko* today.
> (Tanaka et al. 2005:6)

The instruments' expense and difficulty to learn of course feed into the declining interest in their study as well. The *ko-tsuzumi* itself is becoming especially difficult to find, and therefore expensive, with quality well-aged instruments costing upwards from 500,000 yen (U.S.$5,250). The body of the instrument, beautifully fashioned from cherry wood into an appealing hourglass shape, with unique ridges carved inside to enhance its acoustics (*kanname*), and painted in thick lacquer with gold-leaf designs on the outside, is a work of art; one that, when separated from its worn-out skins, unfortunately ends up displayed as a vase in restaurants rather than serving its real purpose. Notoriously temperamental, with horse skins that must be heated and coaxed (by wetting and blowing on them during performance) into producing the desired sound, I resorted to purchasing a student model with synthetic body and plastic skins. This modern invention in no way captures the sound of the original, and without a doubt, demanding teachers such as Tosha feel that practice on such synthetic heads ruins one's ability to play with the proper technique on real instruments. But what it suffers in sound quality, it makes up for in playability in the unpredictable—and unfamiliar—North American climate.

The sound and construction of the *tsuzumi* (both the *ko* and the *ō*) are precisely what attracts people to them. Tosha knows the history of these drums well, as they traveled from India to Japan where the shape changed. He "greatly admires the person who decided to put the *ko-tsuzumi* on the shoulder and strike it in a uniquely Japanese way." There are of course similar types of drums in Africa (for example, the "talking drum" that is struck with a curved stick), but the *ko-tsuzumi* may be unusual in the way one strikes it with the hand. And the fact that both *tsuzumi* are struck with only one hand actually increases their difficulty. Hughes was "told by *kabuki* hand-drummer Mochizuki Tasaku III that hitting the drum was a matter of *jo-ha-kyū*: slowly move the arm back in preparation; begin a steady movement towards the drum skin; finish with an accelerating flick of the wrist," thus placing the motion of the strike within broader Japanese aesthetic ideas (e-mail correspondence January 30, 2014), albeit this does not make it any easier to accomplish. (See Malm 1986 for further discussion of both the construction and technique of the *ko-tsuzumi*.)

But again, the difficulty and detail necessary to produce the particular sound inspires people, including Tosha, to pick up these instruments. One interviewee explains she first developed an interest in *narimono* (the instruments of *kabuki*) when, as a child, her mother took her to see *kabuki* and "the sound stuck in her ears." So much so that when she decided she wanted to learn something "new and different" as an adult, she returned to the sound that had so mesmerized her as a child and found the *ko-* and *ō-tsuzumi*. She has been studying now for twelve years, still motivated by the sound, which makes her "excited" (*waku waku*). She argues that if these instruments were simple she would lose interest, while the challenge of memorizing the music and mastering the precise techniques is good for her mind. So in some ways the motivations for studying these instruments are the same as for the large *taiko* drums.

"Echigojishi" ("The Echigo Lion")

The quality of Tosha's *okeiko*, unique timbre of the *tsuzumi* drums, and overall feel of the music of this world are illustrated in the following exploration of the well-known piece "Echigojishi" ("The Echigo Lion") (Website Example 16; Track 16). An example of *nagauta*, I first learned "Echigojishi" on *shamisen* years ago when studying with Yoshizumi Kosakuro in Tokyo (Malm 1963; Keister 2004). It may be difficult to distinguish between the different *shamisen*-based narrative genres, but this piece feels quite different in comparison to the *kouta* "Kasuga Sanbasō," discussed in Chapter 3 (Track 4).

This *nagauta* performance features a larger ensemble of vocals, *shamisen*, *shinobue* and of course Japanese classical percussion. Deschênes explains *nagauta* is "not the only style used in *kabuki*, but is the most important and most appropriately adapted to stage actions, providing dance accompaniment, songs and background music" (1980).

The music of "Echigojishi" is attributed to Kineya Rokuzaemon IX (1756–1819), and the lyrics to Shinoda Kaneji (1768–1819). Both combined relate the story of itinerant street entertainers featuring a tumbling act in which a child performer wears a carved lion's head. The story sounds cheerful, accompanied by equally energetic music, in the beginning, however, the overall feeling of the lyrics is melancholy. The song is written from the perspective of a young boy named "Kakube," who is a *shishi-mai* dancer (the lion dance introduced in Chapter 1). The original lyrics are included with the *shamisen* notation for the piece in Appendices A and B, with the romanization and English translation below:

越後獅子
"Echigojishi"
("The Echigo Lion")

utsu ya taiko no ne mo sumiwatari
Kakube Kakube to manekarete
inagara misuru jakkyō no
[here the text ends in the *Yoshizumi-ryū* score; end of the sixth line in the *Kineya-ryū* score]
The sound of the *taiko* is clear in the air
Calling my name "Kakube, Kakube"
Watching from a stone bridge

ukiyo o wataru fūgamono
utō mo mō mo hayasu no mo
hitori tabine no kusamakura
[the bottom of the first page of the *Kineya-ryū* score]
I am an elegant creature passing through this transient world
Whether I sing, dance, or play
I sleep by myself with grass as a pillow.

Students come to Tosha's *okeiko* with notation (*gakufu*) on different size papers, some handwritten, others copied, with no uniformity, but many of the manuscripts look like works of art themselves. When he cannot find the notation he wants, Tosha simply writes the piece down again, in what I understand is his own style. An excerpt of Tosha Rōetsu's score for the *ko-tsuzumi* and *ō-tsuzumi* in "Echigojishi" is included in Figure 6.4 (see Appendix C for the complete score). The score is read from top to bottom, right to left in Japanese fashion.

There are numerous symbols used to indicate precise rhythmic patterns—a kind of shorthand to make the process of notating quicker, and perhaps to protect the details of pieces in the past. Tosha provided a key for me (see Figure 6.5), though it was unclear if he extended this courtesy to his Japanese students as well.

Tosha's student and my teacher at the Taiko Center, Yamauchi Reach, graciously provided a translation (for that is what this feels like) of the first half of the original score. An excerpt is included in Figure 6.6 (see Appendix D for the first half of the original in Western notation).

In the Western version, Yamauchi opted to regularly change the meter to best capture the fluid sense of rhythm. The *ō-tsuzumi* and *ko-tsuzumi* parts are notated on two separate lines, with the mnemonics (*kuchishōka*) for the *ko-tsuzumi* below. Vocal calls (*kakegoe*) are inserted between the lines. The *shamisen* part is added when in direct dialogue with the percussion. But as with all notation for traditional Japanese music, this is only an approximation of what the piece actually sounds like.

Listen to the field recording of "Echigojishi" featuring Tosha Rōetsu on *ō-tsuzumi*, his wife Imafuji Misuzu on *shamisen* and vocals, and Yamauchi Reach on *ko-tsuzumi* (Website Example 16). From 3:10, Tosha's *kuchishōka* are clearly audible as he instructs Yamauchi while they are performing, always fine-tuning the rhythm and sound.

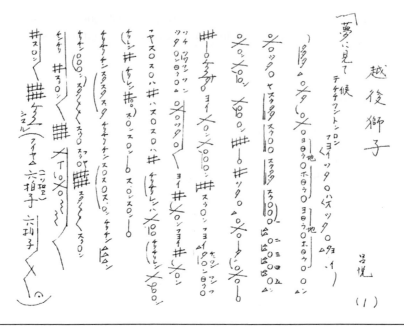

Figure 6.4 "Echigojishi" (Japanese score by Tosha Rōetsu)

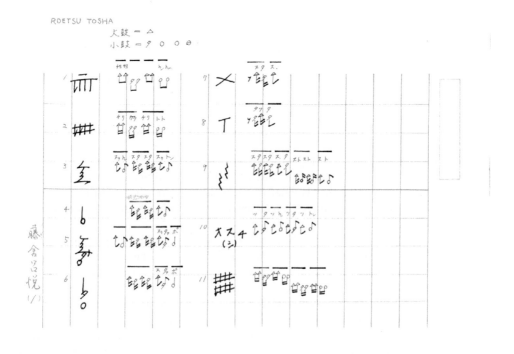

Figure 6.5 Notation key (by Tosha Rōetsu)

Four Case Studies from Kyoto • 189

Figure 6.6 "Echigojishi" (Western score by Yamauchi Reach)

Yamauchi's score, which contains the entire first page of Tosha's original score up until the beginning of the parentheses in the last line, ends at 2:35 in the recording.

Now compare with professional recording (Track 16), a re-release of an original LP by Nonesuch from 1980, which features members of the Ensemble Nipponia with Sugiura Hirokazu and Ōta Yukiko on *shamisen*, Nishikawa Kōhei on *shinobue* and *noh-kan*, Tosha Naritoshi on *ko-tsuzumi*, Ozaki Taichi on *ō-tsuzumi*, and Katada Hiromitsu and Takahashi Akikuni on additional percussion including *taiko* and *kane* (small brass gong). The first example illustrates the bare bones of the piece, while this version presents the complete instrumentation (with the exception of the vocal part).

Summary

Tosha and Imafuji have a critical, even grim view of the current state of *hōgaku*. They repeatedly noted how the number of people interested in seriously pursuing the study of Japanese classical percussion is decreasing for a variety of reasons, including the high degree of difficulty, demands on time from work and family, and the expense of everything from lessons to instruments to *kimono*. Imafuji in particular lamented that young people do not want to put the time into studying, pursing activities that are perhaps more immediately satisfying. Ultimately, these factors are lessening the quality of *hōgaku* in their eyes. And several of Tosha's students conferred that some named professionals are not as skilled as was once required, as teachers award professional titles for monetary gain and not as a real recognition of talent or skill. Kineya Hiroki in fact feels *hōgaku* in general will eventually fade away in Kyoto.

But for now, Tosha Rōetsu's Pontochō *okeiko* offers a remarkable experience. And the environment of the *okeiko*, alienating to some, is one of the primary attractions to others, as several students expressed enthusiasm for both the formality of the *okeiko* and the opportunity to interact with such high-level performers. One of the last times I waited in the holding area for my turn with Tosha, I realized how those of us familiar with the traditional Japanese *okeiko* setting may take this experience for granted. I kneeled in *seiza* with a group of women, several in summer *yukata*—listening intently, tapping along if the piece happens to be one known to them—while Tosha focused intently on the student in front of him. It is truly like being invited into another world, removed from reality, and even if not everyone's cup of tea, for those who enjoy this sort of thing, it doesn't get any better than this. I will forever remember his fantastic ribald sense of humor and amazing vitality, filling that tiny studio with equal doses of humor and musicianship.

Basara and the One-room Schoolhouse

I first found Basara in the fall of 2009 while searching for Japanese ensemble groups on the Internet, which I would later learn, is the same manner in which most of their members discovered the group. Although there were relatively few performers to be found this way in Kyoto, Basara's website stood out as clear and easy to read, with pages both in Japanese and English (a result of the fact that Basara regularly has foreign members rotating through its ranks who in the past wrote the English pages). Fujiwara Aki, a former student of Tosha Rōetsu, and two current members of the group, Ōtsuka Takeshi, who took several courses at the Taiko Center years ago, and Nakai Kunihiko, established the group in 1991. In this way, both the network of Tosha Rōetsu and the Taiko Center, completely unconnected with each other, intersected, if only in a most cursory way, in the group Basara.

Sadly Fujiwara passed away in the late 1990s, but the group still keeps her memory alive, the website explaining how "Her performance held the power to invigorate the withering soul and arouse a controlled society" (Basara n.d.a). Fujiwara chose the "name 'Basara' [which] comes from 'Basara Daisho.' He is one of the twelve guards who protect Buddha" (Basara n.d.b). And the group still uses her drums and performs many of her pieces.

Rehearsals in a One-room Schoolhouse

They practice every Saturday afternoon in the village of Iwakura, approximately one hour north of the city of Kyoto proper, in a one-room schoolhouse nestled between rice paddies, complete with a pony whinnying next door. The location itself immediately creates an unreal atmosphere for both rehearsals and many of their rather informal live performances, as one disembarks from the local bus into a rapidly disappearing rural

Figure 6.7 Basara rehearsing

Japan. The rehearsal schedule is relaxed, with members, who pay a modest 3,500 yen (U.S.$37.00) a month fee to support the group, arriving as early as 11 a.m. to start a fire in the woodstove in the cold months (the only source of heat in the room) or open windows and light the mosquito coils in the humidity of the summer. The early arrivals will chat, eat lunch and slowly move to the drums. Around 2 p.m., the members with less familiarity, or questionable skills on the *taiko* despite many years' experience, start to warm-up under the direction of Ōtsuka, the groups "unofficial" leader, practicing the basic rhythms and arm gestures that they favor. Older and more advanced members will trickle in later in the afternoon when everyone is more likely to be working on actual pieces, with rehearsal wrapping up around 6 p.m. A few members are very committed to practicing every weekend, while others participate less frequently. Everyone understands that other obligations take precedence and all the members miss rehearsal now and then.

In addition to performing the "lion dance" (*shishi-mai*) described in the context of *kagura* in Chapter 1, Basara periodically receive requests to perform at various events in the Kyoto area, from joining festivals (*matsuri*) to providing entertainment at dinner celebrations. Several organizations that contacted them during the year I worked with them, however, would not pay the fee Basara requested and instead they performed shows primarily for visitors of their own members. For such performances in the schoolhouse, Basara clears away chairs, toys and other random items, draping a black wall hanging with "Basara" written in Japanese characters in gold paint behind the drums. In 2010, when few public gigs came their way, Basara turned to recording videos of their performances and posting them to the Internet, both as a means of providing a goal for rehearsals, and promoting the group even further. Nonetheless, some members consider themselves semi-professional because they request and accept money for performances, primarily to support the high cost of drums, the rent and to cover travel expenses. But they do not make a living playing *taiko*, and do not practice the same hours or with the same discipline one would expect of a professional group.

Members and the Identity of Basara

Basara has several core members who have been playing for years, but does experience a high turnover of new people, which of course means constantly having to learn their pieces over again. This situation may prevent the group from moving forward and truly obtaining the high level of skill many of them desire; however, with each new member comes fresh energy and interest, which no doubt has helped the group survive now for close to 25 years.

Basara comprises a wide variety of both male and female members of varying ages, the youngest in his twenties and the oldest in his sixties. The members are all unusual in their own ways, although in general they are all educated, either currently attending or having graduated from respectable colleges. They pursue a variety of professions, from dentistry to directing a non-profit organization, but many members are educators, ranging from college-level professors to junior high school teachers. These varied individuals come together primarily for the sheer joy of performing with each other.

In general, interviewees refer to the typical member as "nice" and "friendly," compared to other groups where people may be more "intense." Far too serious players really would not fit the ethos of Basara. To illustrate, one interviewee explained that several years ago a young man joined the group who refuses to speak. Initially his mother brought him and picked him up from rehearsals afterwards. The interviewee felt it would have been really difficult for the young man to join the group at first if everyone was really severe. But he "learned so much in just a few years" that he is now able to fully participate in rehearsals and performances with Basara, "speaking through the drums rather than his voice ... Players who can welcome someone like this young man are the heart of Basara."

The story of this individual illustrates another interesting characteristic of Basara members—that they are all *different* in some way—indeed "aroused from a controlled society" as founder Fujiwara is described on the website. In interviews, people regularly used words such "unusual," "strange," or "unconventional" to describe themselves and others in the group. As one member explains, "Conventional people think you need money for happiness, but Basara members don't feel this way," noting how one of the older men even quit his safe and secure salaryman position to go into business for himself, which is certainly an exceptional thing to do. Because Basara comprises people who embrace and encapsulate difference, someone like this young man can participate; his *difference* becomes a *commonality* shared amongst everyone.

Another member describes them as "so weird but in a really good way." She does not feel that "one can participate all day if you are worried about what you are doing or how you look." Instead, these are people who are not self-conscious, which she finds unusual in the context of Japan. They might be a little nervous and self-aware when they first find this makeshift studio in the hills, but they quickly move past these misgivings. Several participants expanded this idea, explaining that the typical member is in general a person who is more concerned with others than themselves (in my opinion illustrated by the large number of teachers and especially the person involved in the non-profit organization). This constant service to others may in fact inspire interest in Basara, where people can leave the demands of their day jobs at the door.

Of course, as performers, these people are also attracted to the music of *taiko*, but even this too serves as a means to emotional catharsis. One man explains that he was in a "funk" in his late twenties, feeling mentally and physically down and thought the "dynamism and rhythm" of *taiko* would energize him, especially given the demands of his job (working with emotionally and physically disabled people). Everyone is able to come to rehearsal and be themselves without concern for the outside world. The pressures of Japanese society to conform are not present here.

Gender, Foreigners and Inclusivity

The group therefore values both individuality and inclusivity, which extends to ways in which they view the roles of men and women as well. The group at times has more female members, while at other times male, but they feel that their pieces can be performed equally well by both men and women. Basara were invited to play at a gig in Kyoto in 2009 for 95,000 yen (U.S.$1,000), but the event organizer wanted to know if they performed "sound with impact" (*hakuryoku*). After some discussion, they responded that yes, they felt they had "*hakuryoku*," but the organization asked if they could bring only men just the same. The group considered this again and decided that they would just not play for this event—they are a group with both men *and* women and therefore would not fulfill this sponsors' request. One member exclaimed, "You don't just kick the women out because someone doesn't like how they play *taiko*!" The decision apparently was unanimous, even though it meant the group lost a great deal of money.

The acceptance of difference within welcoming space, as well as, to a lesser degree, the fine website in English, have attracted a number of foreign women in the past (including myself). One young American woman, at the time conducting research on her Ph.D. dissertation, explained she felt unconnected and isolated from actual Japanese people, particularly given the long hours she was spending in the library. She therefore wanted to do something she felt she could only do in Japan, and that in turn would bring her into contact with other Japanese people. She found Basara "really welcoming to foreigners," not practicing the typical Japanese habit of constantly making the distinction between Japanese and foreign. In her words, "They don't mention how well you use chopsticks." She really felt for the first time in Japan as if she was being "treated like a human being." As a foreigner:

> You spend your whole day being treated like a novelty... and this was the one space where I showed up and it was like oh you are just a regular person, who can play the drums, cool, let's be friends. It was awesome... It completely changed my experience in Japan. It was like night and day, I was so miserable, and then I joined Basara, and I had friends, and I was involved in something local. And they were just super nice people. And we could share. And I was not 100 percent happy to be here still, but it was much better.

She finds Basara to be "kind of a refuge from the world," a feeling clearly shared by many of the members.

Whatever one's motivations for joining the group, the general consensus is that it doesn't matter who you are outside rehearsal—standard hierarchical social organization is dropped (for example,. the *senpai* (older) and *kōhai* (younger) relationship common within other areas of Japanese life). When you are with Basara everyone is there to play the drums and therefore equal no matter what age, gender, nationality, or profession.

Collective Teaching

This egalitarian approach extends to the leadership and transmission of technique and repertoire, albeit with varied results. Several members feel the group has no defined leader and no clear goal, which makes them inclusive, but at the same time hinders their ability to really grow. Ōtsuka is generally perceived as responsible for the administration, but not as the musical director. Choices are always made by consensus as to what gigs they will take and which pieces they will perform in what one member describes as "democratic decision making." Another person explains, "Nobody has a monopoly on being able to give an interpretation on what's wrong with what we are doing." Rather, dialogue ensues and whoever insists on their opinion the most seems to affect change. The group does not follow a typical hierarchical structure, common in other music settings, but may enact Japaneseness nevertheless in their egalitarian approach to the management and musical direction of the group, relying on communal decisions reached through consensus. This may in fact be a rather common management system amongst amateurs both in Japan and other areas of world, present in numerous *taiko* groups in North America, for example. Nevertheless, this approach abroad more likely results from local needs as opposed to connecting with the practice in Japan.

In rehearsal, people often good-naturedly pointed out each other's mistakes and discussed ways to improve the overall performance in a warm collaborative spirit. Founding member Ōtsuka, however, has taken on the responsibility for teaching the desired position and technique, as well as transmitting the group's pieces (hence his recognition as the "unofficial leader"), but not without some concerns.

Figure 6.8 Ōtsuka Takeshi of Basara on *shinobue*

Ōtsuka is a gentle teacher, focused on precise rhythm and articulating the large arm gestures Basara favors, even at rapid tempos (See Figure 6.9). He often employs a metronome to help everyone strike the rhythms together, a practice some members found "conservative," and not allowing for flexibility. But Ōtsuka is thoughtful about this choice. He really believes that "since using the metronome people's ears have improved and people should listen to the metronome rather than each other." I mentioned how I give a beat and count when leading my own ensemble, to which he responded if he "had a teacher–student relationship with the other members" then he too could do that. But since he doesn't, he finds it awkward to critique others. With the metronome, there is no argument or friction—he can say someone is not matching the metronome without asserting a hierarchical relationship, without authority. Thus the metronome diffuses potential tension. He feels he is not really the "teacher," but acknowledges that he runs the rehearsals and has put a lot of time into thinking about how to do so without appearing as the teacher. For Ōtsuka, "the metronome is the teacher."

For the most part, everyone agrees that playing rhythms precisely together and improving listening to each other is a desirable goal. One member explains, "Without everyone being all together, *taiko* becomes a lot of noise, but when everyone is totally together you feel the vibrations of the drums—it is visceral!" This sensation is one of the things that first attracted her to the drums, especially given that her regular days were "so devoid of physical activity that practicing and playing the drums was amazing." She appreciated "feeling her body ache." But to create this "togetherness you have to listen. If you are not together something is missing . . . and it is not just 'playing together' but having to feel connected with each other," highlighting again the importance of inclusivity and camaraderie that characterizes Basara.

Performance

Given this approach to managing the group, it is no surprise that several of the players prize teamwork in performance, one person going so far as to describe the ideal as "for everyone to play together—for everyone to come together in one heart." Although perhaps not an uncommon goal in *taiko* performance in general, Basara also works to create a great atmosphere (*fun'iki*), which differs depending on the piece; sometimes creating fun and festive feelings, and sometimes telling a more serious story. A Basara performance is an "event," and expression of an image is important. Their pieces are highly original and offer great variety, with interesting layers of rhythm. One member applauds the fact "Basara's style is free and doesn't really fit with any specific form. They are able to play freely, with no rules, and they don't follow any specific model." In this way, difference is celebrated in the music of Basara as well.

They wear simple costumes made common in ensemble drumming by Ondekoza, consisting of the typical workman's bib and pants over a white shirt (one member preferring to wear red instead), and sometimes top the look off with a white headband (*hachimaki*), as pictured in Figure 6.9 at a performance at Higashi Hongan-ji, a major temple in Kyoto. The performance was actually part of a charity event to feed the homeless—a *mochitsuki*, or festival to pound rice into fresh sticky "*mochi*" patties. There were 100–200 people coming and going, some homeless, some serving them, some just stopping by, who ate, pounded the rice and socialized, reminding us that the homeless are human as well. The event took place in the park by the temple, with the drums squeezed

196 • Focusing In: Identity, Meaning and Japanese Drumming in Kyoto

Figure 6.9 Basara performing "Narushima"

into a narrow space in front of a large fountain (visible in the background). At noon, Basara performed the "*shishi-mai*" dance yet again, plus three additional pieces, including "Narushima" ("Roaring Island"), a piece by Kodō, with great enthusiasm.

Their costume allows freedom of arms and shoulders that facilitate their particular performance styles. Basara appreciates a low body stance common to *taiko*, but as noted above with very large arm gestures even at rapid tempos and fast rhythmic durations. During rehearsal, Ōtsuka tries to instill some uniformity in these moves, but not surprisingly in performance I found that each member expressed him or herself rather uniquely, some keeping shoulders and elbows aligned with the core of their bodies and others breaking at the elbows with energetic and exaggerated arm movements. Members are able to move their arms how they wish and express some individuality. The group relied almost exclusively upon long and fat, albeit light sticks (*bachi*) made of fragrant cypress wood (*hinoki*), resembling the type of *bachi* used for solos on large drums (ō-daiko) made famous by performers such as Hayashi Eitetsu of Kodō (Bender 2010). In the case of Basara, these *bachi* further elongated the line of the arms.

Despite Basara's emphasis on diversity, they actually rely on rather standard *taiko* instrumentation with most pieces performed primarily on barrel drums (*nagado-daiko*) and the Japanese equivalent of the snare (*shime-daiko*), supported sometimes by a brass gong struck with a deer horn (*atarigane*) and small cymbals (*chappa*), and featuring transverse bamboo flute (*shinobue*). They used this relatively simple configuration, however, to create what most of the members considered especially "melodic" pieces, absolutely creating rhythmic melody through the *taiko*, and typically weaving two contrasting sections (that is, alternating A and B) over a driving groove (*ji*) on the *shime-daiko*.

"Semi Shigure" ("Cicada Rain," referring to the collective cries of many cicada that sound like rain) by Banba Tomoko expresses the musical identity of Basara well (Website Example 17). I initially videoed them rehearsing "Semi Shigure" the first time I visited in fall 2009 and was immediately struck by their artistic vision and performative style. The video in Website Example 17 was made almost a year later in June 2010, in that same one-room schoolhouse as I nearly completed my research.

The African shakers that open the piece echo the sound of the cicada outside as the *shime-daiko* begin with extended arms and driving rhythms. The main part on the *nagado-daiko* and *okedo-daiko* (a large doubled-headed drum with skins affixed by ropes) primarily alternates between A and B melodies, interspersed with brief rests or mimicking of the *shime-daiko*. Basara often create a "lilting" quality in their melodies, here enhanced by the choreography as the performers rock back and forth, punctuated by the baseball bat on the larger *nagado-daiko* in back. The *shinobue* adds a festive feel; in particular, the joyful exchange between the women dancing is obvious on their faces.

In most ways, Basara very much fits expectations of traditional *taiko*, in general instrumentation and costumes, for example. Their songs are from varied sources, ranging from pieces attributed to other famous *taiko* groups, to new works composed expressly for them, just as with Kodō. Their performative style, however, with the exaggerated arm gestures even at rapid tempos, and particularly "lilting" melodic quality, stood them apart from any other *taiko* group I encountered in Kyoto.

Summary

The majority of Basara's members do not feel the group connects with Kyoto in any way. Most of them are not even from Kyoto, but first moved to the city for college or work, and ended up settling there permanently. Most of the *taiko* in Kyoto usually has an association with temples and shrines, and village festivals, but Basara performs something quite different than the musics heard in these contexts. They may be connected to Kyoto through their performance space, which is rather remarkable, and several of their pieces are set in specific locations around Kyoto, including "Semi Shigure," which evokes the sound of summer on Yoshida Mountain. Although referring to an earlier rehearsal space (they moved to the current schoolroom in the early 2000s), the website makes clear a connection between this piece and Kyoto:

> Our practice place "Moan" is located in the top of Mt. Yoshida. It is covered with trees, we can be refreshed and gain composure. This building—"Moan" is also beautiful. It was built at the end of the Taisho era, so about eighty years

ago. It is in harmony with the surroundings. We love this place. In summer, we enjoy the continuous chorus of cicadas. One of our members Miss [Banba] has composed ["Semi Shigure"], so you too can hear this chorus. We will compose a suite, which represents seasons at "Moan." ["Semi Shigure"] is a part of summer and the first piece in this creation. We are looking forward to presenting you the other parts in the near future.

(Basara n.d.c)

Basara might not see a strong connection with Kyoto, however, they do see a strong connection with each other—one member beautifully remarking "this is 'wa' daiko after all"—invoking the other common way of referring to this general ensemble style in which the "wa" means "Japanese," but also translates as "peaceful."

Matsuri-shū and the Kyoto Taiko Center

According to Higashi Munenori, founder of the Taiko Center, Matsuri-shū were actually the first professional *taiko* group in Kansai, western Japan, and at the time of research, were still the only truly professional group in Kyoto (they have since disbanded). Founded in 1986, "Matsuri-shū" is actually a contraction of their full name: "Fūryū" (Elegant Soothing Styles) "Dagaku" (Percussion Music) "Matsuri-shū" (Festival People); also written as "f.d.m." (Matsuri-shū n.d.). But they were most often referred to as simply "Matsuri-shū" by their fans, many of who regularly worked with them at the Taiko Center.

Matsuri-shū's position in the broader *taiko* world was indeed complicated by their association with the Taiko Center, with many of the members also teaching at both the Kyoto and Osaka branches. In fact, my two main teachers at the Taiko Center—Kawarazaki Yoshihiro and Yamauchi Reach—were in Matsuri-shū at the time I started my research, although both retired from the group to devote more time to other professional projects. Members, comprising both male and female career musicians, did regularly rotate in and out of Matsuri-shū, bringing new creative energy with them (see Figure 6.10).

Matsuri-shū required tremendous commitment from its members, as the group rehearsed for six hours every day in a studio approximately one hour's drive west of central Kyoto, located on a mountain top in an artist's commune (see Figure 3.5). Despite the relatively isolated location, they still had to finish rehearsing by 9 p.m. due to the noise. This is particularly demanding given that Matsuri-shū typically only performs two major concerts a year, one in December and one in July or August, both of which were always well-attended by their students from the Taiko Center.

The Ultimate Artist: Yamauchi Reach

Yamauchi Reach is originally from Tottori prefecture north-west of Osaka (interview, May 9, 2010). He came to Kyoto to attend Kyoto City University of Arts (a respected arts college) and graduated in 1996 with a degree in Western percussion. He also performs *tsugaru-jamisen* (see Figure 3.5) and what he calls "*gendai hōgaku*" (contemporary *hōgaku*), or works for traditional Japanese instruments in a European compositional style. After graduating, moved by a performance of Ondekoza, he consulted his primary percussion teacher about playing *taiko*, who recommended he first study *tsuzumi* with Tosha Rōetsu. He has not formally studied *taiko* with anyone; nevertheless, his training

Four Case Studies from Kyoto • 199

Figure 6.10 Matsuri-shū performing "Konjichō"

Figure 6.11 Yamauchi Reach on *shime-daiko*

in both Western and classical Japanese percussion permeates his teaching, composition and performance styles.

Kawarazaki Yoshihiro (to be further discussed below) recruited Yamauchi in 2000 to serve as the new music director of Matsuri-shū. Yamauchi is also active with several other professional projects, including Fluegel, a "jazzier" group, Wakana, heard performing "Yaraiya" (Track 7), and the trio Wa San Bon. Yamauchi composes pieces and plays *tsugaru-jamisen*, in addition to percussion, for all of these groups.

In the Classroom and on the Stage

Yamauchi was offered an instructor's position at the Taiko Center after joining Matsuri-shū, and his enthusiasm for teaching is apparent as he draws out precise rhythmic articulations, emphasizing the importance of mnemonics (*kuchishōka*). He summarizes his philosophy as "*koe o dasu*" (literally "draw out the voice")—referring to the need to learn to "speak" the rhythms aloud, through which one actually internalizes them more deeply, as opposed to just playing notation. He equates this process to "little children reading a picture book, where they read aloud to actually learn the language." Students in Yamauchi's beginner-level *shime-daiko* class described his style as methodical and thoughtful, and I too found him incredibly in tune with the nuances and details of drumming (see Figure 6.11). He was extremely concerned with proper technique, but only commented when someone was really struggling, otherwise usually ending each exercise with polite thanks instead.

Yamauchi believes that an ideal performer must embrace "*mu*," a concept rather like *satori*, a Buddhist idea of "becoming nothing." This is a most difficult level to obtain, which he himself has not reached yet, implying he still consciously "thinks" while making music. Although this may sound profound, it is a rather everyday way of thinking in Japan; one must simply "do" without consciousness coming in the way, and rather in line with traditional approaches to teaching music discussed earlier. According to Yamauchi, students new to *taiko* specifically have too much "strength" (*chikara*) when they play. Yamauchi therefore tries to make them understand that in order to play well, they have to relax and find a "neutral" or "zero point" to release the *chikara*. And personally I found his playing—fluid and gentle, but really tight—surely exemplified this. He compares this approach to playing to when a "car is in neutral, and then the stick shift can go in any direction." And he is always thinking about how to be natural or "neutral"—to find his zero point or "*mu*." You can only perform really well when you are no longer there.

Even though he did enjoy teaching at the Taiko Center, he sometimes felt in conflict with the school as a business, concerned about interference from management with his classes, presumably with directives to keep the students happy and paying. Apparently, although the classes are expensive, the teachers do not make all that much money. And some instructors may feel inhibited from offering constructive criticism in classes, as this may alienate those students who are there primarily for fun and not necessarily to improve. He was always careful with his comments about the Taiko Center, but nevertheless stopped teaching there in fall 2010 when he left Matsuri-shū.

Not surprisingly, Yamauchi focuses on the "color of sound" (*neiro*), just as Tosha Rōetsu, and a rich "sound" (*onryō*) expressed through layers of timbre and rhythms. He feels his own compositions are influenced by the precise layering of harmony and rhythm characterized by European-style art composers including J.S. Bach and Steve Reich, illustrated in his piece "Shimensoka," which he claims was influenced by a Bach Violin Suite (not included with the accompanying audio-visual materials). Thus Yamauchi mixes elements of *hōgaku* with European compositional techniques in *taiko*. While "Yaraiya" (Track 7; see further discussion in Chapter 3) does not reflect Bach or Reich, it does clearly connect with a swinging jazz, and illustrates his precise rhythmic sense, while he creates melodic contour through dynamic changes, further enhanced through subtle differences between *staccato* and *legato* articulations on the drums. His students recognize his musicality, referring to him as the consummate "artist."

The Star of the Stage: Kawarazaki Yoshihiro

Kawarazaki Yoshihiro is from the Arashiyama area of Kyoto (interview, April 27, 2010). As a child, both of his parents worked, so he spent afternoons at a neighborhood community center, at which he began playing *taiko*. Higashi of the Taiko Center actually suggested this community center formalize the group into Arashiyama-daiko, which is still active today. Higashi also is responsible for bringing Kawarazaki to the Taiko Center and fostering his career as a professional.

Kawarazaki originally intended to go to college and possibly run his own business, but when he failed his entrance exam, he realized he actually was not that motivated to go to college anyway. Higashi told him "If you are going to bang on the drum, I will give you money." And he began performing with Matsuri-shū and teaching at the Taiko Center over 25 years ago.

As a professional player, he did have the opportunity to perform with Leonardo Eto (another former member of Kodō and now globally recognized "superstar" on the flashy double-headed string-drum *katsugi-oke-daiko*) in 1994. At the time of research, Kawarazaki was appearing in several groups, including one called Beat Press, where he performs with his wife (and fellow *taiko*-player and teacher), and the all-male trio San Kyodai (three brothers). His identity as a teacher and performer continue to intertwine (see Figure 6.12).

Figure 6.12 Kawarazaki Yoshihiro on *katsugi-oke-daiko*

In the Classroom and on the Stage

Kawarazaki feels his ability to play *taiko* is "something special," a gift which he should use to move people, whether students or in an audience. He is happy both teaching and performing, although he does love playing in front of people. He thus is not sure where he will find himself in the future, but he knows he will keep making music in his own way.

He explains that the way of playing *taiko* in Tokyo is dominant—"standing low and hitting rapidly"—but his approach is a little different. He really does not want to be boxed into one style, which can prevent a performer from growing and improving. He illustrates this by talking about the details of playing: "If you widen the stance 1mm the sound will change; if you stress a different finger on the *bachi*, the sound will change, etc." So everyday he changes the "details in an attempt to change the sound." When he holds a *bachi*, however, no matter what style, he thinks of it as an extension of his hand and tries to imagine his nerves passing through the wood to the tip.

He believes people outside of Japan expect *taiko* to be performed with lots of choreography, including "the bowing and quickly thrusting one's arms into the air at the end of a performance." These audiences are too interested in the visuals—the beauty of the form (*kata*)—and not enough in the sound. He refers to the importance of *kata* in other Japanese arts, such as *karate*, where form is important, saying "this is a very Japanese thing to do"—confirming the comments from scholar-musicians above about the emphasis on the body and form. But when he created Beat Press, he wanted them to sound like a "jam session," the implication being he desired to make a group that just focused on the music. To him what Beat Press does "*is* music"; it is all about "enjoying the sound."

His compositional process is also very much focused on sound, which may seem rather obvious in the context of music, but within *taiko*, with its extreme emphasis on image, the sound is sometimes secondary. When creating a new piece, Kawarazaki first finds a rhythm "without thinking," then adds on additional rhythmic patterns that match. He feels the music rather "lands on him" (*orite kita*), as he reworks rhythms around a main theme, one that people hopefully remember and take with them. He equates this artistic expression to adding "color to a drawing." When he was young, he liked drawing, but not coloring. When he "started coloring things the drawing became something else" from what he initially envisioned. He liked pencil drawing—"having just black and white contrast is enough—it is easy to understand." So adding layers and layers obscures the main rhythmic melody.

Continuously repeating the basic parts creates groove (*nori*). His piece "Densha Hātobīto" ("Train Heartbeat") for Beat Press illustrates this making-the-maximum with-minimal-sounds approach, which of course is not uncommon in much music making in Japan (not included in the supporting audio-visual materials). He explains the main rhythm is actually inspired by a *hōgaku shime-daiko* pattern—"tenten tsuketen tsuketen teretsuku" (mnemonics for *shime-daiko*)—to which he added other rhythms. Although this compositional process, involving a main theme to which other musical ideas are added, is perhaps not all that unique, the result in Kawarazaki's hands is truly *grooving*. He envisions an "old guy in full Japanese formal dress (*montsuki hakama*) playing this rhythm on *shime-daiko*. But as he is drawn into the groove, becoming more and more excited, he begins dancing while playing the rhythm." The point is to have fun.

His ideas of what *taiko* can be and the way to create music permeate his approach in class. He wants students to have a good time, to "feel" the groove, but also wishes to motivate people to work harder—"so for two hours [he pushes] them so they leave class and go practice." He wants people to feel frustrated (*kuyashisa*) when not doing well, which in turn should inspire them to practice even more (and this was certainly true in my case). Both he and his students ultimately find joy with how much they change week after week, seeing how they "grow and expand." He therefore is quite strict, explaining that class is not the time to practice, and scolding those who obviously have not done so. If "normal" people taught this way, they would look arrogant in his opinion. But he has a place in the broader professional *taiko* world, and therefore can be demanding. Students not only accept, but also expect him to assert his authority in this way. People otherwise may feel that he is not living up to his reputation. He thus is actually quite thoughtful about his teaching, not necessarily doing what he wants, but instead what he thinks is appropriate for his position. But he also is severe because, quite simply, it works. He pushes his students, especially those more advanced in the class, trying to challenge everyone; otherwise their style becomes "servile" or "obsequious" and their skill does not continue to blossom.

Many of the students in Kawarazaki's class on *shime-daiko* and *katsugi-oke-daiko* (the only class at the Kyoto Taiko Center that meets weekly and, albeit labeled "intermediate," was widely considered the most advanced), are extremely loyal to him, taking the class multiple times, one student even enrolling twelve times over the past six years. Many of his students study only with him, referring to his classes as "special" amongst the offerings at the Taiko Center. One student explained she was initially hesitant in his classes, but after two years, had grown "much stronger and gained confidence." And student after student warmly acknowledges how Kawarazaki's demanding classroom demeanor has made them both better musicians and better performers, which are not always the same thing in this context. In this way, Kawarazaki is generating a loyalty similar to that fostered by *hōgaku* master Tosha Rōetsu. And indeed, he might object to the assessment, but I nevertheless found his methods resonating with those found in typical formal Japanese *okeiko*.

The requirements within class certainly ensured improvement, but the Taiko Center allows anyone to register for the course. Thus a complete beginner is dropped into a clearly well-established and advanced group. This of course is not ideal pedagogically as it holds back advanced students and slows everyone down, while new students feel overwhelmed and frustrated with the realization they are holding people back (a feeling that welled up in my heart numerous times throughout the year). On the flip side, students who had taken the class numerous times often assumed classic *senpai* roles, instructing the newer *kōhai* and in turn deepening their own understanding of the rhythms. Kawarazaki, however, was clearly concerned with the level of the course, noting that the Taiko Center at the time was not restricting enrollment; instead they were more concerned with "filling the class," a further indication of their identity as a business.

Kawarazaki nevertheless believes his approach to both performing and teaching is fostering young people's interest and skills in *taiko*. He always wants to maintain an image that he is the best among his followers, inspiring them to call out "Yoshihiro! Yoshihiro!"—and certainly does not want to disappoint them; thus he will maintain his high standards. He acknowledges that someday his students "will be better than him," but even then he wants to be the "chairman." Whether in the classroom or performing for an audience, he wants to be the star of the stage.

Matsuri-shū

Their respective approaches to music making and teaching are entirely different, nevertheless, Yamauchi's and Kawarazaki's distinct creative energies mingled in Matsuri-shū. Yamauchi, however, was responsible for most of Matsuri-shū's compositions while they worked together, but even here they came to influence each other. Kawarazaki explains that at first he did not really understand Yamauchi's vision. Kawarazaki was in fact "intimidated by Yamauchi's talent," but this actually inspired him to practice hard and improve his skills so he could perform the difficult pieces. In turn, he feels Yamauchi began composing pieces to match his improving skill. So Kawarazaki thinks he must have been learning, on a subconscious level, Yamauchi's style and vice versa. And each other's improvement and understanding shows through Matsuri-shū's performances.

Taiko Resource places Matsuri-shū's artistic vision within the immediate culture of Kyoto: "In Kyoto, there are many resources for traditional performing arts. Matsuri-sh[ū] researched the culture and traditional performing arts of Kyoto to create performances that move the people of today" (Leong n.d.), quickly revealing the way this group combines traditional elements in a modern mixture. Matsuri-shū's goal of capturing Japanese cultural identity as a whole is further elucidated in an excerpt of a letter written by Yamauchi to a European promoter regarding a possible tour in 2010 (I translated this letter into English for him at the time):

> We express "*Fūryū*," by creating music that is unconventional, while still moving with the traditional essence of Japan. *Wadaiko* is usually described as "soulful," but we go one step beyond, delivering a performance that is subtle, but also strikingly powerful. We create a new style of *wadaiko* combining traditional Japanese musical elements with hints of genres and rhythms from all around the world.

The professionals of Matsuri-shū thus clearly connect with the stereotypical image of *taiko*, but also play with traditional iconography, bringing in global sounds.

Matsuri-shū does so by using relatively simple staging with the basic backdrop of black curtains. In a live performance that I saw in December 2009 at the Kyoto Prefectural Center for Arts and Culture, the largest drum loomed on the back of the stage, waiting its turn in the darkness, as audience members, many of whom I recognized from classes at the Taiko Center, gradually filled the seats. The ambience was enhanced only with colored lighting and fog machines, but nothing more; a simplicity that allows the drums themselves to become the primary props on the stage.

The costumes were similarly simple, although typically reflected a common theme for each concert. They start with a black base, such as flowing pants, and then add some flash of color in the form of body paint or bright *kimono* fabric, playing with the association of Kyoto with traditional Japan through clothing. Lower bodies are thus usually covered, while torso and arms are revealed to varying degrees, again allowing unrestricted movement. Hairstyles support this blend, the women with hair up in funky ponytails or cornrows, while the men wore hair long or at one point even shaved patterns along their scalp. Jewelry, wrist and upper arm cuffs, and bare feet (as opposed to the more common traditional split-toe footwear (*tabi*)) all supported the simultaneous earthy, funky image of the group. Matsuri-shū were at once completely Kyoto and globally connected. Yamauchi agrees that the clothing captured the essence of Kyoto, in that

Matsuri-shū did not just "turn *kimono* straight into costumes," instead cutting them up and refashioning them in hip ways. "Kyoto's mentality is to create something new while keeping the tradition alive," which he also tried to do in the music for the group. But this is not possible "unless you have studied the traditional arts as well," which make him uniquely qualified to meld these musical styles.

First and foremost for Matsuri-shū was creating an interesting sound, either through laying a strong groove or interlocking intricate rhythmic patterns or both (depending on which member was primarily responsible for creating the particular piece). But under Yamauchi's influence, they incorporated musical elements from classical Japanese music to African drumming. In my research, I found Matsuri-shū to have the most relaxed and natural-looking arm gestures and extremely fluid play. They do not perform simultaneous and obviously choreographed gestures. Their bodies break lines in unexpected and visually appealing ways. They also use a variety of *bachi*, ranging from baseball bats to tympani mallets, never feeling constrained by convention.

Their instrumentation also relied on some unusual *taiko*, for example *magewappa-daiko*, large drums, 3–4 feet in diameter, from Akita prefecture in northern Honshū, and quite rare in the world of ensemble drumming, which are suspended from shoulder straps in performance. They also occasionally employed non-Western instruments serving as special effects, such as wind chimes and a rain stick. However, they did not often, if ever, incorporate non-Japanese instruments into the main melodies, instead staying well within Japan—indeed, well within Kyoto—but finding creative ways to pull sound from these native instruments and traditional techniques.

Several of these elements are highlighted in their piece "Konjichō," composed by former Matsuri-shū member Yura Hidenori (Website Example 18). This piece exhibits Matsuri-shū at play with the traditional and the modern. Yamauchi, for example, employs classical drumming techniques in the way he holds his *bachi*, here playing a *shime-daiko* and not actually the *taiko* of *noh-hayashi*, and the vocal calls (*kakegoe*) at 3:10, a traditional flute (*nohkan*) intermittently floats above at times invoking images of classic *noh* plays, at 2:55 and again with a piercing call at the end, but at other times circling on new melodies. The virtuosic solos that begin as Kawarazaki moves to the front of the stage with a double-headed drum at 3:25 are decidedly outside the realm of traditional Japanese music, however, harkening more to *taiko*'s origin in jazz, as the entire piece spills forth over a driving groove. There is play within tropes of *taiko* as well, with the position of a barrel-shaped *nagado-daiko* on its side, and struck on both heads as if a *katsugi-oke-daiko*. Yura, who is playing this drum, is an accomplished *katsugi-oke-daiko* player who developed an innovative style in which both arms cross over the body to the opposite head (as opposed to the standard style in which only the right arm strikes the left head). And one cannot miss the formal *obi*—the elaborate belt used to secure *kimono*—but here wrapped around a young woman's tank top, her midriff clearly apparent.

Summary

Matsuri-shū lean towards "world beat" in their costuming and overall aesthetic feel, somewhat like Gocoo; nonetheless, the sense of "tradition" is still very much present, precisely because Yamauchi is highly trained in classical Japanese techniques while others, including Kawarazaki, have long performed in the professional *taiko* world.

Matsuri-shū presents their own vision of *taiko* as grooving, varied and open to vast manipulation. Nonetheless, they rely much on Japanese instrumentation standard in *taiko*, although here too they actively seek instruments that stand out in some way.

Both in this piece composed by Yura, and others by Yamauchi, Matsuri-shū were able to create a connection with Kyoto through their music. Yamauchi did so at times rather overtly, including rhythms from the *Gion-bayashi* or other well-known *matsuri*. He expands: "There is a strong image of *kabuki* and *maiko* associated with the image of Kyoto, and my music includes *kabuki* rhythms through *tsuzumi* and *shime-daiko*, even if most people do not recognize them." And with the decline in *hōgaku* this is likely true. Through the costumes perhaps the connection is more obvious, as Yamauchi reminds us: "At first they look like regular clothes, but if you look more closely you see the costumes are made from *kimono*. It is easy to do this in Kyoto whereas this would be harder for a group like Kodō in Sado. Everybody in Japan relates *kimono* to Kyoto." Matsuri-shū have thus wrapped modernity in traditional garb yet again.

Murasaki Daiko and the Proper Dōjō (Studio)

Murasaki Daiko also present themselves as a professional *taiko* group although they perform a drastically different style in distinct contexts than other performers in Kyoto. The group's leadership is split between a creative director, Akane Fujino, and her husband and former hotel manager, Nishimura Shirō, who handles administrative duties. Murasaki Daiko is in fact very much focused on the business aspects of performing, which constantly permeate Akane's artistic vision.

Murasaki Daiko was founded in 2004 and named after Murasaki Shikibu (late tenth century to early eleventh century), the author of *Genji Monogatari* (*The Tale of Genji*), the epic tale set in Kyoto at the height of the Heian period. The company (for that is what the management feels like) creates elaborate promotional materials including glossy brochures and fliers, featuring photographs of the performers in their various ornate costumes floating on soft purple backgrounds ("*murasaki*" literally refers to a shade of purple), draped with vines of wisteria flowers or cherry blossoms. Within these materials, Murasaki Daiko primarily describes their dancing in which they perform

> ... "Kyoto *jūnihitoe buyō*" [Kyoto twelve-layered-robe dancing] and features original music and dance inspired by the classic Japanese novel *Genji Monogatari* [*The Tale of Genji*], which continues to move our souls even though it was written 1000 years ago. Our group regularly performs around Kyoto at various vernacular venues, while also performing pieces dedicated to the gods at both Heian Shrine every spring and Kamigamo Shrine every New Year's season.
>
> The dances included in this program all reflect parts of this iconic novel about the great lover Prince Genji and his various escapades throughout Kyoto and neighboring towns.

Many perceive Murasaki Daiko as actually a dance troupe, as opposed to a drumming ensemble, despite the prominent position of *taiko* on the stage in most of their pieces, and the group as a result attracts many performers who are primarily interested, and in some cases, previously trained in dance.

Figure 6.13 Osoda Miho of Murasaki Daiko performing at Heian-jingū

Murasaki Daiko includes exclusively female students, some of whom become part of the professional group, currently comprising young women in their late teens to mid-twenties (see Figure 6.13). Murasaki Daiko recruits its professional performers largely through advertisements at local colleges. These young women are considered "employees" as well as students, and are quickly taught the pieces for public, meaning paid, performance. Akane's impression is that Kyoto women do not find *taiko* "elegant" and are unwilling to play (interview, April 23, 2010). Nishimura adds:

> Since classic times, there has been the saying—"the men from Tokyo are stylish and the women from Kyoto are womanly" (*azuma otoko ni kyō onna*)—so the general public in Japan has an image of Kyoto women as "womanly." Things are changing now, but people have been told over and over this image—which might make some women not want to play *taiko*.
>
> (interview, April 23, 2010)

Taiko's physicality, in their view, may prevent the typical Kyoto woman from joining their group; albeit an opinion that clearly does not take into consideration the high number of women performing at the Taiko Center and other groups I encountered. Akane, nevertheless, recruits college students coming to Kyoto from other parts of the world, who she feels are more likely to want to come play *taiko*. And according to interviewees, at the time of my research, none of the professional members were actually from Kyoto, but from other areas of Japan or even China. Perhaps these young women feel more connected to Kyoto themselves through performing Murasaki Daiko's interpretations of scenes from *Genji Monogatari*, although no one ever made this explicit connection.

Ideally, Akane looks for performers who are "smart" in terms of appearance, "slim" and "proud standing," but they must also be "someone who enjoys life." She further envisions the young performers like characters in a video game, so they must have "cool" personalities on stage. She continually refers to the ideal performance as "sexy," which is achieved through entertaining and exciting choreography and costuming. But performances must remain "amusing," as being too serious will alienate the audience.

Several interviewees described the ideal Murasaki Daiko performer as "cute," "healthy," and with great vitality. The performers most often describe themselves, and are described by others, as women who want to "show themselves," who like attention, with "strong personalities and confidence." And not surprisingly many of the performers list their motivations for joining as a desire to move people through their performance, to be on stage.

Women Outside the Box

In the mid-2000s, Akane began teaching a group of mature women all in their sixties, with whom I actually spent most of my time during my research. The group offered all the women, including Akane, an important opportunity to regularly meet, to maintain physical and mental health, and perhaps even more importantly, a much appreciated opportunity to socialize, as they met before lessons to share tea and sweets, and gathered for dinners together on numerous occasions. These women all combated the traditional image of a typical Japanese housewife—each being spectacularly unique in their own way. The wife of a fishmonger, a voracious reader, recognized that studying *taiko* was rare amongst her friends and she loved feeling unusual. While another member who ran a café, decorated with her own paintings of famous *maiko* and *geiko*, practiced jazz singing to challenge her mind, and found *taiko* provided a "balance" for her body, bringing together exercise, music and mental work. Another member actually performed professionally with the younger women, until management at Murasaki Daiko decided that she should no longer do so (presumably because they wanted to promote the attractive image of the young women), but she enjoyed playing with this relaxed, older group, describing them as women who want more—"more studying, more learning, more living. . . ."

Unlike many groups who must practice outside of city limits because of the noise, Murasaki Daiko rehearses in a small, second-floor studio in central Kyoto, although they must mute the drums with rubber mats in order to do so (see Figure 6.14).

Towards the end of my research, Akane arranged for us to rent studio space, transported over drums, and rehearsed without mutes with the "mature" amateur students. Murasaki Daiko performs professionally, but it was nevertheless extremely difficult for the "pro-members" to coordinate schedules and rehearse adequately together, hindering their ability to truly develop and tighten details of performance. High turnover was

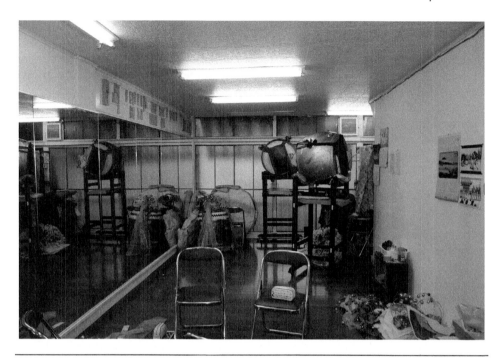

Figure 6.14 Murasaki Daiko *dōjō*

another common problem amongst professional players as well. The older students, however, consistently met once a week for several hours.

Once a year, Murasaki Daiko perform during cherry blossom season at Heian-jingu (a large shrine in Kyoto) (see Figure 6.13) and cultural centers; even so, the group's bread and butter is made performing at hotels essentially as dinner theater. In fall 2009, I was invited to attend one of these professional performances at a large resort on nearby Lake Biwa. The performers, once dressed in Murasaki Daiko's extravagant costumes, ascended a small stage in the lobby and settled into seated positions, appearing like the traditional dolls displayed on Girl's Day (*hina-ningyō*). A few minutes later, the hotel staff suddenly came to life scurrying here and there as the first of several large tour buses pulled up to the door. Throngs of senior citizens descended from the buses to a flurry of solicitous behavior from the staff. Nishimura raised the volume of pre-recorded music and the young women of Murasaki Daiko came to life, greeting the tourists and then moving through a sampling of the dances they would perform later that evening. Some travelers stopped to watch, and take photos or video footage, while others barely glanced at the dancers, as they quickly passed on their way to the soft cotton robes and hot baths that awaited them. Nishimura explained later that this "live welcoming" was quite "unusual," an opinion with which I wholeheartedly agreed.

After the last of the tour buses arrived and all the passengers left the lobby, the young women then proceeded to the room where they would be performing that evening—a large banquet hall, with a narrow raised stage at the far end. After preparing the space, rolling out large drums and various other decorations and props stored in a back room, they took a few minutes to rest and recuperate before the performance proper began.

The show took place on the stage while the tourists sat on the floor, drinking and eating at the tables in front of them, chatting loudly. The music featured a sampling of very short pieces on the drums interposed with Akane's electronic, modern-sounding synthesized interpretations of traditional Japanese music (see further discussion below). To my surprise, the young women, initially dressed from head to toe, by the end were wearing rather revealing costumes (see further discussion below). Twenty minutes into the program, three older gentleman were invited onto the stage and allowed to briefly "solo" on the drums, taking away small gifts at the end of their mini-performances. The total event lasted a brief 27 minutes before the 200 or so revelers went straight into *karaoke* without missing a beat.

Doing Things the Right Way

Whether in a lesson or a public performance, even including the one just described, Akane strives to create a "proper" atmosphere, connecting with traditional Japanese performance practices. She does not think of Murasaki Daiko as a formal school (*ryū* or *ie*), in the strict sense (for example, collecting exorbitant fees from students to obtain titles and progress upwards within the line); however, she does consider this a new school of performance and expects her students to learn her pieces as belonging to "Akane-ryū." In order to be taken seriously as a business, both she and Nishimura also decided she needs to be referred to as an *iemoto*, or head of this school. Despite the image of Murasaki Daiko in the hotel setting, which seems far removed from traditional Japan on the surface, Akane is most concerned with creating a formal environment, expecting appropriate behavior from students at all times and treating both the lesson (*okeiko*) and studio (*okeikoba*) with a great deal of respect.

She insisted, for example, that I clean the studio each day when I arrived in order to allow "the gods (*kami-sama*) to enter" both the space and my playing. According to Akane, devotees in *kendō* (a Japanese martial art involving long wooden "swords") or Takarazuka Revue (all-female musical theater), clean the *dōjō* (the space where martial arts are practiced) to clear the heart for the *kami-sama* to enter. So one must "clean the space to clean the heart" as *kami-sama* will only then enter, thus connecting her philosophy with traditional Japanese conceptions of purity and Shintoism. For Akane, *taiko* is like martial arts, hence her use of "*dōjō*" as opposed to "*okeikoba*" to refer to the studio, and therefore those who practice this art should follow the *samurai* code (*bushidō*). One must therefore think of the "*bachi* as a sword (*katana*) and treat it as such in performance. The *kami-sama* appear when you strike the *taiko* with a clean heart in a proper *dōjō*."

Lessons begin and end with formal exchanges (*aisatsu*), she in a chair and students kneeling on the floor in *seiza*, with *bachi* precisely placed in front, and a low bow with the forehead grazing the floor. She bemoans the decreasing awareness of such social graces amongst young people and consequently distributes a list of expected behaviors to new students, the content of which affirms traditional relationships between junior students (*kōhai*) and their seniors (*senpai*), as well as establishing her own position as head of this school (*iemoto*). The list includes such directives as for new students to carry heavy things; let senior students enter the elevator first and push the button for them; to use only *keigo* (formal Japanese) in the studio; to be humble about level and skill, and of course to ask Akane for permission to speak and, in a modern twist, to respond to her e-mails punctually. She believes that people should learn to "do things the right way"—upholding the image of Kyoto.

Figure 6.15 Akane Fujino

Akane Fujino, a Bright Ball of Energy

Without a doubt, of all my teachers Akane was the most generous with her time both in lessons and without, as she shared her most developed aesthetic and pedagogical philosophies (see Figure 6.15). Perhaps this was simply her personality, or because both she and Nishimura recognized the potential gains of promotion by a foreign scholar (I prefer not to present her as quite so opportunistic), or simply a result of the fact that she was my only female teacher, eager to share her artistic vision with another woman. Regardless of the reasons, she clearly revealed Murasaki Daiko's highly theorized, if unusual performance style.

Akane is a Kyoto-native who studied language and visual design in London. As a child, she was exposed to a great variety of arts, including the *koto*, so she feels comfortable working in both Japanese and Western music systems. She first tried *taiko* in her late twenties, while playing percussion in an ensemble. Although she never studied formally, she saw many professional performers, which informed her vision of *taiko*. While working as a promoter of performing groups, she came into contact with a wide variety of global percussion, particularly that of Senegal and Martinique, which she wanted to connect with Japanese *taiko*. When she founded Murasaki Daiko, she therefore had these global percussive sounds in mind.

Murasaki Daiko is actually the combined creation of her artistic vision and the business sense of Nishimura, whom she met while promoting a group at a hotel he was managing at the time. The two together decided to start their own performing group. As an artist, she "respects and accepts any kind of music," but he ultimately settled on drums as their primary instrumentation because they are "exciting" and "sexy," recognizing their potential to attract audiences. In the end, she wanted to use *taiko* to do something "different," to not feel limited by expectations of "what *taiko* should be," which she feels is enforced by various *taiko* associations. Akane finds that "Japanese drummers tend to be hardheaded, fixated, and are not flexible—probably because they are mostly men." Whether this is true or not is not the point, rather Akane's comments here clearly reveal her conscious decision to position Murasaki Daiko out of the mainstream of *taiko* performance.

Akane brings this appreciation for variety to her teaching. When introducing a new dance, for example, she thinks it is important to recognize everyone's differences—in height, in character, whether someone has a "cute, sharp, or cool face." She strives to draw out each student's individuality. Everyone doing the same thing is amateurish, in her mind, so as professionals she wants each person on stage to highlight her own charismatic features. "Each individual has a beautiful way of doing things from birth," an inner beauty that she hopes to identify and in turn, help young people find themselves through performance.

During the performance, she expects her people to connect with the audience, to keep them enthralled with the power of the performers and constantly surprised by the music and dance. She aspires to make the audience yearn for the next thrill and will do anything to create this feeling. Every aspect of performance is therefore designed to increase the connection between performer and audience, from being sure to make eye contact, rather than the common habit of gazing above the audience's heads or staring intently at the center of the drum, to the flowery props the group employs. Image and atmosphere are most important for her. An extremely expressive talker, peppering her comments with arm-to-full-body gestures, Akane is a bright ball of energy at all times—embodying the excitement she strives for in the performance of Murasaki Daiko.

Murasaki Daiko in Performance

Murasaki Daiko are extremely proud of their homemade staging and costumes, all of which are intended to highlight what Akane sees as elements of *Genji Monogatari*, but reinterpreted in a way that will be appealing—that is, marketable—to contemporary audiences. Staging remains relatively simple in terms of the number of props in view at one time, but all items, from the drums themselves to the scarves attached to poles and

Four Case Studies from Kyoto • 213

Figure 6.16 Murasaki Daiko dancing

flung through the air while dancing, something akin to rhythmic gymnastics, are colorful, sparkling and shiny.

Costumes reinforce this vision. The group typically begins a 20-minute performance with a series of short dances featuring the young women in costumes inspired by court dress, complete with *kimono* that appear to be in many layers, harkening back to the Heian period when women wrapped themselves in twelve *kimono*. In this modern version, however, Nishimura, who makes all the costumes for the group, actually sews twelve hems at the sleeve's edge to make it appear as if there are actually multiple robes. Wigs now provide the floor-grazing hair of women of the court centuries ago (with the exception of one committed member who purposefully grew her hair long). The addition of dramatic gold headpieces and theatrical makeup create the desired illusion (see Figure 6.16). As the show progresses and the performers introduce increasingly demanding drumming, the robes are removed to reveal colorful brocade vests over black hot pants, red *tabi* and spats plus various other shiny accessories (see Figure 6.17).

These young women's bodies are clearly on display as they point their toes, make large, choreographed dance moves that engage the entire body, or wrap themselves around the drums in a suggestive manner. Akane expects their shoulders to continuously move back and forth as they manipulate homemade, very short *bachi* with rubber strips on the handles to help them maintain the unconventional grip she prefers. The uneven lines of their bodies and constant shifting of the center of gravity is most striking, and most difficult to emulate if trained in other forms of *taiko* (see Figure 6.17).

Not surprisingly, Akane has put a great deal of thought into this performance style precisely because her group is all women. Finding it really difficult for women

Figure 6.17 Murasaki Daiko drumming

to perform *taiko* in an equal way with men, she exclaims "they would have to cut their hair and be very buff like GI Jane." So, just as she desires to draw out each performer's unique personality, she developed a style she feels men cannot easily play in the same way, constantly thinking about how she is going to promote these women "as women."

Indeed, the vast majority of people I interviewed, regardless of the group, recognized that men and women's bodies are different and therefore the sound they produce when playing *taiko* naturally varies. But this was accepted as fact and not questioned. If anything, these differences should be recognized, embraced and used to enhance musicality within a performance; one interviewee compared the energy of male and female *taiko* players to "*yin* and *yang*, which need each other to exist in balanced harmony." Most of the *taiko* groups I encountered in Kyoto, from Bachi Holic to Matsuri-shū, are mindful of having men and women play parts they feel are appropriate to the gender, and even when on the same part acknowledge the nuance is subtly to vastly different. This distinction was celebrated rather than seen as potentially limiting. The consensus seemed to be rather than trying to claim that men and women are the same, it is better to acknowledge the dissimilarity, even using this to one's advantage when programming performances. There is a problem of course when these impressions are used to prevent women from playing certain types of *taiko* that are understood as more appropriate for men if they choose to do so, and perhaps vice versa.

But in regards Murasaki Daiko, as Akane succinctly summarizes:

> . . . in some performances, when women play the audience may question why women are there. In Japan a lot of people will question why women are trying to do the same thing as men. Even here, when they try to promote the group people will ask can they hit the drum for real. Since the old days people believe there are things women can't do when it comes to *taiko*. It is rare that there are women who can perform *taiko* better than men . . . So for women to look better than men, they need to make bigger action. And if it is a man he can just show his back and hit the drum, but women need something else. . . .

She proudly exclaims Murasaki Daiko "are not men, they are women!" and therefore require a style that both suits their female bodies and sets them apart. Her desire to highlight the femininity of her performers informs the costumes, technique and position; in short, every aspect of performance. The wide stance of the Taiko Center, for example, is inappropriately broad in her opinion, while she has her performers "wrap hips" around the drum and step forward to create a three-dimensional effect for the audience. The performers are to create long lines from the tip of the *bachi* to the tip of the toe, "lifting a heel and stepping on toes as if wearing high-heels for a pretty affect." And she uses fluid strokes, with active upper bodies. She pays similar attention to the detail of her performers' makeup, which each of the women must learn to apply herself, to highlight their eyes, making them appear more dramatic. Akane pays tremendous attention to the most minute details, which of course are also informed by the desire to attract audiences. Murasaki Daiko's members recognize the emphasis on dance and the costuming as both unique and an important "sales point," acknowledging the business side of the group. But several interviewees also describe both as "elegant," reminding us that this is still an art for Akane.

They perform on large barrel drums purchased in Mongolia, which are significantly less expensive, lighter, and produce a decent sound more quickly than their Japanese counterparts; Akane feels the latter is especially true for female performers who lack the upper body strength of men. But this choice is also informed by economics, as the famous drums made by Japanese makers, such as Asano and Miyamoto, and favored by many players, are so expensive that even "professional performers can't make any money because everything goes to paying for the drums." These therefore convenient

Mongolian drums are painted in silver or gold to which Akane and Nishimura apply crystals that sparkle when the light hits them, adding to the visual impact.

Her artistic sense was influenced by seeing Chinese percussion groups earlier in her career, and she remains amazed by what she describes as "visually stunning performances," appreciating both their musical sensibility and ability to draw the audience into the show. She realized they use other instruments besides *taiko* when they want to move the crowd, and hence Nishimura began fashioning new instruments for the group, of which he is very proud. He is particularly interested in making instruments out of bamboo, a plentiful resource in Kyoto, to expand both the timbre and the texture of the group, but even these are painted silver and gold to match the drums. There is no doubt Akane is most concerned about the affect of the group's appearance on the audience, at times even more so than the quality of sound, truly privileging the visual over the sonic.

As noted above, Akane creates short pieces that blend pre-recorded and live music, a style that many of the Murasaki Daiko members feel really distinguishes the group from other *taiko* ensembles. And she regularly synthesizes interpretations of traditional Japanese music and instruments, including *shamisen* and *koto*, with *taiko*, to varying degrees of success. When asked about her music, she continues to refer to the "personality" and "image," she is trying to create, rather than the "notes" themselves, again emphasizing her visual orientation; she is after all trained as a graphic designer and not a musician, which no doubt feeds into her emphasis on visual impact at every level. Akane nevertheless makes music that reflects what she believes people want to hear, a process that in turn changes her. Ever concerned with pleasing an audience, her creativity is deeply informed by the needs of others.

"Hannya"

Akane's concepts come together in her composition "Hannya" (Website Example 19), a fantastic story about a demon in battle with a shaman. The piece opens with atmospheric, synthesized sounds mimicking a *koto*, the crash of thunder and pouring rain, as the women come to life first dancing on the floor, gradually working their way up to standing positions, with arm thrusts timed to precisely coincide with cues in the music. Once at the drums, the woman in red performs the demon, while the shaman is in white on the other side of the *ō-daiko* up on the stand. The timbre and texture is certainly expanded by the inclusion of one of Nishimura's homemade bamboo instruments, located at the back of the stage, and producing a distinctive "clacking" sound. The hostility between these two characters is created through interlocking parts, but with little repetition and an absence of the groove that characterizes much *taiko*. Akane's music, as a result, can be quite difficult to memorize. Unlike the majority of other *taiko* I have encountered, in which strong beats are typically articulated by the right hand, she alternates between the right and left hands, also furthering the difficulty of mastering her pieces. She finds the conventional approach "easy," however, preferring to use the left hand to start rhythmic melodies in order to allow the right hand to strike on particularly strong beats (much like an "up bow" marking with a Western string instrument). She is particular about dynamics as well (difficult to discern here, given the quality of the video) to create her desired moments of surprise, building the tension through the piece and hopefully drawing in the audience just as the shaman defeats the demon, and the young women return to a group dance.

Summary

Murasaki Daiko is removed from the core identity of *taiko*, both socially and as regards broader aspects of performance. Many involved in *taiko* in Kyoto in fact perceived Murasaki Daiko primarily as a dance troupe. Nonetheless, given where and how often they perform, in front of sometimes hundreds of tourists gathered in nearby Lake Biwa, they significantly contribute to the image of *taiko* in the Kyoto area. Murasaki Daiko's connection with Kyoto is clearly expressed through their choice to enact the scenes of the classical *Genji Monogatari* with a modern ethos, capturing the essence of Kyoto's identity both past and present. Several members recognize Murasaki Daiko as a most modern group that tells a most classic tale, which performs at contemporary hotels as easily as at the oldest of temples. And of course they wear modern interpretations of classical costumes. One interviewee explained how when all the young women take to the stage, "a similar feeling of jealousy and envy as found amongst Prince Genji's women is created," perhaps connecting to the subtly "erotic" and overtly romantic character of not only *Genji Monogatari* but of Kyoto as a whole. Akane consciously imagines Kyoto through the themes and feelings of the pieces, trying to evoke the *miyako* aura that she thinks clients desire; she is manipulating traditional imagery with modern performative techniques to appeal to the paying customer, but in the end creates something uniquely her own.

Some Conclusions

I went to Kyoto looking for a *taiko* "scene," but did not really find one; instead there is great variety and little intersection between performers. Tosha Rōetsu certainly influenced a number of *taiko* groups I worked with, as the teacher of both Basara's founder Fujiwara years ago, and at the time of research, Yamauchi of the Taiko Center and Matsuri-shū. Tosha himself claims that through his work with Ondekoza, who of course impacted the global practice of *taiko* ensemble drumming, he instructed numerous innovators in the genre, including Leonardo Eto, with whom Kawarazaki performed and claims stylistic similarities. But not everyone I interviewed agreed that through Tosha a network of *taiko* emerges, such as Murasaki Daiko, who are truly doing "their own thing," and some even objected to being associated with Tosha's traditional world. The dominant position of the Taiko Center in Kyoto must be noted; however, its problematic reputation prevents it from generating a scene per se, and again, several people did not want to be associated with and were even quite critical of the school, turning elsewhere to make music. *Taiko* in other cities in Japan and other global contexts may produce a greater sense of a cohesive community, and there may be unexplored virtual scenes as well, but more inquiry with these questions in mind would need to be done to make this argument.

Within Kyoto, however, every group I worked with expressed different aesthetic visions and goals, with performance technique, beyond the common use of drums, unique to each. Even the types of *bachi* vary—from the long and fat *bachi* made of light and fragrant *hinoki* wood of Basara, to the homemade short oak *bachi*, with a grip wrapped in sticky rubber of Murasaki Daiko, each type preferred to create the desired aesthetic style exhibited in the illustrative musical examples. The specific mnemonics (*kuchishōka*) and notation hovered in the same realm—everyone uses them—but each in their own way. Tosha's elaborate scoring with its unique characters has already been discussed, but within the *taiko* groups there was no single fixed system of drum tablature used by everyone. For example, even at the Taiko Center, published notation would place a note head above a line to indicate right hand, below the line for left, or "o" for right and "x" for left. But teachers varied these scores considerably in classes. Within Basara, the only group which did not rely on *kuchishōka* to learn new material, notation changed depending on the original source of a piece, and usually initial practices were spent copying down the sticking. Akane had everyone copy down her own mnemonics for a piece, which used "*to*" and "*ta*" to differentiate between non-accented and accented strikes respectively, something no one else did. Although these notations served only as maps, as with traditional music, and did not capture the subtlety of performance, I was nonetheless surprised by the variety, even inconsistency. But I eventually came to see this diversity as an accurate reflection of *taiko* as a whole—rich with variance and innovation—as the practice continues to develop as a genre throughout the world today.

My fieldwork further revealed that not only are musical styles heterogeneous, but so are the ways in which both *hōgaku* and ensemble drumming are transmitted in lessons and rehearsals. The multiplicity of pedagogical styles should combat the mythology of uniformity in Japanese traditional arts, while furthering the reading of *taiko* as a genre really still in its infancy, and several of these individuals are original enough actually to be seen as "creating new schools" of *taiko*. Tosha Rōetsu is easily understood as the consummate traditional teacher, even as he sees this world fading away, but still here we have uniqueness in his individual style, and the use of live *shamisen* at the Pontochō *okeiko*. It took some time to see the similarities, for example, Kawarazaki actually teaches in a very traditional Japanese way, by "showing and not telling" musical elements; he is quick to critique, and his students assume classic *senpai* and *kōhai* relationships.

Akane too maintains formality, in part to assert her legitimacy, as well as to draw clear connections with the classic image of Kyoto. But in contrast to traditional teachers, she is most thoughtful with her explanations of her vision and technique. Yamauchi is similarly concerned with technique, where his training in both Western conservatory and classical Japanese percussion come together, resulting in a highly developed musical sensibility, which he tries to draw from his students. Ōtsuka would likely object to being included in this list of educators at all, but I do so nonetheless as his considerate approach to maintaining a democratic environment while transmitting his knowledge impacted both Basara and myself. Variety, after all, is the spice of life and all the students I interviewed shared a tremendous loyalty to both their individual teachers and the groups with which they each perform. Tosha warned me that I would never become good at anything working with so many teachers, and I have to agree; nevertheless doing so was incredibly enlightening, as each has informed my own style with students in my studio back home.

Most importantly, pursuing so many paths revealed what all these sites had in common: namely an emphasis on each individual's unique identity as performers and as people. In a land where "sameness" is celebrated, Japanese percussion and especially *taiko* may offer a tremendous opportunity to express difference.

References

Basara. n.d.a. "A message from Aki—the founder of Basara." *Geocities* (n.d.): http://www.geocities.jp/wadaikobasara/e-handwri.htm (accessed November 4, 2009).
Basara. n.d.b. "Wadaiko Japanese Drums Basara." *Geocities* (n.d.): http://www.geocities.jp/wadaikobasara/e-index.htm (accessed November 4, 2009).

Basara. n.d.c. "Wadaiko Songs of Basara." *Geocities* (n.d.): http://www.geocities.jp/wadaikobasara/e-song.htm (accessed November 4, 2009).

Bender, Shawn. 2010. "Drumming from Screen to Stage: Ondekoza's Odaiko and the Reimaging of Japanese Taiko." *The Journal of Asian Studies* 69(3):843–867.

——. 2012. *Taiko Boom: Japanese Drumming in Place and Motion*. Berkeley: University of California Press.

Blasdel, Christopher Y. 2005. *The Single Tone: A Personal Journey into Shakuhachi Music*. Tokyo: Printed Matter Press.

Deschênes, Bruno. 1987. Comments on the re-release of *Japan: Kabuki & Other Traditional Music*. Nonesuch Records 72084 (first released 1980): http://www.barnesandnoble.com/w/japan-kabuki-other-traditional-music-ensemble-nipponia/233245?ean=75597208429 (accessed 18 March 2015).

Gillan, Matthew. 2012. *Songs From the Edge of Japan: Music-Making in Yaeyama and Okinawa*. Farnham: Ashgate.

Keister, Jay. 2004. *Shaped by Japanese Music: Kikuoka Hiroaki and Nagauta Shamisen in Tokyo*. New York/London: Routledge.

Leong, David. n.d. "Resource: Japanese Taiko Group" *Rolling Thunder* (n.d.): http://www.taiko.com/taiko_resource/groups_j.html (accessed September 11, 2009).

Malm, William P. 1963. *Nagauta: The Heart of Kabuki Music*. Rutland, VT: Tuttle.

——. 1986. *Six Hidden Views of Japanese Music*. Berkeley: University of California Press.

Matsuri-shū. n.d. "Matsuri-shū Profile." *Matsuri-shū* (n.d.): http://www.matsurishu.com/profile.html (accessed September 18, 2009).

Shimosako, Mari. 2002. "Philosophy and Aesthetics." In R. Provine, Y. Tokumaru and J. Witzleben, eds., *East Asia: China, Japan and Korea. The Garland Encyclopedia of World Music Vol. 7*, pp. 554–555. New York/London: Routledge.

Surak, Kristin. 2013. *Making Tea, Making Japan: Cultural Nationalism in Practice*. Stanford, CA: Stanford University Press.

Tanaka, Takafumi, Mayusa Oda, Kimiko Iwashita, Kiyo Furusaki and Mariko Okeda. 2005. *Performing Arts in Japan: Traditional Music Today*. Translated by ALAYA INC. Tokyo: The Japan Foundation.

Wong, Deborah. 2008. "Moving: From Performance to Performative Ethnography and Back Again." In G. Barz and T. Cooley, eds., *Shadows in the Field: New Perspectives for Fieldwork in Ethnomusicology*, pp. 76–89. Oxford: Oxford University Press.

Conclusion: The Future of Japanese Music

Figure 7.1 Vendors at a *matsuri*

In October 2014, while serving as Visiting Faculty at Kansai Gaidai University in Osaka, I attended the local fall festival at our neighborhood shrine. There were the typical food stalls, *sake* for the adults, games and inexpensive toys for sale for the children (see Figure 7.1); however, the highlight of the two-day festival was the musical performances on the second and final night. We arrived just as members of the community took their turns at "*karaoke* for the gods," performing predominantly well-known *enka* tunes for both their own and the enjoyment of the Shintō deities in attendance. As the sun began to set, the outdoor stage was quickly changed and we enjoyed a lively performance by a local *taiko* group, including Kodō's interpretation of the famous piece "Yatai." After scooting us off our benches, which were transformed into risers on the stage, a full SATB choir, with supporting string quartet (volunteers from the local philharmonic orchestra), electronic keyboard and a conductor decked out in black tie and tails, transported the audience through a collection of well-known songs. Although most of these songs were in Japanese, the one with English lyrics was exceptional in that the vocalists appeared, at least to me, to have a limited idea of what they were singing—rather the language became sound, muted, without proper accent and devoid of actual meaning for both the performers and the audience. The group rallied as they closed their "set" with the famous piece "Shōnen Jidai" ("Boyhood") by Inoue Yōsui, a song about youth.

The evening culminated with *kyōgen*, a stylized comedic performance typically interspersed in longer *noh* plays, the wind whipping the leaves from trees. As the professional actors completed the hilarious scene "Busu," about two retainers who eat the head of the temple's container of sweets while he is away, they received much applause and a spattering of coins wrapped in tissue paper tossed on the stage in a display of appreciation. This performance, just as with all the proceeding, was meant to entertain the Shintō gods, who no doubt were highly amused. As the festival came to a close, the entire audience of perhaps a little over a hundred people joined together with the choir, the conductor, and even the *kyōgen* actors to sing "Furusato," a *shōka* (school song) from 1914 glorifying the connection with one's hometown, and uniting the community in song and ideology.

What amazed me, as I experienced this event, is the way in which the program moved from one style of music to the next, from *karaoke* to *taiko*, choral music to *kyōgen*, without missing a beat. All these musics clearly can and do coexist side-by-side in contemporary Japan, and in so doing, express many of the themes introduced in the preceding pages; an apt conclusion as I finished writing up this book.

The examples both here and in the preceding pages present myriad ways Japanese cultural identity is negotiated through music. Yes, it is possible to argue for Japaneseness in sound—in the scales of *min'yō* and the melodies they produce, heterophonic texture, or form that spills forth through the process *jo-ha-kyū*, but these are difficult arguments to make as these sounds are found in much music around the world. The ability for instruments to express a specific cultural identity has become increasingly incongruous, especially in Japan with its history of acculturation. There certainly is a strong case to be made that the rapid hybridization of imported forms best captures Japaneseness. This process is most apparent in the modern era as Japanese musicians found unique forms of expression in a foreign language, from European art musics to idols, and is particularly well-illustrated in the ongoing development of *taiko* as a genre. The continued negotiation of tradition and modernity characterizes the identity of Kyoto, in which a tremendous variety of percussionists—both classical and much more "outside the box"—coexist. Japanese music, and how we even identify this category, will no doubt serve as important foci through which to watch ever-changing ideas of Japaneseness.

Japanese cultural identity is perhaps more easily recognized in "older" traditional musics (*hōgaku*) yet we may worry that these genres risk being lost, as newer forms of art or popular music come to dominate—but we must remember that the formation of these so-called "traditional" musics that hold the key to cultural identity resulted from and continue to be part of an active process. If we do, then perhaps Tosha Rōetsu's fear that not only the quality of traditional music, but also its very existence is not quite in the actual jeopardy he presumes.

As the world becomes more interconnected, will the boundaries between Japanese and other ethnic and/or national identities disappear? Wade argues to the contrary: that it is precisely the continued importation of cultural forms that inspires Japanese musicians' desire to maintain boundaries in numerous areas of music making (Wade 2005:138). And it is highly likely that the need to distinguish "our" music from everyone else's will keep such boundaries, even if necessarily shifting and at times difficult to define, yet nonetheless in place. It therefore is improbable that distinctions between us and them, *hōgaku* and *yōgaku*, pre-modern and modern, are likely to disappear anytime soon in Japan—even as these musics happily fill the same small stage at the neighborhood shrine.

The Future of Japanese Music

No doubt Japanese musicians will continue looking outside to both frame and better understand who they are within, but Japanese music increasingly has been moving outwards from Japan as well. Various musics from the underground, including Shōnen Knife, the all-female punk group who famously opened for North American grunge legends Nirvana, or the avant-garde of experimental bands like Melt Banana who, in the 1990s, worked with producer John Zorn in Chicago, and in the mainstream, Utada Hikaru, an American-born Japanese who released her pumping dance album *Exodus* in the United States in 2004, are just a few examples. Now, of course, Hatsune Miku has become a household name, well, at least in houses that watch David Letterman. And shortly after Miku's surreal appearance, on October 11, 2014, longtime rock band X-Japan sold out Madison Square Garden with an audience of 15,000 (Anon. 2014b), an accomplishment inconceivable to me certainly fifteen, ten and perhaps even five years ago. New Japanese rock groups, such as One OK Rock, now easily shift between English and Japanese lyrics, reaching global audiences (www.oneokrock.com). And of course Babymetal opened for Lady Gaga in summer 2014 (Anon. 2014a).

We head back to Babymetal now to revisit the performance of "Megitsune" (Website Example 1), which beautifully exemplifies the mixing and melding of styles that has characterized Japanese music throughout this text. The title "Megitsune" refers to the important character of the fox (*kitsune*), a messenger of the Shintō gods, and a common trickster in Japan, but here made female by adding the prefix "*me*." Thus these young women embody "megitsune"—a female fox—as each wears a fox mask. The "live" performance actually occurs on a *noh* stage, complete with a looming portrait of a pine tree behind (a standard symbolic image), while other scenes are shot in what appears to be a traditional-style Japanese home with sliding doors (*fusuma*). The percussion of the *noh-hayashi* including *taiko* and *ko-tsuzumi* replace the snare, tom toms and high hat of a Western drum set, with a larger *nagado-daiko* placed on its side on the floor and struck with a foot pedal as a bass drum.

The piece opens with a simple, even stereotyped Japanese melody constructed on a pentatonic scale, synthesized to sound like *koto*, as the producer plays with orientalist stereotypes of Japan (much as Yellow Magic Orchestra did in the 1980s by including easily recognizable Japanese melodies, silhouettes of pagodas, and other iconographic imagery of Japan (Bourdaghs 2012)). The piece quickly leaps into a J-pop interpretation of metal, a fast tempo driving a thick texture, with glossy guitar effects. The girls call out "*sore*" in encouragement throughout—the *hayashi-kotoba* of so much *min'yō* and *taiko*. Midway through, the feeling changes as "Sakura," one of the most famous songs in all of Japan, is transformed into a metal version with extensive feedback, set with new lyrics as the lead singer repeats that she is a female fox. During this momentary repose, we glimpse a woman in formal *kimono* wearing a fox mask as she performs *nihon buyō*, the classical dance of traditional *hōgaku*. Her formal costuming highlights the playful appearance of Babymetal, once again capturing the spirit of mix and matching that fills the video.

This trio of young teenage girls debuted as Babymetal in 2011 with what they consider as a new genre, melding together J-Pop idol performance with metal. "Su-Metal" serves as the lead singer, as seen in this video, while "Yuimetal" and "Moametal," scream and dance (the roles they play in the group as indicated on Babymetal's official website (Babymetal 2014). Babymetal's ultimate goal is to conquer the world and indeed they have.

If we accept that Japanese musicians are now able to fashion an identity couched within the historical trajectory of Japanese popular music alone (Stevens 2008; Bourdaghs 2012), then "Megitsune" is entirely Japanese with its use of young female idols, who appear as much as fashion models as musicians in the official video of the song, as well as the mash-up of such extreme references as "Baby" and "Metal," despite the complete removal of the sound from that of actual metal—this is J-pop at its bending, blurring, playful and crazy best. This is Japan.

References

Anon. 2014a. "Lady Gaga on Babymetal." *109news* (August 5, 2014): http://109news.jp/entertainment/20140805/9929/ (accessed November 28, 2014).
—— 2014b. "X-Japan live Performance at Madison Square Garden." *e-talent bank* (October 14, 2014): http://news.mynavi.jp/news/2014/10/14/593/ (accessed November 28, 2014).
Babymetal. 2014. "Babymetal Official Website." *Babymetal* (2014): http://www.babymetal.jp (accessed on October 1, 2014).
Bourdaghs, Michael K. 2012. *Sayonara Amerika, Sayonara Nippon: A Geopolitical Prehistory of J-Pop*. New York: Columbia University Press.
Stevens, Carolyn S. 2008. *Japanese Popular Music: Culture, Authenticity, and Power*. New York/London: Routledge.
Wade, Bonnie C. 2005. *Music in Japan: Expressing Music, Expressing Culture*. Oxford: Oxford University Press.

Appendices

Appendix A

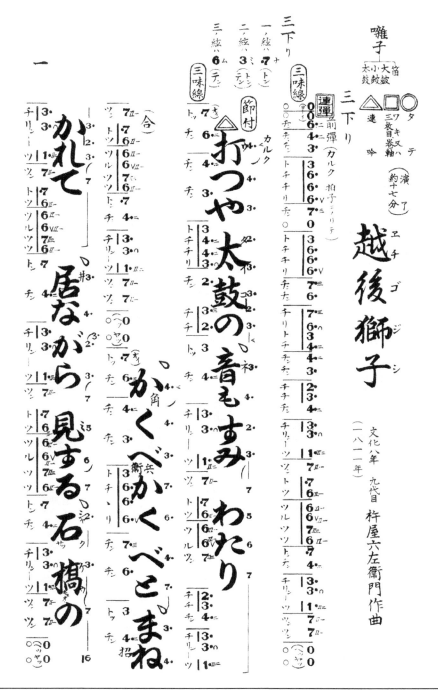

"Echigojishi" (*Yoshizumi Kojūrō-fu* for *shamisen*).

Source: YOSHIZUMI Kojūrō, Nagautashinkeikobon: Echigojishi, Hōgakusha, p.1.

226 • Appendices

Appendix B

"Echigojishi" (*Kineya bunkafu* for shamisen).

Source: KINEIE Yashichi IV, Hōgakusha ed., Shamisenbunkafu Nagauta: Echigojishi, Hōgakusha, p.1.

Appendix C

"Echigojishi," (Japanese score for *ko-tsuzumi* and *ō-tsuzumi*, by Tosha Rōetsu).

228 • Appendices

Appendix D

"Echigojishi," (Western score for *ko-tsuzumi* and *ō-tsuzumi*, by Yamauchi Reach).

Appendices • 229

230 • Appendices

(continued)

Echigojishi 3

Echigojishi (continued)

(continued)

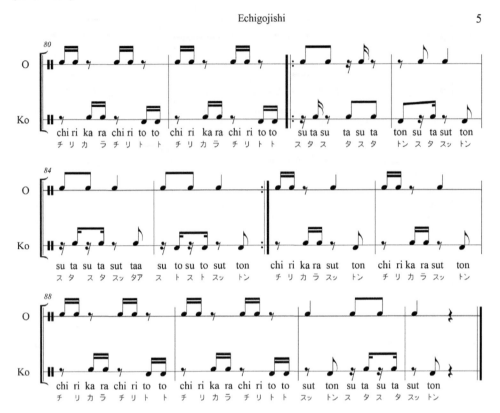

Glossary

aidoru (アイドル) idol in the Japanese popular music system.
Ainu (アイヌ) indigenous people of Japan.
aisatsu (挨拶) salutation.
aji (味) literally means "flavor of food"; here referring to the "flavor" of a person's vocal style.
Ama no Uzume (アメノウズメ) mythical dancer who enticed the goddess Amaterasu from her hiding place.
Amaterasu (天照大神) goddess who trapped herself in a cave.
an (暗) dark mode of a song.
angura (アングラ) underground subculture; here used to refer in general to music produced in these subcultures.
anime (アニメ) Japanese animation.
antecedent and consequent phrases within Western art music, a "period" is a group of phrases consisting usually of at least one antecedent phrase and one consequent phrase totaling about eight measures in length.
Aoi Matsuri (葵祭) one of the three big *matsuri* in Kyoto; occurs annually on May 15.
Ashikaga (足利) name of one of the ruling families in the Muromachi period.
atarigane (当たり鉦) small brass gong.
azuma otoko ni kyō onna (東男に京女) proverb: "Men from Tokyo are manly and stylish, women from Kyoto are womanly and beautiful."
bachi (バチ) general term for a plectrum or drumstick.
bakufu (幕府) private government run by a *shōgun*.
biwa (琵琶) pear-shaped lute.
bon-daiko (盆太鼓) *taiko* performed during *bon-odori*.
bon-odori (盆踊) folk dance usually performed in mid-August during *bon*, a ritual to welcome home the spirits of the dead.

budō (武道) Japanese martial arts in general.
bugaku (舞楽) court dances of *gagaku* and their music.
bunraku (文楽) Japanese puppet theater; also called *ningyō jōruri*.
burakumin (部落民) low or outcaste people.
bushidō (武士道) way of the *samurai*.
butoh (舞踏) type of Japanese dance theater that developed after World War II.
chappa (チャッパ) small hand cymbals.
chiiki (地域) local neighborhood.
Chikamatsu Monzaemon (近松門左衛門) (1653–1725) famous playwright who wrote many plays for *bunraku* and *kabuki* theater.
chikara (力) strength.
chikuzen-biwa (筑前琵琶) specific type of *biwa* and its repertoire.
chōchin (提灯) Japanese lantern.
chōshi (調子) general term for modes; often used as a suffix; also refers to a piece performed to establish the mood of a mode (written as "Choshi" in regards the *shakuhachi* piece discussed in Chapter 3).
chūkan'on (中間音) indeterminate tone between *kakuon*.
chū no mai (中の舞) type of dance music found in *noh*.
daimyō (大名) regional lord in Japan.
dan (段) general term for a section of music.
danmono (段物) form based on a series of *dan* or sections.
danna (旦那) husband; here as a *geiko*'s male patron.
dashi (山車) floats used in festivals.
dentō (伝統) tradition.
deshi (弟子) committed student in Japanese traditional art.
didgeridoo wind instrument developed by indigenous Australians.
do-enka (ど演歌) a subgenre of *enka* considered the "real *enka*."
dogū (土偶) human-like clay figurines made during the Jōmon period.
dōjō (道場) studio for practicing martial arts.
dōyō (童謡) children's songs composed in the modern era.
enka (演歌・艶歌) genre of popular music.
ereki būmu (エレキブーム) electric guitar boom.
fōku songu (フォークソング) term for folk songs from the mid-twentieth century; distinct from Japanese folk song *min'yō*.
fue (笛) general term for transverse bamboo flutes.
fundoshi (ふんどし) Japanese traditional underwear.
fun'iki (雰囲気) musical atmosphere; mood or ambience.
Fujiwara (藤原) powerful family in the Heian period (794–1185).
Fujiwara no Yukinaga (藤原行長) (n.d.) author credited with writing *Heike Monogatari*.
Fuke sect (普化宗) sect of Zen Buddhism with which *shakuhachi* players are associated.
furi (振り) choreography; here arm movements when hitting *taiko*.
furigana (ふりがな) *hiragana* or *katakana* written next to *kanji* to help people read the characters.
furusato (故郷) hometown, usually rural.
fushi or *bushi* (節) term for song; often used as a suffix.
fushiuta (節唄) Okinawa Yaeyama island's classical folk song.
fusuma (襖) sliding doors in a Japanese-style room (*washitsu*).

Futaiken (布袋軒) name of the *komusō* temple in Miyagi prefecture.
gagaku (雅楽) court orchestra and its music.
gaikyoku (外曲) term for *shakuhachi* music adapted from *shamisen* or *koto* music.
gakki (楽器) musical instrument.
gakufu (楽譜) musical score.
gakusei (学制) first education proclamation established in 1872.
gaman suru (我慢する) to suffer patiently through hardship.
gamelan traditional ensemble music from Java and Bali in Indonesia.
ganbaru (頑張る) persevere with patience and determination.
gayageum Korean zither.
geiko (芸妓) or *geisha* (芸者) female conversant in singing, dancing and performing on instruments.
gendai (現代) the modern era from World War II to the present.
gendai-hōgaku (現代邦楽) works for traditional instruments in a European compositional style.
Genji (源氏) powerful clan in Kamakura period; its battles with the Heike clan are recounted in *The Tale of the Heike*.
Genji Monogatari (源氏物語) *The Tale of Genji*; an epic tale of the escapades of Prince Genji attributed to Murasaki Shikibu (late tenth century to early eleventh century).
gidayū (義太夫) narrator for *bunraku* accompanied by *shamisen* music.
gidayū-bushi (義太夫節) narrative *shamisen* genre founded by Takemoto Gidayū (1651–1714).
gion (擬音) onomatopoeia; for Tosha Rōetsu, "artificial sound".
Gion (祇園) district in Kyoto.
Gion-bayashi (祇園囃子) music played at *Gion Matsuri*.
Gion Matsuri (祇園祭) month-long festival held in Kyoto in July.
giri-ninjō (義理人情) social obligations and human feelings.
gunka (軍歌) military songs composed in the modern era.
gurūpu saunzu (グループサウンズ) Japanese rock music genre; "Group Sounds."
guzheng (箏) Chinese zither.
hachimaki (鉢巻) cotton headbands commonly worn in *taiko* performance.
hakama (袴) formal Japanese pants.
hakuryoku (迫力) impact.
haniwa (埴輪) ancient tomb figurines from the Kofun period.
Hanshin (阪神) Osaka and Kōbe area.
hariōgi (張り扇) leather-covered fans struck to keep rhythm in traditional drum lessons.
hayashi or *bayashi* (囃子) general term for ensemble in *hōgaku*; often used as a suffix; also refers to a person who plays *hayashi*.
hayashi-kotoba (囃子詞) chorus interjections found in folk songs; see also *uta-bayashi*.
Heiankyō (平安京) central Kyoto; capital of Japan until the Meiji period, when Tokyo became the capital.
Heike (平家) powerful clan in the Kamakura period; its battles with the Genji clan recounted in *The Tale of the Heike*.
Heike Monogatari (平家物語) *The Tale of the Heike*; written in the thirteenth century, it is the saga of the Heike clan.
Heike-biwa (平家琵琶) specific type of *biwa* and the music for *The Tale of the Heike*.
hen'on (変音) so-called "auxiliary" tones in scales; note that is varied in Japanese scales.

heterophony musical texture involving the simultaneous performance of different versions of the same melody.
hichiriki (篳篥) double-reed oboe-type instrument in the *gagaku* orchestra and *kagura* performances.
hina-ningyō (雛人形) dolls displayed to celebrate "Girl's Day" festival on March 3.
hinoki (檜) cypress wood; used to make *bachi*.
hira-daiko (平太鼓) narrow, barrel-shaped drum suspended in a stand.
hiragana (ひらがな) one of two Japanese phonetic alphabets, this one is for writing Japanese words, as opposed to foreign words.
hōgaku (邦楽) meta-genre label for traditional music for Japanese instruments.
hōgaku **boom** or *būmu* (邦楽ブーム) refers to the recent popularity of musics that synthesize *hōgaku* instruments and musical elements with popular music styles.
Hokkaidō (北海道) northernmost of the five main islands of Japan.
honkyoku (本曲) general term for the fundamental pieces in a particular repertoire; in *shakuhachi* refers to "original" *shakuhachi*, as opposed to *gaikyoku*.
honne (本音) one's true feelings, as opposed to *tatemae*.
Honshū (本州) one of the five main islands of Japan.
honte (本手) basic or main line in a piece for several instruments.
hozonkai (保存会) general term for preservation societies.
ie(家) literally means "house"; a guild or school for traditional art.
iemoto (家元) head of a guild or school for traditional art.
inaka (田舎) countryside.
in **scale** (陰旋) most common scale type in traditional Japanese music since the Edo period (pitches: CDbFGBbC (ascending) CAbGFDbC (descending)).
indīzu (インディーズ) indie (music) produced by independent labels.
iroke (色気) word whose meaning is somewhat equivalent to "eroticism," though not as sexually charged as in the Western use of this term.
Izanagi (イザナギ) in Japanese mythology, male god who created Japan with his sister and wife Izanami.
Izanami (イザナミ) in Japanese mythology, female goddess who created Japan with her brother and husband Izanagi.
janggu Korean hourglass-shaped drum.
Jazu kissa (ジャズ喫茶) tea restaurant with jazz music entertainment.
ji(地) underlying rhythmic pattern; here in reference to *taiko* music.
Jidai Matsuri (時代祭) one of the three big *matsuri* in Kyoto; occurs annually in October.
jiin (寺院) Buddhist temple; also referred to as *tera* or *otera*.
Jimmu (神武) considered the legendary first emperor of Japan.
jimusho (事務所) office; here refers to a idol (*aidoru*) management agency.
jinja (神社) Shintō shrine.
jo-ha-kyū (序破急) tripartite form and aesthetic idea; introduction – breaking apart – rushing.
jōruri (浄瑠璃) general term for narrative *shamisen* music.
joryū (女流) art form performed by women.
kabuki (歌舞伎) popular Japanese musical theater.
kaburaya (鏑矢) special arrow that makes a unique sound.
kadō (華道) flower arrangement; also referred to as *ikebana* (生け花).

kaede (替手) supporting part in a piece for several instruments.
kaiseki (懐石) traditional Japanese multi-course cuisine.
Kansai-ben (関西弁) Japanese dialects from Kansai area.
kagura (神楽) general term for Shintō music.
kakegoe (掛声) term for the calls of drummers and *shamisen* players that help keep time and signal cues.
kakko (鞨鼓) small, double-headed barrel drum used in *gagaku* music.
kaku (格) level or sophistication of things.
kakuon (核音) two stable nuclear tones spaced with a perfect fourth.
kami-dana (神棚) small altars at home or office to enshrine Shintō gods.
kami-sama (神様) spirits or gods in Shintō.
kane (鐘) hand-gong.
kangen (管弦) term for instrumental music in *gagaku*.
kanji (漢字) Chinese characters that have been adopted into Japanese.
kanname (鉋目) patterns carved inside drum bodies to adjust tone; also on the inside of *shamisen*.
kan'on (漢音) one of the ways to read or pronounce *kanji*; established during the Nara and Heian periods.
Kansai (関西) western region of Honshū including Kyoto, Osaka and Kobe.
Kansai-ben (関西弁) regional dialect in Kansai area.
Kantō (関東) eastern region of Honshū including Tokyo, Chiba and Yokohama.
karaoke (カラオケ) type of entertainment in which people are able to supply the vocals to well-known songs; "*karaoke* box" refers to a rented room for people to enjoy *karaoke* privately or in groups.
kata (型) form.
katakana (片仮名) one of two Japanese phonetic alphabets, this one for writing imported foreign words as opposed to Japanese.
katana (刀) sword.
katsugi-oke-daiko (かつぎ桶太鼓) large double-headed drum with skins affixed by ropes, light enough to be played while carried.
kayōkyoku (歌謡曲) popular music, from the end of World War II until the end of the 1980s.
kei (磬) Buddhist, fish-mouthed bronze chime.
keigo (敬語) Japanese honorifics.
keiko-goto (稽古事) lessons for cultural enrichment.
kendō (剣道) Japanese martial art; "way of the sword."
kiai (気合) calls of encouragement.
kigaku (器楽) instrumental music.
kimono (着物) Japanese traditional clothing.
kin (磬) bowl-shaped Buddhist bell.
Kineya (杵屋/稀音家) name of one of the major *shamisen* guilds.
Kineya bunkafu (杵屋文化譜) Kineya *shamisen* notation.
Kinko (琴古) name of one of the major schools of *shakuhachi*.
kindai (近代) the modern era, from the Meiji period to World War II.
kitsune (狐) fox.
Kiyomoto (清元) one of the major *shamisen* genres founded by Kiyomoto Enjudayū (1777–1825).

Kōbō-Daishi (弘法大師) also known as Kūkai (774–835); celebrated founder of Shingon Buddhism.

kobushi (小節) a general term for vocal ornamentation.

koe o dasu (声を出す) saying things aloud.

kofun (古墳) great tombs of the Kofun period.

kōhai (後輩) junior member of a group (school or work) in a reciprocal relationship with a *senpai* (senior).

"Kōhaku Uta Gassen" (紅白歌合戦) "The Red and White Song Contest"; popular television program produced by NHK which airs on New Year's Eve.

Koizumi, a tetrachord system a way to organize Japanese scales and melodic structures identified by Japanese musicologist Koizumi Fumio (1927–83) that emphasizes the tetrachord (*miyako-bushi*, *min'yō*, *ritsu* and *Ryūkyū*).

Kojiki (古事記) oldest known Japanese history book, presented to Empress Genmei in 712, which includes songs.

Kokin Wakashū (古今和歌集) collection of poems from Heian period.

kokoro (心) heart and soul.

koku (石) during Edo period, each *daimyō*'s wealth was measured by how much *koku* of rice their land produced; 1 *koku* = about 278.3 liters.

komagaku (高麗楽) *gagaku* music of Korean origin.

komusō (虚無僧) itinerant Fuke sect priests who developed the *shakuhachi*; they are also referred to as *komosō* (薦僧).

koten (古典) refers to classical arts; often used as a prefix.

koten-chōshi (古典調子) design of *fue* used in traditional Japanese music.

koten-min'yō (古典民謡) classical folk song (in Okinawa); see *min'yō* and *fushiuta*.

koten-teki (古典的) when something is following classic tradition; refined and classical.

koto (箏) Japanese zither.

ko-tsuzumi (小鼓) double-headed hourglass-shaped drum with skins affixed by ropes; held at the shoulder.

kouta (小唄) literally "short song," a genre of short *shamisen* songs.

Kōya-san (高野山) Mt. Kōya, the headquarters of Shingon Buddhism.

kuchishōka (口唱歌) mnemonics used for memorizing music; also referred to as *kuchishōga*.

kuge bunka (公家文化) culture associated with the Japanese aristocratic class related to the imperial court.

Kūkai (空海) (774–835) celebrated founder of Shingon Buddhism; also known as Kōbō-Daishi, his saint name.

kumidaiko (組太鼓) a specific type of ensemble drumming.

kuromisu (黒御簾) room on the side of the *kabuki* stage covered with a black curtain to block view of the musicians from the audience.

Kurosawa Kinko (黒沢琴古) (1710–71) founder of Kinko school of *shakuhachi*.

kuyashisa (悔しさ) to be motivated by one's frustration.

kyōgen (狂言) stylized comedic performance inserted in longer *noh* drama.

Kyo-kotoba (京言葉) Kyoto dialect.

kyōmai (京舞) refers to dances from Kyoto.

kyūtei bunka (宮廷文化) culture associated with the imperial court.

Kyūshū (九州) one of the five main islands of Japan to the west of Honshū.

ma (間) aesthetic idea focused on the space between things.

machi (町) town.

magewappa-daiko (曲げわっぱ太鼓) large drums, 3–4 feet in diameter, from Akita prefecture in northern Honshū.

mai (舞) general term for dance.

maigoto (舞事) long instrumental dances featuring the *noh-hayashi*.

maiko (舞妓) young women in training to become *geiko* in Kyoto.

manga (漫画) Japanese comics.

Man'yōshū (万葉集) famous anthology of poetry (late seventh century to late eighth century).

matsuri (祭) general term for festivals.

matsuri-bayashi (祭囃子) ensemble music for festivals.

mei (明) bright mood of a song.

Meian (明暗) a school of *shakuhachi* playing, also known as "*Myōan*"; also refers to Meian temple.

mikagura (御神楽) Shintō music of the imperial palace.

Miki Rōfu (三木露風) (1889–1964) modern-day poet and writer. His song "Akatonbo" is discussed in Chapter 4.

miko (巫女) female Shintō shrine attendant.

miko-mai (巫女舞) a *miko*'s dance for Shintō gods.

mikoshi (神輿) portable shrine carried in festivals throughout Japan.

min'yō (民謡) general term for Japanese folk song.

Minamoto (源) important clan in Japanese history.

minzoku geinō (民俗芸能) general term for folk performing arts.

miyabi (雅) elegant and refined; invokes the image of the court.

miyako (都) courtly capital.

mochi (餅) sweet rice patties.

mochitsuki (餅つき) to pound steamed sweet rice with a mallet into *mochi* patties.

Monbukagakushō (文部科学省) Ministry of Education, Culture, Sports, Science and Technology, formed in 2001.

Monbushō (文部省) Ministry of Education, Science and Culture, established in 1871.

Monbushō shōka (文部省唱歌) children's school songs, as authorized by the Ministry of Education, Science and Culture; *shōka* is a more general term for songs.

montsuki hakama (紋付袴) full formal Japanese dress.

mōsō (盲僧) blind priest.

mu (無) literally "nothing"; here referring to performing music without thinking.

mūdo enka (ムード演歌) subgenre of *enka* that is considered emotional and sad.

Murasaki Shikibu (紫式部) (late tenth century to early eleventh century) author of *Genji Monogatari* (*The Tale of Genji*).

musume (娘) daughter, or young girl.

Myōan (明暗) school of *shakuhachi* playing, also known as "*Meian*"; also refers to Myōan temple.

nagado-daiko (長胴太鼓) barrel-shaped double-headed drum.

nagauta (長唄) literally "long song," a lyrical genre of *shamisen* music.

naniwa-bushi (浪花節) early twentieth-century popular *shamisen* narrative; also referred to as *rōkyoku*.

narimono (鳴物) instruments of *hōgaku* excluding voice and *shamisen*.

natori (名取) title granted to students of high rank in *hōgaku*.

nehan (涅槃) *nirvana*; state of mind when you have enlightenment; Buddhist belief.
neiro (音色) color of sound; sound quality.
Nihon (日本) Japan.
nihon buyō (日本舞踊) Japanese classical dance.
Nihongi (日本紀) early Japanese history book completed in 720; also referred to as *Nihon Shoki*.
Nihonjin (日本人) Japanese people.
nihonjinron (日本人論) discourse on Japanese identity.
Nihon Shoki (日本書紀) early Japanese history book completed in 720; also referred to as *Nihongi*.
ningyō (人形) general term for dolls or puppets; the puppets in *bunraku*.
ningyō jōruri (人形浄瑠璃) another name for *bunraku* (combines *ningyō* (puppets) and *jōruri* (*shamisen* narrative music)).
nirvana state of mind when you have enlightenment; Buddhist belief; *nehan* in Japanese.
Nodo Jiman (のど自慢) literally, "Proud of My Voice"; long-running and popular NHK amateur *karaoke* contest television show.
noh (能) classical dance-drama.
noh-hayashi (能囃子) the instrumental ensemble in *noh*.
nohkan (能管) a bamboo flute used in *noh-hayashi, kabuki, Gion-bayashi*, etc.
noise or *noizu* (ノイズ) genre of music involving distortion and play with technology.
nori (のり) historically, a theory of rhythm and tempo in *noh*, but today also used to refer to the idea of "groove."
nyōhachi (鐃鉢) Buddhist cymbals.
nyū myūjikku (ニューミュージック) "new music;" genre of singer-songwriters in Japanese popular music.
nyū wēbu (ニューウェーブ) new wave.
obi (帯) sash worn with *kimono*.
ō-daiko (大太鼓) large double-headed barrel-shaped drum; for Tosha Rōetsu, *taiko* as a genre in general.
odori (踊) general term for dance.
ō-gane (大鐘) large Buddhist bell.
ogessha (お月謝) monthly fee for an *okeiko* (lesson).
okagura (お神楽) performances at large national Shintō shrine events.
okedo-daiko (桶胴太鼓) large double-headed drum with skins affixed by ropes.
okeiko (お稽古) lesson.
okeiko-ba (お稽古場) lesson location.
Okinawa (沖縄) southern islands of Japan, also called Ryūkyū.
Izumo no Okuni (お国) (late sixteenth century to early seventeenth century) female shaman and dancer credited with originating *kabuki*.
ongaku (音楽) general term for "music."
onkyō (音響) literally "sound" and "echo"; refers to a performance genre involving sound effects and play with technology.
onnagata (女形) male actor who specializes in female roles in *kabuki*.
onna jōruri (女浄瑠璃) *gidayū* performed by women.
onryō (音量) richness of the sound.
onshitsu (音質) quality of sound.
orite kita (降りてきた) the idea of new music just coming into one's mind.

otera (お寺) Buddhist temple; also referred to as *jiin*.
otera bunka (お寺文化) culture associated with temples.
otokoyaku (男役) women who perform male roles in Takarazuka Revue.
ō-tsuzumi (大鼓) double-headed hourglass-shaped drum with skins affixed by ropes; held at the hip.
parlando rubato relaxed sense of rhythm.
pipa (琵琶) pear-shaped Chinese lute.
Pontochō (先斗町) Hanamachi district in Kyoto, Japan, known for *geiko* and home to many *geiko* houses and traditional tea houses.
popyurā myūjikku (ポピュラーミュージック) popular music.
raibuhausu (ライブハウス) livehouse; establishments devoted to the performance of live music.
rinne (輪廻) reincarnation and continuation of the cycle of life; *saṃsāra*.
ritsu scale (律旋) scale type which developed in the Nara period (pitches: CDFGAC).
rōkyoku (浪曲) early twentieth-century popular *shamisen* narrative; also referred to as *naniwa-bushi*.
rōnin (浪人) masterless *samurai*.
ryo scale (呂旋) scale type which developed in the Nara period (pitches: CDEGAC).
ryōsai kenbo (良妻賢母) "good wife wise mother"; discourse informing gendered identity in the modern era.
ryū (流) literally means "way of doing" things; school in traditional music.
Ryūkyū (琉球) southern islands of Japan, also called Okinawa.
Ryūkyū scale (琉球旋) scale type common in Ryūkyū (pitches: CEFGBC).
ryūteki (竜笛) bamboo flute used in *gagaku*.
sadō (茶道) Japanese tea ceremony.
sake (酒) Japanese rice wine.
sakebi (叫び) screaming.
saṃsāra reincarnation and continuation of the cycle of life; *rinne* in Japanese.
samurai (侍) member of the military class in pre-modern Japan.
sanbasō mono (三番叟もの) type of songs related to noh *sanbasō* pieces.
sangen (三弦) three-stringed plucked lute; also referred to as *shamisen*.
sankyoku (三曲) ensemble and music played by a trio (*shakuhachi*, *shamisen* and *koto*).
sanshin (三線) Okinawan three-stringed lute.
sanxian (三弦) Chinese progenitor to the *sanshin* and *shamisen*.
sararin (サラリン) one of the techniques in playing *koto*.
satokagura (里神楽) performances in community-oriented local folk festivals.
satori (悟り) Buddhist term for enlightenment.
Satsuma-biwa (薩摩琵琶) specific type of *biwa* and its repertoire.
sawari (サワリ) literally "to touch"; refers to the buzzy resonances of the *shamisen* and *biwa*.
seiza (正座) Japanese way of kneeling on the floor.
sen (旋) general term for scales; often used as a suffix.
senpai (先輩) senior member of a group (school or work), in a reciprocal relationship with a *kōhai* (junior).
sensei (先生) general term for teacher or master.
serifu (セリフ) spoken narrative style between verses in a song, akin to recitative.
shakubyōshi (笏拍子) wooden clappers use in *kagura*.

shakuhachi (尺八) end-blown bamboo flute.
shamisen (三味線) three-stringed plucked lute; also referred to as *sangen*.
shigetō (重藤) traditional Japanese hunting bow.
shikitari (しきたり) old tradition.
Shikoku (四国) one of the five main islands of Japan.
shima (島) island.
shimaguni (島国) country of islands.
shimauta (島唄) island songs.
shime-daiko (締太鼓) a double-headed drum with skins affixed by ropes; also known as *taiko* in *noh-hayashi*.
shindō (振動) vibration.
Shingon sect (真言宗) Buddhist sect established by Kūkai and headquartered at Kōya-san.
shinobue (篠笛) tranverse bamboo flute.
Shintō (神道) major indigenous religion of Japan.
shishi-mai (獅子踊り) lion dance.
shishi-odoshi (鹿威し) yard ornament to scare away deer, comprising a bamboo receptacle that captures and pours water.
shō (笙) mouth-organ of the *gagaku* ensemble.
shōgun (将軍) head of the military government or *samurai* before the Meiji period.
shōjin-ryōri (精進料理) vegetarian cuisine made and consumed by Buddhist monks.
shōka (唱歌) school songs.
shōko (鉦鼓) bronze gong used in *gagaku*.
shōmyō (声明) general term for Buddhist chant.
sō (僧) Buddhist monk.
sōkyoku (箏曲) general term for *koto* music.
sōshi-bushi (壮士節) popular political song in the late nineteenth and early twentieth centuries; precursor to *enka*.
suikinkutsu (水琴窟) yard ornament that creates sound as water drips into an upside down pot.
sui zen (吹禅) achieving self-realization through playing *shakuhachi*.
sumie (墨絵) general term for Japanese ink painting.
sumō (相撲) Japanese national sport – wrestling.
Susano-o (スサノオ) Japanese mythical god, Izanami and Izanagi's son, Amaterasu's brother.
suzu (鈴) term for bell in general; small bell tree used in Shintō ceremonies and dances.
tabi (足袋) Japanese traditional split-toe footwear, worn with traditional clothing like *kimono*.
taiko (太鼓) general term for Japanese drums struck with sticks; small double-headed, barrel-shaped drum with skins affixed by skins in *noh-hayashi* and modern secular ensemble drumming; also refers to the broad genre of secular ensemble drumming also known as *wadaiko*.
Takarazuka Revue (宝塚歌劇団) Japanese all-female musical theater group based in Takarazuka.
Takemitsu Tōru (武満徹) (1930–96) well-known twentieth-century Japanese composer.
tamane (玉音) flutter tongue; *shakuhachi* playing technique.
tatami (畳) traditional straw-mat flooring; dwellings are still measured by the size of their tatami mats.

tatemae (建前) one's behavior and opinions in public, as opposed to *honne*.
Tendai sect (天台宗) Buddhist sect established by Saichō (767–822).
tera **or** *otera* (寺) Buddhist temple; also referred to as *jiin*.
tetrachord a perfect fourth and the pitches within.
tōgaku (唐楽) *gagaku* music from China or India.
Tōhoku (東北) north-east part of Japan.
Tōkaidō (東海道) road that stretched between Kyoto and Edo (Tokyo) in the Edo period.
Tokugawa Ieyasu (徳川家康) (1543–1616) important leader in the Tokugawa clan.
Tokyo (東京) capital of Japan, historically also known as Edo and renamed in 1868.
Tokyo-ben (東京弁) regional dialect in Kantō area; dominant form of Japanese transmitted through the media and taught in schools.
torii (鳥居) traditional Japanese gate commonly found at the entrance of or within a Shintō shrine.
tsugaru-jamisen (津軽三味線) folk *shamisen* genre from northern Honshū.
tsuri-daiko (釣太鼓) suspended taiko drum in the *gagaku* ensemble.
tsuzumi (鼓) general term for hand-beaten drums (for example, *ko-tsuzumi* and *ō-tsuzumi*).
uta (歌) general term for singing; often used as a suffix for vocal genres.
uta-bayashi (歌囃子) chorus interjections found in folk songs; see also *hayashi-kotoba*.
utaguchi (歌口) name of an oblique cut across which the player blows into a *shakuhachi*.
utamono **or** *utaimono* (歌物) general term for lyrical *shamisen* music; flute modified to play western scales.
wa (和) "Japan"; also means "peace."
wadaiko (和太鼓) the broad genre of secular ensemble drumming also known as *taiko*.
wagakki (和楽器) Japanese traditional instruments.
wagon (和琴) six-stringed zither found in *gagaku* and *kagura*.
wasei (和製) Japanese style.
washitsu (和室) traditional Japanese-style room.
yabusame (流鏑馬) Japanese traditional archery on horseback.
yamaboko (山鉾) specific type of floats used in *Gion Matsuri* and other festivals.
Yamada Kōsaku (山田耕筰) (1886–1965) well-known twentieth-century composer.
Yamato (大和) important clan in the Kofun period.
yang (陽) sunny; Chinese philosophy.
Yatsuhashi (八橋) *koto* school founded by Yatsuhashi Kengyō (1614–85).
Yatsuhashi Kengyō (八橋検校) (1614–85) founder of the Yatsuhashi *koto* school.
yin (陰) shady; Chinese philosophy.
yonanuki **pentatonic major** (四七抜き音階) scale type developed in the modern era in which scale degrees 4 and 7 are removed from the Western major scale (pitches: CDEGAC).
yonanuki **pentatonic minor** (四七抜き音階) scale type developed in the modern era in which scale degrees 4 and 7 are removed from the Western minor scale (pitches: ABCEFA).
yō **scale** (陽旋) scale type common in *min'yō* (pitches: CDFGB*b*C (ascending) CAGFDC (descending)).
yōgaku (洋楽) meta-genre label for Western music in general.
yose-daiko (寄せ太鼓) *taiko* played at *sumō* wrestling matches.

Yoshizumi (吉住) One of the major schools of *nagauta*.
yukata (浴衣) traditional Japanese summer clothes.
Yoshizumi Kosaburō (吉住小三郎) *nagauta* musician who established Yoshizumi school of *nagauta*.
Yoshizumi Kojūrō-fu (小十郎譜) Yoshizumi *shamisen* notation.
yubikake (指かけ) piece of knitted cloth that allows the left hand to slide on the neck of a *shamisen*.
yubikawa (指革) an *ō-tsuzumi* drummer's leather or papier-mâché finger cover, which creates a wooden clacking sound.
yuri (揺り) specific vocal ornamentation; a wide vibrato.
zaibatsu (財閥) group of wealthy families who control multiple industries and financial firms; conglomerate.
Zeami Motokiyo (世阿弥) (1363–1443) playwright and philosopher of *noh*.
Zen (禅) Buddhist sect founded in China and introduced to Japan in Kamakura period.

Additional Resources

Print Sources

The Ainu

Chiba, Nobuhiko. 1996a. "Ainu no Uta no Senritsu Kōzō Nitsuite [Melodic Structure of Ainu Songs]." *Tōyō Ongaku Kenkyū* 61:1–21.

———. 1996b. "Fujiyama Haru no Tonkori Ensōhō ni Tsuite (I, II) [On the *Tonkori* Technique of Fujiyama Haru (I, II)]." In M. Haginaka and H. Udagawa, eds., *Hokkaidō Tōbu ni Nokoru Karafuto Ainu Bunka I* [*Sakhalin Ainu Culture Remaining in Eastern Hokkaido*], pp. 9–137. Hokkaido: Karafuto Ainu Bunka Hozonkai.

———. 1996c. "Karafuto Ainu no Ongaku [Music of the Ainu Sakhalin]." In The Ainu Museum, ed., *Karafuto Ainu: Kodama Korekushon* [*Sakhalin Ainu: the Kodama Collection*], pp. 49–58. Hokkaido: The Ainu Museum.

———. 1996d. "Nagarashi Iso *no Tonkori* [The *Tonkori* Music of Nagarashi Iso]." *Hokkaidō no Bunka* 68:1–35.

———. 2006. "Nishihira Ume *no Tonkori no Enshō ni Tsuite* [On the *Tonkori* Technique of Nishihira Ume]." In J. Kitahara, ed., *Nishihira Ume to Tonkori*. Hokkaido: The Ainu Museum.

Hanazaki, Kōhei. 1996. "Ainu Moshir and Yaponesia: Ainu and Okinawan Identities in Contemporary Japan." In D. Denoon et al. eds., *Multicultural Japan: Paleolithic to Postmodern,* pp. 117–131. Cambridge: Cambridge University Press.

Kobayashi, Yukio and Kobayashi Kimie. 1987. *Musical Notations in: Hokkaidō Ainu Koshikobuyō, Uta no Kiroku* [*Traditional Hokkaidō Ainu Dances and Songs*]. Hokkaido: Ainu Koshiki Buyō Rengō Hozonkai.

Nihon Hōsō Kyōkai [Japan Broadcasting Co]. 1965. *Ainu Dentō Ongaku* [*Traditional Ainu Music*]. Tokyo: Nihon Hōsō Kyōkai Shuppan Kyōkai.

Philippi, Donald. 1978. *Songs of Gods, Songs of Humans: The Epic Tradition of the Ainu*. Tokyo: University of Tokyo Press.

Tanimoto, Kazuyuki. 2002. "Music of the Ainu, Nivkhi, and Uilta." In R. Provine, Y. Tokumaru and J. Witzleben, eds., *East Asia: China, Japan and Korea. The Garland Encyclopedia of World Music Vol. 7*, pp. 783–788. New York/London: Routledge.

Anti-nuclear Musical Movement

Manabe, Noriko. 2012. "The No Nukes 2012 Concert and the Role of Musicians in the Anti-Nuclear Movement." *The Asia-Pacific Journal* 10(3).
——. 2013. "Music in Japanese Antinuclear Demonstrations: The Evolution of a Contentious Performance Model." *The Asia-Pacific Journal* 11(3).

Children's Music

Imoto, Yoko. 1997. *Best-Loved Children's Songs from Japan*. Tokyo: Heian International Publishing Company.
Kindaichi, Haruhiko and Aiko Anzai, eds. 1977. *Nihon no Shōka [Japanese School Songs]*. Tokyo: Kodansha.
Manabe, Noriko. 2009. "Western Music in Japan: The Evolution of Styles in Children's Songs, Hip-Hop, and Other Genres." Ph.D. dissertation, City University of New York.
——. 2013. "Songs of Japanese Schoolchildren during World War II." In P. Campbell and T. Wiggens, eds., *The Oxford Handbook of Children's Musical Cultures*, pp. 449–465. Oxford: Oxford University Press.
May, Elizabeth. 1959. "Japanese Children's Folk Songs Before and After Contact with the West." *Journal of the International Folk Music Council* 11:59–65.
——. 1963. *The Influence of the Meiji Period on Japanese Children's Music*. Berkeley: University of California Press.
——. 1965. "The Influence of the Meiji Period on Japanese Children's Music," *Journal of Research in Music Education.* 13(2):110–120.

Court Music

Endō, Tōru. 2004. *Gagaku*. Tokyo: Heibonsha.
Garfias, Robert. 1975. *Music of a Thousand Autumns: The Tōgaku Style of Japanese Court Music*. Berkeley: University of California Press.
Geinōshi Kenkyūkai. 1969. *Kagura: Kodai no Kabu to Matsuri [Kagura: The Song, Dance and Festivals of Ancient Times]*. Tokyo: Heibonsha.
Harich-Schneider, Eta. 1954. *The Rhythmical Patterns in Gagaku and Bugaku*. Leiden: Brill.
——. 1965. *Rōei, The Mediaeval Songs of Japan*. Tokyo: Sophia University Press.
Markham, Elizabeth J. 1983. *Saibara: Japanese Court Songs of the Heian Period*. Cambridge: Cambridge University Press.
Masumoto, Kikuko. 2000. *Gagaku Nyūmon [Introduction to Gagaku]*. Tokyo: Ongaku no Tomo Sha.
Ono, Ryōya. 1989. *Gagaku Jiten [Encyclopedia of Gagaku]*. Tokyo: Ongaku no Tomo Sha.
Terauchi, Naoko. 2002. "Gagaku." In R. Provine, Y. Tokumaru and J. Witzleben, eds., *East Asia: China, Japan and Korea. The Garland Encyclopedia of World Music Vol. 7*, pp. 619–628. New York/London: Routledge.
Wolz, Carl. 1971. *Bugaku: Japanese Court Dance*. Providence, RI: Asian Music Publications.

Dance

Fraleigh, Sondra. 2010. *Butoh: Metamorphic Dance and Global Alchemy*. Urbana-Champaign: University of Illinois Press.

Gunji, Masakatsu. 1970. *Buyō, The Classical Dance, Performing Arts of Japan III*. New York: Walker/Weatherhill.
Hahn, Tomie. 2007. *Sensational Knowledge: Embodying Culture through Japanese Dance*. Middletown, CT: Wesleyan University Press.

Festival Music

Ashkenazi, Michael. 1993. *Matsuri [Festival]*. Honolulu: University of Hawaii Press.
Hoshino, Hiroshi and Hideo Haga. 2006. *Nihon no Matsuri Bunka Jiten [Dictionary of Japan's Festival Culture]*. Tokyo: Tokyo Shoseki.
Iguchi, Kawori. 2008. "Reading/Playing Music: The Musical Notations of the Kyoto Gion Festival and the Noh Flute." *Ethnomusicology Forum* 17(2):249–268.

Folk Performing Arts

Arisawa, Shino. 2012. "Dichotomies between 'Classical' (*Koten*) and 'Folk' (*Min'yō*) in the Intangible Cultural Properties of Japan." In K. Howard, ed., *Music as Intangible Cultural Heritage: Policy, Ideology, and Practice in the Preservation of East Asian Traditions*, pp. 181–196. Farnham: Ashgate.
Asano, Kenji. 1966. *Nihon no Min'yō [Japanese Folk Song]*. Tokyo: Iwanami Shoten.
——. 1983. *Nihon Min'yō Daijiten [Great Dictionary of Japanese Folk Song]*. Tokyo: Yuzankaku.
Groemer, Gerald. 1999. *The Spirit of Tsugaru: Blind Musicians, Tsugaru-jamisen, and the Folk Music of Northern Japan, With the Autobiography of Takahashi Chikuzan*. Warren, MI: Harmonie Park Press.
Howard, Keith, ed. 2012. *Music as Intangible Cultural Heritage: Policy, Ideology, and Practice in the Preservation of East Asian Traditions*. Farnham: Ashgate.
Hughes, David W. 2001. "Japan, II.2: Archaeology." In S. Sadie, and J. Tyrrell, eds., *Nyu Gurōvu Sekai Ongaku Daijiten [New Grove Dictionary of Music and Musicians (Japanese Edn.)]* Vol. 12, pp. 819–820. Tokyo: Kōdansha.
——. 2008. *Traditional Folk Song in Modern Japan: Sources, Sentiment and Society*. Folkestone: Global Oriental.
Isaku, Patia R. 1981. *Mountain Storm, Pine Breeze: Folk Song in Japan*. Phoenix: University of Arizona Press.
Johnson, Henry. 2006. "Tsugaru Shamisen: From Region to Nation (and Beyond) and Back Again." *Asian Music* 27(1):75–100.
Koizumi, Fumio and David W. Hughes. 2001. "Japan, VII: Folk Music." In S. Sadie, and J. Tyrrell, eds., *Nyu Gurōvu Sekai Ongaku Daijiten [New Grove Dictionary of Music and Musicians (Japanese Edn.)]* Vol. 12, pp. 871–876. Tokyo: Kōdansha.
Lancashire, Terence. 2006. *God's Music: The Japanese Folk Theatre of Iwami Kagura*. Wilhelmshaven: Noetzel.
——. 2011. *An Introduction to Japanese Folk Performing Arts*. Farnham: Ashgate.
——. 2013. "What's in a Word? Classifications and Conundrums in Japanese Folk Performing Arts." *Asian Music* 44(1):33–70.
Nakai, Kōjirō, Haruo Misumi, and Shinobu Maruyama, eds. 1972. *Nihon Min'yō Jiten [Dictionary of Japanese Folk Song]*. Tokyo: Tōkyōdō.
——, eds. 1981. *Minzoku Geinō Jiten [Dictionary of Folk Performing Arts]*. Tokyo: Tōkyōdō.
Nihon National Trust. 1976. *Nihon Minzoku Geinō Jiten [Dictionary of Japanese Folk Performing Arts]*. Tokyo: Daiichi Hōki.
Peluse, Michael S. 2005. "Not Your Grandfather's Music: *Tsugaru Shamisen* Blurs the Lines Between 'Folk,' 'Traditional,' and 'Pop'." *Asian Music* 36(2):57–80.
Rosenberg, Neil V. 1993. *Transforming Tradition: Folk Music Revivals Examined*. Urbana-Champaign: University of Illinois Press.

Thompson, Christopher S. 2006. "Preserving the *Ochiai* Deer Dance: Tradition and Continuity in a Tōhoku Hamlet." In C. Thompson, and J. Traphagan, eds., *Wearing Cultural Styles in Japan: Concepts of Tradition and Modernity in Practice*, pp. 124–150. Albany: State University of New York Press.
——. 2008. "Population Decline, Municipal Amalgamation, and the Politics of Folk Performance Preservation in Northeast Japan." In F. Coulmas, H. Conrad, A. Schad-Seifert, and G. Vogt, eds., *The Demographic Challenge: A Handbook about Japan*, pp. 361–386. Leiden: Brill.
Thornbury, Barbara E. 1997. *The Folk Performing Arts: Traditional Culture in Contemporary Japan*. Albany: State University of New York Press.

Geisha

Dalby, Liza. 1998. *Geisha*. Berkeley: University of California Press.
——. 2000. *Little Songs of the Geisha: Traditional Japanese Ko-uta*. Rutland: Tuttle.
Downer, Lesley. 2000. *Geisha: The Secret History of a Vanishing World*. London: Headline.
——. 2006. "The City *Geisha* and Their Role in Modern Japan: Anomaly or Artistes?" In M. Feldman and B. Gordon, eds., *The Courtesan's Arts: Cross-Cultural Perspectives*, pp. 223–242. Oxford: Oxford University Press.
Foreman, Kelly M. 2008. *The Gei of Geisha: Music, Identity and Meaning*. Farnham: Ashgate.
Miho, Matsugu. 2006. "In the Service of the Nation: *Geisha* and Kawabata Yasunari's Snow Country." In M. Feldman and B. Gordon, eds., *The Courtesan's Arts: Cross-Cultural Perspectives*, pp. 3–25. Oxford: Oxford University Press.

Instrumental Genres: Biwa

Atsumi, Kaoru. 1962. *Heike Monogatari no Kisoteki Kenkyū* [Basic Research of the Tale of the Heike]. Tokyo: Sanseidō.
——. 1974. "Ozaki-ke Zō Heike Mabushi Kaidai [Introduction to Heike Mabushi held by the Ozaki Family]." In Heike Mabushi Kankōkai. ed., *Heike Mabushi* [Heike True Notation] Vol. 2, pp. 1–52. Kyoto: Daigakudō Shoten.
——. 1977. *Yokoi Yayū Jihitsu Heigo* [Heike Notation in the Hand of Yokoi Yayū]. Tokyo: Kadokawa Shoten.
——. 1978. *Heike Monogatari Hatano-ryū Fushizuke Katari-bon* [Hatano School Notation of the Tale of the Heike]. Tokyo: Benseisha.
——. 1979. *Gunki Monogatari to Setsuwa* [War Tales and Religious Tales], Vol. 122: Kasama Sōsho [Kasama Edition]. Tokyo: Kasama Shoten.
—— and Mitsuo Okumura. 1980. *Heike Mabushi no Kenkyū* [Research on the Tale of the Heike]. Kyoto: Daigakudō Shoten.
——, Mimeko Maeda and Yakashige Ubukata. 1984. *Okumura-ke Zō Tōdōza / Heike Biwa Shiryō* [Resource Materials held by the Okumura Family on the Tōdōza and Heike Biwa]. Kyoto: Daigakudō Shoten.
de Ferranti, Hugh. 1988. *Seiha Satsuma Biwa no Kifuhō to Sono Kinō* [Notations of the Seiha School of Satsuma Biwa and Their Roles in Transmission]. M.A. thesis, Department of Musicology, Tokyo National University of Fine Arts and Music.
——. 1991. "Composition and Improvisation in Satsuma Biwa." *Musica Asiatica* 6:102–27.
——. 1995. "Relations Between Music and Text in Higo Biwa." *Asian Music* 26(1):149–74.
——. 1996. "Licensed to Laugh: Humour in the Zatō Biwa Narrative Tradition of Kyushu." *Musicology Australia* 19:1–15.
——. 1997. "Text and Music in *Biwa* Narrative: The *Zatō Biwa* Tradition of Kyushu." Ph.D. dissertation, Department of Music, University of Sydney.
Fumon, Yoshinori. 1979. *Satsuma Biwa no Yurai to Onchō* [Origins and Scale Systems of Satsuma Biwa]. Kanagawa: Shintaku Daimon.

Hyōdō, Hiromi. 2000. *Heike Monogatari no Rekishi to Geinō* [*History and Performance of the Tale of the Heike*]. Tokyo: Yoshikawa Kōbunkan.
Koshiyama, Seimi. 1984. *Satsuma Biwa*. Tokyo: Perikansha.
McCollough, Helen C. 1988. *The Tale of the Heike*. Stanford, CA: Stanford University Press.
Nakamura, Masami. 1990. *Satsuma Biwa Songs: An Anthology*. Shizuoka: Nishigai Press.
Ōtsubo, Sōjirō. 1983. *Chikuzen Biwa Monogatari* [*The Story of Chikuzen Biwa*]. Tokyo: Asahi Shinbunsha.
Suzuki, Takatsune. 2007. *Heikyoku to Heike Monogatari* [*Music of Heike-biwa and the Heike Monogatari*]. Tokyo: Chisen Shoten.
Tanabe, Hisao and Kenji Hirano. 1989. "Biwa." *Nihon Ongaku Daijiten* [*Encyclopedia of Japanese Music*]. Tokyo: Heibonsha.

Instrumental Genres: Koto

Adriaansz, Willem. 1973. *The Kumiuta and Danmono Traditions of Japanese Koto Music*. Los Angeles: University of California Press.
Johnson, Henry. 2004. *The Koto: A Traditional Instrument in Contemporary Japan*. Leiden: Brill.
Wade, Bonnie C. 1976. *Tegotomono: Music for the Japanese Koto*. Westport, CT: Greenwood Press.
Yoshida, Bungo. 1984. *Nihon no Koto*. Hiroshima: Keisuisha.

Instrumental Genres: Shakuhachi

Blasdel, Christopher Y. 1990. *Shakuhachi Oddesei – Ten no Neiro ni Miserarete* [*Searching for the Single Tone: A Personal Journey into Japanese Music*]. Tokyo: Kawade Shobo Shinsha.
———. 2005. *The Single Tone: A Personal Journey into Shakuhachi Music*. Tokyo: Printed Matter Press.
——— and Yūkō Kamisangō, 1988. *The Shakuhachi: A Manual For Learning*. Tokyo: Ongaku no Tomo Sha.
Casano, Steven. 2005. "From Fuke *Shuu* to *Uduboo*: The Transnational Flow of the *Shakuhachi* to the West." In B. Deschênes, ed., *The World of Music* 47(3):17–33.
Gutzwiller, Andreas. 1974. "*Shakuhachi*: Aspects of History, Practice and Teaching." Ph.D. dissertation, Wesleyan University.
———. 1983. *Die Shakuhachi der Kinko-Schule*. Kassel: Bärenreiter.
Keister, Jay. 2004. "The Shakuhachi as a Spiritual Tool: A Japanese Buddhist Instrument in the West." *Asian Music* 35(2):99–131.
Kitahara Ikuya, Misao Matsumoto, and Akira Matsuda. 1990. *The Encyclopedia of Musical Instruments: The Shakuhachi*. Tokyo: Ongakusha.
Simura, Satosi. 2002. "Chamber Music for *Shakuhachi*." In R. Provine, Y. Tokumaru and J. Witzleben, eds., *East Asia: China, Japan and Korea. The Garland Encyclopedia of World Music Vol. 7*, pp. 701–705. New York/London: Routledge.
Tann, Hilary. 1989. "Coming to Terms: (*Futaiken*) *Reibo*." *Perspectives of New Music* 27(2):52–77.
Toya, Deiko. 1984. *Komusō Shakuhachi Shinan* [*Instructions for Komusō Shakuhachi*]. Fukuoka: Toya Deiko.

Instrumental Genres: Shamisen

Adriaanz, Willem. 1978. *Introduction to Shamisen Kumiuta*. Buren: Frits Knuf.
Asakawa, Gyokuto. 1974. *Nagauta no Kiso Kenkyū* [*Basic Research in Nagauta*]. Tokyo: Nihon Ongakusha.
Fujita, Shun'ichi, ed. 1968. *Tomisaki Shunshō Geidan: Jiuta, Sōkyoku, Sangen no Hanashi* [*Discussions on Art with Tomisaki Shunshō: Jiuta, Sōkyoku and the Shamisen*]. Tokyo: Nihon Ongakusha.
Johnson, Henry. 2010. *The Shamisen: Tradition and Diversity*. Leiden: Brill.
Keister, Jay. 2004. *Shaped by Japanese Music: Kikuoka Hiroaki and Nagauta Shamisen in Tokyo*. New York/London: Routledge.

Malm, William P. 1963. *Nagauta: The Heart of Kabuki Music*. Rutland: Tuttle.
—— and David W. Hughes. 2001. "Japan, II.6: *Shamisen*." In S. Sadie, and J. Tyrrell, eds., *Nyu Gurōvu Sekai Ongaku Daijiten [New Grove Dictionary of Music and Musicians (Japanese Edn.)] Vol. 12*, pp. 836–839. Tokyo: Kōdansha.
Ōtsuka, Haiko. 2002. "Nagauta." In R. Provine, Y. Tokumaru and J. Witzleben, eds., *East Asia: China, Japan and Korea. The Garland Encyclopedia of World Music Vol. 7*, pp. 671–674. New York/London: Routledge.

Japanese Culture, History and Society (General Resources)

Ben-Ari, Eyal, Brian Moeran, and James Valentine. 2011. *Unwrapping Japan: Society and Culture in Anthropological Perspective*. New York/London: Routledge.
Bestor, Theodore C., Patricia G. Steinhoff, and Victoria L. Bestor. 2003. *Doing Fieldwork in Japan*. Honolulu: University of Hawaii Press.
Davies, Roger J. and Osamu Ikeno. 2002. *The Japanese Mind: Understanding Contemporary Japanese Culture*. Rutland, VT: Tuttle.
Fairbank, Jon K., Edwin O. Reischauer, and Albert M. Craig. 1973. *East Asia: Tradition and Transformation*. Boston, MA: Houghton Mifflin.
Gluck, Carol. 1985. *Japan's Modern Myths: Ideology in the Late Meiji Period*. Princeton, NJ: Princeton University Press.
Goto-Jones, Christopher. 2009. *Modern Japan: A Very Short Introduction*. Oxford: Oxford University Press.
Hendry, Joy. 1999. *An Anthropologist in Japan: Glimpses of Life in the Field*. New York/London: Routledge.
——. 2003. *Understanding Japanese Society, 3rd Edn*. New York/London: Routledge.
Ivy, Marilyn. 1995. *Discourses of the Vanishing: Modernity, Phantasm, Japan*. Chicago, IL: University of Chicago Press.
Karan, Pradyumna P. 2005. *Japan in the 21st Century: Environment, Economy, and Society*. Lexington: University of Kentucky Press.
Kingston, Jeff. 2013. *Contemporary Japan: History, Politics, and Social Change Since the 1980s, 2nd Edn*. Malden: John Wiley & Sons Ltd.
Naka, Mamiko. 2002. "Cultural Exchange." In R. Provine, Y. Tokumaru and J. Witzleben, eds., *East Asia: China, Japan and Korea. The Garland Encyclopedia of World Music Vol. 7*, pp. 49–52. New York/London: Routledge.
Rawski, Evelyn S. 2002. "Cultural Interactions in East and Inner Asia." In R. Provine, Y. Tokumaru and J. Witzleben, eds., *East Asia: China, Japan and Korea. The Garland Encyclopedia of World Music Vol. 7*, pp. 9–38. New York/London: Routledge.
Reischauer, Edwin O. and Marius B. Jansen. 1995. *The Japanese Today – Change and Continuity, Enlarged Edn*. Cambridge, MA: Harvard University Press.
Steinilber-Oberlin, E. 2011 (1938). *The Buddhist Sects of Japan: Their History, Philosophical Doctrines and Sanctuaries*. New York/London: Routledge.
Sugimoto Yoshio. 2010. *An Introduction to Japanese Society, 3rd Edn*. Cambridge: Cambridge University Press.
Surak, Kristin. 2013. *Making Tea, Making Japan: Cultural Nationalism in Practice*. Stanford, CA: Stanford University Press.
Tierney, Kenji R. 2007. "From Popular Performance to National Sport (*Kokugi*): The 'Nationalization' of *Sumō*." In W. Kelly, ed., *This Sporting Life: Sports and Body Culture in Modern Japan*, pp. 67–89. New Haven, CT: Yale CEAS Occasional Publications.
Various Authors. 2011. "Why Japan Matters." *Education About Asia* 16(2):61–63.
Varley, Paul. 2000. *Japanese Culture, 4th Edn*. Honolulu: University of Hawaii Press.
Vlastos, Stephen. 1998. *Mirror of Modernity: Invented Traditions of Modern Japan*. Berkeley: University of California Press.

Witzleben, John L. 2002. "A Profile of East Asian Musics and Cultures." In R. Provine, Y. Tokumaru and J. Witzleben, eds., *East Asia: China, Japan and Korea. The Garland Encyclopedia of World Music Vol. 7*, pp. 3–8. New York/London: Routledge.

Japanese Music (Diaspora)

Olsen, Dale A. 1982. "Japanese Music in Brazil." *Asian Music* 14(1):111–31.
——. 2004. *The Chrysanthemum and the Song: Music, Memory, and Identity in the South American Japanese Diaspora*. Gainesville: University of Florida Press.
Odo, Franklin. 2013. *Voices from the Canefields: Folksongs from Japanese Immigrant Workers in Hawaii*. Oxford: Oxford University Press.

Japanese Music (General Resources)

Alves, William. 2013. "Japan." In *Music of the Peoples of the World, 3rd Edn.*, pp. 309–333. Stamford, CT: Cengage Learning.
Bigenho, Michelle. 2012. *Intimate Distance: Andean Music in Japan*. Durham, NC: Duke University Press.
de Ferranti, Hugh. 2000. *Japanese Musical Instruments*. Oxford: Oxford University Press.
—— and Alison Tokita, eds., 2013. *Music, Modernity and Locality in Prewar Japan: Osaka and Beyond*. Farnham: Ashgate.
Fujie, Linda. 2002. "East Asia – Japan" In J. Titon, ed., *Worlds of Music: An Introduction to the Music of the World's Peoples, 4th Edn.*, pp. 331–384. Belmont, CA: Schirmer/Thomson Learning.
Gunji, Sumi and Henry Johnson. 2012. *A Dictionary of Traditional Japanese Musical Instruments: From Prehistory to the Edo Period*. Tokyo: Eideru Kenkyujo.
Harich-Schneider, Eta. 1973. *A History of Japanese Music*. Oxford: Oxford University Press.
Hebert, David G. 2012. *Wind Bands and Cultural Identity in Japanese Schools*. New York/London: Springer.
Herd, Judith A. 1987. "Change and Continuity in Contemporary Japanese Music: A Search for a National Identity." Ph.D. dissertation, Brown University.
Hirano, Kenji, Yūkō Kamisangō and Satoaki Gamō. 1989. *Nihon Ongaku Daijiten* [Encyclopedia of Japanese Music]. Tokyo: Heibonsha.
Hughes, David W. 1993. "Japan." In H. Myers, ed., *New Grove Handbooks in Musicology: Ethnomusicology Vol. 2: Historical and Regional Studies*, pp. 345–63. New York/London: Norton/Macmillan.
Kanetsune, Kiyosuke. 1913. *Nihon no Ongaku* [Japanese Music]. Tokyo: Rokugokan, Hattori Shoten.
Keister, Jay. 2008. "Okeikoba: Lesson Places as Sites for Negotiating Tradition in Japanese Music." *Ethnomusicology* 52(2):239–269.
——. 2013 "Exotic Essence and Contested Boundaries: Traditional Music and Being Japanese in Colorado," Paper Presentation, Society of Ethnomusicology National Conference in Indiana.
Kikkawa, Eishi. 1984. *Hōgaku Hyakka Jiten: Gagaku Kara Min'yō Made* [Encyclopedia of Japanese Music: From Gagaku to Folksong]. Tokyo: Ongaku no Tomo Sha.
——. 1965. *Nihon Ongaku no Rekishi* [History of Japanese Music]. Tokyo: Sōgensha.
Kishibe, Shigeo. 1984. *The Traditional Music of Japan*. Tokyo: The Japan Foundation.
——. 1987. *Nihon Koten Ongaku Bunken Kaidai* [Annotated Bibliography of Source Materials of Japanese Classical Music]. Tokyo: Kōdansha.
Kōdansha Daiichi Shuppan Sentā. 1995. *Nyu Gurōvu Sekai Ongaku Daijiten* [New Grove Dictionary of Music and Musicians (Japanese Edn.)]. Tokyo: Kōdansha.
Koizumi, Fumio. 1958/1960. *Nihon Dentō Ongaku no Kenkyū (1)* [Studies in Japanese Traditional Music (1)]. Tokyo: Ongaku no Tomo Sha.
——. 1974. *Nihon no Ongaku (Japanese Music)*. Tokyo: National Theater of Japan.
——. 1977. *Nihon no Oto: Sekai no Naka no Nihon Ongaku* [Sound of Japan: Japanese Music in the World]. Tokyo: Seidosha.

——. 1989. *Nihon Dentō Ongaku no Kenkyū 1 (Japanese Tradition Music Research)*. Tokyo: Ongaku no Tomosha.

——, Yoshihiko Tokumaru, and Osamu Yamaguchi. 1977. *Asian Musics in an Asian Perspective: Report of Asian Traditional Performing Arts 1976*. Tokyo: Heibonsha.

Kojima Tomiko. 1979a. "Japanese Musical Instruments, Part I." *The East* 15(3/4):8–16.

——. 1979b. "Japanese Musical Instruments, Part II." *The East* 15(3/4):62–68.

Malm, William P. 1959. *Japanese Music and Musical Instruments, 1st Edn*. Rutland, VT: Tuttle.

——. 1986. *Six Hidden Views of Japanese Music*. Berkeley: University of California Press.

——. 1990. "Practical Approaches to Japanese Music." In K. Shelemay, ed., *The Garland Library of Readings in Ethnomusicology, Vol. 2*. New York/London: Routledge.

——. 2000. *Traditional Japanese Music and Musical Instruments*. Tokyo: Kodansha.

Mathews, Gordon. 2004. "Fence, Flavor, and Phantasm: Japanese Musicians and the Meanings of 'Japaneseness'." *Japanese Studies* 24(3):335–350.

McClimon, Sarah J. 2011. "Music, Politics and Memory: Japanese Military Songs in War and Peace." Ph.D. dissertation, University of Hawaii.

Nakamura, Masayuki, and Jeffrey Hunter. 2009. *A Bilingual Guide to Japanese Traditional Performing Arts*. Tokyo: Tankosha.

Nelson, Steven G. 2002. "Historical Source Materials." In R. Provine, Y. Tokumaru and J. Witzleben, eds., *East Asia: China, Japan and Korea. The Garland Encyclopedia of World Music Vol. 7*, pp. 585–591. New York/London: Routledge.

Nihon Ongaku Buyō Kaigi. 1976. *Kindai Nihon to Ongaku [Modern Japan and Music]*. Tokyo: Ayumi Shuppansha.

Piggott, Francis T. 1909. *The Music and Musical Instruments of Japan*. London: B.T. Batsford.

Provine, Robert C., Yosihiko Tokumaru and John L. Witzleben, eds., 2002. *East Asia: China, Japan and Korea. The Garland Encyclopedia of World Music Vol. 7*. New York/London: Routledge.

Simeda, Takasi. 2002. "Music Scholarship in Japan." In R. Provine, Y. Tokumaru and J. Witzleben, eds., *East Asia: China, Japan and Korea. The Garland Encyclopedia of World Music Vol. 7*, pp. 591–595. New York/London: Routledge.

Tanabe, Hisao. 1964. *Nihon Gakki Jiten [Japanese Musical Instruments]*. Tokyo: Sōshisha Shuppan.

——. 1977. *Hōgakuka no Tame no Ongaku Riron [Music Theory for Japanese Musicians]*. Tokyo: Hōgakusha.

Tanaka, Takafumi, Mayusa Oda, Kimiko Iwashita, Kiyo Furusaki and Mariko Okeda. 2005. *Performing Arts in Japan: Traditional Music Today*. Translated by ALAYA INC. Tokyo: The Japan Foundation.

Tokita, Alison. 2013. "The Piano as a Symbol of Modernity in Prewar Kansai." In H. de Ferranti and A. Tokita, eds., *Music, Modernity and Locality in Prewar Japan: Osaka and Beyond*, pp. 93–122. Farnham: Ashgate.

—— and David W. Hughes, eds. 2008. *The Ashgate Research Companion to Japanese Music*. Farnham: Ashgate.

Tsuge, Gen'ichi. 1986. *Japanese Music: An Annotated Bibliography*. New York: Garland.

Urata, Kenjiro, et. Al. 2006. *Chūgakusei no Kigaku [Junior High School Instrumental Music]*. Tokyo: Kyoiku Geijitsu Sha.

Various Authors. 2002a. "Musical Genres in Japan." In R. Provine, Y. Tokumaru and J. Witzleben, eds., *East Asia: China, Japan and Korea. The Garland Encyclopedia of World Music Vol. 7*, pp. 597–749. New York/London: Routledge.

——. 2002b. "Music in Japanese Culture and Society." In R. Provine, Y. Tokumaru and J. Witzleben, eds., *East Asia: China, Japan and Korea. The Garland Encyclopedia of World Music Vol. 7*, pp. 753–777. New York/London: Routledge.

Wade, Bonnie C. 2005. *Music in Japan: Expressing Music, Expressing Culture*. Oxford: Oxford University Press.

Zheng, Su. 2002. "Musical Instruments." In R. Provine, Y. Tokumaru and J. Witzleben, eds., *East Asia: China, Japan and Korea. The Garland Encyclopedia of World Music, Vol. 7*, pp. 79–84. New York/London: Routledge.

Japanese Popular Music and Culture

Allen, Matthew and Rumi Sakamoto. 2006. "Introduction: Inside-Out Japan? Popular Culture and Globalization in the Context of Japan." In M. Allen and R. Sakamoto, eds., *Popular Culture, Globalization and Japan*, pp. 1–12. New York/London: Routledge.

Aoyagi, Hiroshi. 2005. *Islands of Eight Million Smiles: Idol Performance and Symbolic Production in Contemporary Japan*. Cambridge, MA: Harvard University Press.

Atkins, Everett T. 2000. "Can Japanese Sing the Blues? 'Japanese Jazz' and the Problem of Authenticity." In T. Craig, ed., *Japan Pop!: Inside the World of Japanese Popular Culture*, pp. 27–59. New York: M.E. Sharpe.

——. 2001. *Blue Nippon: Authenticating Jazz in Japan*. Durham, NC: Duke University Press.

——. 2003. *Jazz Planet*. Jackson: University Press of Mississippi.

Atton, Christopher. 2011. "Fan Discourses and the Construction of Noise Music as a Genre." *Journal of Popular Music Studies* 23(3):324–342.

Black, Daniel. 2012. "The Virtual Idol: Producing and Consuming Digital Femininity." In P. Galbraith and J. Karlin, eds., *Idols and Celebrity in Japanese Media Culture*, pp. 209–228. Hampshire: Palgrave Macmillan.

Bourdaghs, Michael K. 2012. *Sayonara Amerika, Sayonara Nippon: A Geopolitical Prehistory of J-Pop*. New York: Columbia University Press.

Cahoon, Keith. 1993. "Popular Music in Japan." In A. Campbell and D. Noble, eds., *Japan: An Illustrated Encyclopedia*, pp. 1287. Tokyo: Kodansha.

Chun, Allen, Ned Rossiter and Brian Shoesmith. 2004. *Refashioning Pop Music in Asia: Cosmopolitan Flows, Political Tempos and Aesthetic Industries*. New York/London: Routledge.

Condry, Ian. 2000. "The Social Production of Difference Imitation and Authenticity in Japanese Rap Music." In H. Fehrenbach and U. Poiger, eds., *Transactions, Transgressions, Transformations: American Culture in Western Europe and Japan*, pp. 166–184. New York/Oxford: Berghahn Books.

——. 2006. *Hip-Hop Japan: Rap and the Paths of Cultural Globalization*. Durham, NC: Duke University Press.

——. 2009. "Anime Creativity Characters and Premises in the Quest for Cool Japan." *Theory, Culture & Society* 26(2–3):139–163.

——. 2011. "Post-3/11 Japan and the Radical Recontextualization of Value: Music, Social Media, and End-Around Strategies for Cultural Action." *International Journal of Japanese Sociology* 20:4–17.

——. 2013. *The Soul of Anime: Collaborative Creativity and Japan's Media Success Story*. Durham, NC: Duke University Press.

Craig, Timothy. 2000. *Japan Pop! Inside the World of Japanese Popular Culture*. Armonk, NY: M.E. Sharpe.

—— and Richard King 2002. *Global goes Local: Popular Culture in Asia*. Honolulu: University of Hawaii Press.

Darling-Wolf, Fabienne. 2004. "SMAP, Sex, and Masculinity: Constructing the Perfect Female Fantasy in Japanese Popular Music." *Popular Music and Society* 27(3):357–370.

de Ferranti, Hugh. 2002. "Japanese Music can be Popular." *Popular Music* 21(2):195–208.

Fellezs, Kevin. 2012. "'This is Who I Am': Jero, Young, Gifted, Polycultural." *Journal of Popular Music Studies* 24(3):333–356.

Fujie, Linda. 1989. "Popular Music." In R. Powers and H. Kato, eds., *Handbook of Japanese Popular Culture*, pp. 197–220. New York: Greenwood Press.

Fukuda, Shunji and Masayoshi Kato. 1994. *Shōwa Ryūkōka Sōran* [*The Catalogue of Shōwa Popular Songs*]. Tokyo: Tsuge Shobō.

Furmanovsky, Michael. 2008. "American Country Music in Japan: Lost Piece in the Popular Music History Puzzle." *Popular Music and Society* 31(3):357–372.

Galbraith, Patrick W. 2012. "Idols: The Image of Desire in Japanese Consumer Capitalism." In P. Galbraith and J. Karlin, eds., *Idols and Celebrity in Japanese Media Culture*, pp. 185–208. Hampshire: Palgrave Macmillan.

——— and Jason G. Karlin, eds. 2012. *Idols and Celebrity in Japanese Media Culture*. Hampshire: Palgrave Macmillan.

García, Héctor. 2010. *A Geek in Japan: Discovering the Land of Manga, Anime, Zen, and the Tea Ceremony*. Rutland: Tuttle.

Hegarty, Paul. 2007. *Noise/Music: A History*. New York: Continuum.

Hosokawa, Shūhei. 1994. *Japanese Popular Music of the Past Twenty Years: Its Mainstream and Underground*. Tokyo: Japan Foundation.

———. 1999a. "Salsa no Tiene Frontera: Orquesta de la Luz and the Globalization of Popular Music." *Cultural Studies* 13(3):509–534.

———. 1999b. "Soy Sauce Music: Harumi Hosono and Japanese Self Orientalism." In P. Hayward, ed., *Widening the Horizon: Exoticism in Post-War Popular Music*, pp. 114–145. Sydney: John Libby.

———. 2000. "Rock and National Language: the Japanese Case." In T. Mitchell and P. Doyle, eds., *Changing Sounds: New Directions and Configurations in Popular Music*, pp. 98–101. Sydney: Faculty of Humanities and Social Sciences, University of Technology.

IASPM-Japan. 1990. *A Guide to Popular Music in Japan*. Takarazuka: IASPM-Japan.

Inamasu, Tatsuo. 1989. *Aidoru Kōgaku* [*The Engineering of Idols*]. Tokyo: Chikuma Shobō.

Itoh, Hiroyuki. 2013a. "Hatsune Miku, the New Social Phenomenon," *Wochi Kochi Magazine*. Interviewed and edited by Kanae Rachi. Japan Foundation Information Center: http://www.wochikochi.jp/english/special/2013/02/hatsune-miku.php (accessed on March 15, 2014).

———. 2013b. Public Lecture at the Japan Foundation in New York City on October 8, 2013.

Iwabuchi, Koichi. 2002. *Recentering Globalization: Popular Culture and Japanese Transnationalism*. Durham, NC: Duke University Press.

Karlin, Jason G. 2012. "Through a Looking Glass Darkly: Television Advertising, Idols, and the Making of Fan Audiences." In P. Galbraith and J. Karlin, eds., *Idols and Celebrity in Japanese Media Culture*, pp. 72–96. Hampshire: Palgrave Macmillan.

Kawano, Kei and Shūhei Hosokawa. 2011. "Thunder in the Far East." In J. Wallach, H. Berger, and P. Greene, eds., *Metal Rules the Globe: Heavy Metal Music Around the World*, pp. 240–270. Durham, NC: Duke University Press.

Kitagawa, Junko 1991 "Some Aspects of Japanese Popular Music." *Popular Music* 10(3):305–316.

———. 2009. "Music Culture." In Y. Sugimoto, ed., *The Cambridge Companion to Modern Japanese Culture*, pp. 261–280. Cambridge: Cambridge University Press.

Komota, Nobuo, Yoshifumi Shimada, Tamotsu Yazawa, et al. 1994–95. *Nihon Ryūkōka Shi* [*History of Japanese Popular Song*]. Tokyo: Shakai Shinsōsha.

Lewis, Michael. 2009. *A Life Adrift: Soeda Azembō, Popular Song, and Modern Mass Culture in Japan* [*Original text by Soeda Azembō*]. New York/London: Routledge.

McClure, Steve. 1998. *Nippon Pop*. Rutland, VT: Tuttle.

Milioto Matsue, Jennifer M. 2001. "Underground Music Making in Contemporary Tokyo." *The International Institute for Asian Studies Newsletter* 26:18.

———. 2008a. "The Local Performance of Global Sound: More than the Musical in Japanese Hardcore Rock." In J. Jaffe and H. Johnson. eds., *Performing Japan: Contemporary Expressions of Cultural Identity*, pp. 221–238. Folkestone: Global Oriental Press.

———. 2008b. *Making Music in Japan's Underground: The Tokyo Hardcore Scene*. New York/London: Routledge.

Minor, William. 2004. *Jazz Journeys to Japan: The Heart Within*. Ann Arbor: University of Michigan Press.

Mitchell, Toni, ed. 2001. *Global Noise: Rap and Hip-Hop outside the USA*. Middletown, CT: Wesleyan University Press.

Mitsui, Toru. 1993. "Copyright and Music in Japan: A Forced Grafting and its Consequences." In S. Frith, ed., *Music and Copyright*, pp. 125–45. Edinburgh: Edinburgh University Press.

———. 1993. "The Reception of the Music of American Southern Whites in Japan." In N. Rosenberg, ed., *Transforming Tradition: Folk Music Revivals Examined*, pp. 275–293. Urbana-Champaign: University of Illinois Press.

——. 1998. "Popular Music: Intercultural Interpretations." Graduate Program in Music, Kanazawa University.
——. 2001. "Far Western in the Far East: The Historical Development of Country and Western in Post-War Japan." *Hybridity* 1(2):64–84.
Mitsui, Toru and Shūhei Hosokawa. 1998. *Karaoke Around the World: Global Technology, Local Singing*. New York/London: Routledge.
Nagaike, Kazumi. 2012. "Johnny's Idols as Icons: Female Desires to Fantasize and Consume Male Idol Images." In P. Galbraith and J. Karlin, eds., *Idols and Celebrity in Japanese Media Culture*, pp. 97–112. Hampshire: Palgrave Macmillan.
Novak, David. 2013. *Japanoise: Music at the Edge of Circulation*. Durham, NC: Duke University Press.
Plourde, Lorraine. 2008. "Disciplined Listening in Tokyo: Onkyō and Non-Intentional Sounds." *Ethnomusicology* 52(2):270–295.
Powers, Richard G., Hidetoshi Katō and Bruce Stronach. 1989. *Handbook of Japanese Popular Culture*. Westport, CT: Greenwood Press.
Rao, Mallika. 2014. "Meet Hatsune Miku, The Sensational Japanese Pop Star Who Doesn't Really Exist." *Huffington Post*: http://www.huffingtonpost.com/2014/10/08/hatsune-miku-letterman_n_5956420.html?utm_hp_ref=weird-news&ir=Weird+News (accessed October 19, 2014).
Schilling, Mark. 1997. *Encyclopedia of Japanese Pop Culture*. New York: Weatherhill.
Slaymaker, Douglas. 2000. *A Century of Popular Culture in Japan*. Lewiston, NY: Edwin Mellen Press.
Sterling, Marvin D. 2010. *Babylon East: Performing Dancehall, Roots Reggae, and Rastafari in Japan*. Durham, NC: Duke University Press.
Stevens, Carolyn S. 2001. "Saved by the Love Song: Japanese Rock Fans, Memory and the Pursuit of Pleasure." In J. Hendry and M. Raveri, eds., *Japan at Play: The Ludic and the Logic of Power*, pp. 99–114. New York/London: Routledge.
——. 2008. *Japanese Popular Music: Culture, Authenticity, and Power*. New York/London: Routledge.
Tagawa, Ritsu. 1992. *Nihon no Fōku to Rokku Shi* [*History of Folk and Rock in Japan*]. Tokyo: Shinkō Music.
Takarajima Magazine. 1992. *Nihon Rokku Daihyakka* [*Encyclopedia of Japanese Rock*]. Tokyo: Takarajimasha.
Treat, John W. 1996. *Contemporary Japan and Popular Culture*. Honolulu: University of Hawaii Press.
Tsutsui, William M. 2010. *Japanese Popular Culture and Globalization*. Ann Arbor, MI: Association for Asian Studies.
Various Authors. 1994. Special Issue on Japan. *Popular Music* 10(3).
——. 1999. *Japan Edge: The Insider's Guide to Japanese Pop Subculture*. San Francisco, CA: VIZ Media.
Yano, Christine R. 2002. *Tears of Longing: Nostalgia and the Nation in Japanese Popular Song*. Cambridge, MA: Harvard University Press.
—— and Shūhei Hosokawa. 2008. "Popular Music in Modern Japan" In A. McQueen Tokita and D. Hughes, eds., *The Ashgate Research Companion to Japanese Music*, pp. 345–362. Farnham: Ashgate.
Yasuda, Masahiro. 2000. "Whose United Future? How Japanese DJs Cut Across Market Boundaries." *Perfect Beat* 4(4):45–60.

Koreans in Japan

de Ferranti, Hugh. 2013. "Music-Making among Koreans in Colonial-Era Osaka" In H. de Ferranti and A. Tokita, eds., *Music, Modernity and Locality in Prewar Japan: Osaka and Beyond*, pp. 229–254. Farnham: Ashgate.
Pilzer, Joshua D. 2012. *Hearts of Pine: Songs in the Lives of Three Korean Survivors of the Japanese "Comfort Women"* Oxford: Oxford University Press.
Ryang, Sonia and John Lie, eds. 2009. *Diaspora Without Homeland: Being Korean in Japan*. Berkeley: University of California Press.
Simura, Tetsuo. 2002. "Korean Music in Japan." In R. Provine, Y. Tokumaru and J. Witzleben, eds., *East Asia: China, Japan and Korea. The Garland Encyclopedia of World Music Vol. 7*, pp. 797–800. New York/London: Routledge.

Kyoto

Brumann, Christoph. 2013. *Tradition, Democracy and the Townscape of Kyoto: Claiming a Right to the Past*. New York/London: Routledge.
Horii, Reiichi. 2009. *Oriori no Kyō Kotoba* [*Everyday Kyoto Dialect*]. Kyoto: Kyoto Shimbun Publishing Center.
Kano, Shin. 1994. *Kyō Kotoba Mame Jiten* [*Kyoto Dialect Small Dictionary*]. Kyoto: Kyoto no Shiseki o Tazunerukai.
Mori, Ken. 1995. *Kyō Kotoba Kyō Zaikyō Ei Jiten* [*Kyoto Dialect Phrasebook*]. Kyoto: Uni Plan.
Rowthorn, Chris, et al. 2007. *Lonely Plant: Japan, 10th Edn*. Oakland, CA: Lonely Planet Publications.

Language

Clarke, Hugh. 2009. "Language." In Y. Sugimoto, ed., *The Cambridge Companion to Modern Japanese Culture*, pp. 56–75. Cambridge: Cambridge University Press.
Hosokawa, Shūhei. 1996. "Pidgin Japanisch: Über Japano-Amerikanischen Sprachmischung in der Popmusic." In S. Guignard, ed., *Musik in Japan: Augsäzte zu Aspekten der Musik im Heutigen Japan*, pp. 107–23. Tokyo: OAG.

Meiji Period Music

Eppstein, Ury. 1994. *The Beginnings of Western Music in Meiji Era Japan*. Lewiston, NY: Edwin Mellen Press.
Malm, William P. 1971. "The Modern Music of Meiji Japan." In D. Shively, ed., *Tradition and Modernization in Japanese Culture*, pp. 257–300. Princeton, NJ: Princeton University Press.

Nihonjinron ("Theories of Japaneseness")

Befu, Harumi. 2001. *Hegemony of Homogeneity: An Anthropological Analysis of Nihonjinron*. Melbourne: Trans Pacific.
Dale, Peter N. 1986. *The Myth of Japanese Uniqueness*. New York: St. Martin's.
Reischauer, Edwin O. and Marius B. Jansen. 1995. *The Japanese Today – Change and Continuity, Enlarged Edn*. Cambridge, MA: Harvard University Press.
Sakai, Naoki. 2002. "Nihonjinron." In S. Buckley, ed., *Encyclopedia of Contemporary Japanese Culture*, pp. 356–357. New York/London: Routledge.
Sugimoto, Yoshio. 1999. "Making Sense of *Nihonjinron*." *Thesis Eleven* 57(1):81–96.
——. 2010. *An Introduction to Japanese Society, 3rd Edn*. Cambridge: Cambridge University Press.
Waswo, Ann. 2007. "Modernism and Cultural Identity in Japan." *Asian Affairs* 20(1):45–56.

Performance Theory

Creighton, Millie. 2008 "*Taiko* Today: Performing Soundscapes, Landscapes and Identities." In J. Jaffe and H. Johnson, eds., *Performing Japan—Contemporary Expressions of Cultural Identity*, pp. 34–67. Folkestone: Global Oriental.
Jaffe, Jerry C. and Henry Johnson. 2008. "Introduction." In J. Jaffe and H Johnson, eds., *Performing Japan—Contemporary Expressions of Cultural Identity*, pp. 1–10. Folkestone: Global Oriental.
Madrid, Alejandro L. 2009. "Why Music and Performance Studies? Why Now?: An Introduction to the Special Issue." *Revista Transcultural de Música – Transcultural Music Review* 13:1–14.
Small, Christopher. 1998. *Musicking: The Meanings of Performing and Listening*. Middletown, CT: Wesleyan University Press.

Wong, Deborah. 2008. "Moving: From Performance to Performative Ethnography and Back Again." In G. Barz and T. Cooley, eds., *Shadows in the Field: New Perspectives for Fieldwork in Ethnomusicology*, pp. 76–89. Oxford: Oxford University Press.

Philosophy and Aesthetics

Kikkawa, Eishi. 1984. *Nihon Ongaku no Bitekikenkyū* [*Studies in the Aesthetics of Japanese Music*]. Tokyo: Ongaku no Tomosha.

Shimosako, Mari. 2002. "Philosophy and Aesthetics." In R. Provine, Y. Tokumaru and J. Witzleben, eds., *East Asia: China, Japan and Korea. The Garland Encyclopedia of World Music Vol. 7*, pp. 554–555. New York/London: Routledge.

Religious Music

Amano, Denchu. 1995. *Bukkyō Ongaku Jiten* [*Dictionary of Buddhist Music*]. Kyoto: Hōzōkan.

Arai, Kōjun. 1995. "The Nanzan-shin School of Shingon *Shōmyō*." In *Anthology of Sources of Japanese Music History in Facsimile, Vol. 1*, pp. 128–122. Tokyo: Tokyo Bijutsu.

——. 1996. "The Historical Development of Music Notation for *Shōmyō* (Japanese Buddhist Chant): Centering on *Hakase* Graphs." *Nihon Ongakushi Kenkyū* [*Studies in the Historiography of Japanese Music*] 1:vii–xxxix.

——1999. "The Buddhist Chant of Japan." In *The Buddhist Chant in its Cultural Context*, pp. 295–337. Seoul: National Center for Korean Traditional Performing Art.

Hill, Jackson. 1982. "Ritual Music in Japanese Esoteric Buddhism: Shingon *Shōmyō*." *Ethnomusicology* 26(1):27–39.

Monhart, Michael. 1992–93. "The Use of *Shōmyō* in Shingon Ritual." *Studies in Central and East Asian Religions* 5/6:129–44.

Nelson, Steven G. 1999. "Buddhist Chant of Shingi-Shingon: A Guide to Readers and Listeners." In M. Kuriyama, and F. Koizumi, eds., *Shingi Shingon Shōmyō Shūsei Gakufuhen*. Tokyo: Shingi Shingonshū Buzan-ha Bukkyō Seinenkai.

Ōyama, Kōjun.1959. *Bukkyō Ongaku to Shōmyō* [*Buddhist Music and Shōmyō*]. Mount Kōya: Ōyama Kyōju Shuppan Kōenkai.

Sawada, Atsuko. 2002. "Buddhist Music in Japan." In R. Provine, Y. Tokumaru and J. Witzleben, eds., *East Asia: China, Japan and Korea. The Garland Encyclopedia of World Music Vol. 7*, pp. 611–618. New York/London: Routledge.

Tanigaito, Kasuko. 2002. "Shintō Music." In R. Provine, Y. Tokumaru and J. Witzleben, eds., *East Asia: China, Japan and Korea. The Garland Encyclopedia of World Music Vol. 7*, pp. 607–610. New York/London: Routledge.

Yokomichi, Mario and Gidō Kataoka. 1984. *Shōmyō Jiten* [*Dictionary of Shōmyō*]. Kyoto: Hōzōkan.

Ryūkyū Music (Okinawan/Amami/Yaeyaman)

Gillan, Matthew. 2004. "Multiple Identities in Yaeyaman Folk Music." Ph.D. dissertation, University of London: SOAS.

——. 2008. "Treasure of the Island People: Tradition and Modernity in Yaeyaman Pop Music." *Asian Music* 29(1):42–68.

——. 2012a. *Songs From the Edge of Japan: Music-Making in Yaeyama and Okinawa*. Farnham: Ashgate.

——. 2012b. "Whose Heritage? Cultural Properties Legislation and Regional Identity in Okinawa" In Howard, Keith, ed., *Music as Intangible Cultural Heritage: Policy, Ideology, and Practice in the Preservation of East Asian Traditions*, pp. 213–228 Farnham: Ashgate.

———. 2013. "'Dancing Fingers': Embodies Lineages in the Performance of Okinawan Classical Music." *Ethnomusicology* 57(3):367–396.

Hanazaki, Kōhei. 1996. "Ainu Moshir and Yaponesia: Ainu and Okinawan Identities in Contemporary Japan." In D. Denoon, M. Hudson, G. McCormack, and T. Morris-Suzuki, eds., *Multicultural Japan Paleolithic to Postmodern*, pp. 117–131. Cambridge: Cambridge University Press.

Johnson, Henry. 2001. "Nationalisms and Globalization in Okinawan Popular Music: Nēnēzu and Their Place in World Music Contexts." In R. Starrs, ed., *Asian Nationalism in an Age of Globalization*, pp. 359–373. Richmond: Curzon.

———. 2013. "Old, New, Borrowed . . . : Hybridity in the Okinawan Guitarscape." *Ethnomusicology* 22(1):89–110.

Kaneshiro, Atsumi. 2002. "Ryūkyū Islands." In R. Provine, Y. Tokumaru and J. Witzleben, eds., *East Asia: China, Japan and Korea. The Garland Encyclopedia of World Music Vol. 7*, pp. 789–796. New York/London: Routledge.

———. 2004. *Okinawa Ongaku no Kōzō* [*The Structure of Okinawan Music*]. Tokyo: Daiichi Shobō.

Mitsui, Toru. 1998. "Domestic Exoticism: A Recent Trend in Japanese Popular Music." *Perfect Beat* 3(4):1–12.

Nihon Hōsō Kyōkai. 1990–92. *Nihon Min'yō Taikan: Okinawa, Amami* [*Conspectus of Japanese Folk Song: Okinawa and Amami*]. Tokyo: Nihon Hōsō Kyōkai Shuppan Kyōkai.

Roberson, James E. 2001. "*Uchinā* Pop: Place and Identity in Contemporary Okinawan Popular Music." *Critical Asian Studies* 33(2):211–242.

———. 2011. "'Doin' Our Thing': Identity and Colonial Modernity in Okinawan Rock Music." *Popular Music and Society* 34(5):593–620.

Wang, Yaohua. 1987. *Ryūkyū Chūgoku Ongaku Hikaku Ron* [*Comparison of Ryūkyū and Chinese Music*]. Naha: Naha Shuppansha.

———. 1998. *Chūgoku to Ryūkyū no Sangen Ongaku* [*The Sanxian/Sanshin Music of China and Ryūkyū*]. Tokyo: Daiichi Shobō.

Taiko in Japan (Japanese)

Akiyama, Kuniharu. 1997. "'Monochrome': The Emotional Aesthetic of Japanese Drums and Maki Ishii's 'Non-Musical Time'" In R. Thompson, translation, C. Ishii-Meinecke, ed., *Sounds of West: Sounds of East: Maki Ishii's Music: Striding Two Musical Worlds*, pp. 164–179. Germany: Moeck Verlag Musikinstrumentenwerk.

Alaszewska, Jane. 2001. "*Kumi-daiko.*" In S. Sadie, and J. Tyrrell, eds., *New Grove Dictionary of Music and Musicians Vol. 14*, pp. 21–22. Oxford: Oxford University Press

———. 2008. "Two Different Beats to a Single Drum: An Analysis of Old and New Styles of *Hachijo-daiko*." In S. Mills, ed., *Musiké 4: Analyzing East Asian Music – Patterns of Rhythm & Melody, International Journal of Ethnomusicological Studies*, pp. 1–23. Netherlands: Semar.

Asano, Akitoshi. 1995. "*Oguchi Daihachi ni Kiku – Wadaiko Ongaku no Reimeiki* [Asking Oguchi Daihachi: The Dawn of *Wadaiko* Music]." *Taikology* 11:6–15.

———. 2005. *Wadaiko o Utō* [*Let's Play Taiko*]. Ishikawa: Asano Foundation of Taiko Culture Research.

Asano Foundation for Taiko Culture Research. 2002. *Wadaiko ga Wakaru Hon* [*A Book for Understanding Taiko*]. M. Ono, ed., Ishikawa: Asano Foundation for Taiko Culture Research.

Asano, Kaori. 1996. *Taikoo Utsu!* [*Play Taiko!*]. M. Kawate, ed., Tokyo: Bakushūsha.

Coutts-Smith, Mark. 1997. *Children of the Drum: The Life of Japan's Kodō Drummers*. Hong Kong: Lightworks Press.

Hanai, Kiyoshi. 2001. *Wadaiko ga Tanoshiku naru Hon (Gijutsu-hen)* [*A Book for Enjoying Wadaiko (Technique Volume)*]. Ishikawa: Asano Foundation for Taiko Culture Research.

Hayashi, Eitetsu. 1992. *Ashita no Taiko Uchi e* [*To Tomorrow's Taiko Players*]. Tokyo: Shobunsha.

———. 1999. "Tokushū Hayashi Eitetsu Zenshi 1970–2000." *Taikology* 17:9–79.

———. 2012. *Taiko Jitsugetsu Dokusō no Kiseki* [*Hayashi Eitetsu's Taiko Years: A Path Taken Alone*]. Tokyo: Kōdansha.

Higashi, Munenori. 1989a. "*Taiko Gakufuroku, Dai Ikkai: Chichibu Yatai-bayashi.*" *Taikology* 2:50–51.
——. 1989b. "*Taiko Gakufuroku, Dai Nikkai: Chichibu Yatai-bayashi, Sono II.*" *Taikology* 3:46–47.
Honda, Yasuji. 1990. "*Geinō to Taiko* [Performing Arts and *Taiko*]." In M. Nishitsunoi, ed., *Minzoku Geinō 2 [Folk Performing Arts 2]*, pp. 105–08. Tokyo: Ongaku no Tomosha.
Hoshino, Komaro. 1985. *Kodō*. Tokyo: Nippon Geijutsu Shuppansha.
Inoue, Ryohei. 1996. *Ondekoza, Amerika o Hashiru [Ondekoza, Run Through America]*. Tokyo: Seikyūsha.
Kojima Haruko. 1990. "*Nihon no Taiko* [Japanese *Taiko*]." In M. Nishitsunoi, ed., *Minzoku Geinō 2 [Folk Performing Arts 2]*, pp. 99–104. Tokyo: Ongaku no Tomosha.
Kodō Cultural Foundation. 2011. *Inochi Moyashite, Tatakeyo – Kodō 30 Nen no Kiseki [Light Your Fire and Play – Kodō's 30 Year Journey]*. Tokyo: Shuppan Bunka Sha.
Konagaya, Hideyo. 2005. "Performing Manliness: Resistance and Harmony in Japanese American Taiko." In S. Bronner, ed., *Manly Traditions: The Folk Roots of American Masculinities*, pp. 134–156. Bloomington: University of Indiana Press.
Kono, Yuki. 2001. *Yasashiku Manaberu Wadaiko Kyōhon [A Guide for Easily Learning Taiko]*. Tokyo: Sekibunsha.
Misumi, Haruo. 1990. "*Taikoto Matsuri-bayashi [Taiko and Matsuri-bayashi]*." In M. Nishitsunoi, ed., *Minzoku Geinō 2 [Folk Performing Arts 2]*, pp. 109–113. Tokyo: Ongaku no Tomosha.
Miyake, Satoko, and Hironori Nakagawa. 2001. *Taiko*. Osaka: Kaihou Shuppansha.
——, and Jun'ichi Ota. 1997. *Taiko Shokunin [Taiko Craftsmen]*. Tokyo: Kaihou Shuppansha.
Mogi, Hitoshi. 2003. *Nyūmon Nihon no Taiko: Minzoku, Dentō Soshite Nyūwēbu [A Manual of Japanese Taiko: Folklore, Tradition, and the New Wave]*. Tokyo: Heibonsha.
——. 2008. "Osuwa Daiko (Part 1)." *Taikology* 33:78–82.
——. 2009. "Osuwa Daiko (Part 2)." *Taikology* 34:64–69.
——. 2010. "Osuwa Daiko (Part 3)." *Taikology* 35:74–79.
——. 2010. "Oedo Sukeroku Taiko." *Taikology* 36:34–41.
Nippon Taiko Foundation. 2006. *Nihon Taiko Kyōhon, 4th Edn. [Japanese Taiko Instruction Manual, 4th Edn.]*. Tokyo: Nippon Taiko Foundation.
Nishitsunoi, Masahiro. 1990. "*Nihon no Taiko no Bunrui Kaisetsu* [An Explanation of the Classification of Japanese *Taiko*]." In M. Nishitsunoi, ed., *Minzoku Geinō 2 [Folk Performing Arts 2]*, pp. 118–123. Tokyo: Ongaku no Tomosha.
Nozawa, Toyoichi, and Chihiro Nishijima. 2010. "*Ishikawa-ken Chihō no Kenka Taiko Uchi Kyōgikai: Hi-Japanesuku, Hi-Ekizochishizumu na Chiiki Bunka* [The Drumming Competitions in Noto, Ishikawa: Non-Japanesque, and Non-Exotic Local Culture]." *Ningen Shakai Kankyō Kenkyū [Human and Socio-Environment Studies]* 20:55–71.
Oguchi, Daihachi. 1987. *Tenko: Oguchi Daihachi no Nihon Taiko Ron [Heavenly Taiko: Daihachi Oguchi's Japanese Taiko Philosophy]*. Nagano: Ginga Shobo.
Ohta, Junichi. 1989. *Sado no Kodō [Kodō of Sado]*. Osaka: Center Brain Co., Ltd.
Ono, Mieko. 2005. *Taiko to iu Gakki [The Instrument Called Taiko]*. Hakusan: Asano Foundation for Taiko Culture Research.
Sendō, Shintarō. 2007. *Gendai Wadaiko Sōhō [Contemporary Taiko School]*. Tokyo: Onkyō Publish.
Taiko Center. 1992. *Wadaiko Nyūmon [An Introduction to Wadaiko]*. M. Nishitsunoi. Kyoto: Taiko Center.
Tamura, Takuo. 2001. *Yasashiku Manaberu Wadaiko Nyūmon [An Introduction to Easily Learning Taiko]*. Tokyo: Zen-On Music Co., Ltd.
Tanaka, Kenji. 2003. *Hitome de Wakaru Nihon Ongaku Nyūmon [Understanding at One Glance: An Introduction to Japanese Music]*. Tokyo: Ongaku noTomosha.
Yagi, Yasuyuki. 1994. "*Furusato no Taiko – Nagasaki-ken ni Okeru Kyōdo Geinō no Sōshutsu to Chiiki Bunka no Yukue* [The Drum Troupe Boom as Folklorism: Inventing Local Cultures for Whom?]." *Jinbun Chiri* 46(6):581–603.
Yamamoto, Hiroko. 2002. *Nihon no Taiko, Ajia no Taiko [Japanese Drums, Asian Drums]*. Tokyo: Seikyusha.

Yanagawa, Keiichi. 1972. "*Shinwa to Taiko no Matsuri* [Festivals of Affinity and Opposition]." *Shisō* 582:66–77.
Yūki, Emi. 1995. *Ondekoza ga Hashiru – Boku no Seishun Amerika 15,000 Kiro* [*Ondekoza's Run Across the U.S.A. – My Youthful Days, America 15,000 km*]. Tokyo: Popura-sha.
Za Ondekoza. 1999. *Taiko no Bīto ni Miserarete – Ondekoza Sekai Kōen-ki* [*Enchanted by the Taiko Beat – A Record of Ondekoza's World Performances*]. Tokyo: Ongaku Shuppansha.

Taiko in Japan (English)

Bender, Shawn. 2005. "Of Roots and Race: Discourses of Body and Place in Japanese *Taiko* Drumming." *Social Science Japan Journal* 8(2):197–212.
———. 2010. "Drumming from Screen to Stage: Ondekoza's *Odaiko* and the Reimaging of Japanese Taiko." *The Journal of Asian Studies* 69(3):843–867.
———. 2012. *Taiko Boom: Japanese Drumming in Place and Motion*. Berkeley: University of California Press.
Collins, Glenn. 1990. "Kodō and the Visceral Sound of One Huge Drum Throbbing." *The New York Times*, February.
Creighton, Millie. 1997. "Consuming Rural Japan: The Marketing of Tradition and Nostalgia in the Japanese Travel Industry." *Ethnology* 36(3):239–254.
Endo, Kenny. 1999. "Yodan Uchi: A Contemporary Composition for Taiko." Master's thesis, University of Hawaii.
Fujie, Linda. 1986. "*Matsuri-bayashi* of Tokyo: The Role of Supporting Organizations in Traditional Music." Ph.D. dissertation, Columbia University.
Gould, Michael. 1996. "*Gozo Daiko*." *Percussive Notes* 1996(4):41–46.
———. 1998. "*Taiko* Classification and Manufacturing." *Percussive Notes* 1998(6):12–20.
Hashimoto, Hiroyuki, and David Ambaras. 1998. "Re-Creating and Re-Imagining Folk Performing Arts in Contemporary Japan." *Journal of Folklore Research* 35(1):35–46.
Ishii, Maki. 1981. *Dyu-ha for Kodō, Op. 46*. Celle: Moeck Verlag Musikinstrumentenwerk.
———. 1989. *Monochrome for Japanese Drums and Gongs Op. 29 (1976)*. Celle: Moeck Verlag Musikinstrumentenwerk.
Konagaya, Hideyo. 2007. "Performing the Okinawan Woman in *Taiko*: Gender, Folklore, and Identity Politics in Modern Japan." Ph.D. dissertation, University of Pennsylvania.
McNicol, Tony. 2006. "Drum Songs: The Intoxicating Music of Hachijojima." *Wingspan*, January:31–35.
O'Mahoney, Terry. 1998. "Kodō: Japanese *Taiko* Masters." *Percussive Notes* 6–10.
Otsuka, Chie. 1997. "Learning *Taiko* in America." Master's thesis, University of Tsukuba.
Pachter, Benjamin. 2009. "Displaying 'Japan': *Kumidaiko* and the Exhibition of Culture at Walt Disney World." *Asian Musicology* 14:84–124.
———. 2009. "Drumming for the Mouse: *Kumidaiko* and the Exhibition of 'Japan' at Walt Disney World." Master's thesis, University of Pittsburgh.
———. 2013. "*Wadaiko* in Japan and the United States: The Intercultural History of a Music Genre." Ph.D. dissertation, University of Pittsburgh.
Panalaks, Miyako Saito. 2001. "The *Ma* of *Taiko*." Master's thesis, Dalhousie University.
Schnell, Scott Randall. 1993. "The Rousing Drum: Ritual, Change, and Adaption in a Rural Mountain Community of Central Japan." Ph.D. dissertation, Ohio State University.
Sutton, Anderson R. 1980. "Drumming in Okinawan Classical Music: A Catalogue of Gestures." *Dance Research Journal* 13(1):17–28.
Terada, Yoshitaka. 2008. "Angry Drummers and Buraku Identity: The Ikari Taiko Group in Osaka Japan." In R. Statelova, A. Rodel, L. Peycheva, I. Vlaeva and V. Dimov, eds., *The Human World and Musical Diversity: Proceedings from the Fourth Meeting of the ICTM Study Group "Music and Minorities" in Varna, Bulgaria 2006*, pp. 309–315. Sofia: Bulgarian Academy of Sciences, Institute of Art Studies.

Thornbury, Barbara E. 1994. "The Cultural Properties Protection Law and Japan's Folk Performing Arts." *Asian Folklore Studies* 53(2):211–225.

Tusler, Mark. 1995. "The Los Angeles *Matsuri Taiko*: Performance Aesthetics, Teaching Methods, and Compositional Techniques." Master's thesis, University of California, Santa Barbara.

Varian, Heidi. 2005. *The Way of Taiko*. Berkeley, CA: Stone Bridge Press.

Vogel, Brian. 2009. "Transmission and Performance of *Taiko* in Edo Bayashi, *Hachijo*, and Modern *Kumi-daiko* Styles." Ph.D. dissertation, Rice University.

Taiko in Global Contexts (Japanese)

Izumi, Masumi. 2008. "*Amerika ni Okeru Wadaiko no Kigen to Hatten*: 'Nihon' *Bunka Ishoku no Mitsu no Ruitei* [The Pioneering of *Taiko* Drumming in the United States: An Examination of Three Distinct Routes]." *Gengo Bunka* 11(2):139–68.

Kobayashi, Kim N. 2006. "Asian Women Kick Ass: A Study of Gender Issues within Canadian *Kumi-daiko*." *The Canadian Folk Music/Bulletin de Musique Folkorique Canadienne* 40:1–11.

Konagaya, Hideyo. 2002. "*Taiko no Hyōshō to Masukyurinichī no Kōchiku-minzoku Dentō ni Yoru Nihonjin to Nikkei Amerika-jin no Teikō* [The Representation of *Taiko* and the Construction of Masculinity: Japanese and Japanese American Resistance through a Folk Tradition]." *Pacific and American Studies* 2(3):113–127.

Otsuka, Chie. 1998. "*Beikoku ni Okeru Wadaiko no Hatten* [The Development of *Taiko* in North America]." *Taikology* 16:45–52.

Shimasaki, Atsuko, and Tomiko Kato 1999. *Jugyō no Tame no Nihon no Ongaku, Sekai no Ongaku* [*Japanese Music & World Music for the Classroom*]. Tokyo: Ongaku no Tomosha.

Taiko in Global Contexts (English)

Ahlgren, Angela. 2011. "Drumming Asian America: Performing Race, Gender, and Sexuality in North American Taiko." Ph.D. dissertation, The University of Texas.

Asai, Susan M. 1985. "*Horaku*: A Buddhist Tradition of Performing Arts and the Development of *Taiko* Drumming in the United States." In N. Jairazbhoy and S. DeVale, eds., *Selected Reports in Ethnomusicology, 6: Asian Music in North America*, pp. 163–172. Los Angeles: University of California.

———. 1995. "Transformations of Tradition: Three Generations of Japanese American Music Making." *The Musical Quarterly* 79(3):429–453.

———. 1997. "*Sansei* Voices in the Community: Japanese American Musicians in California." In K. Lornell and A. Rasmussen, eds., *Musics of Multicultural America: A Study of Twelve Musical Communities*, pp. 257–285. New York: Schirmer Books.

Barakan, Peter. 1995. "Discussion: A Woman Playing Japanese Drums." In K. Ikanoshi, ed., *Wadaiko*, pp. 124–135. Tokyo: Kawade Shobō Shinsha.

Bensen, Daniel Maier. 2006. "*Taiko*: The Formation and Professionalization of a Japanese Performance Art." Honors Project, Bowdoin College.

Carle, Sarah. 2008. "Bodies in Motion: Gender, Identity, and the Politics of Representation in the American *Taiko* Movement." Master's thesis, University of Hawaii.

Chan, Erin. 2002. "They're Beating the Drum for Female Empowerment." *Los Angeles Times*, July.

Creighton, Millie. 2007. "Changing Heart (Beats): From Japanese Identity and Nostalgia to *Taiko* for Citizens of the Earth." In C. Kwok-bun, J. Walls, and D. Hayward, eds., *East-West Identities: Globalization, Localization, and Hybridization*, pp. 203–228. Leiden: Brill.

de Ferranti, Hugh. 2006. "Japan Beating: The Making and Marketing of Professional *Taiko* Music in Australia." In M. Allen and R. Sakamoto, eds., *Popular Culture, Globalization, and Japan*, pp. 75–93. New York/London: Routledge.

Fromartz, Samuel. 1998. "Anything but Quiet." *Natural History* March:10–15.

Fujie, Linda. 2001. "Japanese *Taiko* Drumming in International Performance: Converging Musical Ideas in the Search for Success on Stage." *The World of Music* 43(2/3):93–101.

Itoh, Keiko. 1999. *A Journey to Be a Japanese Drama Therapist: An Exploration of Taiko Drumming as a Therapeutic Resource for Drama Therapy*. San Francisco: California Institute of Integral Studies.

Izumi, Masumi. 2001. "Reconsidering Ethnic Culture and Community: A Case Study on Japanese Canadian *Taiko* Drumming." *Journal of Asian American Studies* 4(1):35–41.

Johnson, Henry. 2008. "Why *Taiko*? Understanding *Taiko* Performance at New Zealand's First *Taiko* Festival." *A Journal of Social Anthropology and Cultural Studies* 5(2):111–134.

Kobayashi, Kim Noriko. 2006. "Tracing the Development of *Kumi-daiko* in Canada." Graduate thesis, The University of British Columbia.

Kodō. 2000. "East Meets East: Kodō in Korea and China." *The Kodō Beat* Summer:1–2.

Konagaya, Hideyo. 2001. "*Taiko* as Performance: Creating Japanese American Traditions." *The Japanese Journal of American Studies* 12:105–124.

Malm, William. 2001. *Traditional Japanese Music and Musical Instruments: The New Edn*. New York: Kodansha America, Inc.

Masuda, Ann. 2001. "'The Future of Japanese American *Taiko*': Bryan Akira Yamami." *Taikology* 20.

Miller, Terry E., Susan M. Asai, and Anne K. Rasmussen. "Asian American Musics." In E. Koskoff, ed., *Music Cultures in the United States*, pp. 273–302. New York/London: Routledge.

Navarro, Mireya. 2004. "Young Japanese-Americans Honor Ethnic Roots." *The New York Times*, August.

Powell, Kimberly. 2003. "Learning Together: Practice, Pleasure and Identity in a *Taiko* Drumming World." Ph.D. dissertation, Stanford University.

———. 2004. "The Apprenticeship of Embodied Knowledge in a *Taiko* Drumming Ensemble." In L. Bresler, ed., *Knowing Bodies, Moving Minds*, pp. 183–195. Netherlands: Kluwer Academic Publishers.

———. 2006. "Inside-Out and Outside-In: Participant Observation in *Taiko* Drumming." In G. Spindler and L. Hammond, eds., *Innovations in Education Ethnography: Theory, Methods, and Results*, pp. 33–64. Mahwah, NJ: Lawrence Erlbaum Associates.

———. 2008. "Drumming against the Quiet: The Sounds of Asian American Identity in an Amorphous Landscape." *Qualitative Inquiry* 14(6):901–925.

Seattle Matsuri Taiko. 2005. "Japanese *Taiko*: Drum for Learning About Culture." In M. Kahn and E. Younger, eds., *Pacific Voices: Keeping Our Cultures Alive*, pp. 105–13. Seattle: University of Washington Press.

Shikuma, Stanley. 2000. "Making a Modern Folk Art: *Taiko* in the Pacific Northwest/Canadian Southwest Region." The Nikkei Experience in the Pacific Northwest [Conference]. Seattle, WA.

Terada, Yoshitaka. 2001. "Shifting Identities of Taiko Music in America." In Y. Terada, ed., *Transcending Boundaries: Asian Musics in North America*, pp. 37–59. Osaka: National Museum of Ethnology.

Tusler, Mark. 2003. "Sounds and Sights of Power: Ensemble *Taiko* Drumming (*Kumi Daiko*) Pedagogy in California and the Conceptualization of Power." Ph.D. dissertation, University of California, Santa Barbara.

Wong, Deborah. 2004. *Speak It Louder: Asian Americans Making Music*. New York/London: Routledge.

———. 2005. "Noisy Intersection: Ethnicity, Authenticity and Ownership in Asian American *Taiko*." In U. Hae-kyung, ed., *Diasporas and Interculturalism in Asian Performing Arts: Translating Traditions*, pp. 85–90. New York/London: Routledge.

———. 2006a. "Asian American Improvisation in Chicago: Tatsu Aoki and the 'New' Japanese American *Taiko*." *Critical Studies in Improvisation* 1(3): http://www.criticalimprov.com/issue/view/13.

———. 2006b. "Taiko and the Asian/American Body: Drums, Rising Sun, and the Question of Gender." In J. Post, ed., *Ethnomusicology: A Contemporary Reader*, pp. 87–96. New York/London: Routledge.

Wong, Frances. 2007. "*Taiko* in North America Bibliography Plan." Class Report, University of Hawaii.

Yoon, Paul J. 2001. "'She's Really Become Japanese Now!': *Taiko* Drumming and Asian American Identifications." *American Music* 19(4):417–438.

———. 2007. *Development and Support of Taiko in the United States*. New York: Asia Society.

———. 2009. "Asian Masculinities and Parodic Possibility in *Odaiko* Solos and Filmic Representations." *Asian Music* 40(1):100–130.

Taiko (Internet Sources)

Endo, Kenny. 2011. "*Ātisuto Intabyū*, Vol. 7: *Kenī Endō* [Artist Interview, Vol. 7: Kenny Endo]." Interview by Staff. Miyamoto Unosuke Shōten: http://www.miyamoto-unosuke.co.jp/taiko/artist/07/1.html (accessed November 19, 2014).

Hayashi, Eitetsu. 2011. "Artist Interview: Innovating Drum Music, the Spirit of Eitetsu Hayashi." Interview by Kazumi Narabe. The Japan Foundation Performing Arts Network Japan: http://performingarts.jp/E/art_interview/1103/1.html (accessed November 19, 2014).

Ochi, Megumi. 1997 "What the *Haniwa* Have to Say About *Taiko*'s Roots: The History of *Taiko*": http://www.taiko.com/taiko_resource/history/haniwa_ochi.html (accessed July 1, 2014).

Pachter, Benjamin. TaikoSource.com: http://taikosource.com/library/bibliography (accessed November 19, 2014).

Theatrical Genres: Bunraku

Andō, Tsuruo. 1970. *Bunraku, The Puppet Theater, Performing Arts of Japan I*. New York: Walker/Weatherhill.

Brazell, Karen. 1998. *Traditional Japanese Theatre: An Anthology of Plays*. New York: Columbia University Press.

Chikamatsu, Zenshū Kankōkai. 1985-94. *Chikamatsu zenshū* [Chikamatsu plays]. Tokyo: Iwanami Shoten.

Inobe, Kiyoshi. 1991. *Jōrurishi Kōsetsu* [Studies in the History of *Jōruri*]. Tokyo: Kazama Shobō.

——, Andrew C. Gerstle and William P. Malm. 1990. *Theater as Music: The Bunraku Play 'Mt. Imo and Mt. Se: An Exemplary Tale of Womanly Virtue'* (Michigan Monograph Series in Japanese Studies 4). Ann Arbor: University of Michigan.

Keene, Donald. 1965. *Bunraku*. Tokyo: Kodansha International.

Motegi, Kiyoko. 1988. *Bunraku: Koe to Oto to Hibiki* [*Bunraku: Voice, Sound and Tone*]. Tokyo: Ongaku no Tomosha.

Yamada, Chieko. 2002. "Theatrical Genres: Bunraku." In R. Provine, Y. Tokumaru and J. Witzleben, eds., *East Asia: China, Japan and Korea. The Garland Encyclopedia of World Music Vol. 7*, pp. 663-665. New York/London: Routledge.

——. 2002. "Theatrical Genres: *Gidayū-bushi*." In R. Provine, Y. Tokumaru and J. Witzleben, eds., *East Asia: China, Japan and Korea. The Garland Encyclopedia of World Music Vol. 7*, pp. 675-677. New York/London: Routledge.

Theatrical Genres: Kabuki

Ariyoshi, Sawako. 1972. *Kabuki Dancer: A Novel of the Woman who Founded Kabuki*. Tokyo: Kodansha.

Brandon, James. 1956. *Studies in Kabuki*. Honolulu: University of Hawaii Press.

——. 1992. *Kabuki: Five Classical Plays*. Berkeley: University of California Press.

—— and Tamako Niwa. 1966. *Kabuki Plays*. London: S. French.

Ernst, Earle. 1956. *The Kabuki Theater*. Honolulu: University of Hawaii Press.

Gunji Masakatsu. 1985. *Kabuki*. Revised. Tokyo: Kodansha International.

Halford, A.S. and G.M. Halford. 1956. *The Kabuki Handbook: A Guide to Understanding and Appreciation*. Rutland, VT: Tuttle.

Malm, William P. 2001. "Japan, VI, Theatre Music: *Kabuki*." In S. Sadie, and J. Tyrrell, eds., *New Grove Dictionary of Music and Musicians Vol. 12*, pp. 868–870. Oxford: Oxford University Press.

——, James R. Brandon, and Donald H. Shively. 1978. *Studies in Kabuki: Its Acting, Music, and Historical Context*. Honolulu: University of Hawaii Press.

Mochizuki, Tainosuke. 1975. *Kabuki Geza Ongaku* [*Kabuki Off-Stage Music*]. Tokyo: Engeki Shuppansha.

Scott, Adolphe C. 1999. *The Kabuki Theatre of Japan*. Mineola, NY: Dover.

Toita, Yasuji. 1970. *Kabuki, The Popular Theater, Performing Arts of Japan II*. New York: Walker/Weatherhill.
Tokita, Alison M. 1999. *Kiyomoto-bushi: Narrative Music of the Kabuki Theatre*. Kassel: Bärenreiter.
———. 2002. "*Tokiwazu, Kiyomoto* and Other Narratives." In R. Provine, Y. Tokumaru and J. Witzleben, eds., *East Asia: China, Japan and Korea. The Garland Encyclopedia of World Music Vol. 7*, pp. 679–682. New York/London: Routledge.
Yamada Shōichi. 1986. *Kabuki Ongaku Nyūmon* [*Introduction to Kabuki Music*]. Tokyo: Ongaku no Tomosha.

Theatrical Genres: Noh

Asai, Susan M. 1999. *Nōmai Dance Drama: A Surviving Spirit of Medieval Japan*. Westport, CT: Greenwood Press.
Asami, Masataka. 1993. *Nō no Ongakusei to Jissai* [The Music of *Noh* and its Practice]. Tokyo: Ongaku no Tomosha.
Bethe, Monica and Karen Brazell. 1978. *Nō as Performance: An Analysis of the Kuse Scene of Yamamba*. Ithaca, NY: Cornell University Press.
———. 1990. "The Practice of *Noh* Theater." In R. Schechner and W. Appel, eds., *By Means of Performance*, pp. 167–193. Cambridge: Cambridge University Press.
——— and Richard Emmert. 1992. *Noh Performance Guides*. 7 Volumes. Tokyo: National Noh Theatre.
Emmert, Richard. 1983. "The *Maigoto* of *Nō*: A Musical Analysis of the *Chu-no-mai*." *Yearbook for Traditional Music* 15:5–13.
Keene, Donald. 1990. *Nō and Bunraku: Two Forms of Japanese Theatre*. New York: Columbia University Press.
Komparu Kunio. 1983. *The Noh Theater: Principles and Perspectives*. New York: Weatherhill.
Malm, William P. 1958. "The Rhythmic Orientation of Two Drums in the Japanese *Nō* drama." *Ethnomusicology* 2(3):89–95.
———. 1960. "An Introduction to *Taiko* Drum Music in the Japanese *Nō* Drama." *Ethnomusicology* 4(2):75–8.
Miura, Hiroko. 1998. *Nō Kyōgen no Ongaku Nyūmon* [*Introduction to the Music of Noh and Kyōgen*]. Tokyo: Ongaku no Tomo Sha.
Nishino, Haruo and Hisashi Hata. 1987. *Nō Kyōgen Jiten* [*The Dictionary of Noh and Kyōgen*]. Tokyo: Heibonsha.
Rimer, John T. and Masakazu Yamazaki. 1984. *On the Art of the Nō Drama: The Major Treatises of Zeami*. Translated by John T. Rimer and M. Yamazaki. Princeton, NJ: Princeton University Press.
Takakuwa Izumi. 2002. "*Nō* and *Kyōgen*." In R. Provine, Y. Tokumaru and J. Witzleben, eds., *East Asia: China, Japan and Korea. The Garland Encyclopedia of World Music Vol. 7*, pp. 629–638. New York/London: Routledge.
Tamba, Akira. 1981. *The Musical Structure of Nō*. Tokyo: Tokai University Press.
Tyler, John W. 1992. *Japanese Noh Dramas*. London: Penguin Books.
Yokomichi, Mario, Hiroshi Koyama and Akira Omote. 1987–90. *Nō* and *Kyōgen*. Tokyo: Iwanami Shoten.

Theory, Solfége and Notation

Fujita, Takanori. 1986. "*Kuchishōga*: The Vocal Rendition of Instrumental Expression in the Oral and Literate Tradition of Japanese Music." In Y. Tokumaru and O. Yamaguchi, eds., *The Oral and the Literate in Music*, pp. 239–251. Tokyo: Academia Music.
Hughes, David W. 1988. "Music Archaeology of Japan: Data and Interpretation." In E. Hickmann and D. Hughes, eds., *The Archaeology of Early Music Cultures*, pp. 55–87. Bonn: Verlag für systematische Musikwissenschaft.

———. 1989. "The Historical Uses of Nonsense; Vowel-Pitch Solfège from Scotland to Japan." In M. Philipp, ed., *Ethnomusicology and the Historical Dimension*, pp. 3–18. Beuzlen: Philipp Verlag.

———. 2000. "No Nonsense: The Logic and Power of Acoustic-Iconic Mnemonic Systems." *British Journal of Ethnomusicology* 9(2):93–120.

———. 2001. Japan, I.3: Transmission." In S. Sadie, and J. Tyrrell, eds., *Nyu Gurōvu Sekai Ongaku Daijiten [New Grove Dictionary of Music and Musicians (Japanese Edn.)]* Vol. 12, pp. 817–818. Tokyo: Kōdansha.

———. 2001. "Japan, I.4: Scales and modes." In S. Sadie, and J. Tyrrell, eds., *Nyu Gurōvu Sekai Ongaku Daijiten [New Grove Dictionary of Music and Musicians (Japanese Edn.)]* Vol. 12, p. 818. Tokyo: Kōdansha.

Koizumi, Fumio. 1977. "Musical Scales in Japanese Music." In *Asian Music in an Asian Perspective*, pp. 73–79. Tokyo: Heibonsha.

Komoda, Haruko and Mihoko Nogawa. 2002. "Theory and Notation in Japan." In R. Provine, Y. Tokumaru and J. Witzleben, eds., *East Asia: China, Japan and Korea. The Garland Encyclopedia of World Music* Vol. 7, pp. 565–584. New York/London: Routledge.

Malm, William P. and David W. Hughes. 2001. "Japan, III: Notation." In S. Sadie, and J. Tyrrell, eds., *Nyu Gurōvu Sekai Ongaku Daijiten [New Grove Dictionary of Music and Musicians (Japanese Edn.)]* Vol. 12, pp. 842–849. Tokyo: Kōdansha.

Marett, Allan. 2001. "Mode, V, 5(II), Japan: Chōshi." In S. Sadie, and J. Tyrrell, eds., *Nyu Gurōvu Sekai Ongaku Daijiten [New Grove Dictionary of Music and Musicians (Japanese Edn.)]* Vol. 16, pp. 853–858. Tokyo: Kōdansha.

Western Art Music

Burt, Peter. 2001. *The Music of Tōru Takemitsu*. Cambridge: Cambridge University Press.

Cook, Lisa M. 2014. "Venerable Traditions, Modern Manifestations: Understanding Mayuzumi's Bunraku for Cello." *Asian Music* 45(1):99–131.

Cooke, Mervyn. 1998. *Britten and the Far East*. Suffolk: Boydell Press.

Everett, Yayoi Uno and Frederick Lau. 2004. *Locating East Asia in Western Art Music*. Middletown, CT: Wesleyan University Press.

Galliano, Luciana. 2002. *Yōgaku: Japanese Music in the Twentieth Century*. Lanham, MD: Scarecrow Press.

Minoru, Miki. 2008. *Composing for Japanese Instruments*. Translated by M. Regan, P. Flavin, ed. Rochester: University of Rochester Press.

Ohtake, Noriko. 1993. *Creative Sources for the Music of Tōru Takemitsu*. Aldershot: Scolar Press.

Pacun, David. 2012. "Nationalism and Musical Style in Interwar *Yōgaku*: A Reappraisal." *Asian Music* 43(2):3–46.

Takemitsu, Tōru. 1989. "Contemporary Music in Japan," text adapted for publication by H. Tann, *Perspectives of New Music* 27(2):198–205.

———. 1995. *Confronting Silence: Selected Writings*. Translated and edited by T. Kakudo and G. Glasgow. Berkeley, CA: Fallen Leaf Press.

———, with Tania Cronin and Hilary Tann. 1989. "Afterword." *Perspectives of New Music* 27(2):206–214.

Wade, Bonnie C. 2014a. *Composing Japanese Musical Modernity*. Chicago, IL: University of Chicago Press.

———. 2014b. "Performing Studies of Music in Asian Cultures: Some Personal Reflections on What We Have Been and Are Up To." *Asian Music* 45(2):3–31.

Women and Gender

Coaldrake, Kimi A. 1997. *Women's Gidayū and the Japanese Theatre Tradition*. New York/London: Routledge.

Howe, Sondra W. 1993. "Women Music Educators in Japan During the Meiji Period." *Bulletin of the Council for Research in Music Education* 119:101–109.

———. 1995. "The Role of Women in the Introduction of Western Music in Japan." *The Bulletin of Historical Research in Music Education* 16(2):81–97.

Oshio, Satomi. 2002. "Gender roles in the performing arts in Japan." In R. Provine, Y. Tokumaru and J. Witzleben, eds., *East Asia: China, Japan and Korea. The Garland Encyclopedia of World Music Vol. 7*, pp. 763–766. New York/London: Routledge.

Milioto, Jennifer. 1998. "Women in Japanese Popular Music: Setting the Subcultural Scene." In T. Mitsui, ed., *Popular Music: Intercultural Interpretations*, pp. 485–498. Kanazawa, Japan: Kanazawa University.

Robertson, Jennifer. 1998. *Takarazuka: Sexual Politics and Popular Culture in Modern Japan*. Berkeley: University of California Press.

Watanabe, Hiroshi. 2013. "Takarazuka and Japanese Modernity." In H. de Ferranti and A. Tokita, eds., *Music, Modernity and Locality in Prewar Japan: Osaka and Beyond*, pp. 193–210. Farnham: Ashgate.

Audio-Visual Sources

Angry Drummers: A Taiko Group from Osaka Japan. 2010. 85 minutes.
Bunraku: Masters of Japanese Puppet Theater. 2001. 53 minutes. HAN 30081.
Drumming Out a Message: Eisa and the Okinawan Diaspora in Japan. 2005. 75 minutes.
Gagaku: The Court Music of Japan. 1989. 57 minutes. Early Music Television, University of Oklahoma.
Jazz in Japan. 1999. 30 minutes. Early Music Television, University of Oklahoma.
Kabuki. n.d. 35 minutes. HAN 1559.
Live From Tokyo: A Documentary About Underground Music. 2010. 81 minutes. MVD Visual.
Music of Bunraku. 1991. 29 minutes. Early Music Television, University of Oklahoma.
Nagauta: The Heart of Kabuki Music. 1993. 30 minutes. Early Music Television, University of Oklahoma.
Nova: Japan's Killer Quake. 2011. 60 minutes. PBS. NOVA 6224
Portrait of an Onnagata. 1990. 30 minutes. FFH 3802.
Shinto Festival Music. 1993. 30 minutes. Early Music Television, University of Oklahoma.
Sukiyaki and Chips. 1984. 60 minutes. Shanachie 1213.
The Ondekoza on Sado (Sadono Kuni Ondekoza). 1975. 57 minutes. Shinoda Masahiro, dir.
The Tradition of Performing Arts in Japan: The Artistry of Kabuki, Noh, and Bunraku. 1989. 38 minutes. Japan: the Land and Its People. Nippon Steel Corp.
The Written Face. 1995. 89 minutes. Daniel Schmid, dir.
Tokyo Blues: Jazz and Blues in Japan. 1999. Craig McTurk, dir.
Tsugaru Shamisen: The World of Michihiro Sato. 2003. 48 minutes. Ishiba Akio, dir.

Index

Abe, Shinzō 16
Agatsuma, Hiromitsu 134
aidoru 48, 60, 129–133
Ainu 23–24, 33
Akane, Fujino 206–217, 218
"Akatonbo" 110, 111–114
AKB48 130, 131, 132
Akita, Masami 127
Allied Occupation 47
Alves, William 18, 80, 95, 102
Amaterasu 11, 17
angura 48, 53, 59, 121–129
Aoyagi, Hiroshi 59
Ara, Yukito 33
Arashi 130, 131, 132
Arashiyama-daiko 201
art music 24, 49, 58, 61, 68, 69, 105, 109–116
Asano, Kaoly 140
Ashikaga, Yoshimitsu 13, 95
Asuka period 11
atarigane 18, 141, 197
Atkins, Everett T. 47, 52, 53, 58
authenticity 52, 53, 57

Babymetal 3–4, 222–223
Bach, J.S. 200
bachi 142, 196–197, 202, 205, 210, 213, 217

Bachi, Holic 164–165, 168, 215
Bakan, Michael B. 42, 43
bakufu 13
bamboo instruments 216
Banba, Tomoko 197
Basara 18–19, 165–166, 190–198, 217, 218
bass guitar 116
Beat Press 201, 202
The Beatles 48
bells 19, 22
Bender, Shawn 137, 138
The Berotecs 59, 123, 124
Bigenho, Michelle 57
biwa 90–93, 103
Bjarnason, Kolbeinn 116
Blasdel, Christopher Y. 49, 51, 71–72, 180, 181
body 181
Bolivian music 56–57
Bourdaghs, Michael K. 121–122
Bracey, Marty 139, 173
brass bands 44, 49
Brazil 62
Buddhism 10, 11–12, 16, 19–23, 68; afterlife 17; familial duty 94; Kyoto 157; *ma* 69; *noh* 95; *satori* 200; *shakuhachi* 71; *shōmyō* 37; *see also* Zen Buddhism

268 • Index

buildings 40
bunraku 13, 14, 79, 161, 162
burakumin 23–24, 172
bushidō 12, 210
butoh 83–84

cadences 89, 93
calligraphy 115
"The Calling" 105–106
case studies 175–219; Basara 190–198; Matsuri-shū 198–206; Murasaki Daiko 206–217; Tosha, Rōetsu 176–190
chants, Buddhist 11–12, 20, 21–22
chappa 18, 141, 197
Chiba, Megu 59
Chikamatsu, Monzaemon 14
chikara 200
children: songs for 111–112, 114; teaching *taiko* to 169, 170
China 11, 12, 68, 90; cultural exchange with 38–39; *gagaku* 102; *jo-ha-kyū* 99; *shakuhachi* 71; sutras 22
"Chonrima" 178–179
choruses 26, 49, 221
"Choshi" 73–76, 94, 128
Christianity 23
"Chū no Mai" 95–97
clappers 17, 19
clarinet 118
Confucianism 15, 23
costumes: Basara 195; Matsuri-shū 204–205, 206; Murasaki Daiko 209, 210, 212–213, 215, 217
country music 47
court music 12, 17–18, 25, 38
Crypton Vocaloid software 130, 132, 133
culture 6–7, 52; hybridity 38–40, 51, 134; Kyoto 157, 161, 172
cymbals 18, 22, 141, 197

Dalby, Liza 81
dance 4, 25, 83–84, 184; Basara 18–19, 191, 196; *geiko* 158; *maigoto* 95, 98; Murasaki Daiko 206, 213, 215, 216, 217; Shintō 17–18; *see also kabuki*
De Ferranti, Hugh 46, 98
De Kloet, Jeroen 5
Demi Semi Quaver 123–125
demographic changes 61
Den, Tagayasu 138
"Densha Hātobīto" 202
Deschênes, Bruno 99–100, 186
deshi 179

dialects 26, 27, 32, 157–158
diatonic scale 45, 112–113
difference 57, 218; Basara 192, 193, 195; gender 215; Murasaki Daiko 212
"DKN" 140–141
do-enka 118–119
Downer, Lesley 158–159
dōyō 111–112, 114
drums 3, 18, 102; *jo-ha-kyū* 104; Kirihito 126; *min'yō* 26; Murasaki Daiko 215–216; *noh* 95, 97; *nori* 99; *see also taiko*
Duet 67–69, 141
Duo-YUMENO 101

earthquakes 7, 8
"Echigojishi" 80, 186–189, 225–232
Edo period 10, 13, 14–15, 24, 54, 68, 98; guilds 80; *koto* 100; Kyoto 157; modernity 41; reforestation 6; scales 85; *shakuhachi* 71; women 58, 60, 61
education system 44–45, 51, 169–170
egalitarianism 193, 194
Eguchi, Aimi 131–132
Emi, Eleonola 124–125
Emi-go 124
Emmert, Richard 95, 98, 103–104
emotion 93
Endo, Kenny 67–68, 105, 125, 135, 138, 141–143, 163, 178
enka 4, 38, 47, 48, 55, 56, 116–121, 132
Ensemble Nipponia 189
ereki būmu 50
eroticism 81, 158, 217
"Etenraku" 85, 101–103
Eto, Leonardo 201, 217
European art music 49, 58, 109–116

family 166
Fellezs, Kevin 119–120
femininity 215
"fence" metaphor 51
festivals 4, 17, 18, 153–155, 220–221; Basara 191; Gion Matsuri 149–153, 155, 161, 171–172; minorities 33; *min'yō* 26; *mochitsuki* 195; *taiko* 168, 171–172, 177
fieldwork 166
"flavor" metaphor 52–53
flower arrangement 69, 161
flutes 17, 26, 67, 95, 115–116, 158; *see also fue*; *nohkan*; *shinobue*
fōkusongu 30, 48

Index

folk music 4, 24–34, 48, 77; BachiHolic164–165; *taiko* 138–139; tempo 99; *see also min'yō*
foreign practitioners 73, 119–121, 193
Foreman, Kelly M. 158
form 99–105, 181, 202
Fraleigh, Sondra 84
fue 17, 26, 27, 32, 67
Fujie, Linda 25, 28–29, 69, 72, 77, 80, 88, 90, 93, 101, 117
Fujiwara, Aki 190, 192, 217
Fukuoka 159, 167
Fukushima Daiichi Nuclear Power Plant 7
Funabashi, Yuichiro 139
furusato 29, 55–56, 114, 117
"Furusato" (song) 221
fusuma 40, 90
"(Futaiken) Tsuru no Sugomori" 88, 93–94

gagaku 12, 38, 68, 78, 90, 114; *jo-ha-kyū* 100, 101–102; Kyoto 161; *matsuri* 154; pitch and scales 84, 85
gagaku taiko 102
gaikyoku 71–72
Galbraith, Patrick W. 130–131, 132
Galliano, Luciana 70, 111, 113, 114–115
gaman suru 8
ganbaru 8
gardens 9, 10, 155
gayageum 39–40
geisha/geiko 14, 79, 81, 158–160, 163, 180, 182–183, 184
gendai hōgaku 198
gendai ongaku 109
gender 58–61, 215; *see also* women
Genji Monogatari 12, 206, 208, 212–213, 217
gidayū-bushi 60–61, 98
Gillan, Matthew 31–32, 33, 155, 181
Gion Matsuri 149–153, 155, 161, 171–172, 206
globalization 5
Gocoo 140–141, 205
gongs 18, 22, 26, 102, 141, 151, 197
Goto-Jones, Christopher 41
Great East Japan Earthquake (2011) 7, 8
"groove" 98–99, 202, 205
gurūpu saunzu 48
guilds 80
guitar 4, 33, 49, 116
Gunji, Sumi 71, 90
gunka 44
guzheng 39–40

"The Hack-Driver's Song of Hakone" 88
Hahn, Tomie 83
Haino, Kiyoshi 32
"Hakone Mago Uta" 27, 29
hakuryoku 193
Hanayagi, Michikaoru 83
Handa, Ayako 90
"Hannya" 216
Happy End 121–122, 123
harmonics 40
harmony 89, 110, 113, 117
"Haru Yo Koi" 121–122
Hatsune, Miku 129–130, 132–133, 222
Hattori, Ryūtaro 27
Hawaii 62
Hayakawa, Shunsuke 126
hayashi 18
Hayashi, Eitetsu 138, 196–197
hayashi-kotoba 26, 77, 223
Heian period 12, 85, 153
Heian-jingu 209
Heike Monogatari 90–93
Heike-biwa 90–91
Hendry, Joy 13, 14, 16
hen'on 85, 87
heterophony 89–90, 93, 110, 128, 221
hichiriki 17, 103
Higashi, Munenori 139–140, 167, 168, 169, 170–171, 201
Hikawa, Kiyoshi 118–119
hip-hop 120, 122–123
hira-daiko 142
Hirohito, Emperor 15
Hiroshima 9, 15, 167
hōgaku 24, 49, 58, 68–69, 106, 143, 222; decline of 185, 206; heterogeneous pedagogical styles 218; Kyoto 162, 163, 172; "Megitsune" 223; professional musicians 184–185; Tosha, Rōetsu 176, 177, 178, 179, 189–190; *see also* pre-modern music
hōgaku būmu 109, 134
hōgaku nyū wēbu 133
Hokkaidō 6, 23, 31
honkyoku 71–72, 76, 94
honne 131, 132
Honshū 6, 27, 30–31, 94, 205
Hosokawa, Shūhei 25, 44, 45, 57, 121
Hosokawa, Toshio 114–116
Hughes, David W. 25, 26, 29–30, 31, 85, 87–88, 186

humor 28
hybridity 37, 38–40, 51, 133–134, 140, 221

identity 4–5, 10, 40–44, 51–53, 54, 61–62, 109, 221–222; *enka* 117; festivals 155; homogeneous 24; Jero 120, 121; Kyoto 155, 217; Matsuri-shū 204; *min'yō* 29–30; modern music 110–111; nostalgia 55–56; Okinawan 30–31, 32, 33; pitch and scales 88; religious traditions 16; *sumō* 36; traditionalism 37–38; women 59; *see also* Japaneseness; national identity
"idols" 48, 60, 129–133, 223
Imafuji, Misuzu 163, 177, 183–184, 185, 187, 189–190
imitation 81
imperialism: Japanese 15, 16; Western 41
improvisation 68, 106
in scale 85–86, 87, 88, 100
Inoue, Yōsui 221
Internet 5, 62, 191
intertextuality 78, 98, 130–131, 132
Irish music 56, 89
iroke 81, 82
Isawa, Shuji 56
Iseki, Kazuhiro 100
Ishigaki, Kyoko 32
Ishikawa, Sayuri 117–118
Ishikura, Kōzan 134
Ishikura, Yoshihisa 137
Ishizuka, Yutaka 137
Itoh, Miki 112

Jaffe, Jerry C. 41
Jansen, B. 20
Japaneseness 5, 51–53, 54–55, 61–62, 73, 109; hybridization 221; Jero 120; *jo-ha-kyū* 104, 105; lessons 180–181; modern music 110; *nihonjinron* 43–44, 57, 62; pre-modern music 68–69; *taiko* 135; technology 126; underground music 121; *see also* identity
jazz 47, 52, 58; *nori* 99; *shakuhachi* 71; *taiko* 137; Tosha, Rōetsu 179
Jero 119–121
Jiang, Stanley 78
Jin, Nyodo 76
jo-ha-kyū 99–105, 115, 186, 221
Johnson, Henry 41, 71, 90
Jōmon period 11
J-pop 48, 108, 223

kabuki 13, 14, 24–25, 79, 84, 140, 184; Kyoto 162; Matsuri-shū 206; *nagauta* 186; percussion in 177, 185, 186; Tosha, Rōetsu 179; women 58, 60, 158
kadō 69, 161
"Kagoshima Ohara-bushi" 27–29, 88
kagura 17, 68
"Kagura" 98, 103
kakegoe 77, 95, 97, 105–106; Endo 142; Matsuri-shū 205; *min'yō* 26, 27, 28; notation 187; *taiko* 137, 140; Tosha, Rōetsu 177
kakko 102
Kamakura period 13, 71, 90–91
kami-sama 210
Kamiyama, "Hoppy" 124–126
Kan'ami, Kiyotsugu 13, 95
Kanazawa 159
kane 26, 151, 189
Karan, Pradyumna P. 6, 9, 15
karaoke 4, 48, 55, 210, 221
Karlin, Jason G. 130–131, 132
Kasuga, Toyo 82
Kasuga, Toyoeishiba 80, 88
"Kasuga Sanbasō" 78, 80, 82–83, 88, 89, 186
kata 117, 181, 202
katsugi-oke-daiko 201, 203, 205
Kawarazaki, Yoshihiro 167, 169, 171–172, 198, 199, 201–204, 205, 217, 218
kayōkyoku 25
Kaze 177
kei 22
Keister, Jay 53–54, 103, 105
Kemmu Restoration 13
kendō 210
kiai 77, 140
kimono 117, 157, 158, 159, 161, 204–205, 213
Kimura, Kaori 59
Kimura, Yoko 101
kin 22
Kina, Shokichi 134
kindai ongaku 109
Kineya, Hiroki 163, 177, 183–184, 190
Kineya, Rokuzaemon IX 186
Kineya school 80–81
Kinko 74
Kirihito 126, 135
Kishibe, Shigeo 80, 102–103
Kitagawa, Junko 24, 49, 50
"Kiyari" 138–139
Kobayashi, Seidō 137
Kobe 8, 158, 164
kobushi 26, 27, 77, 116, 119

Kodō 135, 138–139, 142, 143, 173, 178–179, 196–197, 206, 221
Kofun period 11
koha 210
"Kohama-bushi" 32–34
kōhai/senpai relationships 193, 203, 210, 218
Koizumi, Fumio 38, 84, 86–88, 113
Kojiki 11
komusō 71
"Konjichō" 205
Korea 11, 12, 15, 165; Christianity 23; cultural exchange with 38–39; folk songs 26; *gagaku* 102
koten 25
koten-chōshi 44
koto 5, 12, 14, 39–40, 49, 73, 103; fast pace 88; heterophony 90; *jo-ha-kyū* 100, 101; Kyoto 161, 162; "Megitsune" 223; modern music 109; Murasaki Daiko 212, 216; Okinawan music 32; pitch and scales 84, 88; women 58, 61
ko-tsuzumi 142, 158, 163, 177, 178, 185–186; "Echigojishi" 187, 189, 227–232; *geiko* 182; *jo-ha-kyū* 104; "Megitsune" 222; *noh* 95, 97; teaching 185
kouta 79, 80–83, 90
Kōya-san 20
kuchishōka 96, 97, 217–218
Kūkai 20
kyōgen 161, 162, 221
kyōmai 161
Kyoto 9, 12, 147, 149–174, 221; case studies 175–219; festivals 153–155; *geiko* 158–160; Gion Matsuri 149–153, 155, 171–172; musical life of 162–163; *shishi-mai* 18–19; *taiko* in 139–140, 143, 163–173; traditional image of 155–162
Kyūshū 6, 27, 31

Lady Gaga 108–109, 133, 222
Lancashire, Terence 152
language 121, 122–124, 221
lessons 53–54, 166–171, 179–190, 202–203, 210, 218
Letterman, David 129–130, 222
"Lied" 110, 114–116
livehouses 50, 53, 121, 161–162
"Love Maniac" 124–126
lyrics: *enka* 117, 118; *min'yō* 26–27, 30; nationalistic 47; Okinawan music 32–33; rock music 222; underground music 122, 123

ma 69–77, 94, 95, 104, 105, 115, 128, 140
magewappa-daiko 205

maigoto 95, 98, 103
maiko 159–160, 180, 182–183, 184
Malm, William P. 22, 90, 98
Manabe, Noriko 7
martial arts 139, 167, 202, 210
Mason, Luther Whiting 56
Masuda, Ann 8
Mathews, Gordon 5, 51–53, 55
matsuri 4, 17, 18, 106; Basara 191; Kyoto 153–155; Matsuri-shū 206; *taiko* 171–172, 177; *see also* festivals
matsuri-bayashi 18, 141
Matsuri-shū 166, 168, 172, 173, 184, 198–206, 215, 217
"Megitsune" 3–4, 222–223
Meiji period 14, 36, 37, 44, 49, 71, 89, 100, 153
melody 88, 90, 94, 102–103, 197
Melt Banana 222
Merzbow 127
meter 25–26
metronomes 195
Mie 168
military songs 44
Minamoto 13
minorities 23–24, 33–34
Minoru, Miki 40, 77–78, 97
min'yō 25–34, 51, 68, 77, 138–139; fast pace 88; *hayashi-kotoba* 223; scales 221; *shamisen* 79; *yō* scale 87
minzoku geinō 24, 25
Mitome, Tomohiro 138
"Miyake" 138–139, 142
miyako-bushi 87, 88
mnemonics 96, 97, 101, 187, 217–218
mochitsuki 195
Mochizuki, Tasaku III 186
modern music 108–145, 222–223; *aidoru* 129–133; art music 109–116; *enka* 116–121; influence of Western popular music 133–134; *taiko* 134–141; underground music 121–129; *see also* pop music; *yōgaku*
modernity 14, 37, 41–44, 51, 61, 143; Kyoto 160–162; Matsuri-shū 206; musical 44–51; nostalgia 57
modernization 37, 42–43, 44, 46, 55, 58, 176
Mongolian drums 215–216
monophony 89
mu 200
Muchaku, Seikyō 81
Murasaki Daiko 164, 166, 206–217
Muromachi period 13
"Musume Shirasagi" 83

nagado-daiko 142, 171, 197, 205, 222
Nagasaki 15
nagauta 177, 186
nagauta shamisen 84, 163, 183
Nagoya 164
Naka, Mamiko 112
Nakai, Kunihiko 190
Nakajima, Hiroyuki 165
naniwa-bushi 47
Nara period 12, 20, 85, 90, 102
"Narushima" 196
national identity 5, 16–17, 36, 55; see also identity
National Taiko Database 164
National Theatre of Japan 179
nationalism 37, 41, 43, 47
natural resources 6, 7, 9
nature 6, 9, 10, 40, 77
neiro 178
"new music" 48
"new wave" 133
nihon buyō 4, 83
Nihon ongaku 24
Nihon Shoki 11
nihonjinron 43–44, 57, 62
Nishi, Yoko 100
Nishimura, Shirō 206–207, 209–213, 216
noh 13, 14, 70, 78, 84, 116, 221; *Gion Matsuri* 153; heterophony 90; *jo-ha-kyū* 100, 103–104; *ko-tsuzumi* 185; *kouta* 81; Kyoto 161, 162; *nori* 99; organized time 94–98; pitch and scales 84; women 60
noh-hayashi 95, 97–98, 105–106, 125; Kyoto 163; "Megitsune" 222; *nori* 99; *taiko* 177
nohkan 95, 105–106, 142; "Echigojishi" 189; *geiko* 158; *Gion Matsuri* 152; *Matsuri-shū* 205
noizu (noise) 126–127, 128–129
Nomura, Mansai 78
nori 98–99, 202
nostalgia 29, 55–58, 114, 117
notation 75–76, 80–81, 97, 187–189, 217–218
Novak, David 126, 127, 128–129
nuclear power 7
nyōhachi 22
nyū myūjikku 48

ō-daiko 18, 105–106, 177, 178, 185, 196, 216
"Ōgi no Mato" 90, 91–93, 94
Oguchi, Daihachi 137
okedo-daiko 197
okeiko 53, 179–190, 203, 210, 218
Okinawa 37, 56, 133–134
Okinawans 23, 30–33
Okura, Shonosuke 105
older women 208
Ondekoza 135, 138, 173, 177, 195, 198, 217
One OK Rock 222
onkyō 126, 127–128
Onozato, Motoe 137
opera 49
orchestras 49
ornamentation 26
Orquesta de la Luz 57, 122
Osaka 46, 158, 164, 168, 169
Oshio, Satomi 58, 59, 60–61
Osuwa Daiko 135, 137
Ōtsuka, Takeshi 190, 191, 194–195, 196, 218
ō-tsuzumi 105–106, 158, 163, 177; "Echigojishi" 187, 189, 227–232; *geiko* 182; *jo-ha-kyū* 104; noh 95; teaching 185

Pacun, David 110
parlando rubato 94
party songs 26
pedagogy 180, 218
Peluse, Michael S. 134
pentatonic scales 48, 84–85, 112, 116, 223
performance: Basara 195–197; *Matsuri-shū* 204–205; Murasaki Daiko 209–210, 211, 212–216
performative ethnography 175
Perry, Commodore 14, 24–25, 41
"phantasm" metaphor 53, 55
piano 49, 116
pitch 77, 84–85, 88, 89, 94
Plourde, Lorraine 126–128
political songs 47
politics 16
polyphony 26, 89
pop music 4, 24, 30, 38, 46–49; imported styles 45; influence of Western popular music 133–134; *nori* 98; terminology 25; see also *enka*; rock music
popyurā myūjikku 25
pre-modern music 67–107; form 99–105; free rhythm 93–94; *ma* 69–77; melody and harmony 88–89; *nori* 98–99; organized time 94–98; pitch and scales 84–88; texture 89–93; timbre 77–83; see also *hōgaku*
professional musicians 163, 184–185
prostitution 158, 159
puppet theater 14, 60, 98

race 120, 121
radio 46, 47, 55
Rao, Mallika 133
rap music 122–123
recitals 170
rehearsal spaces 162, 173, 190–191, 208
Reich, Steve 200
Reischauer, Edwin O. 20
religion 16–23, 157; *see also* Buddhism; Shintō
resonating bowls 22
rhythm: free 93–94; *min'yō* 25; *nori* 98–99; organized time 94–98; *taiko* 202
"Rishukyō" 85
ritsu scale 20, 85, 87
rituals 17, 102, 155
rock and roll 47
rock music 48, 53, 222; language used in 121, 122; women 59, 60, 61
"Rokudan" 88, 100–101
rōkyoku 47
rōnin 71
Rowthorn, Chris 155
ryo scale 20, 85
ryū 80–81
Ryūkyū islands 6, 23, 30, 31
Ryūkyū scale 31–32, 84, 87
ryūteki 102, 116

sadō 5, 69, 157, 159, 161
"Sagi Musume" 83
"Sai-bo" 126
Sakai, Naoki 43
"Sakura" 223
samurai 12, 13, 14, 58, 210; imperialism 15; Okinawan identity 32; shakuhachi 71
San Kyodai 201
sanshin 32, 37, 133
sararin 101
satori 200
saxophone 116, 118
scales 20, 45, 84–88, 112–113; *enka* 116, 119; *min'yō* 221; pentatonic 48, 84–85, 112, 116, 223; *Ryūkyū* 31–32, 84, 87
Schlefer, James Nyoraku 72–76, 88, 94
seasons 10
seiza 181, 190, 210
"Semi Shigure" 197, 198
senpai/kōhai relationships 193, 203, 210, 218
shakubyōshi 17
shakuhachi 14, 62, 116, 134; "Choshi" 128; *enka* 119; free rhythm 93–94; Kyoto 162; lessons 180; *ma* 70–76; *min'yō* 26; modern music 108, 109; pitch and scales 88
shamisen 4, 14, 47, 89; "Echigojishi" 186, 187, 189, 225–226; *enka* 116; fast pace 88; *geiko* 158; heterophony 90; *kouta* 82, 90; lessons 180, 181, 183–184; *min'yō* 26, 27; Murasaki Daiko 216; *nori* 98; pitch and scales 84, 88; teachers 185; timbre 77, 78–80; Tosha, Roetsu 218; women 58, 182
Shien 168
Shiga 168, 172
Shigin Shunbō-Hakuun no Shiro 118–119
Shikoku 6, 31
shime-daiko 106, 142, 152, 171; Basara 197; Kawarazaki 202, 203; Yamauchi 200, 205, 206
"Shimensoka" 200
Shingon Buddhism 20–22
shinobue 18, 19, 44, 106, 142; Basara 197; "Echigojishi" 186, 189; *geiko* 158; Gion Matsuri 152
Shinoda, Kaneji 186
Shintō 10, 11, 16–19, 68, 98, 210; festivals 221; *gagaku* 102; Gion Matsuri 150; imperialism 15; Kyoto 157; *taiko* 177
shishi 19
shishi-mai 18–19, 191, 196
shishi-odoshi 10
shō 102–103
shōko 102, 103
shōmyō 37, 68, 98; Buddhist chants 11–12, 20, 21–22; pitch and scales 84, 85; voice 77
"Shōnen Jidai" 221
Shōnen Knife 222
shrines 17, 20, 150–151, 153–154; Kyoto 157, 162, 171
"sliding door" effect 90, 98
SMAP 130
sōkyoku 61, 100
sōshibushi 47
sound-color 178, 200
space (*ma*) 69–77, 94, 95, 104, 105, 115, 128, 140
Spiller, Henry 43
Sports 123
Stevens, Carolyn S. 47, 88, 117, 121
sticks *see bachi*
Studio Rag 162
suikinkutsu 10
Sukeroku Daiko 135, 137–138, 173
sumō 36–38
Surak, Kristin 5, 181

sutras 11–12, 20, 21–23
suzu 19, 22, 27
Suzuki, Kyosuke, 105
synthesizers 48

taiko 4, 18, 30, 67, 134–141, 221; Basara 190–198; case studies 175–219; "Etenraku" 103; fast pace 88; *geiko* 158; Kyoto 162, 163–173; Matsuri-shū 198–206; "Megitsune" 222; *min'yō* 26, 27; Murasaki Daiko 206–217; *noh* 95, 97; *nori* 99; Tosha, Rōetsu 176–190; "Yobikake" 105–106
Taiko Center, Kyoto 139–140, 166–171, 173, 187, 190, 198–206, 207, 217, 218
Taishō period 15, 47, 197–198
Takamine, Mitsu 32
Takarazuka Revue 60, 77–78, 210
Takehisa, Ken 126
Takemitsu, Tōru 24, 70, 73, 110–111, 115
Tamako, Hikaru 101
tamane 94
Tamura, Hikaru 10
Tanaka, Seiichi 138
Tanaka, Takafumi 133, 134, 135, 141, 185
Tann, Hilary 74
tatami 40, 61
tatemae 131, 132
tea ceremony 5, 69, 157, 161
Team Kozan 108–109, 134
technology 126, 128–129; Crypton Vocaloid software 130, 132, 133
television 4, 55
temples 20–21, 76, 94, 155, 171
tempo 99, 138
tetrachords 86–87, 88, 113
texture 89–93, 110, 216, 221
theater 14, 25, 60
Tierney, Kenji R. 37
timbre 77–83, 94, 126, 200, 216
time, organized 94–98
Tokita, Alison M. 46
Tokugawa, Ieyasu 13, 23, 71
Tokyo 15, 45, 46, 157; *geisha* 159; Great Kantō Earthquake 8; Irish music 56; men from 207; National Theatre of Japan 179; *onkyō* 127, 128; professional musicians in 163; rock music 53, 59; Sukeroku Daiko 173; *taiko* 137, 138, 167, 202; *Tokyo-ben* 158; underground music 123
"Tomo no Ura Bojō" 132
Tosha, Kiyonari 105
Tosha, Rōetsu 95, 97, 139, 159, 163, 165–166, 176–190, 198, 200, 203, 217–218, 222, 227

Tosha, Rosen 177
tourism 157, 160–161, 171
tradition and traditionalism 3, 36, 37–38, 42–43, 157, 160–161
training 53–55; *see also* lessons
trumpet 116
tsugaru-jamisen 30, 79, 133, 134, 198, 199
"Tsugarukaikyō-Fuyugeshiki" 117–118
tsuri-daiko 102

"Umiyuki" 119, 120
underground music 48, 53, 59, 60, 121–129
United States 14, 15, 52, 122, 180, 181
uta-bayashi 26, 27
Utada, Hikaru 222
utamono 44

The Ventures 48
vibrato 77, 94, 115, 116
violin 49, 116
visual impact 216
voice 77–78; combined with *biwa* 90, 93; heterophony 90; *noh* 95
volcanoes 8

Wa San Bon 199
Wade, Bonnie C. 57–58, 78, 95, 98, 100, 103, 109–112, 114, 122, 222
wagakki 51
wagon 17
Wakana 99, 199
wasei 48
Waswo, Ann 42, 44
Watanabe, Kaoru 44, 67–68, 135, 139, 141–143
Watazumido 10
"ways of doing" 53–55
Western music 24, 44–46, 47, 48–49, 51–52; art music 49, 58, 69, 105, 109–116; *enka* 116; harmony 89; influence of 133–134; melody 102–103; *see also* modern music; *yōgaku*
Westernization 42, 55
Williams, Sean 56, 89
women 58–61, 100; Kyoto 158; Murasaki Daiko 166, 207–208, 210, 213–215, 217; older 208; *taiko* 167–168, 170, 182–184, 193; *see also geisha/geiko*
Wong, Deborah 175
"Woodpecker No.1" 127
World War II 15, 16–17, 43, 47, 157

X-Japan 222

Yaeyama 32–33
Yamada, Kōsaku 111
Yamauchi, Reach 79, 99, 172, 184, 187–189, 198–200, 204–206, 217, 218, 228
Yano, Christine R. 25, 44, 45, 55–56, 116–119
"Yaraiya" 99, 199, 200
"Yatai" 221
Yatsuhashi, Kengyō 24, 100
Yayoi period 11
Yellow Magic Orchestra (YMO) 48, 126, 223
yin/yang 95, 215
yō scale 85–86, 87, 88
"Yobikake" 105–106, 125
yōgaku 24, 49, 222; *see also* modern music; Western music

yonanuki scale 112–113, 116, 119
Yoshida Brothers 134
Yoshizumi, Kosakurō 186
Yoshizumi school 80
young people 30, 47, 51, 163, 190
Yuko, Eguchi 90
Yura, Hidenori 205, 206
yuri 116

Zakuro-Daiko 164
Zeami, Motokiyo 13, 95, 100, 104
Zen Buddhism 13, 14, 20; gardens 10; *ma* 69; *noh* 95; *shakuhachi* 71, 72, 73
zithers 17, 39–40; *see also koto*

eBooks
from Taylor & Francis

Helping you to choose the right eBooks for your Library

Add to your library's digital collection today with Taylor & Francis eBooks. We have over 50,000 eBooks in the Humanities, Social Sciences, Behavioural Sciences, Built Environment and Law, from leading imprints, including Routledge, Focal Press and Psychology Press.

Choose from a range of subject packages or create your own!

Benefits for you
- Free MARC records
- COUNTER-compliant usage statistics
- Flexible purchase and pricing options
- All titles DRM-free.

Benefits for your user
- Off-site, anytime access via Athens or referring URL
- Print or copy pages or chapters
- Full content search
- Bookmark, highlight and annotate text
- Access to thousands of pages of quality research at the click of a button.

Free Trials Available
We offer free trials to qualifying academic, corporate and government customers.

eCollections

Choose from over 30 subject eCollections, including:

Archaeology	Language Learning
Architecture	Law
Asian Studies	Literature
Business & Management	Media & Communication
Classical Studies	Middle East Studies
Construction	Music
Creative & Media Arts	Philosophy
Criminology & Criminal Justice	Planning
Economics	Politics
Education	Psychology & Mental Health
Energy	Religion
Engineering	Security
English Language & Linguistics	Social Work
Environment & Sustainability	Sociology
Geography	Sport
Health Studies	Theatre & Performance
History	Tourism, Hospitality & Events

For more information, pricing enquiries or to order a free trial, please contact your local sales team:
www.tandfebooks.com/page/sales

www.tandfebooks.com